Kay Müller

Investing in Private Equity Partnerships

GABLER EDITION WISSENSCHAFT

Entrepreneurial and Financial Studies

Herausgegeben von
Professor Dr. Dr. Ann-Kristin Achleitner
und Professor Dr. Christoph Kaserer

Die Schriftenreihe präsentiert aktuelle Forschungsergebnisse aus dem Gebiet der Entrepreneurial und Corporate Finance. Sie greift an der Schnittstelle von Wissenschaft und Praxis innovative Fragestellungen der Unternehmensfinanzierung auf.

This series presents research results from the fields of entrepreneurial and corporate finance. Its focus lies on innovative research topics at the interface of science and practice.

Kay Müller

Investing in Private Equity Partnerships

The Role of Monitoring and Reporting

With a foreword by Prof. Dr. Dr. Ann-Kristin Achleitner

GABLER EDITION WISSENSCHAFT

Bibliographic information published by the Deutsche Nationalbibliothek
The Deutsche Nationalbibliothek lists this publication in the Deutsche Nationalbibliografie; detailed bibliographic data are available in the Internet at http://dnb.d-nb.de.

Dissertation Technische Universität München, 2007

1st Edition 2008

Editorial Office: Claudia Jeske

Gabler Verlag is part of the specialist publishing group Springer Science+Business Media.
www.gabler.de

Cover design: Regine Zimmer, Dipl.-Designerin, Frankfurt/Main
Printed on acid-free paper

ISBN 978-3-8349-0934-3

Foreword

The private equity industry has experienced rapid growth on a global scale in recent years. Institutional investors nowadays see private equity as a core element of their portfolios and have increased their allocation to this asset class accordingly.

With the private equity industry becoming more mature and institutional investors becoming more experienced with the asset class, the debate on the industry's transparency has intensified. In order to manage their exposure to private equity effectively, institutional investors demand increased levels of transparency and disclosure from private equity fund managers. Are these calls justified? What information do private equity fund investors actually need? Are private equity fund managers providing sufficient reporting?

Kay Müller's distinguished dissertation sheds light on these questions. For the first time, he provides empirical analysis combining the perspective of private equity fund investors and managers. On the basis of a comprehensive set of interviews with leading European private equity fund investors, he presents an in-depth insight into the monitoring activities of institutional investors and explores their information requirements. These results are then contrasted with the actual reporting by fund managers based on a disclosure study of a unique sample of private equity fund reports. The analysis reveals several important information gaps and provides guidance on areas for improvements.

The focus of this book is the relationship between investors and fund managers, which is at the heart of the private equity industry. It comes at the right time as the industry is facing major challenges as a result of the global credit crunch. Declining returns turn the investors' focus to transparency and governance issues. Effective and open communication between the market participants becomes even more important in order to support long-lasting and trusted partnerships.

I strongly believe that this book offers valuable contributions for the private equity industry and helps to further professionalize the asset class. I am very confident that researchers and practitioners alike will find the results thought-provoking and insightful.

Munich, May 2008

Prof. Dr. Dr. Ann-Kristin Achleitner

Acknowledgements

This book results from intensive research work at the KfW Endowed Chair in Entrepreneurial Finance and the Center for Entrepreneurial and Financial Studies (CEFS), both at Technische Universität München (TUM). It has been made possible with the cooperation and support of many individuals who I want to express my sincere appreciation and gratitude with the following lines.

First of all, I would like to thank my doctoral supervisor Professor Ann-Kristin Achleitner for giving me the opportunity of working together with her for three years. This was a very enriching experience both intellectually and personally. She awakened my interest for private equity as a field of research and thoughtfully guided my research agenda. After the sudden death of my father, her support, trust and encouragement allowed me to finish this dissertation for which I am very grateful.

I am also indebted to several members of the TUM Business School. In particular, I very much thank Professor Christoph Kaserer who was not only acting as referee for my dissertation but was always supportive in various projects that I carried out at the CEFS. I also thank Professor Horst Wildemann for chairing my doctoral examination committee.

Several private equity professionals were especially helpful in my research effort. I am greatly indebted to Jeremy Golding, Hubertus Theile-Ochel and Jakob Schramm from Golding Capital Partners for providing me access to their database as well as for the many insightful discussions we had. Furthermore, I would like to thank Jens-Bisgaard Frantzen, now CEO of Private Advisers UK and at that time CEO of ATP Private Equity Partners, who was very supportive in improving the dataset for my empirical analysis. I also owe special thanks to the large number of private equity professionals for sharing their experience with me in long interviews despite their demanding work load and tight time schedules. I separately list all their names and organizations in the appendices of this book.

This work also benefited to a large degree from the industry experience I was able to gain with the help of a number of people. Whilst being a member of the European Private Equity & Venture Capital Association (EVCA)'s IFRS Task Force, I enjoyed several fruitful discussions with Didier Guennoc and the other members of the Task Force. I would like to thank all of them as they clearly helped to advance my research agenda. Furthermore, I am very much indebted to Marc O. Boheim, J. Christopher Kojima, and their colleagues from Goldman Sachs Private Equity Group who gave me the opportunity to work with them for a couple of months. This was tremendously helpful in order to get real insight into the activities of an institutional private equity fund investor and to ensure practical relevance of my research.

There are also several colleagues from TUM Business School who deserve recognition for both the continuous provision of intellectual and emotional support and the creation of a working environment full of inspiring team spirit. I am very indebted to Annabell Geidner and Dr. Christian Fingerle who not only have become great friends but also took the time to read my entire manuscript. I received thoughtful criticism and insightful feedback and their comments definitely took this book to the next level. I am also grateful to Dr. Simon Wahl, Dr. Eva Nathusius, Dr. Thorsten Groth, Martin Brixner, Dr. Benjamin Moldenhauer, Oliver Klöckner, Peter Heister, Markus Ampenberger, Svenja Jarchow, Stephanie Schraml, and Marco Bender for valuable discussions, advice and other contributions to my work. I would also like to thank Monika Paul since she supported me in so many aspects of my daily work. Furthermore, I was also fortunate to enjoy the help of Andreas Heubl who was an excellent student, assisted in collecting data, and provided stimulating ideas for my research.

The emotional support of my family and friends allowed me to complete this dissertation. My deepest and sincere thanks go to Julia Leuffen for her love, encouragement and patience especially in the final phase of writing this book. She has always been there when I needed her most. Furthermore, she is also a great editor and gave insightful comments and reviewed my work diligently.

Above all, none of this would have been possible without my family. I will always be grateful to my parents, Gerhard and Ilsabeth Müller, and my brother Jan-Gerd, for their love and emotional support over all the years. I am just very sorry that my father did not live to see this work finally come to fruition. I dedicate this book to him.

Munich, May 2008

Dr. Kay Müller

Table of Contents

Table of Figures

Table of Abbreviations

AcSEC	Accounting Standard Executive Committee
AFIC	Association Française des Investisseurs en Capital
AFS	Assets available for sale
AICPA	American Institute of Certified Public Accountants
BVCA	British Venture Capital & Private Equity Association
CalPERS	California Public Employees' Retirement Systems
CEO	Chief Executive Officer
CF	Cash flow
DCF	Discounted cash flow
DPI	Distribution to paid-in
EBIT	Earnings before interests and taxes
EBITDA	Earnings before interests, taxes, depreciation and amortization
EV	Enterprise value
EVCA	European Private Equity & Venture Capital Association
FASB	Financial Accounting Standards Board
FOIA	Freedom of Information Act
FV	Fair value
FVTPL	Assets at fair value through profit and loss
GAAP	General Accepted Accounting Standards
GIPS	Global Investment Performance Standards
GP	General partner
IAS	International Accounting Standard
IASB	International Accounting Standards Board

IFRS	International Financial Reporting Standards
IPO	Initial public offering
IRR	Internal rate of return
LP	Limited partner
LPA	Limited partnership agreement
M	Mean
NASDAQ	National Association of Securities Dealers Automated Quotation System
NAV	Net asset value
NPV	Net present value
NVCA	U.S. National Venture Capital Association
PC	Portfolio company
PE	Private equity
PEIGG	Private Equity Industry Guidelines Group
PME	Public market equivalent
PPM	Public placement memorandum
RVPI	Residual value to paid-in
SD	Standard deviation
SECA	Swiss Private Equity & Corporate Finance Association
SFAS	Statement of Financial Accounting Standard
S&P	Standard & Poor's
TVPI	Total value to paid-in
U.S.	United States of America

Table of Symbols

Chapter 3

t	Time period
T	Lifetime of the fund
CF	Cash flow
IRR	Internal rate of return
NAV	Net asset value
n	Number of remaining time periods
λ	Distribution scaling factor
S_+	Total number of index shares bought over time
S_-	Total number of index shares sold over time
S_N	Final number of index shares
R_{It}	Net return of a public market index in period t
cf_t	Normalized positive cash flow of private equity fund in period t

Chapter 4

I_0	Initial investment
V_0	Post-money valuation including the initial investment
TD	Total disclosure score
d_i	Disclosure item
M	Maximum amount of information items

1 Introduction

1.1 Relevance of Topic

The global growth of the private equity industry has been spectacular over the last years. According to PRIVATE EQUITY INTELLIGENCE, private equity funds worldwide raised USD 432 billion in 2006 which is an increase of 38% on the already strong 2005 figure of USD 313bn.[1] In 1985, global fundraising has been only USD 5bn indicating an annual growth rate of around of 24% of the asset class over the last more than 20 years.[2] The private equity universe, i.e. the total private equity assets under management, accounted for around USD 1,400 billion in 2006.[3] The growth of the asset class also reflects in the trend for larger fund sizes.[4] The ten largest funds in 2006 together raised USD 100bn. Six of them were among the largest private equity funds of all times.[5] As these funds use typically high leverage ratios when investing in portfolio companies, their actual economic impact is even greater as these figures suggest.[6] As a result, the industry has developed significantly in the past years to the extent that it is not longer regarded as the niche sector it once was. Today, private equity has "moved from the fringe to the centre of the capitalist action"[7] and private equity investors are shaping entire industries with their investment strategies.

Many new investors have started to make allocations to private equity and existing investors are increasing their allocations to this asset class. With these investments, they intend to generate high returns and at the same time to improve the diversification of their entire portfolios.[8] Several other growth drivers of the asset class can be identified: The volatility of public stock markets, especially in the years after the tech bubble had burst, has made the allocation to public equity as source of consistent returns less at-

---

1 See Private Equity Intelligence (2007a), p. 3.

2 See Phalippou (2007), p. 1.

3 See Private Equity Intelligence (2007b), p. 13.

4 In 2006 for example, Blackstone raised a USD 15.6bn fund, Texas Pacific Group a USD 15.0bn fund, or Permira a USD 14.7bn fund. Moreover, in 2007, Goldman Sachs Capital Partners is for example expected to close a USD 19bn vehicle. See Smith (2007).

5 See Private Equity Intelligence (2007a), p. 3.

6 See Phalippou (2007), p. 1.

7 Bishop (2004), p. 2.

8 See Bance (2004), p. 5.

tractive. Many investors have become more risk aware and increasingly search for absolute return investment opportunities. Coupled with record long-term low real yields on government bonds, these factors have made many institutional investors consider a higher allocation to private equity.[9]

The majority of the private equity investments are invested via specialized intermediaries that are typically organized as independent limited partnerships.[10] Professional fund managers as general partners are responsible for investing and managing the fund's money. Their fund investors are limited partners and provide the financial capital but are not involved in the active management of the fund.

Fund investors face several challenges when investing in private equity funds. First of all, their investments are blind pool investments. At the launch of the fund, there is no ability to preview the portfolio assets because they have not yet been identified. Furthermore, after the fund has made portfolio company investments, it is typically very difficult for the limited partners to value these investments and to assess their performance. They rely on information provided by the fund mangers.

After the burst of the tech bubble and disappointing absolute and relative returns for many funds, many fund investors felt, however, that they were mislead by the information provided to them. With the increasing professionalism of the asset class, fund investors in private equity partnerships therefore have focused their attention on investor rights and have asked for more accountability of the fund managers. More accountability requires better information on the development and performance of the private equity funds. Furthermore, sophisticated private equity fund investors nowadays try to capture, categorize and interpret historical performance data more accurately. They use the results in order to construct meaningful benchmarks. In addition, they try to map cash flows on a forward-looking basis more reliably and potentially employ risk-return optimization models.[11] Fund investors typically also have a fiduciary responsibility to understand their investments. New investors that run new private equity programs may have to reassure their sponsors and trustees that all is going according to plan.[12] All

9 See Achleitner/Fingerle (2006), p. 729.

10 See Phalippou (2007), p. 1.

11 See Borel (2004), p. 45.

12 See Private Equity Intelligence (2005), p. 2.

these developments have led to greater demands from fund investors to get more rigorous and in-depth reporting.[13]

It seems, however, that fund managers are reluctant to provide the required level of detail in their reporting to fund investors. Some fund managers for example note that more disclosure would bring in short-term targets to an asset class where patience and long-term orientation is a critical success factor.[14] They also argue that regular revaluation of portfolio companies using a fair value model rather than holding the investment at costs means that a fund's performance gets artificially volatile. Or they simply may try to avoid allocating resources to regularly capture, collate and distribute the required information.[15]

This struggle for more transparency between both parties in private equity funds is surprising, because, in general, hiding information should not be optimal. Fund managers have to pay for secrecy by offering superior performance in equilibrium.[16] It is therefore interesting to know more about how fund investors actually monitor their fund investments after having invested in a fund and what their specific information needs are. Furthermore, a realistic assessment is required about whether these information needs are actually fulfilled by the fund managers' reporting or not. This dissertation is intended to shed more light on these issues.

Against the background of the growth and relevance of private equity as an asset class, it is astonishing that academic research does not yet provide a sufficient answer to the conflict between fund managers and their investors concerning the necessary information flow. Over the last years, private equity has become a focus area for many scholars. Due to the existence of fund vehicles as intermediaries in the private equity market, the private equity investment process is typically described in two sets of relationships – the ones between the private equity fund managers and the portfolio companies in which they invest and the others between the private equity fund managers and their fund providers.[17] Previous academic research has concentrated mainly on the first type

13 See Meek (2005b), p. 36.

14 See Meyer/Mathonet (2005), p. 277.

15 See Anonymous author (2004), p. 42.

16 See Phalippou (2007), p. 11.

17 See Achleitner (2002a), 145; Robbie/Wright/Chiplin (1997), p. 9.

of relationship between fund managers and the private equity-backed portfolio companies and has neglected the relationship between fund managers and their investors.[18]

Existing studies on the relationship between fund managers and their investors focus on three fields of interest. First, many studies analyze the performance of private equity fund investments.[19] This strand of research covers topics such as the optimal performance measures for the asset class, the actual return and risk of fund investments, the outperformance of private equity fund investments over public market indexes, or the implications of risk-return characteristics for portfolio allocation decisions of investors. The second field of interest has been the organizational structure between fund managers and their investors. In a seminal paper, SAHLMAN describes and analyzes the fund structure and its compensation system from a principal-agent theory perspective.[20] Based on his findings, many other researchers have focused on the contractual covenants in limited partnerships, on the non-tradability of the fund stakes, or on the compensation structure.[21] The fund selection process from the perspective of the fund investors and the corresponding fundraising process from the perspective of the fund managers have been the third field of interest for researchers.[22] Relevant studies examine the process and criteria used by fund investors in the selection of private equity funds or the determinants of successful fundraising by fund managers.

While these three fields of interests have been explored in some detail, there is a lack of academic research examining the *post*-investment relationship between fund managers and their investors and the information flow in terms of the fund managers' re-

---

18 See Phalippou (2007), p. 2; Robbie/Wright/Chiplin (1997), p. 9.

19 Four important research papers focus on the on risk-return relationship from the fund investors' perspective: Kaplan/Schoar (2005); Phalippou/Zollo (2005); Kaserer/Diller (2004c); Ljungqvist/ Richardson (2003).

20 See Sahlman (1990).

21 Feinendegen/Schmidt/Wahrenburg (2003) and Gompers/Lerner (1996) for example pursue an empirical study on private equity limited partnership covenants. Lerner/Schoar (2004) examine reasons for the restrictions on fund investors' ability to transfer funds and provide evidence. Gompers/Lerner (1999) propose a learning model to explain variations in compensation of fund managers by fund investors and provide empirical evidence.

22 For the fund investors' selection process see Tausend (2006); Barnes/Menzies (2005). Studies on the fundraising include for example Balboa/Marti (2006); Burton/Schierschmidt (2004); Gompers/Lerner (1998).

ports.[23] Again, this is astonishing given the practical importance of this issue. Fund investors regard the lack of performance transparency as one of the top risks of investing in private equity.[24] This dissertation, however, intends to fill the identified research gap. Its strength and its distinguishable feature from previous research is that it explicitly focuses on the fund manager-fund investor dyad and thereby takes each partner's side and position explicitly into account.

1.2 Aims of Analysis and Research Approaches

This dissertation intends to contribute to the understanding of the post-investment relationship between private equity fund managers and their fund investors. It concentrates on the role of the information flow between both parties. Specifically, it examines the fund investors' monitoring of the fund investments on the one hand, and the fund managers' reporting to their investors on the other hand. Three explicit research aims are followed:

The first aim is to elaborate on the role of the information flow between private equity fund managers and their fund investors after the latter have invested in the fund. In the common view, fund investors are - due to their status as limited partners - usually perceived as being entirely passive after having invested in a private equity partnership. Therefore, they are seen as though they only need limited information about their fund investments. By analyzing the characteristics of a private equity partnership, as well as highlighting the governance of such a partnership and the fund investors' investment process, it will be demonstrated that and how this view can be rejected. Moreover, several theoretical explanations for the role of information are provided. In order to achieve the first aim of this analysis, the available current literature on private equity partnerships is thoroughly examined.

Based on these general and theoretical explanations of the information flow between fund managers and their investors, the specific information needs of fund investors are

---

23 Only a few studies examine this issue. See for example Kemmerer/Weidig (2005); Böhler (2004b).

24 This has been found in a survey of large UK investors. Investors gave equal weighting of 3.7 (highest scores) to lack of liquidity and lack of performance transparency when asked to rank perceived risks on a scale of one (low risk) to five (high risk). See CMBOR/Adveq (2005) cited in Skypala (2005).

identified. Therefore, an understanding of their monitoring approaches and their respective use of the information is necessary. Consequently, *the second aim is to elaborate the current best practices of private equity fund investors with respect to monitoring their fund investments and to identify their specific information requirements.* In order to get detailed insight into their monitoring processes, the author carried out semi-structured interviews with 28 European private equity fund investors. His intention was to explore the current best practices. Therefore, the sample includes both leading institutions investing in private equity and designated experts in that field. Conclusions are drawn from the fund investors monitoring approaches resulting in the development of several implications for the specific information content.

After exploring and outlining the information requirements of fund investors, the analysis will focus on the perspective of the fund managers. *The third aim of this analysis is to investigate whether fund managers actually fulfill the fund investors' information needs with their fund reporting or not.* Fund reports are perceived to be an integral part of the communication and seen as most important information sources for fund investors.

Heading for the third aim, however, three derived subordinated aims need to be achieved. Parts of the fund reports are statutory financial statements which are based on accounting regulation. As the International Financial Reporting Standards (IFRS) are becoming more important for private equity funds, the *first subordinated aim is to describe and discuss the requirements of the IFRS especially in regard to the accounting for portfolio company investments.*

The valuations of the fund's portfolio company investments are an essential input not only to the statutory financial statements, but also to the fund managers' reports. Fund managers are required to carry out periodic valuations of their investments. In the past, it has been common practice among industry participants to report these typically illiquid and non-listed investments at costs. Today, the fair value measurement of these investments is required not only by accounting standards, but also by valuation guidelines which were developed by private equity industry associations. *The second subordinated aim is therefore a detailed elaboration and discussion of the fair value measurement requirements of portfolio company investments.*

In order to achieve these two subordinated aims, the respective accounting standards and industry valuation guidelines, the accompanying commentary and the relevant academic literature need to be thoroughly examined. Data gathered from four in-depth interviews with leading international private equity fund accounting and portfolio company valuation experts assures that practical insight and experience is integrated in the analysis and discussion.[25]

As statutory financial statements alone do not provide a comprehensive picture of the performance and current state of private equity investments, fund managers disclose additional information to the fund investors. *The third subordinated aim is to develop a comprehensive framework for the additional investors reporting, to measure the level of disclosure in the fund reports based on this framework and to identify relationships between the level of disclosure and selected fund characteristics.* In order to measure the level of additional disclosure, a so-called disclosure index will be developed. This technique has been proven to be a valid and frequently used research methodology in empirical accounting research. For the first time, it will be employed to analyze the additional disclosure to investors in private equity fund reports. The necessary data to empirically test the actual extent of disclosure was gathered from two leading European fund-of-funds investors who provided full access to all fund reports from their investments. The findings on the content of private equity fund reports will be finally compared with fund investors' information requirements in order to identify and discuss any potential information gaps.

This in-depth analysis of the post-investment relationship and the information flow between fund managers and investors will be useful for practitioners who have to understand the requirements of various players involved in the private equity market. In addition, it may also form the basis for further future theoretical research on the issue.

1.3 Structure of Analysis

The dissertation proceeds as follows: After the introduction in *chapter 1*, *chapter 2* provides an overview of investing in private equity partnerships with the intention to examine the role of information between the partners. Chapter 2.1 features the fundamentals of private equity by providing a general definition of private equity invest-

25 In addition, results of a study conducted on behalf of the European Private Equity & Venture Capital Association on the differences between private equity entities and non-investment companies are integrated in the analysis and discussion. For this study 21 semi-structured interviews with leading private equity experts were carried out. See Achleitner/Müller (2004).

ments and an introduction to private equity funds as intermediaries. As the vast majority of private equity funds are organized as a limited partnership, the characteristics of this organizational form are discussed in chapter 2.2. Its generic structure, its typical life cycle and the roles of both partners in such a partnership - private equity firms as general partners and fund investors as limited partners – will be disclosed. Based on these findings, the characteristics of private equity partnership investments from the fund investors' perspective are briefly analyzed in chapter 2.3. Based on the findings in the three precedent chapters, the challenges of governing the relationship between limited and general partners are subject to chapter 2.4. It is demonstrated which potential conflicts of interest could arise between both partners, and how these conflicts are addressed by direct means of control and by performance incentives. Before being able to elaborate the role of information in the private equity partnership, it is necessary to turn again to the perspective of the fund investors. Chapter 2.5 describes the private equity fund investors' investment process with respect to their allocation decision, their portfolio construction processes and their portfolio monitoring and portfolio management. Any institutional differences with respect to this process and the impact on the fund investors' investment success are discussed in chapter 2.6. All these preceding elaborations finally form the basis for the theoretical reflections on the role of information in the relationship between fund managers and their investors in chapter 2.7. A decision-supporting role, a governance-enabling role and a relationship-building role of the information between both parties will be discussed.

Chapter 3 concentrates on how fund investors monitor their fund investments and thoroughly analyzes resulting information requirements. After introductory remarks in chapter 3.1, chapter 3.2 presents the research methodology and the data for the exploratory study. Chapter 3.3 explains the relevance and specific objectives of fund investors' monitoring. As discussed in chapter 3.4, a fundamental basis for all other monitoring purposes is provided by a thorough investigation of performance not only of the single fund investments, but also of the fund investor's entire portfolio. The common return measures for private equity investments are introduced, the relevance of interim return measurement and resulting challenges of interim fund valuations are revealed, and the possibilities to benchmark these returns are presented. However, fund investors are interested in risk-adjusted returns. Therefore, the risks of fund investments are discussed and, finally, also the costs of fund investments are presented. In chapter 3.5 the monitoring and fund governance of individual fund investments is addressed, i.e. the advisory board representation of fund investors, their potential value adding to funds as well as the management of any arising crisis. In chapter 3.6, the author discloses how the monitoring can support the re-investment decision in a subsequent fund of the same fund managers. Chapter 3.7 highlights the monitoring for portfolio management purposes which includes steering the portfolio diversification and liquidity as well as using secondary market transactions to be able to do so. Finally, chapter 3.8 summarizes the resulting information requirements of fund investors to fulfill the monitoring purposes and formulates implications for the content of the fund managers' reporting.

Chapter 4 turns to the perspective of the fund managers and elaborates the fund managers' reporting to investors. Following the introduction in chapter 4.1, this chapter comprises three parts. First of all, in chapter 4.2, the statutory financial statements are analyzed and their relevance for fund investors is discussed. The descriptions emphasize the accounting for portfolio companies as main part of the financial statements. Secondly, the fair value measurement of the portfolio company investments of the funds is subject to an in-depth analysis in chapter 4.3, as the valuations are an integral input of the reports to fund investors. Especially the appropriateness of the fair value measurement in comparison to the more conservative cost-based approach is discussed. Finally, chapter 4.4 comprises a detailed empirical analysis of the actual content of the additional voluntary disclosure, i.e. the investors reporting. Based on the content implications of the fund reports developed in chapter 3, which were drawn from a review of the employed literature as well as on the recommendations of reporting guidelines from industry association, a comprehensive private equity investor reporting framework is developed. Within this framework, a sample of fund reports serves to measure the actual level of disclosure. It is tested whether various fund characteristics have an influence on the level of disclosure. Finally, the results are presented and interpreted.

Chapter 5 concludes, discusses and reveals further implications for private equity practitioners as well as the research community. Figure 1 summarizes the structure of the analysis.

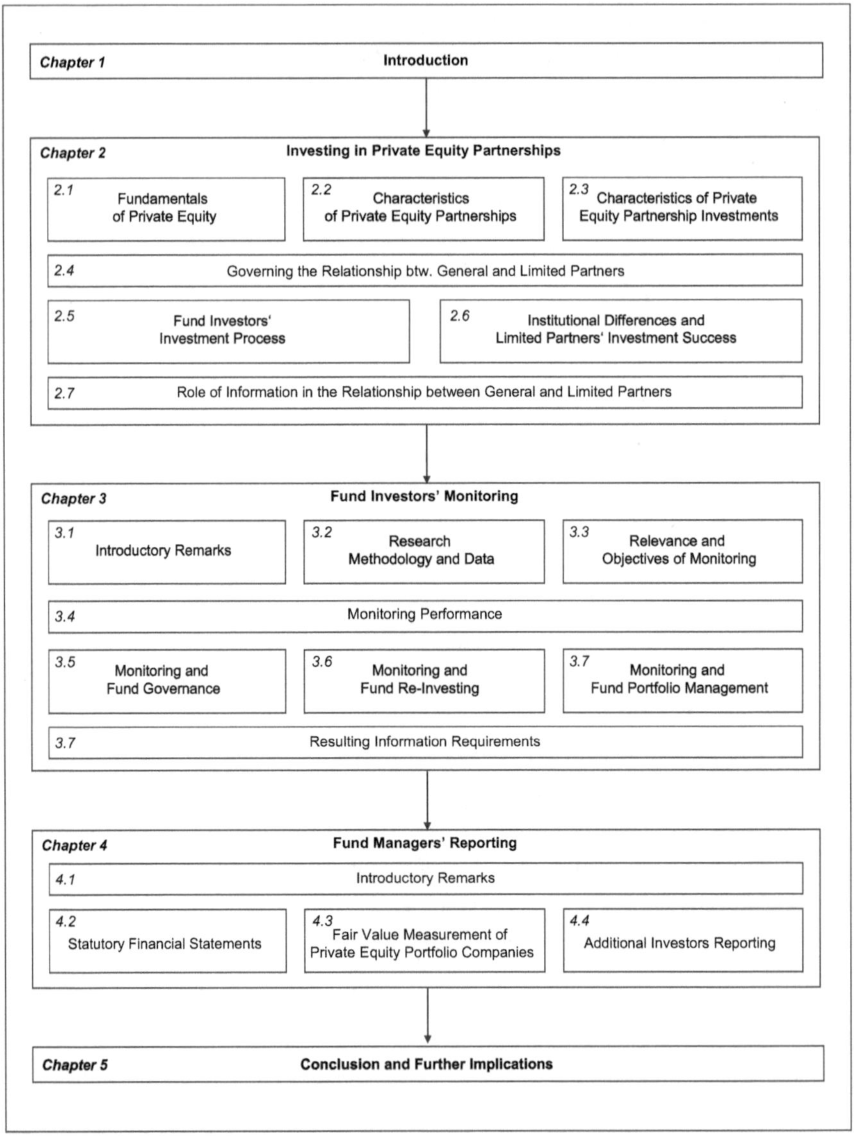

Figure 1: Structure of analysis

2 Investing in Private Equity Partnerships

2.1 Fundamentals of Private Equity

2.1.1 Definition of Private Equity Investments

Private equity investments comprise all equity investments[26] in non-public[27], closely held companies that face a transformational situation in their corporate development.[28] Apart from providing financial resources, private equity investors offer additional management support mainly by advising the management teams of the portfolio companies.[29] The objective of the investors is to generate an optimal risk-adjusted rate of return of their investments. The primary reward of the investors is typically a capital gain which is only rarely supplemented by dividend yields. In order to realize that capital gain, the investors typically plan for an exit of the company investment already at the time of the initial investment. The holding period of the investments lasts usually five to seven years.[30]

According to the stage of the companies that receive the financing, private equity investments are typically split into different sub-segments.[31] Broadly defined, these sub-segments are venture capital, i.e. early stage investments, on the one hand, and buy-

---

26 Equity investments are any form of securities that have an equity feature, e.g. common stock, convertible preferred stock, or subordinated debt that include conversion privileges or warrants. See Fenn/Liang/Prowse (1995), p. 2. If an investment has both equity and debt characteristics it is also called mezzanine capital.

27 The majority of private equity investments are in unquoted companies. However, private equity investors have historically also pursued private investment in public equity, so-called *PIPE investments*. These transactions are typically structured as minority investments in a publicly listed company. See Kuzneski/Landen (2006). EVCA therefore defines the term private equity more broadly as "*investing in securities through a negotiated way.*" Bance (2004), p. 2.

28 See Hagenmüller (2004), p. 12; Wright/Robbie (1998), p. 526; Bader (1996), p. 11. In addition to equity capital, investors may provide debt to the companies.

29 See Wright/Robbie (1998), p. 525. Private equity investors may for example take an active role as member of the advisory boards.

30 See Achleitner/Müller (2004), p. 15; Levin (2002), p. 102.

31 Most categorizations of private equity investments build upon the stage of corporate development in which the portfolio companies is. See for an overview of different conceptualizations of the stages in the literature Fingerle (2005), p. 24.

outs, i.e. late stage investments, on the other.[32] *Venture capital* encompasses all equity investments in start-up companies intended to finance the launch, early development or expansion of a business.[33] The financing may be required for developing business plans, product development, initial marketing activities, or the commercialization of products and their production. The portfolio companies typically belong to high growth industries, e.g. technology or biotech. Due to their inherent risks, these firms have very limited financing alternatives other than equity financing provided by venture capitalists.[34] The source of the return to the equity provider typically comes from revenue and profit stream growth.

Buyouts or late stage investments comprise investments in established companies. These companies are considered to have stable business or to face matured growth.[35] As these companies normally have positive and predictable cash flows, the financing structure of the transactions allows for additional leverage of the investments through debt. The potentially high returns to equity providers are mainly sourced from financial structuring, cost reductions and improving efficiencies.[36]

The *purposes* for financing companies with private equity can be distinguished as follows. On the one hand, private equity is used to finance growth, e.g. by providing capital to develop new products, to expand operations, or to make acquisitions. This is typical for venture capital investments, but could be also relevant for later stage companies. Private equity can further resolve ownership and management issues. A succession in family-owned companies or the buyout or the buyin of a company by ex-

---

32 For further details on the sub-segmentation see for example Schefczyck (2000), p. 37 or Sahlman (1990), p. 479. The boundaries of the different development stages are blurred.

33 See Grabenwarter/Weidig (2005a), p. 19. Venture capital investments are often distinguished in seed, start-up and expansion capital. *Seed capital* finances the research, assess and development of a product. *Start-up capital* serves to finance the set-up of a company and the further development and initial marketing of the product. When the business reaches break-even or is profitable, *expansion capital* might be provided to finance further growth, e.g. the increase of production capacity, market development or providing working capital. See Bance (2004), p. 3; Sahlman (1990), p. 479.

34 See Fingerle (2005), p. 28.

35 Their growth is usually lower than that of venture capital-backed companies.

36 See Tuck (2003a), p. 6. The investors usually acquire a controlling stake of the company.

perienced managers may be achieved by using private equity. In some cases, private equity capital is used to strengthen a company's balance sheet, e.g. in turnarounds.[37]

In the subsequent analysis, the term *private equity* refers to private equity investment as asset class in general. This term comprises all respective sub-segments of the asset class such as venture capital or buyout investments. Where it is appropriate and necessary to emphasize further distinctions, these sub-segments of private equity are explicitly mentioned.

2.1.2 Private Equity Funds as Intermediaries

Investors in private equity are typically institutions and high net worth individuals who can invest in long-term, illiquid investments.[38] These investors have different opportunities to gain exposure to private equity. This is outlined in Figure 2.

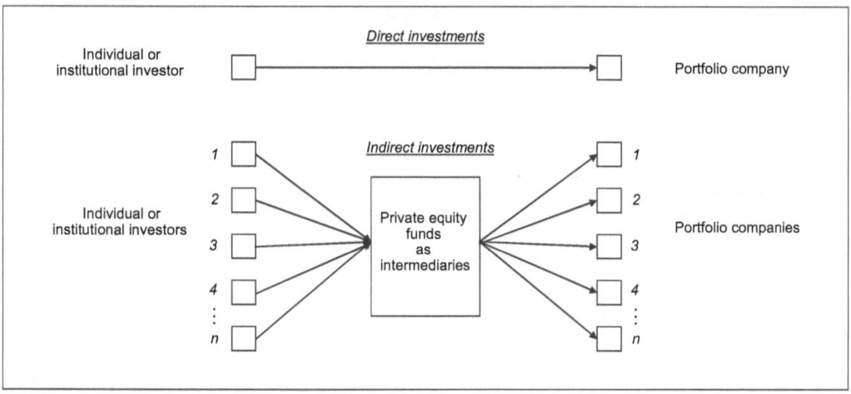

Figure 2: Direct and indirect investing in the private equity market[39]

One way is investing directly in securities of issuing companies. However, most of the investors neither have the professional staff nor the expertise to make such invest-

[37] See Grabenwarter/Weidig (2005a), p. 18. Kraft (2001) provides an in-depth analysis of the management of private equity investment in turnarounds.

[38] For more details see chapter 2.2.3.2.

[39] Based on Fenn/Liang/Prowse (1995), p. 4; Gompers/Lerner (2004), p. 11. A third way is investing via fund-of-funds who themselves invest in other intermediaries. See more details in chapter 2.2.3.2.

ments.[40] Another way is therefore investing indirectly via intermediaries in the portfolio companies. These specialized intermediaries offer the service to their investors to professionally manage the private equity investments.[41] This indirect way of investing is focus of the analysis at hand.

Three major players are interacting in the private equity financing process: the fund investors, the intermediaries, and the portfolio companies. ACHLEITNER conceptualizes and structures the interrelatedness of the various players in a model covering three perspectives: the perspective of the actual providers of the financial means (investors' investment process), the perspective of the intermediaries who pool, professionally invest and manage the fund investors' money (private equity firms' investment process), and the perspective of the companies or entrepreneurs that ultimately receive the financial resources and issue securities in return (corporate development process).[42]

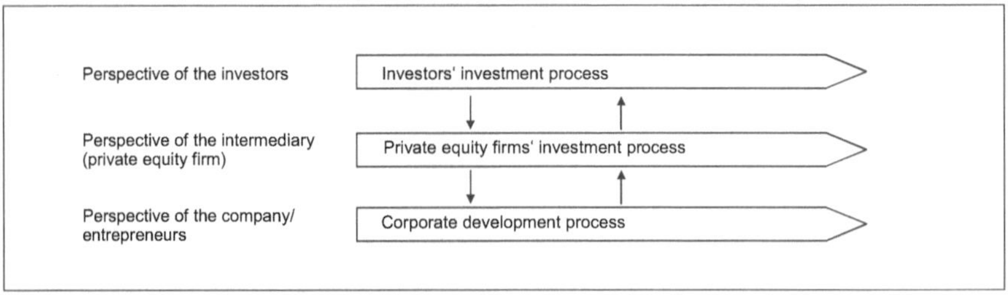

Figure 3: Three perspectives of private equity investments[43]

The role of intermediaries in the private equity market has been well documented in the relevant theoretical literature.[44] Intermediaries resolve adverse selection and moral hazard problems that arise when outside investors provide financial resources to a

---

40 See Povaly (2006), p. 14.

41 See Fenn/Liang/Prowse (1995), p. 2. In comparison, the *informal private equity market* comprises all investments in privately held companies by investors that are not professionally managed and which are typically only occasionally pursued. This may also include *business angel capital investments* in small, new companies by wealthy individuals who may advise the entrepreneurs but who are not as active as professional managers in monitoring the company and taking control. See Wright/Robbie (1998), pp. 530 et seq. for more information on business angel.

42 See Achleitner (2002a), p. 145.

43 Based on Achleitner (2002a), p. 145.

44 See for example Amit/Brander/Zott (1998); Fenn/Liang/Prowse (1995); Sahlman (1990).

company and, due to the separation of ownership and management, high informational asymmetry between insiders and outsiders exists.[45] *Adverse selection* occurs since firm owners and managers as insiders are typically better informed about the condition of the business than outsiders and since these insiders may have an incentive to misrepresent the information. Following the arguments of AKERLOF, the market for private equity could break down in case of information asymmetry.[46] Investors face the risk that the investment may be not as promising as expected and therefore may refrain from investing at all. The problem of *moral hazard* arises after having invested due to the separation of ownership and management. As the outside investors cannot observe the actions taken by the management,[47] and the outcome of the investment may largely depend on external conditions, it is not possible to infer the management's actions from the outcome. Managers or entrepreneurs may therefore have the opportunity to benefit themselves at the costs of the outside investors while running the company.

Through intensive pre-investment due diligence and subsequent post-investment monitoring the adverse selection and the moral hazard problems may be mitigated.[48] However, these tasks require considerable expertise from outside investors. Intermediaries specialized in assessing and monitoring companies provide this expertise to investors.[49] Thereby, they offer institutional investors or high net worth individuals access to investment opportunities in private equity. Both types of investors would otherwise not be able to undertake the necessary activities in an efficient way since the resource needs to successfully pursue a private equity investment strategy may be too high.[50]

The use of intermediaries, however, causes similar adverse selection and moral hazard problems between managers of the intermediaries and their investors. If the investors must employ the same resources to solve these problems as solving the problems when

---

45 See Prowse (1998), p. 28. Other words for adverse selection and moral hazard are sorting and incentive problems. See Amit/Brander/Zott (1998), p. 443.

46 See Akerlof (1970), pp. 488 et seq. AKERLOF describes the problem of adverse selection using the example of the used car market.

47 See Sanders/Boivie (2004), pp. 274 et seq.

48 See Prowse (1998), p. 27; Amit/Brander/Zott (1998), p. 444.

49 See Schefczyck (2000), p. 146.

50 See Barnes/Menzies (2005), p. 210; Fenn/Liang/Prowse (1995), p. 28.

directly investing in the companies, the use of an intermediary may be not efficient.[51] The effects of specialization, however, make intermediaries more efficient. The potential problems that may arise between intermediaries and their investors will be discussed in more detail in subsequent chapters. As a prerequisite, however, the characteristics of the most common form of private equity intermediaries, i.e. the limited partnership, needs to be analyzed.

2.2 Characteristics of Private Equity Partnerships

2.2.1 Generic Structure of the Limited Partnership

The most common organizational form of intermediaries in the private equity market is the limited partnership, composed of investors as limited partners and the fund managers as general partner. [52] Its generic structure is shown in Figure 4.[53]

The *limited partners* are either individual or institutional investors who provide almost all of the partnership's capital. The *general partner* contributes only a marginal share to the fund, typically 1%.[54] He is, however, responsible for the active management of the partnership. In order to avoid a personal unlimited liability of investment professionals that are general partners, the general partner himself is commonly structured either as a limited liability company or as a stock corporation. Typically, the general partner appoints an associated entity, i.e. an investment managing company that provides advice to the general partner.[55] This investment management company is often

[51] See Diamond (1984), p. 393.

[52] See Sahlman (1990), p. 487; Fenn/Liang/Prowse (1995), p. 1. There are other organizational structures available. An alternative organizational form may be a corporate holding structure in which a management company and the investment fund form one entity with infinite lifetime. See Fingerle (2005), p. 58. Listed private equity vehicles typically take this legal form. However, only a few private equity funds are listed.

[53] A detailed discussion of the legal and tax structures of private equity partnerships in different jurisdictions goes beyond the scope of this analysis. Only the key aspects of a limited partnership are explained in general. These aspects, however, apply under various legal structures. For a detailed legal and tax analysis of U.S. private equity partnerships see for example Levin (2002).

[54] See Hagenmüller (2004), p. 18. The general partner's contribution is intended to align interest between the partners. For more details see 2.4.3.

[55] See Schell (2006), p. I/17; Fingerle (2005), p. 58; BVCA (2002), 4.

called the private equity firm.[56] Throughout this dissertation, the expression *fund manager* is used in general to refer to those running the fund without especially distinguishing between the general partner, the private equity firm or the individual investment professionals running the private equity firm.

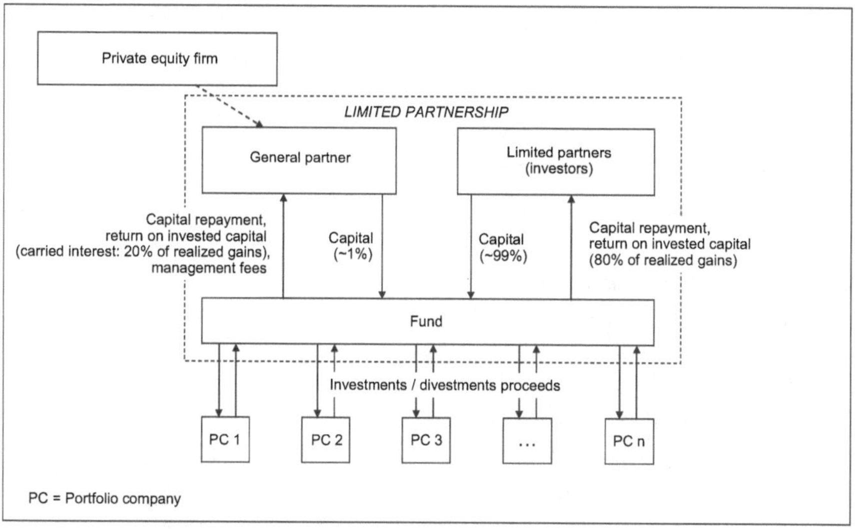

Figure 4: Generic structure of a limited partnership[57]

Limited partners commit a certain amount to the fund. Whenever the fund manager wants to invest in a company, he draws down parts of the committed capital from the investors. For his activities and services, the general partner is compensated with an annual management fee.[58] Furthermore, he receives a share of the profits, the so-called

---

56 One may distinguish private equity firms and venture capital firms, respectively venture capitalists. The latter refers to investment management companies that manage venture capital investments. Private equity firms may mean only those investment firms that manage late stage funds. However, the term private equity firm used here subsumes both.

57 Based on Bader (1996), p. 156; Meyer/Mathonet (2005), p. 28; Levin (2002), chap. 10, p. 3.

58 Typically, this is 2.0% to 2.5% of the committed capital. See Hagenmüller (2004), p. 19.

carried interest. This is typically 20% of the realized gains.[59] And, of course, he participates in the profit sharing along his stake in the fund.

For investors, the limited partnership is an attractive organizational structure mostly due to liability and tax reasons.[60] The liability for the debt and other obligations of the partnership is limited to their capital contribution.[61] This is essential for investors in order to manage the risk.[62] Investors also want to avoid double taxation when investing in private equity. Double taxation means, first of all, the taxation on the fund level when the fund receives dividends or realizes capital gains. It is, secondly, the taxation of the return on the fund investor level.[63] Typically, limited partnership structures offer a tax-exemption or a tax transparency for the limited partners. The investors in the fund are treated as if they were direct investors in the portfolio companies.[64] Thereby, the structure is suitable to all kinds of different investors, i.e. tax-exempt and not tax-exempt ones.[65] Limited partnerships typically offer these features. However, this depends on the legal, regulatory and tax framework the fund operates in.

2.2.2 Life Cycle of the Limited Partnership

According to their lifetime, private equity limited partnerships can be structured as either open-end or closed-end funds. *Open-end funds*, or evergreen funds, have no finite life time and the returns of the investments are usually reinvested in the fund. *Closed-end funds* have a contractually fixed lifetime which is generally around ten years.[66] Re-

---

59 Further details of the performance incentives of the general partners, e.g. a hurdle rate of return that they need to achieve before getting a share of the profits, are discussed in chapter 2.4.3.

60 The actual treatment depends on the jurisdiction the fund operates in. For U.S. private equity partnership law see Levin (2002); Schell (2006). For an introduction of legal and regulatory aspects of private equity funds in Europe see EVCA (2004).

61 If they participate in the control of the partnership, the limited liability status may be lost. See Gompers/Lerner (2004), p. 65.

62 See Grabenwarter/Weidig (2005a), p. 68. However, the limited liability could be also achieved by other organisational structures such as a limited corporation.

63 See Blake (1999), p. 84. An investor in a fund should not pay more taxes than an investor who made an investment directly in the portfolio companies.

64 See Brooks (1999), p. 107.

65 See Blake (1999), pp. 84 et seq. Parallel structures where several vehicles co-exist and co-invest are common in private equity but increase both the complexity, e.g. relating to governance issues, and administrative costs, e.g. audit fees for each vehicle. See Grabenwarter/Weidig (2005a), p. 69.

66 See Lin/Smith (1998), p. 244.

turns from the investments are directly distributed to the investors, at the latest through a liquidation of the fund at the end of the fund's lifetime. In order to have enough capital resources to invest in new companies, private equity firms that manage close-end funds have to regularly raise new funds from outside investors. As the fund investors only re-invest in a subsequent fund after a good performance, a finite lifetime of the fund mitigates agency problems between the fund investors and managers. It forces the fund managers to act in the interest of the fund investors.[67]

The life of an independent closed-end private equity partnership typically starts with the *fundraising*. The fund managers seek investors who commit to the fund. This may take up to one or two years depending on the demand in the fund.[68] An upper and lower size limit are usually applied to the fund. The fund managers close the fund as soon as enough investors have committed to the fund. Funds have typically more than one closing. The first closing is when sufficient investors commit to invest the required minimum aggregate amount for the fund to be established.[69] The first closing communicates to the investment community that a fund has been successfully raised, implying a favorable evaluation of the fund by those that have already committed.[70] The fund managers may then draw down the capital and start to invest in companies (start of the *investment period*). The year of the first investment made by the fund is usually called the vintage year of the fund. After the final closing, no other investor can commit to the fund anymore.

The investment period usually lasts up to four to five years. In the following four to five years, the fund managers are typically not allowed to make any new investments but have time to manage and to exit the investments (*realization period*).[71] During that time the fund managers' efforts are concentrated on realizing or selling the investments. At the end of the lifetime, the fund managers are typically forced to sell the remaining fund investments (liquidation). However, an *extension* of typically up to two years of the fund's lifetime may be approved by a majority vote of the fund investors.

---

67 For more details see chapter 2.4.3.

68 See Hagenmüller (2004), p. 84.

69 See BVCA (2002), p. 7.

70 See Fenn/Liang/Prowse (1995), p. 36.

71 The exact period of time for both the investment and realization period is subject to negotiation between fund managers and investors.

In such a case, the management fees may be reduced or cut to zero in order to stimulate exits.[72] Fund managers raise a follow-on fund when the subsequent fund has been nearly fully invested. The typical life cycle of a private equity limited partnership is shown in Figure 5.

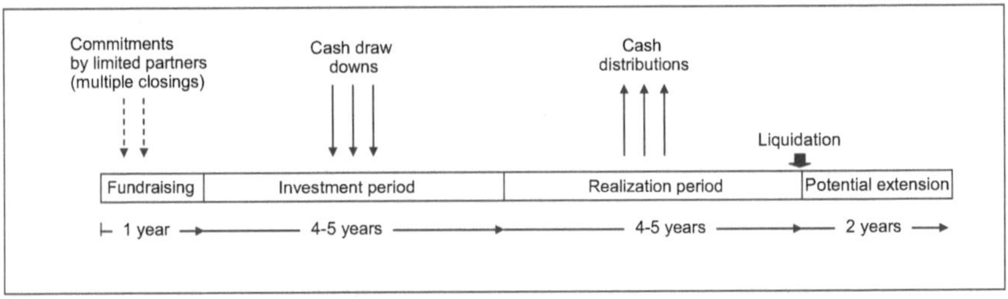

Figure 5: Life cycle of a closed-end private equity partnership

2.2.3 Partners in the Limited Partnership

2.2.3.1 Private Equity Firms as General Partners

The role of the private equity firms as general partners in the life of a partnership starts with raising the fund, proceeds with investing in companies, and ends with exiting the investments, including returning the capital to investors.[73] Then, the process starts all over again with raising a subsequent fund.[74]

The investment activities comprise three stages.[75] *Selecting* the companies to invest in is the first stage. The fund managers originate, screen and evaluate investment opportunities. In a second step, they structure the transaction. *Structuring* includes an agreement on the valuation of the company, the financial instruments that are used and the additional investor rights that will define the formal relationship between the fund and the portfolio company.[76] The third step is the *monitoring* of the investments. The fund

---

72 See Meyer/Mathonet (2005), p. 31. Normally, the approval is given annually, not for two years in advance.

73 See Gompers/Lerner (2004). The authors describe the role of private equity firms over a cycle, the so-called venture capital or private equity cycle.

74 See Gompers/Lerner (2004), pp. 3 et seq; Fenn/Liang/Prowse (1995), p. 28.

75 For the investment process see also Wright/Robbie (1998), p. 535; Fried/Hisrich (1994), p. 31; Tyebjee/Bruno (1984), p. 1053.

76 See Fingerle (2005), p. 77.

managers' objective is to add value by providing a variety of services and advice to the portfolio investments.[77] To realize a return on the investment, *divesting* or *exiting* the investment is an integral part of the whole investment process of a private equity fund manager.[78] After subtracting the profit share of the fund managers, the proceeds of the sales are distributed to the investors. The role of private equity firms is summarized as process in Figure 6.

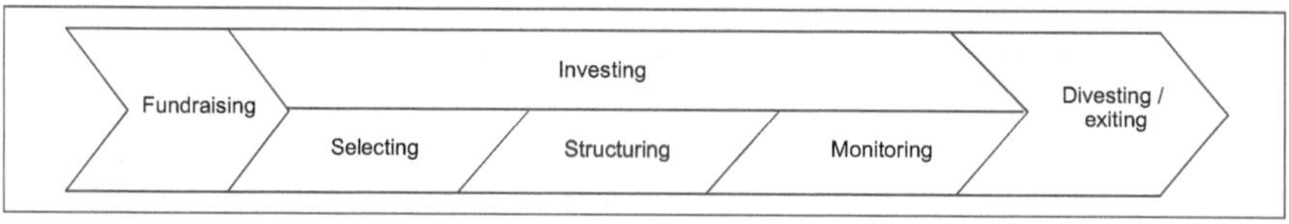

Figure 6: Role of private equity firms[79]

The degree to which the general partners are involved in monitoring and advising the management, the respective value-adding activities can vary. Some fund managers are rather active, often referred to as *hand-on* investors. Other fund managers are rather passive with respect to their involvement in the management of the portfolio companies. They are called *hands-off* investors.[80]

Private equity firms can be classified according to the *strategies* that they employ and pursue. With respect to the investments they target, one can, for example, distinguish between those that focus on venture capital investments and those that focus on late stage companies. Typically, the latter are also called buyout funds. Within these sub-segments of private equity, funds may specialize in one industry or invest generally across industries. According to the size of the investments that they target, one can distinguish between large-cap and mid-cap funds.

Depending on the influence that fund investors have on the investment policy of the fund, private equity firms can be distinguished in captive, semi-captive and independ-

---

77 See Fenn/Liang/Prowse (1995), pp. 33.

78 See Smith/Smith (2004), p. 546. An exit of the private equity investment is possible via an *initial public offering*, a *trade sale* to a strategic buyer, a *secondary sale* to another financial-oriented buyer, e.g. another private equity fund, a *buyback* of the stake of the former owners, or - in case of a failure - via a *liquidation* of the company. See Weitnauer (2001), p. 259.

79 Based on Berg (2005), p. 110; Achleitner (2002b), p. 748; Zehmke (1995), p. 103.

80 See Wright/Pruthi/Lockert (2005), p. 142.

ent funds.[81] *Captive funds* are characterized by having a financial institution as majority investor who controls the entity.[82] These are often banks or insurance companies.[83] *Semi-captive funds* are backed by a small group of investors with no controlling protagonist among them, but with one investor contributing a large part of the capital.[84] *Independent funds* are backed by many different investors but none of them has significant influence or is associated with the private equity firm.[85] There is no formal relation between fund investors and fund managers. As most private equity funds are independent funds, the analysis at hand concentrates on the relationship between investors and fund managers in this kind of funds.

2.2.3.2 Fund Investors as Limited Partners

Fund investors provide the capital required to carry out the investment strategies of the funds. Being the limited partners in the partnership, they are not involved in the active management of the fund. One typically distinguishes private and institutional investors. Figure 7 provides an overview of the relevant investors in European private equity funds.

Private individuals only play a minor role as investors in European private equity funds. In 2005, they provided 6% of the funds raised. Far more important are the institutional investors. Among those, public and private *pension funds* are the largest contributors (25% of funds raised in 2005).[86] They have long-term liabilities and limited requirements for liquidity. Private equity is therefore an attractive asset class for them.[87] *Banks* still contribute 18% of the total assets, however, over the years their

---

81 See Weitnauer (2001), p. 266.

82 See Osnabrugge/Robinson (2001), p. 27. Usually, these captive funds can still operate autonomously.

83 In case venture capitalists are controlled by an industrial organization, one speaks of a *corporate venture capital fund.* In addition to financial interests, corporate venture capital funds can also pursue strategic goals, e.g. access to new technologies, access to new products or services. RÖPER provides a detailed overview over corporate venture capital in Germany and the U.S. See Röper (2003).

84 Often semi-captive funds evolve from captive funds when these have a proven track record and their parent company takes third party money by inviting other investors to co-invest into the fund. See Bader (1996), p. 154.

85 See Osnabrugge/Robinson (2001), p. 25.

86 In the U.K., pension funds play a more important role in providing capital to private equity funds.

87 See Brooks (1999), p. 100.

share of total raised funds has been falling. *Insurance companies* have a stake of 11% in the capital raised. *Government agencies* (10%) also play a role although their shares seem to vary over the years. Corporate investors (5%) in total contribute smaller parts but may play an important role for venture capital funds.[88] The role of *capital market entities* (1%) and *academic institutions* (3%) as investors in European private equity funds is only marginal. This is different to the U.S. where university endowments contribute large sums to private equity.[89]

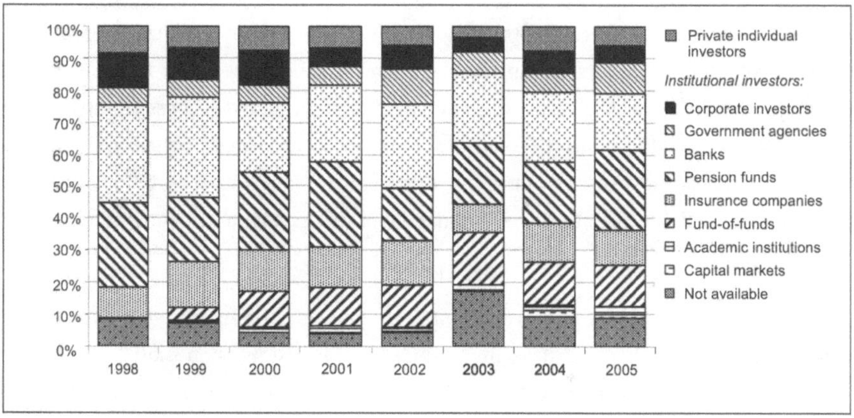

Figure 7: Contributions to European private equity funds by type of investor[90]

The *fund-of-funds* play a special role as fund investor. They are vehicles that pool money from their investors which they invest on their behalf in several private equity

---

[88] MAYER/SCHOORS/YAFEH who investigate the relation between the sources of funds and the investment activities of private equity funds find that funds which are mainly backed by corporate and private individuals target rather venture capital investments. If the funds are mainly backed by pension funds, insurance companies or banks, they tend to invest more in later stage activities. See Mayer/Schoors/Yafeh (2003), p. 4.

[89] Including the university funds, endowments have contributed 11% of total funds raised by independent venture capital funds in the U.S. in 2002. See Gompers/Lerner (2004), p. 11. In 2004, Yale's university endowment had 18% of its asset under management in private equity, Harvard 13% and Stanford 10%. See Avida Advisors (2005), p. 13.

[90] EVCA (2006c); EVCA (2002a). The figures show the distribution of different types of investors in European funds in percent raised from 1998 until 2006. However, they do not show the contribution of different investors to the total investment by all European investors in private equity. Unfortunately, these figures are not available.

funds.[91] The contribution of independent fund-of-funds to European private equity funds (13% in 2005) has increased over the years. Many investors prefer investing in private equity via these specialist vehicles rather than managing their own private equity program. Fund-of-funds can add value in various ways. For investors who only want to invest small amounts in private equity, fund-of-funds offer the possibility to diversify their allocation. Those who lack the in-house expertise to select funds can outsource this service by employing a fund-of-funds manager. Some investors, e.g. public pension funds, may not be able to build the in-house expertise because they are unable to offer appropriate incentives.[92] A high compensation structure might cause culture problems within their organizations. Appropriate incentives for investment professionals are, however, necessary to retain the experienced and successful staff within the investor's investment team. Therefore, these investors should better contribute to fund-of-funds instead. A disadvantage of investment through fund-of-funds structures is, however, that it leads to an additional layer of management and performance-related fees.[93]

According to the source of their own capital, private equity fund investors themselves can be classified into balance sheet investors, hybrid investors or specialist investors.[94] *Balance sheet investors* are part of a large financial institution and invest their parent's capital in the funds. Depending on the size of their total allocation, they have dedicated investment teams that manage the private equity allocation with more or less operating autonomy. Typically, pension funds are balance sheet investors. *Hybrid investors* invest not only their parent's capital, but have also third party money from external sources under management. Banks or large insurance companies follow hybrid ap-

---

91 See Grabenwarter/Weidig (2005a), p. 146.

92 See Meyer/Mathonet (2005), p. 48; Weidig/Mathonet (2004), p. 2.

93 See for a discussion of the benefits and costs of fund-of-funds for example Lai (2005); Meyer/Mathonet (2005), pp. 47 et seq. Once a decision to invest in private equity has been made, the investor needs to decide whether the portfolio is managed internally by its own staff or externally, through independent fund-of-funds managers. Alternatively, investors can use advisors or managed accounts to gain access to the asset class. Whereas advisors only assist the investor in selecting funds, managed accounts provide additional administrative support such as implementing control and reporting systems. The difference to investing in fund-of-funds is that investors still decide on the investments themselves. See Avida Advisors (2005), p. 17.

94 See for this and the following Barnes/Menzies (2005), p. 213.

proaches. *Specialist investors* manage external money only and are therefore depending on raising funds. Independent fund-of-funds are specialist investors.[95]

Although being a limited partner in a private equity fund and being not involved in active management, fund investors are not necessarily only passive. The active ones among them closely monitor their fund investments, they attend annual investors' meetings, or they serve on advisory boards.

The structure of a private equity limited partnership, its typical life cycle, and the special roles of both fund managers and investors that have been elaborated in this chapter result in unique characteristics of these private equity partnership investments. They will be discussed next.

2.3 Characteristics of Private Equity Partnership Investments

Investors in private equity partnerships have to consider the unique characteristics of these investments. Some are the results of the special type of the underlying private investments, and some are due to the private equity partnership structure (Figure 8).

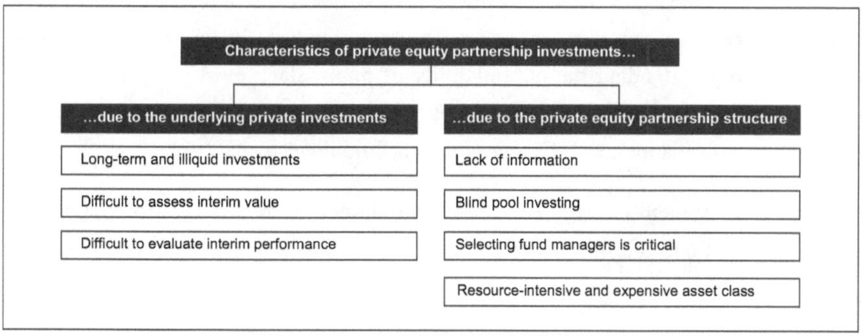

Figure 8: Characteristics of private equity partnership investments

95 BARNES/MENZIES argue that when investment teams mature and become more experienced, they establish a reputation and are able to raise external money. Consequently, there might be an evolutionary pathway for private equity investors from balance sheet over hybrid investors to specialist investors. This evolution is driven by the investment professionals at the institutions who are attracted by increased decision-power and increased remuneration. See Barnes/Menzies (2005), pp. 216 et seq.

First of all, private equity fund investments are *long-term and illiquid investments*. The lifetime of a single fund is typically contractually fixed at around ten years. Although a secondary market for the limited partnership stakes exists,[96] a quick sell at a fair market value is unlikely during the lifetime of the fund. One of the main reasons for the complexity to sell a partnership stake during the life-time is the *difficulty to determine its interim value.* While the fund is still in progress, the net asset values of the unrealized portfolio company investments need to be determined. However, as there are no publicly available market values for these portfolio company investments, a value is typically ascribed to them by the general partners. Private equity partnership investments are therefore subject to the valuation policy of the fund managers.[97] As a true value can hardly be defined, it is also very *difficult to evaluate the interim performance* of the fund. A definite return can only be calculated when a fund is liquidated and all investments are realized.[98] A benchmarking of the partnership during the lifetime of the fund investment's performance is therefore challenging.

As fund managers of private equity partnerships do not have disclose their performance or any other information in the public, there is in general a *lack of information* in and about the industry.[99] This does not only make benchmarking very difficult, but also complicates or deters the use of quantitative analysis in investment allocation planning. Notwithstanding the unavailability of public data, even limited partners of single partnerships depend more or less on the willingness of the general partners to satisfy their information needs concerning their fund investment.[100]

Whilst the investment strategy is outlined and agreed on before the limited partners commit to the fund, the fund investors leave the actual decision to select a particular

---

[96] See for an introduction of the secondary markets for example von Daniels (2004); Clark/Kojima (2003). Chapter 3.7.3 examines the usefulness of the secondary market for fund investors' active portfolio management.

[97] See Meyer/Mathonet (2005), p. 13. As will be outlined in more detail in chapter 4.3 which deals with the valuation of private equity investments, fund managers are discrete in determining a value for the investments.

[98] See Burgel (2000), p. 5.

[99] See Robbie/Wright/Chiplin (1999), p. 204. Due to the Freedom of Information Act in the U.S., public private equity investors such as public pension funds have been under pressure to disclose information on the performance of their private equity fund investments.

[100] The amount of provided information is typically fixed in the limited partnership agreement, for example by reference to industry reporting standards.

investment to the fund managers. Private equity fund investing is therefore also called *blind pool investing*. At the launch of the fund, there is no ability to preview the portfolio assets because they have not yet been identified. After the fund has been established, the limited partners have usually no possibility to review and decide on investments.[101] Therefore, *selecting fund managers is critical* for private equity partnership investors. The skills of the fund managers are regarded as key performance driver for generating attractive returns.[102]

Taking all that into account, private equity funds are a far more *resource-intensive and expensive asset class* than investing in the public market instead.[103] The special characteristics of private equity partnership investments require that investors are highly active. Selecting the most promising fund managers requires extensive research based on expertise and experience. In addition, in order to reduce the information deficiency between them and the fund managers, fund investors are required to carefully monitor the investments over the fund's lifetime. The remuneration of the general partner is high and further contributes to the fact that private equity is overall an expensive asset class.[104] As will be outlined next, this intensive monitoring and the alignment of interests are, however, necessary to govern the relationship between limited and general partners.

2.4 Governing the Relationship between Limited and General Partners

2.4.1 Potential Conflicts of Interest

Once the limited partners have selected to invest in a fund, they fully delegate the operational management, especially the investment decisions to the general partner and his fund managers. The general partner acts as agent who performs work for its princi-

---

[101] See Bance (2004), p. 7; Grabenwarter/Weidig (2005a), p. 10.

[102] See Meyer/Mathonet (2005), p. 60. In fact, there is evidence of a large dispersion of returns of different funds. See for example Kaserer/Diller (2004d), p. 9.

[103] See Bance (2004), p. 7; Grabenwarter/Weidig (2005a), p. 10. If investors want to pursue an in-house private equity management program, it is therefore required that they commit significant amounts of capital to the asset class in order to realize necessary economies of scale.

[104] On average, investors in European private equity funds pay 14.7% of their invested capital as management fee. See Feinendegen/Schmidt/Wahrenburg (2003), p. 1177. Additionally, the fund investors usually get 20% of the net realized gain as profit share.

pals, the limited partners.[105] Agency problems arise when the objectives of the principal and the agent conflict and when - due to asymmetric information - it gets difficult to verify what the agent is actually doing and if he behaves appropriately.[106] The information asymmetry *after* the investors have selected the fund manager exists in the form of *hidden action* that causes moral hazard.[107]

This theoretical analysis explains the *conflicts of interest* that potentially arise during the lifetime of the partnership and that fund investors have to deal with. There is a whole bunch of potential conflicts of interests in the relationship between fund managers and investors – as the following differentiations show:

Conflicts of interest relating to the risk level and the strategy of the fund

There is an incentive for the general partners to maximize the partnership's risk when investing in their portfolio companies. The performance related compensation, i.e. the carried interest, is an option-like claim on the fund's assets. The fund managers could intend to maximize the expected value of their carried interest rather than optimizing the fund's risk adjusted expected rate of return by increasing the fund's risk.[108] The risk taking may be even more excessive with a deal-by-deal carry interest scheme in comparison to a fund-as-a-whole carry system. In a *deal-by-deal* carry system, the carried interest is payable if the rate of return for an individual deal exceeds the hurdle rate or preferred return. With a *fund-as-a-whole* scheme previous losses and the overall performance are also taken into account.[109]

Instead of complying with the strategy of the fund, they could also invest in other asset classes. This causes concerns for investors, mainly for three reasons. First of all, the fund managers - unintentionally backed by the fund investors - may opt to gain experience in asset classes where they currently have no expertise. Secondly, fund managers

---

105 For fundamentals of the *agency theory* see Jensen/Ruback (1983); Eisenhardt (1989). SAHLMAN analyzes the principle agent relationship between general and limited partners. See Sahlman (1990), pp. 493 et seq.

106 See Eisenhardt (1989), p. 58.

107 See Eisenhardt (1989), p. 61.

108 Based on Black/Scholes (1973) the value of a call option is positively correlated with the volatility of the value of the underlying asset. See Sahlman (1990), p. 496.

109 See Meyer/Mathonet (2005), p. 33.

charge management fees on assets for which the compensation they receive might be inappropriately large.[110] Last but not least, fund investors may end up with a different asset allocation than their target ones.

Conflicts of interest relating to other activities of the general partner

Limited partners fear that fund managers could spend too little effort in monitoring and advising portfolio firms. In addition, fund managers may simply aim at maximizing their fee income. In case general partners propose consulting services to their portfolio companies on a fee basis, the fund investors should be concerned as the general partners get paid for this. The fund managers may argue that they thereby increase the value for investors. However, as the limited partners have already mandated them to manage the portfolio companies and therefore pay the management fee and a profit share, the fund managers thus intentially charge twice for the same service.[111]

With respect to own investment activities, limited partners should be attentive to whether general partners pursue selective co-investments in portfolio companies. This could lead the fund managers' full attention to these assets only.[112] Besides, they might also reserve the most attractive investment opportunities for themselves.[113]

Conflicts of interest between different funds managed by the same fund managers

Investors dislike fund managers raising new funds although the current one is not yet invested. First, fundraising costs valuable time of the fund managers that should be better allocated to the current fund. In addition, having raised the new fund may lead the focus of the managers' investment activities to the new fund. This is especially the case, when the performance of the old fund does not allow the managers to get any profit share. Additionally, when a follow-on fund of the same fund manager co-invests in financing rounds of the predecessor fund, there are severe conflicts of interest be-

---

110 See Gompers/Lerner (1996), p. 483. Some fund investors argue that it may be not appropriate to charge a management fee of 2.5% and 20% of the profits if private equity firms invested in public securities as the investors could do that cheaper by themselves. However, this depends on the actual strategy of the funds and, of course, on the agreement between fund investors and managers.

111 See Grabenwarter/Weidig (2005a), p. 78.

112 However, the general partners' contribution of 1% of the whole fund is generally required. See Sahlman (1990), p. 490.

113 See Prowse (1998), p. 31.

tween the investors of both funds since value could be shifted from one fund to the other, depending on the valuation of the financed company.[114]

These potential conflicts of interest caused by the delegation of the active management of private equity partnerships to the general partners have to be addressed in the mechanisms that govern the formal relationship between fund managers and investors.[115] The fund investors need to assure that the general partners do not act against their interests. An appropriate legal and incentive structure mitigates some of the governance related problems. The framework that governs the relationship between investors and fund managers is the limited partnership agreement.[116] Conflicts of interest are mitigated by mechanisms that relate to direct means of control or mechanisms that relate to performance incentives for the general partners (Figure 9).[117] They will come up in detail in the following two chapters. However, it is worth noting that not all potential issues can be regulated upfront. Private equity market participants therefore always stress that in addition to the formal agreements, there is also a need for a good personal relationship between the fund managers and their investors which is based on trust.[118]

---

114 See Grabenwarter/Weidig (2005a), pp. 78 et seq.

115 See Sahlman (1990), p. 493.

116 FAMA/JENSEN state that in order to mitigate agency problems the principal and the agent sign a contract that specifies the rights of the agent, clarifies the performance criteria on which the agent will be evaluated, and defines the payoff functions for both parties. See Fama/Jensen (1983), p. 302.

117 See Fenn/Liang/Prowse (1995), p. 38; Prowse (1998), p. 3. In public equity financing, the *market for corporate control* would also mitigate conflicts of interest between managers and investors. JENSEN/RUBACK describe it as a market where alternative management teams compete for the right to manage corporate resources. See Jensen/Ruback (1983), p. 6. In public corporations, the threat of a takeover might put pressure on the management teams to perform. However, the relevance of the market for corporate control as a mechanism to solve governance problems in private equity partnerships is still marginal. The secondary market for limited private equity partnership stakes is rather illiquid and, although a change of the management through the general partner could be triggered typically by a qualified majority vote of the limited partners, this rarely happens in reality. See Böhler (2004b), p. 77. However, as the private equity market evolves and the fund investors get more active, it is at least not unthinkable that the market for corporate control as a mechanism to solve governance issues becomes more important.

118 More information on the role of trust is provided in chapter 2.7.4.

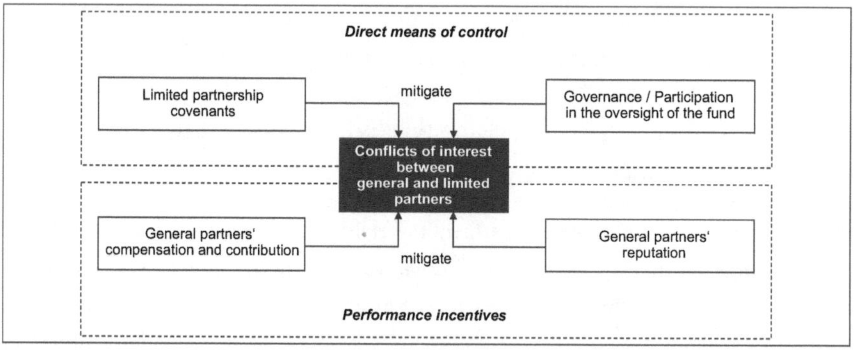

Figure 9: Means for mitigating conflicts of interests in private equity partnerships[119]

2.4.2 Direct Means of Control

Mechanism of direct control can be split in limited partners' participation in oversight of the fund and in up-front rules, such as covenants that place restrictions on a partnership's investments and on other activities of the general partners.[120]

Covenants

Contractual covenants address potential conflicts of interest that cause concern for investors. Restrictions on the investments are intended to ensure that the general partners follow the initially agreed investment strategy.[121] Restrictions on the activities of the general partners make sure that they are committed to the success of the actual fund and limit the possibility to pursue their own or other fund's interests under their management.

Key-man and removal clauses are protective clauses that cut investors' risks if things get off track due to issues in the management team of the fund.[122] *Key-man clauses* address the investors' concern about a potential turnover of certain named fund man-

---

[119] Based on Fenn/Liang/Prowse (1995).

[120] See Prowse (1998), p. 32.

[121] Investment opportunities are not automatically excluded when they are in breach of the covenants. If fund managers think that it is still a good opportunity that the fund should pursue, the limited partnership agreement often allows that the investment proposal is subject to an extraordinary approval of all investors or their representatives in the advisory board.

[122] See Grabenwarter/Weidig (2005a), p. 70.

agers. If a partnership is faced with general partner turnover and the key-man clause is triggered, limited partners may, for example, cease any further commitments or even terminate the partnership. The limited partnership agreement specifies in detail when this is the case, either if specific individuals or a combination of key people leave the fund's management team.[123]

Removal clauses give the limited partners the right to terminate the general partners, i.e. to change the management team.[124] *Removal clauses for cause* specify circumstances that allow the limited partners to exercise their right to terminate the general partner by a majority vote. It is nearly impossible to define ex-ante all situations in which limited partners desire to do so. Therefore, fund investors also ask for *removal clauses without cause* which give them the right to change the general partners without any specific reason. Removal clauses without causes are typically triggered by a 75% qualified vote.

Conflicts of interest		Covenants in the limited partnership agreement
Conflicts of interest relating to the risk level and the strategy of the fund	⇨	• Restrictions on the size of a portfolio company investment • Restrictions on the use of debt • Restrictions on the type of investment
Conflicts of interest relating to other activities of general partners	⇨	• Restrictions on co-investments by general partners • Restrictions on the sale of partnership interests by general partners • Restrictions on other activities of general partners
Conflict of interest between different funds managed by general partners	⇨	• Restrictions on co-investments of general partners' earlier or later funds • Restrictions on new fundraising by general partners
General misalignment of interests	⇨	• Key-man clauses • Removal clauses for cause and without cause

Figure 10: Conflicts of interests and examples for mitigating covenants[125]

For fund investors, these contractual control rights are a very powerful tool to influence the development of their investments. Examples and the respective conflicts of interest that they address are provided in Figure 10.

---

123 See William M. Mercer Inc. (1997), pp. 117 et seq.

124 See Grabenwarter/Weidig (2005a), pp. 72 et seq.

125 Based on Gompers/Lerner (1996), p. 484; Feinendegen/Schmidt/Wahrenburg (2003), pp. 1171 et seq; Hagenmüller (2004), p. 181.

Contracting is costly since the details of the contracts have to be negotiated and the adherence to the contractual agreement needs to be monitored. The benefits of restricting the activity of the general partner need to be therefore greater than the costs.[126] GOMPERS/LERNER find evidence in an analysis of U.S. private equity limited partnership agreements that the number and type of covenants depend on both the variations in the need of oversight and the supply and demand conditions in the private equity market.[127] The more severe the potential agency problems and the need for oversight between fund managers and investors, the higher are the benefits from writing covenants. In years with greater inflow in the industry, fewer restrictions are found in the limited partnership agreements.[128] FEINENDEGEN/SCHMIDT/WAHRENBURG pursue a similar study with limited partnership agreements of European private equity funds. They find great heterogeneity with respect to the type and number of covenants and the use of more covenants over time. However, they do not confirm the relevance of supply and demand conditions in the market.

Participation in the oversight of the fund

In addition to the covenants, limited partners may have some degree of oversight and control of the partnership through advisory boards or special committees such as a valuation committee.[129] These governance bodies are typically composed of the largest investors. They offer the investors a formal platform of dialogue with the general partners. Advisory boards and committees may review the fund's investment activity, the investment strategy, or the valuation policy applied by the fund managers. They also may decide on any conflicts of interest.[130] However, they typically do not take a role in the daily operations of the funds.[131]

---

[126] See Gompers/Lerner (1996), p. 470.

[127] See Gompers/Lerner (1996), p. 464.

[128] See Feinendegen/Schmidt/Wahrenburg (2003), p. 1190.

[129] See Sahlman (1990), p. 493; Fenn/Liang/Prowse (1995), p. 41.

[130] See Grabenwarter/Weidig (2005b), p. 83. Chapter 3.5.1 provides insight about the role of advisory boards for monitoring the partnership.

[131] See chapter 3.5.1 for more details on advisory boards.

2.4.3 Performance Incentives

Even more important to overcome agency problems are the economics of the partnership agreement and the alignment of interests between investors and fund managers through performance incentives.[132] General partners are given incentives to perform in the interest of the fund investors through the structure of their compensation package for the fund. Additionally, as they need to raise follow-up funds, fund managers need to care about their reputation. Therefore, they are subject to ongoing market discipline.[133]

General partners' compensation and contribution

The general partners' compensation comprises two parts: a fixed management fee and a share of the partnership's profits, the so-called carried interest.[134] The *management fee* shall cover the actual cost of managing the fund. It is determined by multiplying a fee percentage, e.g. 2.0-2.5%,[135] with a certain fee base. Fee bases are typically the committed capital during the investment period of the fund and the invested capital at cost afterwards.[136] Investors need to analyze and monitor the possible incentives for fund managers resulting from the management fee. Increasing fund sizes or the management of multiple funds may lead to excessive surpluses on the management fee. As the management fee income is independent on the effort of the fund managers, moral hazard problems as described earlier may arise. High fee income may decrease the motivation of the fund managers to earn the performance depending carried interest.

The *carried interest* is the general partners' share of the partnership's profit. Usually, it is 20% of the net return of the entire fund.[137] Distribution clauses (also *called water-*

---

132 See Meyer/Mathonet (2005), p. 30.

133 See Smith/Smith (2004), p. 481.

134 See Fenn/Liang/Prowse (1995), p. 38.

135 See Feinendegen/Schmidt/Wahrenburg (2003), p. 1176. In a study of European partnerships, the authors find that around 80% apply a management fee of 2.0% or 2.5%.

136 See Grabenwarter/Weidig (2005a), p. 58. In practice, the total actual paid management fees vary across different funds, depending on the fee bases that are applied. See Feinendegen/Schmidt/Wahrenburg (2003), p. 1177.

137 See Feinendegen/Schmidt/Wahrenburg (2003), p. 1177; Gompers/Lerner (1999), p. 15. Under earlier agreements, the carried interest was sometimes based on the performance of individual investments (deal-by-deal carry) rather than based on the performance of the entire fund (fund-as-a-whole carry). However, with a deal-by-deal carry system fund managers were more focused on

fall structure) in the partnership agreements specify how the proceeds from portfolio companies are distributed, i.e. paid to the partners. It has become a standard term that investors receive a minimum rate of return (*hurdle rate* or *preferred return*) before the fund managers receive their share of any profits.[138] The advocates of a hurdle rate argue that fund managers should earn at least an equivalent to the cost of capital of the funds provided before getting any carry. A catch-up mechanism typically defines the following when proceeds occur:[139] First of all, the limited partners receive their invested capital back plus the preferred return. Then, all subsequent distributions are allocated to the general partners until they have received an amount equal to their profit share of the amount already distributed to limited partners. Thereafter, any distribution depends on the split agreed between limited and general partners. If a fund makes early distributions, there is a risk that the general partners receive carried interest although the overall performance of the fund may be below the hurdle rate or even negative.[140] This leads to so-called *clawback* liabilities against the fund managers. To mitigate the credit risk for investors in the case of overdistributions to fund managers, the latter may be forced to allocate all or part of the received carry to escrow accounts.[141]

The option-like claim on the fund profits may lead to an excessive risk taking by the general partners when investing for the fund. In order to mitigate these risks, fund managers are typically required to contribute a significant part of their personal wealth to the fund. Thereby, they are exposed to losses of the fund and discouraged from taking inappropriate risk or even leaving the fund.[142]

---

maximizing returns of the most successful investments than of the total fund return. See Fenn/Liang/Prowse (1995), p. 39.

138 See Meyer/Mathonet (2005), p. 33. The hurdle rate is usually set at 6%-8%.

139 See Grabenwarter/Weidig (2005a), p. 62.

140 See Grabenwarter/Weidig (2005a), p. 64.

141 See Schell (2006), pp. 2/22 et seq. The details are set out by claw-back provisions in the limited partnership agreement.

142 See Meyer/Mathonet (2005), p. 34. Typically, a contribution of 1% of the fund's capital is regarded as appropriate. This depends on the personal wealth of the general partners and the size of the fund.

General partners' need to build up a reputation

A bad fund management and opportunistic behavior damages the fund managers' reputation and makes it more difficult for them to raise new funds.[143] Due to the finite lives of the independent closed-end partnerships, the fund managers must regularly raise new funds in order to stay in business.[144] It is important that they are able to continuously make investments in order to generate and keep a sufficient deal flow.[145] Therefore, the new fundraising starts typically already before the former fund is fully invested. Raising funds is costly and time consuming. In order to reduce these costs, fund managers generally prefer their existing investors to also participate in the new fund. Their existing investors are most familiar with the performance and behavior of the management team. It would be difficult for the fund managers to attract new investors, if the former experienced investors withdrew from investing in the new fund.[146]

Fund managers therefore have an incentive to build a reputation[147] which claims that they are not only high performing investment managers, but that they are also trustworthy to work with. Fund managers and investors agree to work together for a long period of time where many unforeseen events may happen and a fair behavior is required. Reputation and trust are advantageous and extremely important in these situations.[148] Within the principal-agent-framework, reputation can be seen as a security given by the agent to the principal.[149] Misbehavior or actions against the interests of the principal may reduce the agent's capital. For fund managers, this means that their opportunities to raise future funds would decline. The fear to loose a high reputation may have effects on the compensation terms and the need for covenants. The reputation may substitute explicit contractual terms.[150]

---

143 See Balboa/Marti (2006), p. 5.

144 See Fenn/Liang/Prowse (1995), p. 36.

145 Without the possibility to make any investment, fund managers may loose their network to potential sellers of companies, i.e. owners, advisors, investment banks, or others.

146 See Fenn/Liang/Prowse (1995), p. 36.

147 Reputation is a collective construct describing aggregate perceptions of third parties about the performance of the private equity company and its reliability. See Fingerle (2005), p. 35.

148 See Holmström/Tirole (1989), pp. 76 et seq.

149 See Schmidt/Wahrenburg (2004), p. 8.

150 See Smith/Smith (2004), p. 495.

2.4.4 Importance of Provisions in the Limited Partnership Agreement

The limited partnership agreement plays an important role in the relationship between general and limited partners in private equity partnerships. Both parties largely agree on the relevance of specific provisions.

A study by the TUCK SCHOOL OF BUSINESS ranks the importance for specific provisions perceived by general and limited partners.[151] The respective ten most important provisions are shown in Figure 11. Of highest importance for both partners are clauses that relate to economic terms, i.e. provisions with respect to the carried interest, claw-back or management fees. The relevance of the general partners' personal capital commitment is also stressed by both parties. General partners rank the provisions addressing the limitation of their liability very high. They also find indemnification clauses important which exclude the general and limited partners' personal liability when acting by order of the partnership, e.g. as member of portfolio companies' advisory boards. Limited partners ascribe greater importance to provisions addressing governance than general partners, e.g. conflicts of interest or key-men clauses.[152] Limited partners also rank side-letters as one of the ten most provisions. Side-letters set out specific individual agreements between general and limited partners, e.g. with respect to management fees, advisory board seats, or co-investment rights.

General partners	Limited partners
1. Waterfall structure, carried interest calculations	**1. Waterfall structure, carried interest calculations**
2. Management fees	**2. Claw-back provisions**
3. Claw-back provisions	3. General partners conflict issues
4. General partners' capital commitment	4. Key-man provisions
5. Limitations of liability for general partners	**5. Management fees**
6. Indemnification clauses	**6. General partners' capital commitment**
7. Investment strategy, limitations and guidelines	7. Side-letters
8. Fundraising period, investment period & term	**8. Investment strategy, limitations and guidelines**
9. Permitted activities of general partners	**9. Permitted activities of general partners**
10. Limited partners' approval rights	10. Portfolio company fee offsets

Note: Issues of agreement in bold

Figure 11: Top ten ranked most important provisions in limited partnership agreements[153]

---

151 See Tuck (2004b). The authors base their results on a survey among general partners (n=117) and limited partners (n=97) in the U.S.

152 See Tuck (2004b), p. 4.

153 See Blaydon/Wainwright (2004b), p. 19.

Given the fact that limited and general partners agree on the importance of at least six out of the ten most important provisions, the question arises why no standard limited partnership agreements exist. Creating and negotiating the limited partnership agreement is a detailed and time consuming task.[154] BLAYDON/WAINWRIGHT have raised the question in a survey among U.S. industry participants, whether a standard or model document would benefit the industry.[155] It might reduce negotiation time and costs, facilitate due diligence, or increase the liquidity of the secondary market for partnership interests. However, their results are not clear. Limited partners tend to favor a development of a model agreement, whereas general partners rather disagree with the importance of such a model.[156] The bottom line of the discussion is that instead of a standard document which decreases the flexibility in setting the terms, it is important that the process is transparent. Each partner needs to be able to easily understand how he is being affected by the different aspects of the limited partnership agreement.[157]

While the discussion so far has considered both the perspective of the fund managers and the fund investors, in the following the fund investors' investment process will be analyzed in more detail.

2.5 Fund Investors' Investment Process

2.5.1 Overview

When describing and analyzing the activities of the fund investors with respect to their investment process, it is appropriate to conceptually distinguish two different levels: the individual fund investment level and the portfolio of funds level, also called fund-of-fund level (Figure 12).

The *individual fund investment level* illustrates the relationship between the fund investor and the individual fund. The activities of the fund investor are the fund selection, the monitoring and governing of the fund investment and the divestment of the

---

154 See Tuck (2004a), p. 3. On average, the legal costs for a limited partnership agreement are $260,000 for general partners and $18,000 for limited partners. See Tuck (2004b), p. 7.

155 See Blaydon/Wainwright (2004b), p. 217. For detailed results see Tuck (2004b); Tuck (2004c); Tuck (2004d); Tuck (2004a).

156 See Tuck (2004b), pp. 3 et seq.

157 See Tuck (2004a), p. 9.

fund investment.[158] The fund investor, however, does not only invest in one fund but diversifies over a number of funds. The respective activities cannot be analyzed without taking into account that portfolio of funds.

The *portfolio of funds* comprises all the individual fund investments. The four tasks on the portfolio of funds level are (1) the asset allocation decision, (2) the portfolio construction, (3) the portfolio monitoring, and (4) the portfolio management. It is pictured in Figure 12. These tasks and any respective interdependencies between the activities on the portfolio of fund level and the individual fund level will be elaborated in detail in the next chapters.

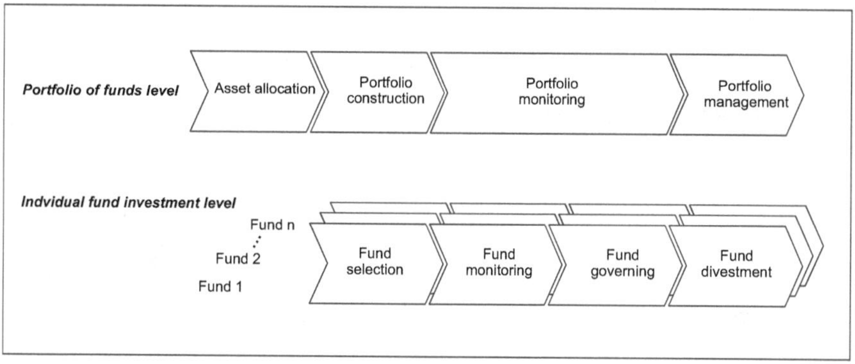

Figure 12: Fund investors' investment process

2.5.2 Asset Allocation

According to SHARPE, the asset allocation decision states how to distribute an investor's portfolio across a number of 'major' asset classes.[159] From an investor's perspective, private equity competes with other asset classes for an allocation from the available financial resources.[160] Public equity and fixed income securities are traditional as-

---

158 The divestment typically happens automatically as the fund managers exit the portfolio company investment and distribute the proceeds to their fund investors.

159 See Sharpe (1992), p. 7. An asset class comprises all investments that have similar characteristics, attributes and risk-return relationships. See Reilly/Brown (2003), p. 35.

160 Fund-of-funds investors have a certain amount of capital available that was allocated to them by their clients. They do not have to decide about how much they allocate to private equity. However, their clients need to address this question.

set classes. Private equity is part of the so-called alternative asset classes.[161] In the process of asset allocation, the private equity investor needs to address the following two questions:[162]

- How much of an entire portfolio shall be allocated to private equity?
- How shall the private equity program be implemented and managed?

Determining the portfolio allocation to private equity

In portfolio theory, the investor defines the appropriate weighting for each asset class that maximizes the risk-adjusted return based on the expected returns of the different asset classes, the respective expected risk, and the expected correlations between the different asset classes.[163] For each asset class, the investor therefore needs to estimate its future return, risk and correlation. The higher the risk-adjusted return and the lower the correlation to other asset classes, the higher is the weight of the asset class in the optimal portfolio.[164]

Estimating these input factors for private equity investments is problematic. The private equity industry lacks transparency as privately owned funds are not legally obliged to publish their performance.[165] Only few empirical research studies exist that examine the risk and return characteristics of private equity. And these different stud-

---

161 See Achleitner/Fingerle (2006), p. 3. There is no commonly accepted definition of the universe of alternative assets. Typically, it includes private equity, hedge funds, infrastructure investments, real estate, and other investment assets such as commodities, fine art, or wine.

162 See Hagenmüller (2004), p. 32; Gompers/Lerner (2001), p. 1; Bader (1996), p. 248.

163 See Markowitz (1952). Tax and legal constraints also need to be considered in the allocation decision. See Gompers/Lerner (2001), p. 2. However, these aspects are neglected here.

164 See Grabenwarter/Weidig (2005a), p. 34. For an introduction to portfolio theory and the assumptions see for example Reilly/Brown (2003), pp. 209 et seq.

165 Instead, two commercial data vendors provide the main source of data on the venture capital industry, VentureXperts from Venture Economics and VentureSource from VentureOne. *Venture Economics* comprises cash flows from around 2,500 U.S. and European funds. *VentureOne* is a database on direct venture capital investments. It includes more than 17,000 financing rounds involving more than 8,000 companies. See Grabenwarter/Weidig (2005a), p. 108. These databases mostly rely on the voluntary reporting of the funds and their investors. Other databases that academic researchers may have access to are provided by large investors. However, these databases are not published on an ongoing basis.

ies are based on different time periods, use different databases, filter out young funds in different ways, or measure performance in different ways.[166]

It is furthermore important to consider the perspective of these studies when interpreting their results. Some of them examine the return distribution based on portfolio company data.[167] Other studies analyze the return distribution of investments in private equity funds.[168]

Private equity and benchmarks	Net IRR p.a. as of 31.12.2005			
	1 year	3 years	5 years	10 years
European venture capital [a]	36.5	1.7	-3.0	6.4
European buyouts [a]	31.7	9.1	6.1	14.3
European all private equity [a]	33.8	6.3	2.0	11.4
U.S. venture capital [b]	15.6	7.5	-6.8	23.7
U.S. buyouts [b]	31.3	16.3	5.2	9.2
U.S. all private equity [b]	22.6	13.1	1.5	12.3
Morgan Stanley European Equity Index [a]	16.6	13.2	-3.7	2.9
HSBC Small European Equity Index [a]	15.8	33.5	13.0	11.1
NASDAQ [b]	5.2	14.2	-2.2	7.7
S & P 500 [b]	6.3	10.1	-1.1	7.3

Figure 13: Private equity returns and benchmarks[169]

With respect to fund return data, the private equity industry associations together with an independent data service company, VentureXperts, are providing benchmarks. As

166 See Grabenwarter/Weidig (2005a), p. 27. The authors provide a comprehensive list of existing risk-return studies in private equity. See Grabenwarter/Weidig (2005a), pp. 28 et seq.

167 These studies are mainly based on VentureOne data. They examine the gross-of-fee return of individual venture capital investments. COCHRANE for example bases his analysis on financing rounds of 7,765 companies and calculates mean average returns to be 59% with a standard deviation of 107%. See Cochrane (2005), p. 5. Other studies are for example Quigley/Woodward (2003); Woodward/Hall (2003); Peng (2001).

168 Important studies are Phalippou/Zollo (2005); Kaplan/Schoar (2005); Kaserer/Diller (2004b); Ljungqvist/Richardson (2003); Jones/Rhodes-Kropf (2003).

169 See a: EVCA/Thomson Financial (2006), p. 12; b: NVCA/Financial (2006), p. 2. The data is provided by VentureXperts. The comparison of returns of private equity with the benchmarks is made by calculating equivalent IRR returns for the benchmarks assuming the same cash flows as for the "all private equity" asset classes. For detailed information on the methodology see 3.4.3.2.

can be seen in Figure 13, over a ten years period the net internal rate of returns (IRR) of European and U.S. private equity funds outperform the public asset classes. The return of U.S. venture capital is higher than U.S. buyout investments which should be expected due to the inherent higher risk of venture capital companies. This is not the case in Europe which suggests an inefficient risk-return allocation between various sub-segments.[170]

The presented data is based on net asset values[171] of the fund investments. As there are no observable market prices for the fund investments, a value must be assigned to the unrealized and illiquid investments. This complicates performance measurement, as fund managers may value their investments differently from each other.[172]

Therefore, several authors base their studies on the performance of private equity funds preferably on cash flow data. LJUNGQVIST/RICHARDSON, for example, analyze the cash flows of 73 liquidated U.S. funds. The authors find an average internal rate of return (IRR) of 20% over the period from 1981-1993 with a standard deviation of 22%.[173] They show that this is an excess return of 5%-8% to the aggregate market return of the S&P 500.[174] KAPLAN/SCHOAR base their results on cash flows from 746 U.S. funds between 1980 and 2001. They calculate an average IRR of 17% with a 31% standard deviation. In order to circumvent the problems associated with the IRR,[175] they focus on the public market equivalent approach. On average, they find a public market equivalent[176] of 0.96 compared to the S&P 500.[177] Net of fees, private equity

---

170 See Grabenwarter/Weidig (2005a), p. 20.

171 The net asset value is the value of the portfolio company investments plus any additional assets minus any liabilities.

172 See Gompers/Lerner (2001), p. 3. Some fund managers might be conservative in their approach to value investments whereas others are more aggressive.

173 See Ljungqvist/Richardson (2003), p. 15. The returns are net of any management fees and carried interests and therefore represent the actual return to the limited partners.

174 See Ljungqvist/Richardson (2003), p. 28. They interpret this as a premium for the illiquidity of the portfolio company investments.

175 Chapter 3.4.1 discusses the problems associated with the use of the internal rate of return as return measure in private equity.

176 A public market equivalent (PME) compares an investment in a private equity fund to an investment in public equity, usually a capital market index. KAPLAN/SCHOAR implement the PME calculation by investing all cash outflows of the fund at the total return to the S&P 500 and comparing the resulting value to the value of the cash inflows to the fund invested using the total return to

has slightly underperformed the S&P 500 over the sample period. KASERER/DILLER calculate cash flow based returns from 201 European private equity funds.[178] On average they report an IRR of 12% and a standard deviation of 17%. The sample outperformed the equity index MSCI Europe by 4% and the J.P. Morgan Government Bond index by 5%.[179] They found an average PME of 0.93.[180] PHALIPPOU/ZOLLO analyze the performance of 983 U.S. private equity funds raised between 1980 and 1996 and officially liquidated until 2003.[181] They show that the return of private equity funds after corrections for sample selection-bias of the database is 12% and therefore lower than the return of the S&P by more than 3%. To sum up, based on these divergent results of various studies, so far no definite conclusion for the performance of private equity fund investments can be drawn.[182]

Besides of return and risk, the correlation of returns between private equity and other asset classes is another important factor in order to assess the optimal portfolio allocation for investors. The lower the correlation, the higher is the diversification effect of adding private equity to a portfolio consisting of other asset classes. There are, however, again major difficulties in estimating correlations. Returns on private equity are typically measured using the internal rate of return. In public market, time-weighted returns are used. If public and private equity returns shall be compared, one has to calculate private equity time-weighted returns. The reported net asset values are used as beginning and ending inputs of a period. Due to conservative accounting methods and infrequent valuation, the calculated correlation may be artificially low.[183] Several authors try to overcome this problem with different methods.[184] KASERER/DILLER report

the S&P 500. A fund with a PME that is smaller than one underperforms the S&P 500. See Kaplan/Schoar (2005), p. 1797. For more information on the PME method see chapter 3.4.3.2.

177 See Kaplan/Schoar (2005), p. 1798. Their returns are also net of any fees.

178 See Kaserer/Diller (2004c), p. 49. Their sample includes all funds that are liquidated or non-liquidated with a residual value not higher than 10%. Returns are net of any fees.

179 See Kaserer/Diller (2004c), pp. 50 et seq.

180 See Kaserer/Diller (2004b), p. 54. Their approach assumes that returns from private equity funds are reinvested in the public market index.

181 See Phalippou/Zollo (2005), p. 8.

182 See Grabenwarter/Weidig (2005a), p. 31.

183 See Grabenwarter/Weidig (2005a), p. 33. Gompers/Lerner call this the *stale price problem*. See Gompers/Lerner (2001), p. 3.

184 See for example Gompers/Lerner (2001).

a correlation coefficient with a fixed income index to be 0.75 and with a public equity index to be 0.84.[185] Other studies also find non-zero but rather moderate to high correlation.[186]

The quantitative analysis provides insights in the key determinants in portfolio allocation. KASERER/DILLER, for example, calculate based on the characteristics of European private equity funds that an optimal portfolio may contain in addition to bonds and public equity 5% venture capital and 3% buyout investments.[187] However, KASERER/ACHLEITNER/WAGNER conclude that the empirical understanding of the risk-return characteristics of private equity investments is still incomplete.[188] A well-founded, in-depth understanding of this matter is yet a prerequisite for a purposeful asset allocation decision.

As a result of the difficulties in using the traditional allocation techniques, investors typically apply qualitative approaches to budget an allocation to private equity.[189] Very often it is said that around 5%-10% of the total assets should be allocated to private equity.[190] Investors need to consider their liquidity needs. If they have a long-term horizon, their allocation to private equity may be higher.[191]

Implementing the private equity investment program

The question of how large the allocation to private equity in absolute size should be is related to the decision of how to implement the private equity program. The investor has the choice to invest in direct investments, private equity funds, or fund-of-funds.[192]

---

185 See Kaserer/Diller (2004b), p. 42. They assume that returns from private equity are reinvested in the indices.

186 See Grabenwarter/Weidig (2005a), p. 33 for more details.

187 See Kaserer/Diller (2004c), p. 70.

188 See Kaserer/Wagner/Achleitner (2003), p. 275.

189 See Avida Advisors (2005), p. 23. Based on a survey among 32 European investors, the authors found that 57% use qualitative approaches only.

190 See Kaserer/Diller (2004c), p. 71; Meyer/Mathonet (2005), p. 83.

191 Foundations may have infinite investment horizons. Very often, they distribute returns to various purposes. Due to the infinite investment horizon, they may afford to allocate more resources to private equity.

192 Fund managers sometimes offer their fund investors to co-invest alongside the fund directly in a specific company. This is often the case, when the amount to be invested in the company exceeds

WEIDIG/MATHONET simulate the return distributions of these different possibilities in order to demonstrate the respective risks. They show that by investing in professionally managed funds, investors are able to reduce the risks associated with the stand-alone investments. Fund-of-funds investments even more decrease the risk.[193] Figure 14 illustrates the risk profiles of different investment types by showing their return distributions.

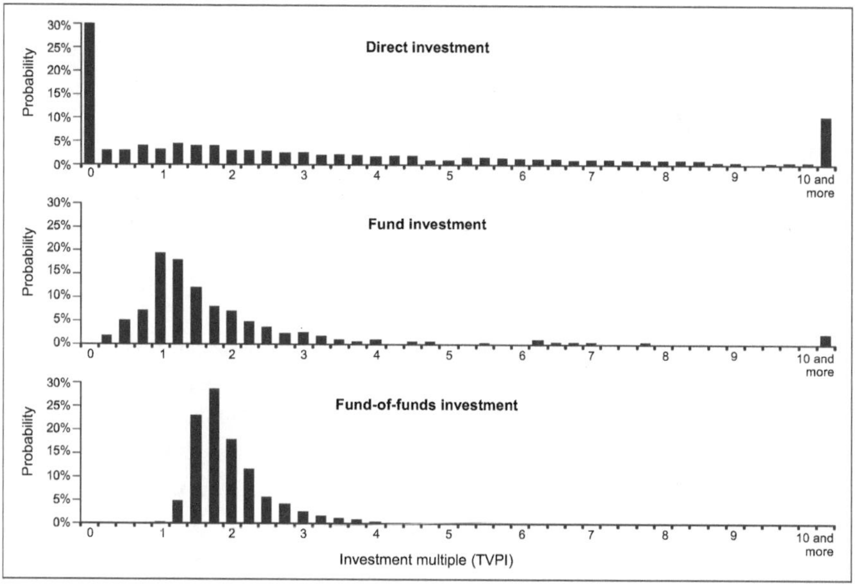

Figure 14: Return distribution of direct, fund and fund-of-funds investment[194]

---

the investment limit set by the partnership agreement. Pursuing co-investments offers the fund investors the possibility to get more exposure to specific assets. Often, they do not have to pay management fee and carry on these investments.

193 See Weidig/Mathonet (2004), p. 6.

194 See Weidig/Mathonet (2004), p. 28. For the way in which the data is presented see Fingerle (2005), p. 93. The data is based on U.S. and European venture capital investments and on simulations for fund-of-funds investments. Return measure is the investment multiple *total value to paid-in capital (TVPI)*. The total value including total distributions to fund investors plus the net asset value of the fund investment is related to the paid-in capital. See chapter 3.4.1 for more details on return measures in private equity.

From an organizational point of view, the investors need to determine whether they want to build up own resources for investments in private equity, to use an investment advisor or to outsource the investment tasks to a fund-of-funds. This decision depends on the evaluation of various criteria as is summarized in Figure 15.

	Build up own resources	Use of investment advisor	Invest in fund-of-funds
Time needs	high	medium	low
Resource needs	high	medium	low
Access to quality funds	medium	low	high
Individuality of program	high	medium	low
Fees	medium	high	high

Figure 15: Comparing different forms of organization for the private equity program[195]

The build-up of own resources may require a high level of commitment from the investors as this needs to be a long-term program. Usually, it is very difficult for new investors to get access to quality funds.[196] Investment advisors, i.e. consultants, can help in constructing a portfolio. Access to top funds may be, however, provided only by top advisors which are very well connected in the private equity industry. An advantage in comparison to the fund-of-funds approach is that the investor may still decide about the investments himself. Using a fund-of-funds, the investment decision is completely outsourced. However, fund-of-funds are already accessible with lower investment sums.[197] High-qualitative fund-of-fund managers typically have good relationships with top-quartile general partners. Therefore, they may offer access to these funds.[198] Obviously, the decision about which of these three ways investors prefer depends very much on their individual circumstances.

---

195 See Laib (2003), p. 27; Hagenmüller (2004), p. 35.

196 See Laib (2003), p. 28.

197 Of course, the decision to select a fund-of-funds manager remains.

198 See Bance (2004), p. 10.

For the remainder of the analysis, it is assumed that investors either build up and manage their own program or are fund-of-funds managers who offer this service to clients.

2.5.3 Portfolio Construction

After having decided about the target size of the private equity portfolio, the construction of the portfolio of private equity funds starts. MEYER/MATHONET distinguish between a top-down and bottom-up approach.[199]

The *top-down approach* is based on strategy research. Investors following this approach focus on the choice of the sub-segments, e.g. venture capital and buyout. They focus also on the choice of management styles, e.g. active or passive, or on the selection of countries and investment sectors. They also consider the diversification over vintage years.[200] The investors determine the asset allocation based on their analysis of the macroeconomic environment, including an assessment of the political, economic and currency opportunities and risks. The outcome of this process is a commitment planning depending on the investors' desired exposure level, risk tolerance and his available resources for investing. Only thereafter, the investor will look for funds that fit the defined allocation. The objective of this approach is an optimal risk-return profile of the portfolio.[201]

Since the performance spread in private equity funds between top-quartile and lower-quartile managers is high,[202] it is critical to select fund managers that can generate above-average returns. Many investors therefore pursue a *bottom-up approach* in portfolio construction. This approach is fund manager research-based. The investors focus on the quality of the fund management team rather than worrying about the fund strategy and diversification of the portfolio. By selecting a sufficient number of funds and avoiding concentration in a single fund, the investors seek to control for risk. The ob-

---

199 See Meyer/Mathonet (2005), pp. 83 et seq.

200 The vintage year is the year of fund formation and first drawdown of capital. Vintage year diversification means spreading investment across time periods. It reflects the different pricing and liquidity cycles of the private equity and exit markets.

201 See Meyer/Mathonet (2005), p. 85.

202 KASERER/DILLER show for their sample of European funds a first quartile return to be 4.47% and the third quartile return to be 17.13%. See Kaserer/Diller (2004a), p. 30. LJUNGQVIST/RICHARDSON calculate a first quartile return of 9.85% and a third quartile return of 28.59%. See Ljungqvist/Richardson (2003), p. 35.

jective is to identify and select those funds from the fund manager universe that have the highest expected performance.[203]

Following only a bottom-up approach causes problems. An opportunistic investment path can lead to an unbalanced portfolio that carries significantly more risks than expected.[204] However, the main problem of the top-down approach is that an exact achievement of a targeted allocation in private equity is not feasible. The identification of and access to a sufficient number of superior managers that fit into the predetermined strategy might be impossible in a given vintage year.[205] Therefore, most investors follow a combined approach as demonstrated in Figure 16. They target the best fund managers and simultaneously aim at diversifying according to strategies.

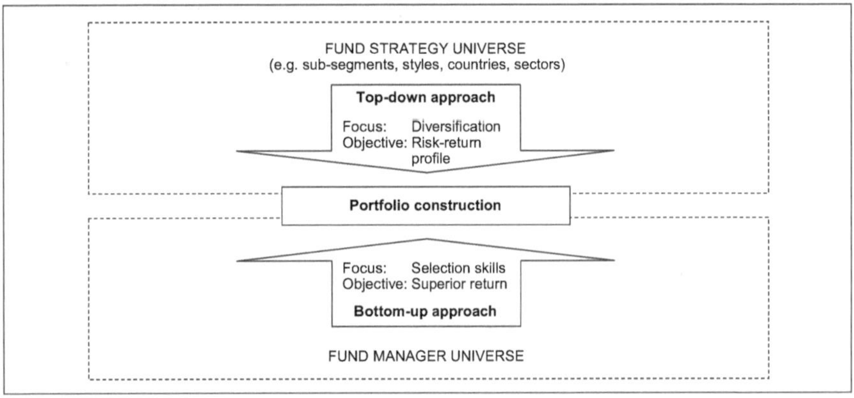

Figure 16: Portfolio construction approaches[206]

So far, the analysis has focused on the portfolio of fund level. With respect to the individual fund level, investors utilize a quite standardized process to select a fund. This process is shown in Figure 17.

[203] See Meyer/Mathonet (2005), p. 84.

[204] See Meyer/Mathonet (2005), p. 84.

[205] See Meyer/Mathonet (2005), p. 85. In fact, some high-quality fund managers may not allow new investors to invest into their new funds as the commitments from existing investors already exceed the fund's targeted size.

[206] Based on Meyer/Mathonet (2005), p. 86.

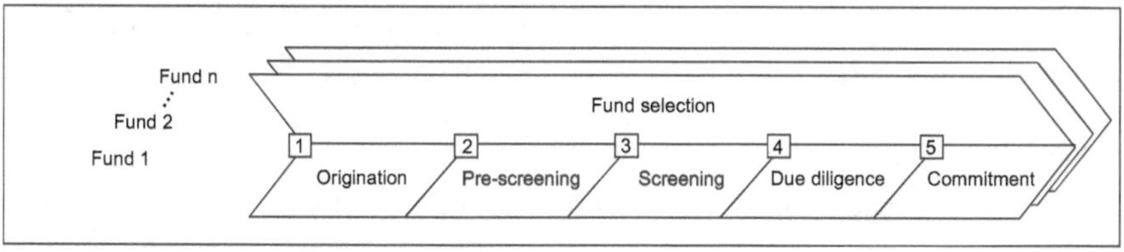

Figure 17: Individual fund selection process[207]

The selection of an individual fund follows fives stages. The first stage is deal *origination*. Funds are sourced via a number of sources, including active searches by the investors, referrals from other investors, or direct approaches by the fund managers and their placement agents.[208] In a second stage, the *pre-screening*, investors review the private placement memorandum and make a first assessment.[209] On average, one third of the funds typically get to the third step, the so-called *screening phase*, in which the investors meet the team.[210] Some fund investors attempt to meet as many teams as possible at this stage. They claim that this is a very effective way of forming early relationships with the fund managers they may choose to invest in at future point of times.[211]

In the *due diligence* stage, the fund investors check and negotiate in detail the commercial, legal and tax characteristics. This includes the investment strategy, the team members, their track record, the fee structure, and the proposed limited partnership agreement. At this stage, investors require further documents from the fund managers. Personal meetings, often on-site visits at the fund managers' office, take place. In or-

---

207 Based on Barnes/Menzies (2005), p. 214; Tausend (2006), p. 48.

208 See Barnes/Menzies (2005), p. 218. Some established investors follow a core group of fund managers whose performance they track. They already begin to form a view on them before the funds start their fundraising process.

209 The *private placement memorandum* is the core marketing document of a new fund. It typically highlights the opportunity of the fund, including market conditions and investment strategy, details on the team, the investment process, the track record and covers the structure and operations of the fund. See Brooks (1999), p. 112.

210 See Hagenmüller (2004), p. 39.

211 See Barnes/Menzies (2005), p. 218.

der to get other views on the team, the investors conduct reference calls with other investors, portfolio company managers or other industry experts.[212]

Following due diligence, the investor decides whether to *commit to invest in the fund* or not and how much capital he is willing to allocate to the individual investment. Typically, he invests in around 4% of the funds from which he had received a public placement memorandum.[213]

2.5.4 Portfolio Monitoring and Portfolio Management

Once a commitment to a limited partnership has been made, the investor does not actively participate in the operational management of the partnership. However, it is not true that fund investors totally ignore their investment once it has been made.[214] Chapter 3 deals in detail with the fund investors' monitoring and its implications for the fund portfolio management. For the moment, only the fund investors' major tasks shall be summarized.

The investor needs to monitor both the individual funds and the portfolio of funds. First, a constant *performance measurement* of the fund investments is necessary. Furthermore, on an individual fund level, the fund investor *monitors the individual fund* investment activity of the fund managers and its compliance with contractual terms. Fund investors may participate in the governance of the fund, e.g. by taking a seat in the advisory board.[215] This should help to identify potential crisis on fund level at an early step. Detailed fund monitoring furthermore forms the basis for re-investment decisions.

The fund investors also *monitor the overall fund portfolio* on an ongoing basis in order to assure that the portfolio is well balanced with respect to the desired diversification

---

212 See Hagenmüller (2004), p. 40. BARNES/MENZIES find a ranking of four key evaluation criteria that investors base their decision on: the team, the team's track record, the fund investment strategy, and the terms for investing in the fund. See Barnes/Menzies (2005), pp. 219 et seq.

213 See Hagenmüller (2004), p. 48.

214 See Fried/Hisrich (1989), p. 268.

215 See Meyer/Mathonet (2005), p. 64. For more details on the relevance of monitoring see chapter 3.2.

level.[216] Furthermore, it is essential to track and forecast the liquidity of the portfolio as most investors need to forecast their liquidity needs.

If required, the fund investor should take necessary actions, i.e. *manage the portfolio* by making appropriate adjustments to the portfolio structure. This can be achieved through the selling of existing partnerships or by steering the new commitments to other investment targets. On an individual fund level, it could be necessary to restructure poor performing or distressed funds, e.g. through the removal of the existing fund managers.

2.6 Institutional Differences and Limited Partners' Investment Success

Among institutional fund investors, large differences with respect to the overall sophistication of the investment processes seem to exist.[217] LERNER/SCHOAR/WONG find that different types of investors have achieved significantly different returns from their private equity fund investments. They examine a sample of 7,587 fund investments made by 417 limited partners in 1,398 worldwide funds raised between 1991 and 2001. The average fund in their sample has an annual internal rate of return of 6.7%.[218]

As demonstrated in Figure 18, the funds in which endowments have invested, have had by far the best overall performance with an average internal rate of return of 20.5%. They outperform the average fund by around 14 percentage points. Public and corporate pension funds have reached on average an internal rate of return of 7.6% and 5.1%. Insurance companies have realized an average of 5.5%. Funds that are picked by fund-of-funds and banks show only poor results with an average of -1.8% and -3.2%, respectively.[219]

---

216 See Meyer/Mathonet (2005), p. 65.

217 See Lerner/Schoar/Wong (2005), p. 9.

218 See Lerner/Schoar/Wong (2005), p. 15. As it is typical for private equity returns, the authors find a great amount of dispersion: The worst fund returned -94%, while the best performing fund showed an internal rate of return of more than 500%.

219 These results are robust even after employing a variety of controls and specifications, e.g. the time periods in which the fund investments were made, their risk profiles or the early access to superior funds that some investors may have. See Lerner/Schoar/Wong (2005), pp. 3 et seq.

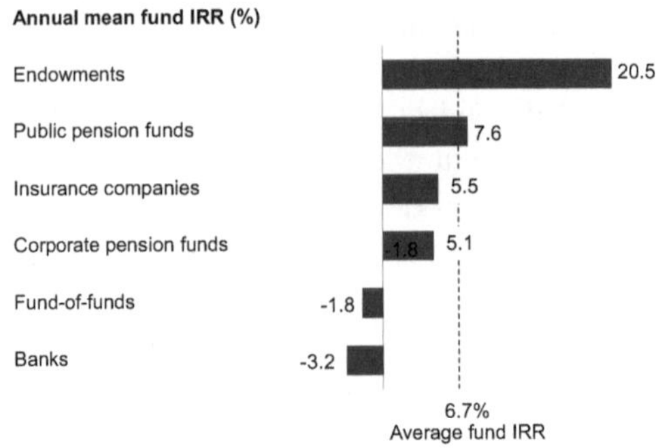

Figure 18: Performance by type of private equity fund investor[220]

These puzzling results may be attributed to various factors. The *experience* of the fund investors certainly plays an important role in explaining differences in investment performance. The fund investor needs a capable high quality team with the right skill set.[221] Endowments and universities in the U.S. were among the earliest investors in private equity and frequently have a deep understanding of investments in this asset class.[222] The *access* to funds very often correlates with the experience. The longer a fund investor has been active in the private equity market, the better usually his access to new funds raised by leading fund managers is.[223]

Furthermore, explaining the negative returns of banks, LERNER/SCHOAR/WONG speculate that banks may also *pursue non-financial aims* when investing in new funds. They might also try to attract lending and advisory business.[224] HELLMANN/LINDSEY/PURI find evidence that banks invest in direct venture capital investments for strategic rea-

---

220 See Lerner/Schoar/Wong (2005), pp. 14 et seq. The results do not represent the overall performance of the investors' portfolios as the calculation does not reflect the actual size of allocations to each of the different funds.

221 See Schmidt (2003), p. 259.

222 See Lerner/Schoar/Wong (2005), p. 10.

223 LERNER/SCHOAR/WONG state that some of the performance differences they find for endowments may be due to the early access of theses institutions to superior funds. See Lerner/Schoar/Wong (2005), p. 39.

224 See Lerner/Schoar/Wong (2005), p. 40.

sons, namely to build relationships at an early step.[225] The same may apply to indirect fund investments.

The *institutional governance* at fund investors' institutions has to be considered when explaining differences in the investment and monitoring behavior. Private equity programs require long-term support and objectives. If the overall impact of the fund investor's private equity program to his entire investment return is marginal, trustees and senior executives may take only a minimal effort to govern their internal fund investors. If fund investors' institutions require and support rather short-term performance perspectives, managers at these institutions have often only a three to four year time horizon. This is inadequate for private equity investments as sponsorships to funds reveal a long-term nature.[226]

The *incentive structures* for individual investment professionals are important.[227] If the remuneration is not tied to the investments' performance at all, the monitoring might be rather neglected.[228] Also, the relative level of compensation is of relevance. Compared to the standards of the financial services industry, many public pension funds, for example, offer only modest compensation levels. Consequently, they face high turnover among their investment professionals and a relatively lower average level of experience.[229] On the other hand, some U.S. university endowments, specifically Yale or Harvard, have been very successful at preventing their investment managers from leaving by offering them a variety of financial and non-pecuniary benefits.[230]

The above mentioned results shed light on the overall performance of fund investors' entire investment activities including the selection decision. There is, however, also empirical evidence that some investors are more capable to monitor and to use the information gathered from existing fund relationships *after* the investment decisions in a fund have been made. LERNER/SCHOAR show that fund investors in general are able to

---

225 See Hellmann/Lindsey/Puri (2004), p. 22.

226 See Osnabrugge/Robinson (2001), pp. 31 et seq. With respect to sub-segments of private equity, short-term oriented fund investors may eschew venture capital investments as they typically have even longer payback periods than buyout investments.

227 See Schmidt (2003), p. 260.

228 See Robbie/Wright/Chiplin (1997), p. 10.

229 See Lerner/Schoar/Wong (2005), p. 10.

230 See Lerner/Schoar/Wong (2005), p. 10.

acquire and use inside information about the quality of a partnership during the investment holding period.[231] LERNER/SCHOAR/WONG find differences in the ability of institutional investors to select better future performing funds.[232] Funds in which endowments decide to re-invest have a much higher performance than those they decide to skip (IRR of 31% versus 7%). The authors suggest that endowments proactively use the information they gain from being an inside investor. Other limited partners seem less willing or able to use information they obtained as an existing fund investor.[233]

These results reveal that the information flow between fund managers and fund investors seem to play an essential role in their relationship. The next chapter thus examines and stresses the theoretical role of this information flow especially after fund investors have invested in a partnership. It thereby lays the theoretical foundation for the analysis in the subsequent chapters on fund investors' monitoring (chapter 3) and fund managers' reporting (chapter 4).

2.7 Role of Information in the Relationship between General and Limited Partners

2.7.1 Overview

In the private equity market, the information between the market participants is not equally shared. Whereas public listed companies have to disclose financial information which analysts quickly take up in order to publish their opinions, private equity fund managers are not obliged to publish their cash flows, performance or other information. Historical market prices for private equity transactions are therefore not available.[234] Furthermore, private equity fund investors do not have direct access to the fund's portfolio companies. They need to rely on the fund managers to inform them about the developments.[235] Private equity investors, however, naturally require a wide-

---

231 See Lerner/Schoar (2004), p. 37. The authors find in a sample of 92 funds provided by two institutional investors that the returns for the funds that were subsequently dropped by the investors are significantly lower than for those that were continued.

232 See Lerner/Schoar/Wong (2005), p. 27.

233 See Lerner/Schoar/Wong (2005), p. 39.

234 See Grabenwarter/Weidig (2005a), p. 101.

235 See Kemmerer/Weidig (2005), p. 88.

ranging and high amount of information that allows them to monitor the developments of the individual funds and their portfolio of funds effectively.

General and limited partners normally agree that fund managers provide wide-ranging information to fund investors about the state and performance of their fund investments. Part of the information flow is channeled through legally required statutory financial statements.[236] Other parts of the information flow are either subject to a formal agreement, e.g. a special note in the limited partnership agreement, or submitted through informal sources such as calls and meetings.

In the following, the reasons why general partners provide this information and the need of limited partner for that information will be analyzed from a theoretical point of view. Conceptually, the information flow has three different but interdependent roles (Figure 19). For public markets, GJESDAL distinguishes two objectives of information production, from an accounting and reporting perspective.[237] In private equity, a third but very important role needs to be added.

First of all, information is of value to investors in order to make investment decisions. This is called the *decision-supporting role* of information. Secondly, since fund investors delegate the decision making to managers, there is a demand for information about the actions that are taken by their managers. The purpose of this information is the controlling and governing of the managers. This is called the *governance-enabling role* of information.[238] The third role is what can be called the *relationship-building role*. It relates to the fact that communication and information between partners may enhance trust and co-operation among them. As will be demonstrated, this role is very important in the context of private equity partnerships between limited and general partners.

---

236 Statutory financial statements are governed by the law of the jurisdiction in which the partnership is established and the limited partnership agreement by which it is constituted. See EVCA (2006b), p. 5.

237 See Gjesdal (1981), p. 208.

238 With respect to the role of financial accounting, the governance role of information is also called the *stewardship demand* for information. See Gjesdal (1981), p. 208; Beaver (1987), p. 48.

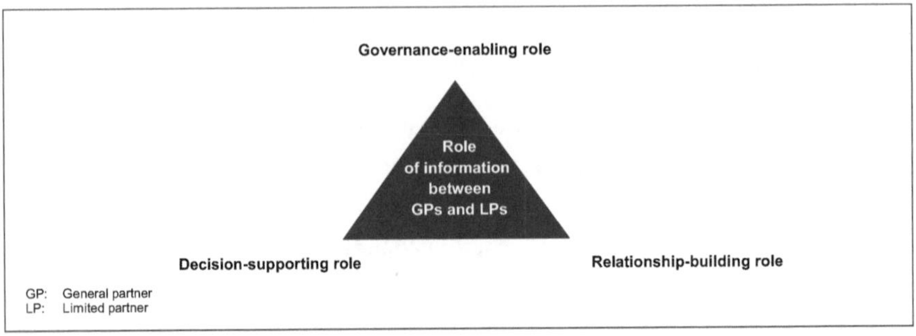

Figure 19: Role of information in the relationship between general and limited partners

In addition to these three general roles of information between fund managers and investors, private equity fund investors themselves typically face own reporting requirements. They have to inform their investors, trustees or sponsors about the status and development of the investments. Therefore, also for this reason they require an appropriate information flow from their fund managers.

2.7.2 Decision-supporting Role

Information given to investors in private as well as in public capital markets intends to solve information problems that investors face when making decisions.[239] Existing and potential investors as outsiders have typically fewer information about the state of the investments than insiders such as the managers. This could cause adverse selection problems where investors cannot distinguish between good and bad investments.[240] Financial reporting may solve this problem by providing information to present and potential investors that is useful to their decision-making process.[241] The information is intended to supply investors with the risk and return information required to facilitate optimal portfolio management decisions.[242] Information helps investors to identify and evaluate future investment opportunities. If reliable and accessible information

239 See Healy/Palepu (2001), p. 407.

240 See Healy/Palepu (2001), p. 408. AKERLOF demonstrates how a market may break down if the differentiation between good and bad opportunities is not possible. Buyers are only willing to pay average prices, leading good sellers to leave the market. The remaining opportunities are only of bad quality, inducing the buyers to further decrease their offered prices. See Akerlof (1970), pp. 488 et seq.

241 See Beaver (1987), p. 4.

242 See Sloan (2001), p. 336.

were absent, the efficient flow of capital towards sectors having high returns and away from sectors having poor prospects would be impeded.[243]

This decision role of information is more obvious in public capital markets with liquid assets where investors are able to easily sell and buy investments and where regular transactions prices can be observed.[244] In fact, the value-relevance of accounting information in public markets has been subject of many research studies.[245]

Unlike public equity, however, non-listed private equity fund investments are long-term and illiquid. There is no liquid market such as a stock exchange where partnership stakes can be instantly bought and sold. Thus, the fund investors are typically unable to react quickly to new information.[246] Furthermore, the importance of regular reporting to determine prices in private equity transactions is limited. When investors buy private equity funds, e.g. on the secondary market, they typically make an in-depth due diligence. They do not only rely on reported information as it is the case for most of the public equity investors.[247]

Nevertheless, the information that is regularly spread by the funds is nevertheless very useful for the fund investors' decision-making, mainly due to two reasons: First of all, with respect to the individual fund, fund investors regularly make re-investment decisions into follow-on funds of the same fund manager. According to LERNER/SCHOAR, the fund investors' effort to monitor the partnership investments is largely driven by their objective to get better information to support the re-investment decision.[248] LERNER/SCHOAR/WONG furthermore suggest that in order to improve their investment

---

[243] See Bushman/Smith (2003), p. 67.

[244] KASERER/WAGNER/ACHLEITNER demonstrate that this is not the case for private equity investments. See Kaserer/Wagner/Achleitner (2003), p. 261.

[245] KOTHARI provides a review on capital markets research in accounting. See Kothari (2001). The main topics of interests for researchers in this field appear to be the test of market efficiency with respect to financial accounting, e.g. accounting methods and accruals, fundamental analysis and accounting-based valuation, and value-relevance of financial reporting. See Kothari (2001), p. 107.

[246] See Meyer/Mathonet (2005), p. 281.

[247] This is different of course for investments in publicly traded private equity vehicles.

[248] See Lerner/Schoar (2004), p. 5.

decisions, some investors are better in proactively using the information they gain as inside investors. Other LPs seem less willing or able to use this information.[249]

Secondly, private equity fund investors make portfolio management decisions with respect to their portfolio of funds. They steer the degree of diversification and the liquidity of the portfolio mainly in order to optimally allocate their resources dedicated to private equity investments. Information concerning their fund investments allow them to calculate aggregate portfolio measures on which decisions to manage and adjust the portfolio can be based.

2.7.3 Governance-enabling Role

Once fund investors have invested in a fund and the management is delegated, they face the risk that the fund managers have incentives to expropriate their funds.[250] The importance of direct means of control and performance incentive schemes in order to mitigate this agency problem has been already featured in chapter 2.4. However, also by releasing information and thereby creating transparency, some of the governance-problems between fund investors and managers may be minimized or even solved.

In line with BUSHMAN/SMITH, the governance-enabling role of information can therefore be defined as the use of data in control mechanisms that promote the efficiency of corporations.[251] A continuous information flow from general partners towards limited partners allows the latter to monitor and control the appropriate use of the resources.[252] As a direct result, the information lowers information asymmetries and thus potential agency conflicts between the two partners.[253] Indirectly, the information can be used to fulfill the governance role in advisory boards and to control the adherence to the limited partnership agreement.

There may be reasons for the fund management to suppress unfavorable facts and figures which may reduce the quality of information.[254] This could, for example, happen

249 See Lerner/Schoar/Wong (2005), p. 3.

250 See Healy/Palepu (2001), p. 409.

251 See Bushman/Smith (2001), p. 238. In their review, the authors focus on financial accounting information rather than information in a broader sense.

252 See Gjesdal (1981), p. 208.

253 See Kemmerer/Weidig (2005), p. 88.

254 See Beaver (1987), p. 195.

when fund managers plan to raise a new fund. Auditors are typically hired as independent experts to testify the accuracy of the prepared financial statements. However, for the non-obligatory parts of the reporting it is not yet common to engage an auditor.

2.7.4 Relationship-building Role

Open communication between partners enhances co-operation and relationship-building. Several researchers have focused on the importance of co-operative behavior in the relationship between the private equity firm and the management of the portfolio company.[255] Co-operation is, however, also important for the relationship between general and limited partners.

Limited partners have little influence on the management of the fund and therefore have limited possibilities to be not co-operative during a fund's lifetime. However, as already mentioned, they may decide not to participate in a subsequent fund organized by the same general partners. This behavior causes problems for the general partners due to the following reason: Assuming that being an inside investor is the best way to find out about the quality and returns of fund managers, insider investors are natural candidates to invest in the general partners' next fund.[256] If they do not re-invest, outsiders will perceive this as a bad signal. However, the former investors could simply have other reasons for not re-investing. They may face a liquidity shock, being unable to participate in follow-on funds.[257] They may also have allocation strategy reasons. As outsiders cannot differentiate the reasons, they may assume, however, the fund manager is of low quality.[258]

But instead, limited partners might also be quite co-operative. If they are unable to re-invest due to reasons that are not caused by the performance of the fund managers, the current fund investors might still recommend the new fund to other limited partners.[259] Furthermore, even if the fund has not performed as expected, investors may still re-

---

255 See for example Cable/Shane (1997); Sapienza/Korsgaard (1996); Steir/Greenwood (1995); Timmons/Bygrave (1986).

256 See Lerner/Schoar (2004), p. 9.

257 See Lerner/Schoar (2004), p. 4.

258 See Lerner/Schoar (2004), p. 9. In order to still persuade the outside investors, the fund managers may make special confessions.

259 Many limited partners may place a lot of confidence in a general partner recommendation from another reputable limited partner.

invest in the next fund. They typically have a certain degree of tolerance for failures and mistakes of the fund managers.[260] This is especially the case, when fund managers recognize their failures and are able to change things going forward to maximize the chance of future success.[261] In a few cases, the fund investors might provide advice to the fund managers on how to develop the strategy and the organization of the partnership. To conclude, fund managers greatly benefit from a loyal and reliable investor base and therefore are interested in a good relationship with their investors. The questions remains, however, what the conditions are that promote the creation of a good relationship.

When examining the relationship between private equity fund managers and the management teams of their portfolio companies, several authors suggest the importance of building trust.[262] The same is likely to be true for fund managers and their respective investors. CABLE/SHANE question the appropriateness of agency theory alone to explain the relationship. Fund managers, i.e. the agents, also depend on the co-operative behavior of their investors. The authors therefore suggest using the *prisoner's dilemma framework* to analyze the co-operation decision.[263] Essentially, this framework states that each actor who does not know the other party's strategy has an incentive to act opportunistically, even though all actors are collectively better off, i.e. receive higher rewards, if they work together.[264] Based on the existing research dealing with the prisoner's dilemma, the authors conceptually model how the parties should structure their relationship in order to maximize mutual co-operation and minimize defection. Co-operation is enhanced when information about the supportive behavior of one party can be gathered easily by the other.[265] The information transfer is affected by communication and social relationships. CABLE/SHANE propose that the probability of co-operative relationships increases with the quality and frequency of their communica-

---

260 See Meyer/Mathonet (2005), p. 25.

261 See Hellman/Katz (2002), p. 5.

262 See Shepherd/Zacharakis (2001); Cable/Shane (1997); Sapienza/Korsgaard (1996).

263 See Cable/Shane (1997), p. 145.

264 See Cable/Shane (1997), p. 145.

265 See Cable/Shane (1997), p. 157. Other factors that affect the probability of co-operative behavior are relate to the personal similarity of the parties, the transaction procedures, the time pressure to reach an agreement and the payoff from co-operation. See Cable/Shane (1997), p. 153.

tion processes. The existence of a positive social or business relationship improves the quality of information transfer and thereby the co-operation itself.[266]

SAPIENZA/KORSGARD refer to *procedural justice in relationships*. This theory deals with individuals' reactions to decisions in which they are personally involved but which they cannot directly of fully control.[267] Individuals value 'just and fair procedures', as these allow indirect control when direct control is not possible. Procedural justice is an important determinant of attitudes and behavior relevant for the relationship between two parties, especially when the outcome of a decision is unfavorable. Although a decision has a negative outcome, fair procedures allow individuals to feel that their interests are protected in the long run.[268] Limited partners do not have direct control over the decisions of the fund managers. The perception of procedural justice may determine their attitudes and behaviors and affect the relationship to the general partners.

Following the argumentation and the cited research by SAPIENZA/KORSGARD, procedural justice can be related to the following attitudes and behaviors of the limited partners: trust in the fund managers, commitment to their decisions, monitoring of the fund, and willingness to re-invest. The fund investors' perception of procedural justice is affected by the fund managers' provision of immediate and on-time feedback to the fund investors and the fund investors' actual level of influence on the decisions. The timely feedback allows the fund investors to stay up to date on the fund's performance. It is an important sign of a decision maker's openness and honesty.[269] A lack of feedback may undermine the fund investors' trust in the fund managers and decrease the commitment to the decisions the fund managers are taking. Timely feedback should reduce the need for monitoring. It signals the investors that their interests are protected.[270] If the influence to affect an outcome is low, as this is the case for limited

---

266 See Cable/Shane (1997), p. 167.

267 See Sapienza/Korsgaard (1996), p. 547. Although the authors also analyze the relationship between the fund managers and entrepreneurs, this situation also fits to the relationship between fund limited and general partners.

268 See Sapienza/Korsgaard (1996), p. 547.

269 Timely feedback relates to both the general consideration of investors needs and the actual provision of information that are critical to investors' ongoing interests. See Sapienza/Korsgaard (1996), p. 548.

270 See Sapienza/Korsgaard (1996), p. 550.

partners, the decision making processes become even more critical.[271] To conclude this discussion, the general partners' management of the information flow has a positive impact on the relationship with their fund managers.

SHEPHERD/ZACHARAKIS more generally focus on the balance of control and trust in the relationship between venture capitalists and entrepreneurs.[272] Their results may also mirror the situation between general and limited partners. The authors propose a model of building trust between partners that highlights the importance of signaling commitment and consistency, being fair and just, obtaining a good fit with the partner, and maintaining frequent and open communication.[273] Offering adequate explanations and timely feedback can increase trust in a relationship. Frequent and open communication acts as catalyst for other trust building factors. The better the communication, the clearer may be the commitment to the relationship and the closer the parties may be brought together.[274]

To summarize, it has been shown that an immediate and qualitative information flow between general and limited partners will strengthen their relationship. Open communication builds trust on both sides. This is critical in maintaining a strong relationship. Instead of being reluctant to share information, clear, direct and constructive communication is in the interest of both partners.

Chapter 2 described the fundamentals of investing in private equity partnerships from the fund managers' and fund investors' perspective. The role of information in their relationship has been theoretically analyzed. Based on these results, chapter 3 will deal in detail with the aspect of the fund investors' monitoring in order to elaborate fund investors' information requirements.

---

271 See Sapienza/Korsgaard (1996), p. 548.

272 See Shepherd/Zacharakis (2001), p. 129.

273 See Shepherd/Zacharakis (2001), p. 131.

274 See Shepherd/Zacharakis (2001), p. 138.

3 Fund Investors' Monitoring

3.1 Introductory Remarks

Chapter 3 investigates the post-investment relationship between private equity fund investors and their fund managers. More specifically, it analyzes the monitoring of private equity fund managers by their respective fund investors. So far, this issue has been largely neglected by academic researchers.[275] Due to the increasing role that private equity investments play in the overall investment allocation of institutional investors, however, it is important to understand the nature and extent of the monitoring and the resulting information requirements.

The objectives of this analysis are therefore twofold. On the one hand, it targets to *investigate the current best practices with respect to monitoring the fund investments*. On the other hand, the study aims to *elaborate the information requirements of best-practicing fund investors*. In other words, it will be analyzed which sort of information market participants that have best-practice process in place need in order to fulfill their monitoring roles.

Once an investment in a limited partnership has been made, the fund investor does not actively participate in the daily operations of the fund.[276] However, that does not mean that he is only passive and ignores the fund investments entirely. In contrast, the fund investor carefully monitors the development of the each fund investment, including the individual underlying company investments. He pays attention to the development of his entire portfolio of funds.[277]

Investment *monitoring* can be defined as routinely and systematically collecting information about the investments in a planned and organized way.[278] However, monitoring is not a purposeless or self-fulfilling task. The gathered information needs to be

---

275 A study of Robbie/Wright/Chiplin is an exemption. However, the authors mainly focus on the way how the fund investors gather information. See Robbie/Wright/Chiplin (1997). Two books recently published by practitioners also address the management of private equity fund programs. See Grabenwarter/Weidig (2005a) and Meyer/Mathonet (2005).

276 See Fried/Hisrich (1989), p. 268.

277 See Bader (1996), p. 300; Hagenmüller (2004), p. 44.

278 See Meyer/Mathonet (2005), p. 272.

evaluated and, if any problems are identified, actions have to be taken to make changes and improvements.[279] Therefore, this analysis does not only focus on the gathering of information, but takes an integrated process view on monitoring which includes the actions that are taken by fund investors to solve problems. The implications of these monitoring requirements for private equity fund investors are discussed in the following chapters.

This chapter proceeds as follows: The monitoring of the performance of private equity funds will be looked at in chapter 3.4, as this forms the basis for other decisions. Then in chapter 3.5, the monitoring and governing of the individual fund investment will be addressed. How the monitoring can support the re-investment decision in a subsequent fund of the same fund managers will be subject of the analysis in chapter 3.6. Finally, the monitoring for portfolio management purposes will be discussed in chapter 3.7.

3.2 Research Methodology and Data

To answer the research questions, the author conducted expert interviews with representatives of leading European-based institutions investing in private equity funds.[280] The study followed a two-step approach in gathering data. First of all, four in-depth open interviews with private equity fund investors were conducted. Based on the outcomes and an intensive literature research, the author developed a structured questionnaire including closed and open questions. In a second step, this questionnaire was deployed in a series of 24 in-depth interviews with fund investors.[281] The interviews took place on a one-to-one basis via on-company visits or via telephone between September 2005 and August 2006.

This two-stage approach seems to be more successful in generating high qualitative data than simply mailing questionnaires.[282] Especially, as the intention was to discover best-practices, it was considered not to be appropriate to send questionnaires to the population of all private equity fund investors. In order to identify best practices and

---

279 See Meyer/Mathonet (2005), p. 64.

280 For a list of the interview partners see Appendix A.

281 A sample of the questionnaire is provided in Appendix B at the end of the book.

282 See Barnes/Menzies (2005), p. 212. Based on their experience, the authors state that senior executives at private equity investors were unlikely to complete mailed questionnaires and often pass them to more junior colleagues.

the resulting reporting requirements, the interview partners had been carefully selected rather than randomly chosen. A first selection criterion was the size of the investment program in private equity funds the institutional investors were responsible for. It is assumed that larger institutions have the resources to implement state-of-the-art practices in managing their portfolios. Secondly, the interview partners were selected according to their expertise. Investors who were speakers or panelists at leading industry conferences specifically covering the topics governance, monitoring and reporting in private equity over the last years, had been contacted and invited to participate in the study.

The participants of the study represent institutions that are among the largest investors in private equity in Europe. According to a list of the top 20 European investors provided by PRIVATE EQUITY INTELLIGENCE, the sample includes 12 out of 20 of the largest investors in Europe, including the eight largest ones.[283] In terms of asset under management in private equity, these 12 fund investors cover 79% of the total asset under management of the top 20 investors. The respondents represent in total more than €120 billion assets under management in private equity, with individual portfolios ranging from €150 million to €30 billion.[284]

In order to get an understanding about how well the sample represents the market, one can look at the amount of invested capital in the European private equity market.[285] As of 2005, the total invested capital measured at cost of European private equity funds is €173 billion.[286] In 2005, European funds invested around 68% in buyouts, 27% in venture capital and 5% in other sub-segments.[287] In total, the participating fund investors state that they allocate 71% in buyout, 21% in venture capital and 4% in other sub-segments.

---

283 See Private Equity Intelligence (2006), p. 54.

284 Six of the 28 investors did not disclose their assets under management.

285 See EVCA (2006c). The data only serves as an indication as it is not directly comparable. EVCA reports data provided by private equity funds that are their members. Their respective investors are not only European-based. The respondents in this study, however, are European investors who invest globally.

286 See EVCA (2006c). As only members of the EVCA have been surveyed, this is probably a conservative estimation.

287 See EVCA (2006c). Venture capital includes seed, start-up and expansion capital.

In 2005, European funds raised 13% of their capital from fund of funds, 11% from insurance companies, 25% from pension funds, 18% from banks, and the rest from other organizations.[288] As presented in Figure 20, in the sample of this study, fund of funds managers are overrepresented as they are usually among the largest investors. Most of these fund of funds managers are located in Switzerland.

Participants by type		Participants by country	
Fund of funds manager	14	Switzerland	12
Insurance company	5	Germany	4
Pension fund	2	Great Britain	5
Family office	1	France	1
Bank	2	Netherlands	1
		Sweden	1
Sum	24*	**Sum**	24*

* In addition, four investors participated in open interviews at the first stage of the study. At two institutions two representatives participated. In total, 30 experts were interviewed.

Figure 20: Sample selection

As has been said, it was the intention to explore the current best practices of fund investors' monitoring and the resulting information requirements. Against this background it should not be claimed that the results are representative for the population of all private equity fund investors. The sample rather includes the largest institutions and designated experts.

All interviewed experts were professionals at European-based private equity fund investors, most of them senior fund managers.[289] Interviewees were sent a copy of the questionnaire in advance of the interview appointment. At the beginning of each interview, they were specifically asked to report the institutions' perceptions rather than their individual approaches. Interviews lasted between 45 and 90 minutes each.

By applying a structured questionnaire with some open questions during the interviews, the data was gathered in both a quantitative and qualitative way.[290] According

---

288 See EVCA (2006c). 9% of the investors were not identifiable.

289 One analyst and two controllers were among the interviewees. The others were investment managers or more senior.

290 See Easterby-Smith/Thorpe/Lowe (2002), p. 130, for a distinction of qualitative and quantitative research.

to ESTERBY-SMITH/THORBE/LOWE, this approach offers some flexibility and allows the views of the interview partners to become known whilst following a fairly standardized set of questions.[291] Due to the explorative nature of the study, this type of interview was regarded as appropriate, as responses could be explored and clarified. This process added a degree of confidence to the given answers which is not a feature available in questionnaires.[292]

In the following chapters, the results of the study will be presented.[293] In order to distinguish between empirical results based on the data gathered through the interviews and additional information gained by desk research, the empirical results are presented in each chapter but are separated from the rest of the text. Quantitative results are displayed in figures where it is appropriate.

3.3 Relevance and Objectives of Monitoring

Monitoring can be differentiated with respect to the individual fund and the overall portfolio composition. It may trigger decisions or actions, again with respect to the individual fund or the whole portfolio.

On an individual fund level, the investor monitors the fund's performance, and the fund managers' adherence to the strategy and the terms of the partnership agreement.[294] Through the monitoring of the individual fund investment, the fund investor can rarely enhance the upside performance potential of the fund investment. This task has been outsourced to the fund managers.[295] In some cases, he might be able to add some value, e.g. by giving advice to the fund managers. However, the fund investors could decrease the risk of losses by detecting early warning signals for things going wrong and by quickly taking action to rescue or secure their single fund investment

---

291 See Easterby-Smith/Thorpe/Lowe (2002), p. 86.

292 See Easterby-Smith/Thorpe/Lowe (2002), p. 86. Furthermore, non-verbal clues which are present in the inflection of the voice or facial expressions and which provide additional insight could be identified.

293 As not all interviewed fund investors answered each question, the results are presented including a note on how many fund investors actually responded. The results are based on the 24 in-depth interviews. Therefore, the maximum number of respondents is N=24.

294 See Hagenmüller (2004), p. 44.

295 See Grabenwarter/Weidig (2005a), p. 84.

(crisis management).[296] A very important decision, nevertheless, is whether the investor is going to re-invest in the next fund of the fund managers. This decision can be promoted by monitoring existing fund relationships.

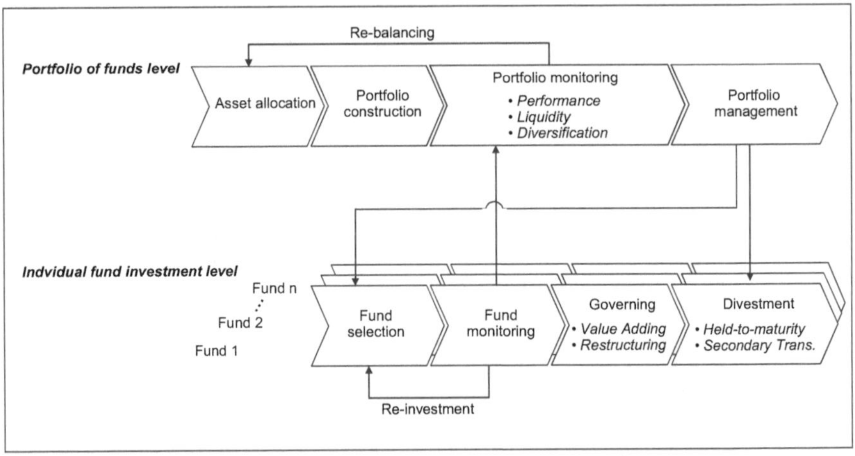

Figure 21: Integrated process view on monitoring

Investors can, however, create value through monitoring and action taking *at the portfolio of funds level.*[297] Performance measurement is necessary to evaluate the success of the entire investment allocation in private equity and might be used to compare the performance with other asset classes. By effectively managing liquidity, the returns for the private equity program can be further enhanced. In addition, the fund investors observe and ensure an appropriate degree of diversification of their entire portfolio. If imbalances are discovered, this may actually have an influence on the fund investors' asset allocation. In addition, the portfolio management may lead to secondary transactions to increase or decrease specific positions in funds. Figure 21 provides an integrated process view on monitoring the portfolio of fund level and the individual fund investment level and shows the various linkages.

[296] See Grabenwarter/Weidig (2005a), p. 84. There are few occasions where investors really restructure funds.

[297] See for this and the following Meyer/Mathonet (2005), p. 276.

The *primary objective* of post-investment monitoring including management of private equity fund investments is to optimize the return-risk relationship of the private equity fund investment program over time. This objective is fulfilled by achieving the *secondary objectives*. The basis for all decisions is the performance measurement of the individual fund investment as well as the portfolio of funds. This is in fact a challenge in private equity as will be discussed later on. Regarding the individual fund investment, the fund monitoring should ensure value-capturing in cases the existing individual investment faces a crisis. A restructuring of the fund may avoid losses. Furthermore, it should enable better subsequent re-investment decisions. Taking into account the portfolio of funds, the monitoring should enable an optimized portfolio diversification. In addition, it should increase the efficiency of the capital employed in the private equity fund investment program by liquidity management. The objectives are summarized in Figure 22.

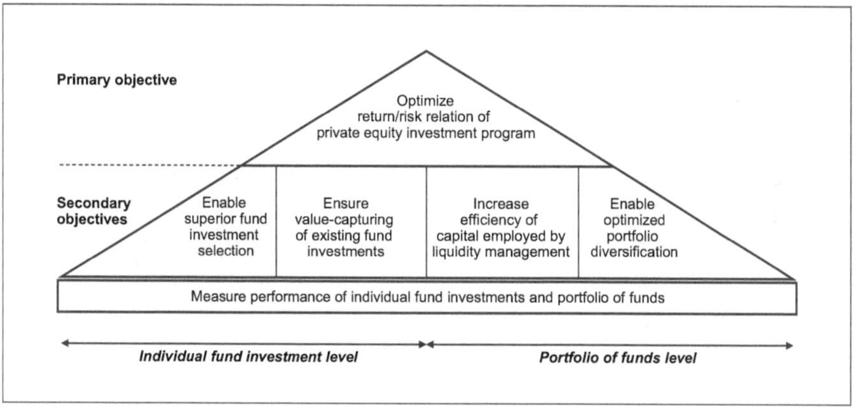

Figure 22: Objectives of private equity fund monitoring

Some fund investors believe that fund deal sourcing and due diligence should be the primary focus of their resources. They consider monitoring a secondary function.[298] In order to assess the relevance of monitoring, the interviewed fund investors have therefore been asked how much resources they allocate to monitoring and what the optimal number of general partner relationships per investment professional is.

---

298 See McKinsey (2003), p. 26.

Empirical results

The interviewed fund investors (N=22) spend an average of 58% of their time on selecting new investments. The remaining time (42%) is allocated to monitoring the existing fund relationships.[299] This confirms that monitoring is perceived to be less important than the selection decision. There are some investors who even spend up to 70% of their time to monitor the existing funds. However, there is no relationship between this decision and certain characteristics of the fund investors. The number of funds that an investment professional in the fund investors' institutions should monitor is stated to reach an average of 13 funds. 20% of the interviewed fund investors say that it should be even less than ten funds per professional. These results demonstrate that the monitoring of private equity fund investments is resource intensive. However, the interviewed fund investors are all willing to spend these resources and believe it is worth the costs.

3.4 Monitoring Performance

3.4.1 Return Measures of Fund Investments

An assessment of the performance of an asset includes determining both its return and its risks. Monitoring and evaluating both is challenging for private equity fund investments, especially in comparison to investments in listed assets, e.g. bonds or stocks, due to their unique characteristics.[300] Before dealing with the measurement of risks in chapter 3.4.4., the different possibilities to calculate the return of fund investments need to be elaborated.

The most important obstacle to calculate returns is the fund investments' private nature, i.e. lack of a liquid market for both the funds and their underlying portfolio companies.[301] Consequently, the fund's asset values can be reliably observed only at two

---

299 The question asked to the interviewed fund investors neglects the fact that some fund investors have to spend time on their own fundraising themselves, e.g. fund-of-fund managers, in order to enhance comparability among all types of fund investors.

300 See chapter 2.3.

301 See Kaserer/Wagner/Achleitner (2003), p. 261. It is typically rather impossible to transact the investments at any point in time and/or only with incurring substantial transaction costs, e.g. high costs of searching potential buyers and sellers. See Kaserer/Wagner/Achleitner (2003), p. 260. This is true for the fund itself as well as for the underlying portfolio companies.

points of time: when fund investors pay in their capital and when the fund investments are completely liquidated.[302] In the meantime, there are typically no reliable market prices available[303] that allow determining interim market-proven returns.[304] To a certain extent, however, interim returns could be inferred from accounting based asset values. Private equity funds typically disclose net asset values (NAV) of their investments on a quarterly or semi-annual basis.[305]

Typically, two types of return measures are used by the private equity industry: the internal rate of return and multiples of invested capital.

Internal rate of return

The internal rate of return (IRR) is the most commonly used performance measure for private equity fund investments.[306] It is the rate of discount that sets the net present value (NPV) of all cash flows (*CF*) from an investment accrued over period *t* equal to zero. If *T* is the lifetime of the fund, the final IRR of a liquidated fund is calculated as follows:[307]

$$\sum_{t=0}^{T} \frac{CF_t}{(1+IRR)^t} = 0$$

The final IRR of a fund investment can only be calculated when the fund is fully liquidated. Over the lifetime of a fund, the general partners report an interim IRR using the NAV as last cash flow. The NAV may be regarded as proxy for the current value of

---

302 See Kaserer/Wagner/Achleitner (2003), p. 262.

303 If a new financing round including a third party transaction for a portfolio company stake comes up, the resulting price for the stake of the company may reflect a market price. Whereas new financing rounds are typical for venture capital investments, they are rather atypical for buyout investments.

304 A secondary market for limited partnership interests exists. However, transactions only take place occasionally. Some fund managers are especially dedicated to secondary market investments. Major secondary investment firms include *Coller Capital, Landmark Partners* or *Lexington Partners.*

305 See Kemmerer/Weidig (2005), p. 88.

306 See Burgel (2000), p. 33. A study of German private equity companies finds that 98% of the participants use the IRR to measure their performance. See Haarmann Hemmelrath/Universitaet Leipzig (2002), p. 8.

307 See Kaserer/Diller (2004c), p. 37; Grabenwarter/Weidig (2005a), p. 23; Brealey/Myers (2005), p. 91.

expected future cash flows and the interim IRR as a proxy for the final IRR.[308] If n is the number of remaining time periods, the interim IRR is calculated as follows:

$$\sum_{t=0}^{n} \frac{CF_t}{(1+IRR)^t} + \frac{NAV_n}{(1+IRR)^n} = 0$$

In the investment-management industry usually the *time-weighted rate of return* is preferred. This measure is not affected by cash withdrawals and additions to the investment. It simply measures the geometric growth of € 1 invested over a given period T. Each time interval bears the same weight independent of the amount of money that is invested. The IRR, however, is a *value-weighted (or money-weighted)* rate of return. It accounts for the amount and timing of all cash flows to and from the investment. Therefore, it is heavily influenced by the time pattern of the respective cash flows used for calculation.[309]

The value-weighted rate of return is preferred for private equity investments for at least two reasons: First of all, since the decisions relating to timing and the amount of cash flows to and from the investments are mainly left to general partners' discretion, a value-weighted measure is appropriate.[310] Secondly, the use of a time-weighted measure, i.e. the computation of periodic returns, involves the employment of net asset values of the fund over time. However, these net asset values are subject to valuation bias and do not accurately reflect the true value.[311]

The IRR has its drawbacks. One is a simple mathematical problem. The calculation may result in more than one possible figure.[312] More importantly, the IRR implicitly assumes that all capital distributions which occur before the whole investment is exited can be reinvested at the fund's IRR.[313] From an investor's point of view, this assump-

---

308 See Troche (2004), p. 30.

309 See for more details Defusco et al. (2001), pp. 81 et seq; Rouvinez (2003b), p. 34; Kaserer/Diller (2004b), p. 37.

310 See zu Knyphausen/Kittlaus/Seeliger (2003), p. 549. Limited partners cannot influence either the call of committed capital by or the timing of any distributions from their general partners.

311 See Rouvinez (2003b), p. 35. Chapter 3.4.2.2 discusses the difficulties of fund valuations.

312 In cases in which over time a mix of positive and negative cash flows occurs may be more than one internal rate of return. See Gottschalg/Zollo/Loos (2004), p. 37.

313 See Gottschalg/Phalippou/Zollo (2004), p. 9.

tion is unrealistic as an equivalent investment opportunity with the identical rate of return can rarely be found.[314] Comparing two or more fund investment leads to different reinvestment rates at the same time.[315]

Portfolio Internal Rate of Return

In order to measure portfolio returns, there are several ways how the single fund investments can be aggregated. Thus different outcomes for the fund's internal rate of return are possible.[316] One possibility is to calculate an *average IRR* which equally weights the IRR of all individual fund investments. However, it does not reflect the overall performance of the portfolio, since it attaches equal weight to all funds irrespective of the amounts under management. To solve this issue, the portfolio manager could calculate a *capital-weighted IRR* based on his fund commitments in order to reflect the size differences of funds. This method, however, ignores the different time periods that the money has been under management. Therefore, the most appropriate method is the *pooled IRR* where the portfolio manager pools the cash flows from all funds, e.g. on a monthly basis.[317]

From the fund investors' perspectives there may be a second issue related to the IRR. It does not account for the committed, but not yet invested capital. Thereby, it measures only the efficiency of the fund manager, not of the fund investors. The latter may have opportunity costs holding capital in low-return investments in order to be able to quickly respond to capital calls. The effective return from a portfolio perspective may be therefore lower than the portfolio IRR suggests.[318]

---

314 Even if another private equity fund is raising capital at the time when the distribution occurs, the investment in the new fund is rarely immediate. See Gottschalg/Phalippou/Zollo (2004), p. 9.

315 See Kaserer/Diller (2004b), p. 38. To overcome these problems HIELSCHER/ZELGER/ BEYER suggest a *modified IRR* that discounts the investment of committed capital at money-market rate and the distributed cash before the exit at a rate that depends on investors risk attitudes and investment opportunities. See Hielscher/Zelger/Beyer (2003), p. 500.

316 The same mechanics are also true for a single fund comprising several investments. As a result, a given fund's IRR should be regarded with immediate suspicion. Sophisticated fund investors carefully verify general partners' information on realized internal rates of return. Typically, they make their own calculations which require transparency on the exact dates and amounts of any occurring cash flows.

317 See Burgel (2000), p. 33. Gull (1999) and Hagenmüller (2004), p. 119 provide sample calculations.

318 See Grabenwarter/Weidig (2005a), p. 24.

Investment multiples

Multiples of invested capital are regarded as complementary measures to the IRR. These measures show what multiple of invested (or drawn-down) money has been returned to the investor. Multiples neglect that the timing of cash flow affects the return due to the time value of money. But they describe how effective an investment was in terms of returning money to the investor.[319] Typically, the following multiples are calculated:[320]

$$\text{distribution to paid–in}\,(DPI) = \frac{\text{cumulative distributions}}{\text{paid–in capital}}$$

This multiple shows how much of the invested capital is already returned to the fund investors. If the DPI multiple results in greater one, the fund has broken even.

$$\text{residual value to paid–in}\,(RVPI) = \frac{\text{residual net asset value}}{\text{paid–in capital}}$$

The RVPI multiple shows how much capital is still unrealized. It of course depends on the age of the fund.

$$\text{total value to paid–in}\,(TVPI) = \frac{\text{total value}}{\text{paid–in capital}}$$

The TVPI is the sum of DPI and RVDI. It expresses the total return of the investment.[321]

It is industry standard to analyze the internal rate of return and investment multiples in conjunction. By only looking at each measure by itself, the performance cannot be compared on a consistent basis. Further research could concentrate on developing a single figure that actually reflects the fund returns.

Payback period as return-indicating measure

---

319 See Grabenwarter/Weidig (2005a), p. 22.

320 See for the following Troche (2004), pp. 28-29; Hagenmüller (2004), pp. 117-118.

321 See Urwyler/Wilde (2001), p. 204.

In addition to the internal rate of return and investment multiples, industry practitioners may use other measures that early indicate the return of funds.[322] The *payback period* for example measures the time required to break even on an investment without taking unrealized investments into account.[323] FREI/STUDER demonstrate that short payback periods of funds indicate a very good performing portfolio and raise the prospects of additional distributions later in fund.[324]

Regarding any further empirical results, the fund investors were asked in an open question whether they apply any other measure to evaluate the individual fund investments in addition to the IRR and investment multiples.

Empirical results

All of the interviewed fund investors calculate the internal rate of return and the investment multiples to evaluate performance. The vast majority does not use any further measures. Only one fund investor cites the payback period as additional indicator for the performance. Some investors underline the importance of looking also at distribution of the returns of the individual portfolio companies. Thereby, they identify whether the return has been equally generated over all returns or by only some of the holdings. One large fund investor studies the portfolio composition of the fund with respect to deals within or beyond the strategy as well as with respect to write-offs and exits. The challenge of valuing the funds to measure interim returns has been pointed out by most of the interviewed investors.

3.4.2 Interim Returns and the Relevance of Fund Valuation

3.4.2.1 J-curve Pattern of Interim Returns

When analyzing and interpreting the return of funds, it is important to question the reliability of the interim figures in relation to the final outcome of liquidated funds.[325] Irrespective of the return measure that is used, the interim return tends to be zero or negative during the early years of a fund's lifetime. Only over time, it converges to-

---

322 See for a discussion of several measures Anonymous author (2002), pp. 32 et seq.

323 See Frei/Studer (2004), p. 30.

324 See Frei/Studer (2004), p. 30. The authors analyze the relation between the IRR of a fund and the payback period for a sample of more than 500 U.S. and European private equity funds.

325 See Burgel (2000), p. 34.

ward the fund's final return. This pattern of the fund's return over time is called the J-curve effect and is illustrated by Figure 23.

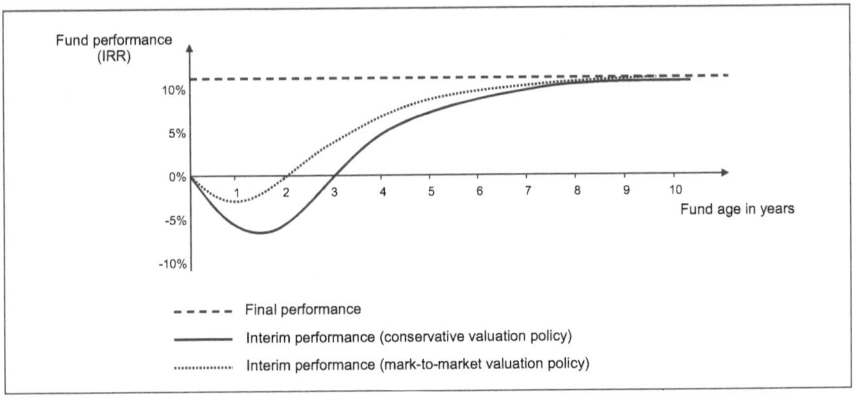

Figure 23: Schematic J-curve pattern of a fund's performance[326]

The J-curve is determined by two factors: management fees and set-up costs on the one hand and a valuation effect on the other. The *management fee* and the fund's *set-up costs* have to be paid by the fund investors and are typically financed out of the first draw-downs. As a result, parts of the sum of these draw-downs in the first years do not create net book value of the limited partnership and the overall performance of the partnership is negatively impacted. The later the fund manager starts to invest, the higher is the negative effect.[327] Fund investors therefore carefully watch the investment pattern of their managers.

The *valuation of the portfolio companies* is the second factor that causes the J-curve pattern.[328] In order to measure the interim performance, the unrealized net asset value of the fund investments has to be taken into account.[329] Many fund managers typically

326 Based on Burgel (2000), p. 35; Meyer/Mathonet (2005), p. 12.

327 See Burgel (2000), p. 34.

328 See Meyer/Mathonet (2005), p. 13.

329 As demonstrated for the internal rate of return calculation for example, the net asset value is used as the last cash flow.

take a conservative approach when valuing their portfolio company assets.[330] A conservative valuation approach only allows positive adjustments of the investments when the portfolio company has witnessed a substantial increase in value. Otherwise, the portfolio company shall be carried at cost.[331] If investments do not perform as expected, they have to be written off. These losses usually impact earlier on the fund performance than successful realizations. Consequently, the interim return of funds - even that of future top performers - tends to be very low or negative in the early years.[332]

The valuation effect may be smoothed if the current economic value of the portfolio investments is determined. In recent years, accounting standards like the *International Financial and Reporting Standards (IFRS)* or *US General Accepted Accounting Principles (US GAAP)* require fair value measurement for investments.[333] Without a conservative bias in valuation, the J-curve effect could be mitigated. For illustration purpose, this effect is indicated by the dotted line in Figure 23.

The remaining unrealized fund values, or so-called carrying values, have a significant influence on the interim performance. The questions to be answered in the following therefore are how the fund investors should determine the fund's value during the lifetime of the fund and what the inherent pros and cons of the different methodologies are.

3.4.2.2 Interim Fund Valuation

Three generic methodologies of fund valuation exist. One of them, the net asset value method, has two different specifications.

The first method uses *prices of funds recently obtained in secondary market transactions*.[334] This method is simple to use if prices of the same fund are obtainable and reliable. However, secondary market prices have to be carefully treated as indictors of a true value for the fund. The seller might be forced to sell, e.g. due to liquidity short-

---

330 See Fort Washington (2006); Achleitner/Müller (2005), p. 69. In fact, the conservative valuation policy had been proposed or required by many private equity and venture capital industry associations for many years. For more details see chapter 4.3.4.

331 See Blaydon/Horvath (2003), p. 48.

332 See Burgel (2000), p. 34.

333 For more details see 4.3.3.

334 See Bane (2005), p. 5.

ages or regulatory constraints, resulting in a discounted price.[335] Furthermore, the prices may not be relevant anymore as too much time elapsed since the transactions. Finally, there are simply not enough secondary transactions in the market and often transaction prices are not publicly available.[336]

Current market practice is the second generic method, the *net asset value method.* Basically, the net asset value is an aggregation of the values of the underlying investments and other net assets or liabilities of the fund (bottom-up valuation).[337] Two different approaches are possible: The fund investors can either use the net asset value reported by the fund's general partner or adjust the reported values if necessary to arrive at a fair value-based net asset value.[338]

Using net asset values provided by general partners to determine the fund's interim value is simple and practical, but has several drawbacks which lead many authors to conclude that these values seldom reflect true market prices, i.e. prices that sellers would receive in an open market transaction.[339] Fund managers may calculate the values along different accounting standards and valuation principles. Some apply conservative approaches that require fund managers to carry the investments only at cost less impairment. This may underestimate their true economic value. Other fund managers may be required to determine values that reflect the fair value of the investments and that are determined within a mark-to-market framework.[340] However, even if determined along the same rules, fund managers cannot entirely avoid valuation errors or may have strategic reasons and incentives to manipulate the values.[341] As long as the

---

335 See Guennoc (2006), p. 122.

336 See Kinsch/Petit-Jouvet (2006).

337 See Bane (2005), p. 6; Meyer/Mathonet (2005), p. 154. There are typically only few other net assets or liabilities of private equity partnerships. See Böhler (2004b), p. 204.

338 According to IFRS, the fair value can be defined as "*the amount for which an asset could be exchanged, or a liability settled, between knowledgeable, willing parties in an arm's length transaction*" (IAS 39.9). For further details see chapter 4.3.1.

339 See for example Kaserer/Wagner/Achleitner (2003), p. 263.

340 As will be shown in chapter 4.2, the IFRS require the determination of fair values. The *International Private Equity & Venture Capital Valuation Guidelines* issued by industry associations demonstrate how to determine the fair value of investments.

341 See Kaserer/Wagner/Achleitner (2003), p. 263. For example during fundraising for subsequent funds, general partners may write up investments in order to be able to show a better track record.

calculation of the asset values is solely subject to the fund managers' discretion, the comparability between different funds is limited.

In order to overcome the problem related to different fund valuation policies, the fund investors themselves could adjust the reported values so that all of them reflect fair values (*adjusted NAV method*).[342] Therefore, the fund investors should determine first, whether the reported fund values are fair value compliant or not. If not, a re-valuation to correct the deficiencies is appropriate. To be able to do this, fund investors need enough information which they can get through fund reports and monitoring calls with general partners. However, with the increasing application of the *International Private Equity & Venture Capital Valuation Guidelines* which require fair value determination throughout the industry, fewer adjustments to the net asset values reported by the general partners should be required. It should become more straightforward for fund investors to produce consistent fair value compliant net asset values for all their fund investments.[343]

Another problem is, however, that the fund reports are distributed to investors several months after the general partners' valuation date. This often causes the reported fund net asset value to be outdated.[344] All important and material events as well as all further contributions or distributions that occurred since the reporting date should be reflected consistently in the fair values.[345]

The third generic method is a *fund valuation model based on estimating the fund's future cash flows*. This method addresses the necessity to differentiate between the values of the funds themselves and the aggregated values of the underlying portfolio companies.[346] The main argument for this third method is that the bottom-up approach of the net asset value method neglects the future value of several components of a

342 See Kinsch/Petit-Jouvet (2006).

343 See Kinsch/Petit-Jouvet (2006).

344 See Clark/Kojima (2003), p. 78.

345 See Kinsch/Petit-Jouvet (2006).

346 See Guennoc (2006), p. 122. The net asset value method implicitly assumes a break-up of the fund whereas in reality the fund is still hold.

fund, most importantly the undrawn commitments, the fund manager's role in adding value, i.e. the quality of the mangers, and the future expenses.[347]

The fund value is not only the net asset value, but also the future expected cash flow of undrawn commitments. Fund investors must correctly quantify the potential (or liability) associated with these uncalled obligations.[348] The ability to create value out of undrawn commitments and to significantly impact the value of portfolio companies depends, however, on the quality of the fund managers.[349] The potential value add should be also reflected in the fund's value. Furthermore, future expenses such as management fees and carried interests reduce the expected cash flow and thus the fund's value.[350]

MEYER/MATHONET develop a fund valuation model and estimate future cash flows based on quantitative and qualitative factors including a grading and classification of the partnerships' management teams, their strategies and the fund structures.[351] By discounting these expected cash flows they derive the funds' present values.[352] The main advantage of such an approach is the incorporation of additional qualitative aspects besides the net asset value. However, thereby one cannot remove subjectivity, as the different criteria have to be assessed and scored. These models lack successful backtesting, and the analytical resources and the amount of information that is required may be obstacle to a broader application.[353]

---

347 See Meyer/Mathonet (2005), p. 154. CLARK/KOJIMA add that also the legal arrangements in the partnership agreements and the alignment of interest between general and limited partners contribute to the value of the fund perceived by fund investors. See Clark/Kojima (2003), p. 84.

348 See Clark/Kojima (2003), p. 84.

349 For high-quality and successful (low-quality) fund managers the fair value of the existing portfolio may underestimate (overestimate) the total value to be created. See Meyer/Mathonet (2005), p. 154.

350 See Meyer/Mathonet (2005), p. 155.

351 See Meyer/Mathonet (2005), pp. 180 et seq. They call their approach *Grading-based Economic Model (GEM)*.

352 A major challenge is the determination of an appropriate discount rate for private equity fund investments as standard approaches, e.g. the capital asset pricing model (CAPM), fail due to the unavailability of necessary data. MEYER/MATHONET conclude that different rates should be used, depending on the context. For valuation purposes they suggest a discount rate at the level of the public market plus a risk premium of 100-300 basis points. See for a detailed discussion of the private equity fund discount rate Meyer/Mathonet (2005), pp. 253 et seq.

353 See Kinsch/Petit-Jouvet (2006).

Fund valuation method	Pros	Cons
1 Use of secondary market prices	• Simple to use if obtainable	• Practical difficulties due to lack of enough transactions and information on these transactions • Distorted prices due to possible forced sale positions of sellers • May be not timely enough
2 Net asset value method: *a) GP reported NAV*	• Easy to obtain	• Subject to different accounting standards and valuation principles • Fund managers have discretion in valuation • Not comparable • Delay in reporting
b) Adjusted (fair value) NAV	• Simple and practical • Comparable to other funds applying this method • Adjustment for delay in reporting possible	• Requires information to be able to make adjustments • Neglects future cash flows with respect to undrawn commitments, expenses and the quality of fund managers
3 Future cash flow model-based fund valuation	• Based on the fund's future cash flows • Incorporates the value of undrawn commitments, future expenses and the quality and capabilities of the fund managers	• Cannot remove subjectivity • Lack of successful back-testing • Requires substantial analytical resources • Requires significant information

Figure 24: Fund valuation methods[354]

Figure 24 summarizes the different approaches of fund valuation. The appropriateness of the use of the different models depends on the current age of the funds and the purpose of valuation. The younger the fund is, the higher the uncalled commitments and the more relevant are qualitative criteria to assess a true economic value.[355] For older, mature funds with few or no uncalled commitments, the net asset values seem to be good proxies for the economic value and therefore the results of this method appear to be sufficient.[356] For internal purposes such as portfolio and risk management, the model-based fund valuation methods suggested by MEYER/MATHONET may be an interesting and promising approach. Due to the lack of broadly accepted common standards regarding these grading-based approaches, the benchmarking of performance based on values derived in such a way is less useful as funds would not be comparable.

---

354 Based on the discussion in Kinsch/Petit-Jouvet (2006); Meyer/Mathonet (2005), pp. 154 et seq; Kojima (2005), p. 42.

355 MEYER/MATHONET correctly do not use the calendar age, but a proxy based on the actual drawdowns. See Meyer/Mathonet (2005), p. 186.

356 See Lossen (2006), p. 13.

3.4.3 Benchmarking Returns

3.4.3.1 Peer Group Benchmarking

The absolute return measures, e.g. the IRR or any multiples, are not sufficient in order to evaluate the success of the investment in the private equity fund from a fund investor's perspective. In addition to neglecting the risks associated with the investments, they do not say anything about the fund investor's success to select the right funds. Thus, the important question for a fund investor is whether his investments have outperformed the benchmark or not. This can be analyzed in two ways: the out-performance over a peer group or the out-performance over public benchmarks.[357]

In order to compare a private equity fund's performance with other funds, it is important to identify a meaningful peer group. It is common in private equity to use peers which are similar with respect to the vintage year. *Comparing funds by vintage year* is an attempt to account for the effect of both the public market conditions and the fund age. Public market conditions at entry and at exit are critical for the outcome of a private equity portfolio company investment and comparable vintage year funds share these conditions. The fund age is important as younger funds may not yet have had a chance to write up or exit investments, whereas more mature funds may have been already realizing and generating returns.

In addition to the vintage year, it is appropriate to restrict the comparison to funds with the same strategy, geographic focus and targeted industry sectors, i.e. the same sub-asset class. The results of the comparisons are typically expressed in terms of the quartile that the fund belongs in relation to the peer group.[358] Fund investors are typically aiming at investing in "top quartile funds", i.e. funds that belongs to the top 25% of the respective peer group.

Several problems are associated with peer group benchmarking. First of all, many fund managers claim to be *top-quartile performers*. Hence, it is very important to understand which benchmark is used. Several services providers offer public benchmarks re-

---

[357] See Frei/Studer (2006), p. 137.

[358] See Meyer/Mathonet (2005), 168.

turns for private equity investments.[359] However, the relative scarcity of data on private equity returns is still a problem for the industry. It even increases when one looks at specific sub-segments of the industry.[360] The quality of the benchmarking data provided by data services also has to be questioned. Typically, benchmarks suffer from a selection bias which arises if the data is self-reported and funds stop reporting when returns worsen.[361]

Another major problem is the inconsistency in the way, how private equity funds value their investments. There are conservative and less conservative approaches applied by the general partners. While in reality the long-term performance may not be different, private equity groups that use less conservative approaches report superior performance when interim returns are compared.[362] The less standardized the methodologies used to value investments are, the less reliable is the comparison with the benchmark. Many fund investors therefore argue that the benchmarking only starts to become reliable towards the end of a fund's lifetime when the proportion of unrealized investments is lower.

Furthermore, the use of vintage year performance may not be exactly precise. Deals occur at different times, even for private equity funds of the same vintage year. The actual points of time of the investments made by two funds from subsequent vintages years are overlapping by more than 50%.[363] It is therefore questionable whether a 1997 vintage fund should be compared to all funds with vintage year 1997, or to all funds with vintages in 1996-1998.

---

359 The most common used providers of fund performance data are VentureXperts from Thomson Financial and Cambridge Associates. They collect data from funds and institutional investors. These data are used to calculate annual and quarterly returns.

360 See Guennoc (2006), p. 121.

361 See Ljungqvist/Richardson (2003), p. 1; Kaplan/Schoar (2005), p. 1811. According to COCHRANE, the problem of a selection bias is especially a problem when analyzing exited individual private equity investments. These investments are far more likely to go public when they are successful. See Cochrane (2005), pp. 4 et seq. CHEN/BAIERL/KAPLAN argue that this is a minor problem when analyzing funds. Return data by private equity funds includes both successful and unsuccessful investments. See Chen/Baierl/Kaplan (2002), p. 85.

362 See Gompers/Lerner (2000). 251.

363 See Gottschalg (2006), p. 203, who cites a study from HEC School of Management.

Finally, a return measure on fund level comprises the success and failure of each single fund investment. They are pooled and do not give any insights about the dispersion of the returns of each single investment within the fund and whether the performance is driven by single investments.[364]

Empirical results

Over 80% of the interviewed fund investors (N=24) benchmark their fund investments with a peer group based on publicly available data. Most of them use VentureXperts from Venture Economics. However, nearly all of them state that the results have to be carefully interpreted. The samples with comparable funds are typically very thin. Therefore, a quarter of the interviewed fund investors have built-up their own database which they believe is more comprehensive and representative. Some of the interviewed investors also pursue a comparison between the different funds within their portfolio. However, this may neglect the different risk levels.

Interestingly, two fund investors mention that they also compare and benchmark the development of the individual portfolio companies that the fund managers invested in. They have gathered a proprietary database which allows analyzing and assessing the value generation relative to other private equity investments. However, no further details were given.

3.4.3.2 Public Market Benchmarking

The benchmarking of performance with different asset classes is typically also a challenge for private equity fund investors, as the internal rate of return is a value-weighted return. In public markets, however, returns are measured in a time-weighted way.

One possibility to compare private equity and public market equity is, therefore, the calculation of *time-weighted returns* for private equity investments using net asset values. As mentioned earlier, these net asset values are sensitive to the accounting policy chosen as well as to infrequent valuation processes.[365]

---

[364] See Gottschalg (2006), p. 202.

[365] See Frei/Studer (2006), p. 132.

An alternative attempt to compare private equity returns with quoted stock returns is the so-called *public market equivalent (PME)*. LONG/NICKLES suggest a method for comparing private market internal rates of return to public market index returns.[366] The idea of their methodology is a duplication of private equity cash flows on a chosen quoted market index. Every time a private equity drawdown is made, the same amount is invested in a specific index. If a distribution occurs, the same amount is exited from the quoted market index.[367] The cash flows of both the private equity fund investment and the index investment are the same. The result is simply a money-weighted return for the index, assuming the same cash flow pattern as in the private equity fund. This IRR of the index can then be compared with IRRs of the private equity investments.[368] The difference in the IRR comes only from the difference in the remaining value of the index investment.[369] If it yields a positive (negative) balance, the public market shows a higher (lower) performance than the private equity fund investment.[370] An example for two different private equity fund cash flow cases is provided in Figure 25.

Period	PE fund cash flow (case A)	PE fund cash flow (case B)	Public market index return	Index value	PME net asset value (case A)	PME cash flow (case A)	PME net asset value (case B)	PME cash flow (case B)
t=0	-300,000	-300,000		100.0	300,000	-300,000	300,000	-300,000
t=1	-200,000	-200,000	10%	110.0	530,000	-200,000	530,000	-200,000
t=2	-450,000	-450,000	5%	115.5	1,006,500	-450,000	1,006,500	-450,000
t=3	-300,000	-300,000	-10%	104.0	1,205,850	-300,000	1,205,850	-300,000
t=4	0	0	-5%	98.8	1,145,558	0	1,145,558	0
t=5	0	0	10%	108.6	1,260,113	0	1,260,113	0
t=6	0	0	40%	152.1	1,764,159	0	1,764,159	0
t=7	2,000,000	3,000,000	30%	197.7	293,406	2,000,000	-706,594	3,000,000
t=8	0	0	30%	257.0	381,428	0	-918,572	0
t=9	0	0	30%	334.1	495,856	0	-1,194,144	0
t=10	3,150,000	3,150,000	30%	434.4	644,613	644,613	-1,552,387	-1,552,387
IRR PE	21.94%	26.32%			PME IRR	13.05%	PME IRR	5.62%

Figure 25: Public market equivalent according to LONG/NICKLES[371]

---

[366] See Long/Nickels (1995).

[367] See Guennoc (2006), p. 123.

[368] See Long/Nickels (1995), p. 4. This methodology is adopted by Thomson Financial and EVCA for measuring and comparing industry returns. See Guennoc (2006), p. 123. Figure 13 shows current performance results for the industry.

[369] See Grabenwarter/Weidig (2005a), p. 24.

[370] See Rouvinez (2003b), p. 35.

[371] Based on Long/Nickels (1995), p. 11.

In both cases A and B the private equity fund investments outperform the respective public market investments. The advantage of this method is its simplicity and transparency. However, it has a serious conceptual problem. If the private equity investment is outperforming the index, the index yields a negative value. A negative index value, however, means that the investor runs a short position to match the private equity distributions. A strong performance of the index in such a situation actually works against the investor. By contrast, when the public markets decline, investors having a short position would collect gains. This is exemplified in case B in Figure 25. The distribution in t=7 (case B) causes the net asset value of the public market equivalent to become negative. As a result, the strong index performance from t=8 until t=10 with 30% p.a. works actually against the public market investor. The outperformance of the PE fund cash flow is therefore much lower than in case A. Given the cash flow of fund A and B, this result is counterintuitive. The shift from a long to a short position impedes the benchmarking process as comparing a long private equity portfolio with a short position in the public market obviously does not make sense.[372] In addition, any correlation studies based on such a public market equivalent is erroneous.[373]

To overcome this problem, ROUVINEZ introduces the so-called *PME+ approach*.[374] This method tries to avoid running a short position by multiplying the private equity fund's distributions by a coefficient (so-called distribution scaling factor) so that the ending PME+ net asset value and the ending net asset value of the private equity investment have the same values.[375] Both cash flows are then compared. Figure 26 provides an example.

The distribution scaling factor λ is a function of the total number of index shares bought over time (S_+), the total number of index shares sold (S_-) over time, and the final number of index shares (S_N). The number of index shares that is sold and bought is received by dividing the private equity cash flow by the index value in the respective period. As the final value of the PME+ net asset value has to match the net asset value of the PE fund investment at the end of the period, there is a linear equation for the

---

372 See Rouvinez (2003a), p. 26.

373 See Rouvinez (2003b), p. 36. The negative value at the end of the measurement period even might cause the IRR to be undefined as there is no discount rate that brings the net present value to zero.

374 See Rouvinez (2003b), pp. 34 et seq.

375 See Grabenwarter/Weidig (2005a), p. 25.

distribution scaling factor λ: $S_+ - \lambda * S_- = S_N$ (which results in $\lambda = (S_+ - S_N)/S_-$).[376] The PME cash flow can be then derived by multiplying the distributions with the scaling factor.

Period	PE fund cash flow	Public market index return	Index value	Index shares bought/ sold	PME net asset value	PME cash flow
t=0	-300,000		100.0	3,000	300,000	-300,000
t=1	-200,000	10%	110.0	1,818	530,000	-200,000
t=2	-450,000	5%	115.5	3,896	1,006,500	-450,000
t=3	-300,000	-10%	104.0	2,886	1,205,850	-300,000
t=4	0	-5%	98.8	0	1,145,558	0
t=5	0	10%	108.6	0	1,260,113	0
t=6	0	40%	152.1	0	1,764,159	0
t=7	3,000,000	30%	197.7	-15,174	1,609,209	684,198
t=8	1,000,000	30%	257.0	-3,891	1,863,905	228,066
t=9	0	30%	334.1	0	2,423,077	0
t=10	3,150,000	30%	434.4	S_N = 7,252	3,150,000	3,150,000
			Scaling factor λ	0.2281		
IRR PE	29.37%				PME+ IRR	16.40%

Figure 26: Public market equivalent (PME+) according to ROUVINEZ[377]

The ending values for the private equity fund cash flow and the PME cash flow are the same. The private equity fund investment (IRR 29.37%) outperforms the PME (16.40%). Due to the scaling procedure, it can be avoided that this outperformance results in a short selling of the benchmark. In this respect, this procedure makes more sense than in the PME approach developed by LONG/NICKELS. The scaling can be interpreted as creating a "similar exposure" in both the private equity and the index investment over time.[378]

An objection to the PME+ approach is, however, that the cash flow patterns of the private equity and the benchmark investment are not exactly matching. Given the identi-

---

376 See Rouvinez (2003a), p. 28. In Figure 26, the scaling factor (=0.2281) can be derived by adding all shares bought (=11,600), subtracting the final number of index shares (=7,252) and divide the result by all shares sold (=19,065).

377 Own calculations based on the methodology presented in Rouvinez (2003a); Rouvinez (2003b). For the derivation of the scaling factor see Rouvinez (2003a), p. 24.

378 See Frei/Studer (2006), p. 141. Although the PME+ scaling procedure mitigates a potential negative exposure and ensures a positive ending balance, it does not guarantee a constant positive exposure over the entire investment period. See Rouvinez (2003b), p. 37.

cal timing, in-flows and the fact that a fixed proportion of outflows are identical, ROUVINEZ, however, concludes this argument is mitigated.[379]

A different approach is suggested by KASERER/DILLER, in order to overcome the reinvestment hypothesis used in calculating the IRR.[380] They propose a public market equivalent measure using a public market reinvestment hypothesis.[381] Basically, they define their PME as the ratio of the terminal wealth of a private equity fund investment - obtained under the assumption that distributions (cash inflows) are reinvested in the public market - compared to the terminal wealth obtained when investing the same amounts of money in the given public index.[382] Mathematically, the PME is expressed as follows, whereby R_{It} is the net return[383] of a public market index in period t, and while cf_t is the normalized positive cash flow of the private equity fund in period t:[384]

$$PME = \frac{\sum_{t=1}^{T} cf_t \prod_{i=t+1}^{T} (1 + R_{Ii})}{\prod_{t=1}^{T} (1 + R_{It})}$$

By dividing the positive distributions of any period with the present value of all investments (all negative cash flows), the positive cash flows are normalized. In doing

---

379 See Rouvinez (2003b), p. 38.

380 See Kaserer/Diller (2004c), p. 38; Diller (2007), pp. 95 et seq. For the criticism of the reinvestment hypothesis see also Ljungqvist/Richardson (2003), p. 19; Kaplan/Schoar (2005), p. 1797. The IRR method assumes that cash flows generated by the fund investment and distributed to investors can be reinvested at an interest rate equal to the IRR. This is unrealistic since, first of all, it is not possible to reinvest the distribution at an identical return and, secondly, it leads to different reinvestment rates for cash flows accruing at the same time.

381 Different authors use different alternative reinvestment hypotheses to overcome the mentioned problem with the IRR. LJUNGQVIST/RICHARDSON, for example, calculate ex post net present values of investments in a fund by discounting realized cash outflows at the risk-free rate of return and at the cost of capital for inflows. The net present values are then scaled by the present value of the investment, giving a so-called profitability index. See Ljungqvist/Richardson (2003), p. 19.

382 See Kaserer/Diller (2004c), pp. 40 et seq. for more details. KAPLAN/SCHOAR use a similar approach modified only because their public market equivalent is the ratio of the discounted value of all cash outflows (using the total return of a public index) and the discounted value of all cash inflows.

383 Typically, only gross returns of public market returns can be observed. In order to correctly compare these returns with private equity fund returns, one need to adjust these public market returns for any fees.

384 See Kaserer/Diller (2004c), p. 40.

so, the cash flows are normalized to an initial investment with a present value of EUR 1. Figure 27 provides a numerical example.

This PME than can also be interpreted as the amount of money that an investor would have to invest in a public index in order to end up with the same terminal wealth as if he had invested the present value of one currency unit in the private equity fund.[385] In the example, the investor would have to invest 1.5 currency units in the public index in order to derive a terminal value of 6.5 currency units. If he had invested one currency unit in the private equity fund investment in t=0, he would have received a terminal value of 6.5 in t=10. This PME is a relative performance measure, meaning that funds with higher performance relative to the index have higher PMEs.[386]

Period	PE fund cash flow	Public market index return	Index value	Positive normalized cash flows	Terminal wealth (in t=10) of positive normalized cash flows
t=0	-300,000		100.0		
t=1	-200,000	10%	110.0		
t=2	-450,000	5%	115.5		
t=3	-300,000	-10%	104.0		
t=4	0	-5%	98.8		
t=5	0	10%	108.6		
t=6	0	40%	152.1		
t=7	2,000,000	30%	197.7	1.72	3.79
t=8	0	30%	257.0		
t=9	0	30%	334.1		
t=10	3,150,000	30%	434.4	2.72	2.72
		Final public market return	4.34	Sum	6.50

$$\text{PME} = \frac{6.50}{4.34} = 1.5$$

The present value of all negative cash outflows (discounted by the public market index) is 1,160,029.

Figure 27: Public market equivalent according to KASERER/DILLER[387]

All mentioned methodologies still depend on net asset values of the funds if one compares interim performance, i.e. assuming that at the time of measurement not all in-

385 See Kaserer/Diller (2004c), p. 40. This can be calculated by dividing the terminal value of the private equity investment in t=10 (7,544,000) by the present value of all cash outflows in t=0 (1,160,029).

386 See Kaserer/Diller (2004b), p. 40. The presented PME+ example assumes that the respective private equity fund is not fully liquidated. If the fund is fully liquidated, the net asset value is zero and S_N equals zero. In these cases, ROUVINEZ's scaling factor is the reciprocal value of KASERER/DILLER's PME. Both approaches are quite similar, only different with respect to calculation and interpretation.

387 Own calculations based on the methodology described in Kaserer/Diller (2004c).

vestments are exited.[388] As a last cash flow, one would use the provided net asset values, which are subject to the already mentioned valuation problems. In addition, using the net asset values indirectly assumes that the private equity investor can immediately exit the fund at that value.

Finally, a crucial problem relevant for all comparisons with the public market equivalent method is that the risk structure of the index is typically not similar to the private equity fund investments.[389] Venture capital investments are typically younger than the average company in an index and therefore more prone to default risk. Buyout investments typically have a higher leverage and therefore a higher financial risk than the average company in indices.[390] Fund investors need to be very careful in concluding whether a higher performance of the private equity investments in comparison with a public index actually corresponds to an outperformance or to a normal compensation for a higher risk.[391]

Empirical results

The majority of the interviewed fund investors are very sceptical about the outcome of benchmarking exercises with public markets. Most of them emphasize that a given market index may be not comparable. Others criticize that due to the different methodologies that could be applied it is possible to "play with the numbers". Especially, some fund-of-fund investors doubt that the comparison is valuable. However, given the need of their customers to get this benchmarking, these fund-of-funds managers still typically provide this service.

3.4.4 Risks of Fund Investments

3.4.4.1 Different Types of Risks

The private equity fund investors must accept risk in exchange for potential superior returns. Thus, any performance measurement should take the risks of the investments

---

388 See Rouvinez (2003b), p. 35; Grabenwarter/Weidig (2005a), p. 24.

389 See Kaplan/Schoar (2005), p. 1797. If the private equity investments' systematic risk is higher (lower) than the index, i.e. its beta is higher (lower) than 1 with respect to the index, the PME will overstate (understate) the true risk-adjusted returns to private equity.

390 See Gottschalg (2006), p. 204.

391 See Guennoc (2006), p. 125; Kaplan/Schoar (2005), p. 1797.

into account. For private equity fund investments, different types of risks have to be addressed.

The *cash flow risk* comprises the uncertainty about the timing and amount of capital contributions and distributions. Many factors influence these amounts and timings which are unknown to the fund investor. The uncertainty with respect to the timing originates from the decision to delegate the investment activity to the fund managers. They decide about when to invest in a company and when to exit. The amount of cash flow that the investor receives (distributions) very much depends on the performance of the underlying portfolio company investments. This cash uncertainty may lead to an inefficient use of resources or undesired allocations. Therefore, liquidity planning and allocation management require sophisticated cash flow modeling processes.[392]

Liquidity risk arises as private equity is naturally an illiquid asset class. It is associated with the cash flow risk. The long holding period, infrequent valuations, low transparency and transfer restrictions are obstacles that hinder the fund investors to easily realize their fund investments during the life of the funds – at least at a fair value.[393] An adjustment to portfolio holdings in order to react on changing circumstances is difficult.[394]

A key driver of return in buyouts is the leverage on the investment.[395] However, in recent years, the leverage in private equity transactions has been rising substantially.[396] This increased *leverage risk* that fund investors face may lead to more downgrades and even defaults of companies.[397] Associated with leverage risks are *interest risks*. A sud-

---

392 In chapter 3.7.2, the issue is described in more detail.

393 See Frei/Studer (2003), p. 207. If the fund investors for example anticipate a decline in value before market participants, they may therefore not be able to act on such information. There are no quickly exercisable secondary transactions possible. On the opposite, if the fundamental outlook of a fund is promising, it may be impossible or very difficult to increase the exposure. See Frei/Studer (2003), p. 207

394 For opportunities and challenges of a secondary market for fund partnerships see chapter 3.7.3.

395 Typically, private equity funds themselves are not leveraged as the limited partnership agreement prevents the general partner from taking this additional risk. See Gompers/Lerner (1996), p. 480.

396 See Financial Service Authority (2006b), p. 37. The leverage is typically measured with the debt/EBITDA ratio.

397 A detailed discussion of the negative but also positive aspects of excessive leverage is provided in Financial Service Authority (2006b), pp. 59 et seq.

den increase in the cost of debt, i.e. interest rates, could cause significant losses to companies and investors alike.[398] However, the interest exposure may be hedged on portfolio company level which mitigates the risk.

Due to the illiquidity and the lack of an organized market for the asset class, private equity fund investors face significant *valuation risks*. The reported value of the fund investment might be very different from the "real" value. Given the significant impact these "real" values have on commitment planning, secondary transactions in portfolio management, or simply performance measurement and reporting, it is necessary to determine them as accurately as possible.[399]

Currency risks arise from exchange rate fluctuations. This volatility may affect both the fund investor liabilities due to his commitments and his investment value, respectively the size of proceeds he may receive from the investments.[400] For example, European fund investors who commit to U.S. funds face the risk that the dollar appreciates before the money has been actually drawn down.[401] In such a situation, however, the realisation of U.S. dollar investments may result in higher proceeds in terms of Euro currency. The fund investor has to decide whether he wants to hedge his private equity exposure or not. In order to implement a hedging strategy, he needs to gather as much information as possible about his actual exposure. Furthermore, he needs to know about any existing hedging strategy at fund level.[402]

Style drift risk can be defined as the fund investors' risk that their fund managers deviate from stated objectives in terms of the focus for investments at particular stages of entrepreneurial development, their industry or geographical location.[403] As these different investment foci significantly differ in terms of risk and return, a style drift may change the planned risk-return relationship of the fund investor's entire portfolio. Due to the illiquidity of the assets, the fund investor cannot easily and timely adjust his

---

398 See Financial Service Authority (2006b), p. 57.

399 See Frei/Studer (2003), p. 209.

400 See Frei/Studer (2003), p. 209.

401 Taking into account both the high volatility of currency markets and the long investment periods of funds (e.g. up to four years), the effect can be significant.

402 It is possible that the general partner already hedges his foreign portfolio.

403 See Cumming/Fleming/Schwienbacher (2005), p. 2.

portfolio if the general partner undertakes investments inconsistent with the declared strategy.[404]

The performance of the fund investments depends very much on the quality of the fund managers which leads to significant *manager risk* for the fund investors.[405] The selection of a good team is probably the most important task fund investors have to fulfill and should be a significant part of the fund due diligence.[406] But even after having selected high-quality people, the fund investors need to monitor whether the team run effective and disciplined investment processes, and has monitoring and oversight systems in place. The team stability, its culture including career and succession planning as well as incentive structures are important. Figure 28 summarizes the discussed risks.

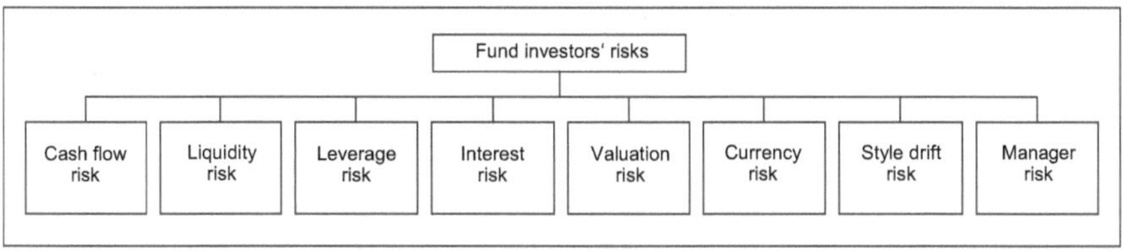

Figure 28: Different types of fund investors' risks

Obviously, all these risks are overlapping. They are finally linked to the uncertainty of the cash flows paid-in and received from a fund investment. In order to understand the relevance of these different types of risks, the study addresses this question to the fund investors.

Empirical results

Figure 29 provides evidence on the perceived risks of private equity fund investments. The manager risk is perceived as the highest risk. Over 80% judge it as important (or very important). This evaluation is triggered by the utmost importance of the quality of the fund manager for the success of the fund. The concern over a fund managers' po-

---

404 See Cumming/Fleming/Schwienbacher (2005), p. 4.

405 A wide gap between top- and bottom-quartile fund managers is evidence for this. See Schmidt (2003), p. 256.

406 See Grabenwarter/Weidig (2005a), p. 94.

tential style drift is high: Over 75% mention that it is at least important. This can be explained by the fact that the fund managers are selected to pursue a chosen strategy and should not deviate from it. The assessment of their quality and the fit of the strategy with the overall portfolio have been selecting criteria. Nearly equally important to the interviewed investors are leverage and interest risks. This high relevance may be biased due to the high leverage that is used in current transactions.

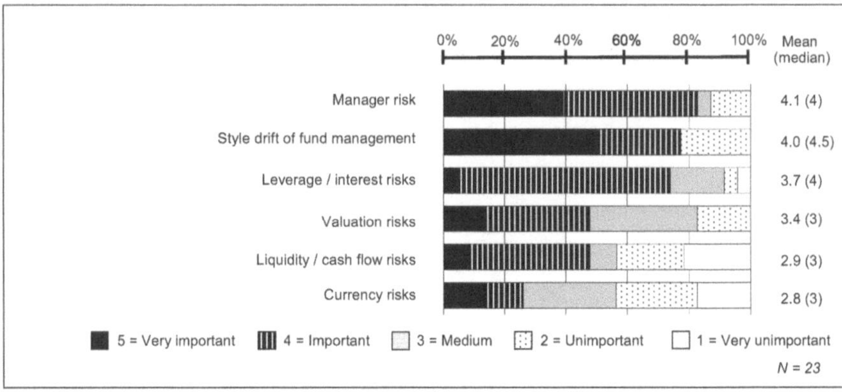

Figure 29: Importance of different fund investments risks

Nearly 50% of the fund investors say that valuation risks are important. This is still a considerable number demonstrating the uncertainty of the valuation inherent in the asset class. Liquidity and cash flow risks are also regarded as considerably influential. The lowest risk weight is given to currency risks which less than 30% of the interviewed investors value as being important. Many fund investors explicitly diversify their assets over different currencies. Others use hedging strategies where possible.

3.4.4.2 Measurement of Risks

The importance of risks has been demonstrated. There is also a need to measure the risk of private equity investments due to two reasons: Any performance measurement and evaluation should be done in the context of risk. Once the risk has been measured, the investor is able to determine if a realized return was sufficient relative to the risk incurred.[407] The risk has significant influence on investment decisions. Understanding

[407] See Atkins/Giannini (2003), p. 226.

a fund investment's risk allows a more reasonable estimation of the required return. To measure the risk level of the fund investment and/or the entire portfolio, either quantitative or more qualitative approaches may be applied.[408]

Quantitative Approaches

In order to quantify the risk of an investment, estimations of its returns and the volatility of these returns are required.[409] To measure the risk in a portfolio context, also the correlation with other assets is needed. The volatility is given by the standard deviation of a time series of market prices.[410] In private equity, there are no time series of market prices available.[411] In order to overcome this problem, some authors suggest calculating a series of time-weighted returns based on the net asset values.[412] The funds' net asset values, however, are no reliable replacement for a market price for two reasons: the subjectivity in valuation (managed pricing) and the artificially low fluctuation over time (stale pricing).[413] The first results from fund managers' discretion in valuations. The second leads to an underestimation of the inherent risk.[414] Whereas stock prices constantly react to new information, private equity net asset values are typically only adjusted every quarter. They do not constantly incorporate all new available information and thus the respective returns appear to be less volatile. The process of smoothing returns leads to an underestimation of volatility and an underestimation of the correlation with other asset classes such as public equity.[415]

---

408 See Atkins/Giannini (2003), p. 226.

409 See Atkins/Giannini (2003), p. 217.

410 See Grabenwarter/Weidig (2005a), p. 26.

411 See Kaserer/Wagner/Achleitner (2003), p. 262. The internal rate of return does not allow the estimation of a standard deviation of returns, and a correlation of returns to other asset classes. See Buchner/Kaserer/Wagner (2006), p. 3.

412 See for example Gompers/Lerner (1997), pp. 5 et seq. The authors suggest a marking to market valuation of the portfolio companies to overcome conservative valuation biases.

413 See Buchner/Kaserer/Wagner (2006), p. 3.

414 See Artus/Teiletche (2004), p. 8.

415 See Artus/Teiletche (2004), p. 8. The authors conclude that in these cases, the risk of the fund investment is individually underestimated (via the standard deviation) or collectively with other assets (via the correlation).

Alternatively, a cross-sectional analysis can be applied to measure risk.[416] Thereby, the standard deviation is measured as a distribution parameter of a sample of funds. This measure is the degree by which the individual fund returns deviate from the average of returns.[417] If data for the individual funds is available, e.g. provided by data services, this analysis is usually easier than estimating the volatility of a time series of market prices.

A general issue with quantitative risk assessment is that it is based on historic data. As discussed earlier, however, the analysis of these measures is limited in private equity due to the relatively short time series and lower quality of the publicly available data.[418]

Qualitative Approaches

Due to the difficulties in quantifying risks in private equity, fund investors may use qualitative approaches. In such an approach, the fund investor makes a relative assessment of the various portfolio company risk characteristics including the stage of development, the size of the targeted companies, the financial leverage applied, the geographical region or the sector.[419] Alternatively or additionally, an assessment could be based on fund level characteristics such as the quality of the management, the investment strategy, the internal investment, or the monitoring and exiting processes.[420] Using scoring models enables the assessor to put different weights to the pre-chosen risk characteristics.[421]

The main disadvantage of qualitative approaches is the dependency on subjective evaluations. However, it is an attempt to incorporate an assessment of future developments. Whereas quantitative analysis relies solely on historic returns, qualitative approaches enable the fund investors to assess and forecast the fund investment's ability to generate future cash flows.

---

416 See Burgel (2000), p. 60; Kaserer/Diller (2004c), p. 42.

417 See Grabenwarter/Weidig (2005a), p. 26.

418 See Meyer/Mathonet (2005), p. 81. For more details see also the discussion in chapter 2.5.2.

419 See Atkins/Giannini (2003), p. 226.

420 See Jugel (2003), p. 20.

421 See Helwing/Hummel (2005), p. 43. The authors develop a scoring model based on institutional characteristics of private equity funds to measure risks.

Empirical results

All interviewed fund investors acknowledge the difficulties of measuring risks in private equity. However, 84% of them (N=19) have some approaches in place that shed light on the different risk profiles of the funds. These approaches are, however, rather qualitative assessments judging on a list of factors. Many investors simply assess the risk level depending on fund characteristics such as the strategy, region, team etc.

Half of the interviewed investors also look at the portfolio companies of the funds and not only at the fund level. The distribution of company returns, the value concentration of companies in a fund, the number of write-offs, the financial leverage of single transactions (also aggregated on fund level) are, for example, factors they consider in a risk evaluation.

It must be recognized that measuring the risks in private equity investments is still an issue to which most of the sophisticated fund investors have no sufficient answer yet. A quantification of the risks, or a "scientific approach" as one investor put it, has not been developed yet.

3.4.5 Fund Investment's Costs

The performance measurement of private equity fund investments cannot be pursued without the consideration of the costs related to the investment activity. With respect to the success of their fund investments, fund investors need to monitor both the gross return on all portfolio company investments and the net return. The *gross return* on investments considers all the cash flows which take place between the fund and its portfolio company investments.[422] It demonstrates the ability of the fund managers to successfully choose, manage and divest portfolio companies. The *net return* is the actual return after cost. Costs include fund manager's carried interest, the management fees paid to fund managers and all other applicable charges which are paid out by the fund manager in the course of investing, managing and divesting from its investment portfolio. The net return proves the overall cost efficiency with respect to the fund man-

422 If not all investments are realized, the valuation of the unrealized portfolio should be considered. The gross return according to *EVCA Reporting Guidelines* neither includes any fees paid by the portfolio company either to the fund or the fund managers, nor fees paid to lawyers, accountants or other advisors. See EVCA (2006b), p. 29.

agement tasks.[423] This is the ultimate interest of investors. Private equity is an expensive asset class.[424] When comparing the performance of funds with peers or other asset classes, the costs of the respective investments should always be considered.

As already indicated in chapter 2.4.3, the *carried interest* is the fund managers' share of the partnership's profits and is typically 20% of the net return, after a minimum return (hurdle rate) has been paid to investors. The *management fee* shall cover the actual costs of managing the fund and comprises during the first years typically 1.5-2.5% of the committed capital.[425] Some fund investors may want to move towards budgeted management fees instead. Thereby, the management fee is charged against an annual budget which may be approved by the fund's advisory board.[426] The use of budget management fees serves the alignment of interest concept because it ensures that the main source of significant compensation for the general partners is the carried interest.[427] However, using a percentage approach currently still remains the industry norm.

The partnership agreement needs to clarify two important aspects. First of all, it must state which types of expenses are covered by the management fee and which items may be additionally charged to the fund investors.[428] Secondly, it needs to establish rules concerning the set-off of potential fee income against the management fee. Currently, there seems to be no industry standard concerning these terms.[429]

The private equity funds often incur material out-of pocket expenses relating to the investments. Many external parties such as lawyers, accountants, consultants and other professional advisors usually help and assist in negotiating and pursuing the transactions. When a transaction is consummated, these *deal expenses* might be reimbursed or

423 See EVCA (2006b), p. 28.

424 The net present value of management fees and other charges over the life of a fund alone may sum up to around 12-15% of the committed capital. See Sormani (2006), p. 45; Feinendegen/Schmidt/Wahrenburg (2003), p. 1177.

425 After a specified investment period, most funds calculate the management fee based on the purchase costs of the remaining portfolio. This reflects the perceived level of activity necessary to manage the remaining portfolio. See Schell (2006), chap. 2, p. 31.

426 See Meyer/Mathonet (2005), p. 32.

427 See Schell (2006), chap. 2, p. 27. A budgeted management fee shifts power towards limited partners and is typical for captive funds.

428 See Grabenwarter/Weidig (2005a), p. 59.

429 See Sormani (2006), pp. 45 et seq; Schell (2006), chap. 2, p. 36.

paid by the portfolio company. In case the transaction did not materialize, the so-called *broken-deal expenses* have to be paid either by the fund or by the general partner out of the management fee. Other expenses relating to the fund can be summarized as *organizational expenses* and include the set-up costs of the fund structure, e.g. legal cost for drafting the fund documentation, or auditing costs.[430] Fund investors should carefully review the outsourcing behavior of a fund manager with respect to due diligence services, especially when these costs are not covered by the management fee.[431]

In same cases, fee income may be generated. For example, if the fund enters into an agreement to acquire a portfolio company, the acquisition may include provisions which allow the target to accept a higher price from a third party, but also require a payment in the event the third party offer is accepted (*break-up fee*). More importantly, general partners may charge *transaction fees* to the new portfolio companies for arranging and negotiating the financing structure, including the debt financing.[432] *Monitoring fee income* may be generated by providing general advisory or consulting services to the portfolio companies following the acquisition. This could include compensation for serving on the boards of directors of the portfolio companies. This potential fee income may cause conflicts of interests between the fund managers and the investors if an offset against the management fee is not ruled out. On the one hand, limited partners will argue that fund managers should not be paid twice for the same services. On the other hand, significant potential fee income may lead to transactions that the fund managers exercise not because of the potential return, but rather to secure ongoing fee income.[433]

By monitoring the detailed costs of the funds investment, the fund investor can assure that the fund managers follow the fee-related provisions specified in the partnership agreements. Furthermore, they are able to detect and assess any newly arising conflicts of interests. Last but not least, they can better understand the cost dynamics of their fund investments and evaluate the net return the fund managers deliver.

---

430 A controversial issue might be the treatment of placement fees which should cover the fundraising costs of the general partners. Fund investors normally do not accept that these fees should be reimbursed by the fund. See Schell (2006), chap. 2, p. 40.

431 See Grabenwarter/Weidig (2005a), p. 59.

432 See Schell (2006), chap. 2, p. 36.

433 See Grabenwarter/Weidig (2005a), p. 60.

The performance measurement of the individual private equity fund investments and of the portfolio of funds which has been discussed in this chapter forms the basis for the other monitoring objectives. Information on the performance of a fund is, for example, a prerequisite to effectively govern the fund manager, to detect whether the fund investment is off track and to find the right decisions if the fund investment faces a crisis situation. The monitoring and fund governance will be discussed next.

3.5 Monitoring and Fund Governance

3.5.1 Advisory Board Representation

Integral elements of the fund governance are annual general meetings of all investors and the participation of some investors in advisory boards of the partnerships. Monitoring the partnership enables the fund investors to fulfill their roles in these governance bodies more efficiently as they have a better understanding of the on-going developments. Vice versa, by participating in these governance bodies, fund investors may be provided with inside information they otherwise would not get.

The *annual general meeting,* which all investors are invited to attend, is rather a communication tool than an effective governance instrument. The agenda usually comprises a review of the partnership activities of the last year and a comment on the plans for the future. Presentations of the management of portfolio companies are standard features of these meetings.[434] With growing fund sizes and an increasing number of portfolio companies, the effectiveness of annual general meeting as an information source decreases.[435]

For many fund investors, the *advisory board* fulfills a more important role than the annual general meeting. It usually meets twice a year.[436] The composition of fund investors in an advisory board is determined by the general partner and is based either on the size of the commitment or the strategic value the fund investors are perceived to bring to the fund.[437] Habitually, three to nine investors are appointed.[438] The tasks of

---

434 See Fried/Hisrich (1989), p. 269.

435 See Hagenmüller (2004), p. 115.

436 See Toll (2003), p. 59. Some boards meet quarterly. See Fried/Hisrich (1989), p. 268.

437 See Schell (2006), chap. 9, p. 13; Thomson (2005), p. 16.

438 See Toll (2003), p. 59.

an advisory board vary from one fund to the next. They are set out in the limited partnership agreement.[439]

For general partners, the advisory board is an instrument to get approval from fund investors without having to take a vote from all investors. Asking every investor may be burdensome from a time-related and logistical point of view.[440] It might be easier to present and discuss issues orally with a smaller circle of investors.[441] It can also be used as early warning system to figure out through a representative group of investors what occupies the mind of all investors.[442]

In order to get a better understanding of the reasons why fund investors participate in an advisory board, its purposes and the actual board representation have been subject of discussion with the surveyed limited partners. So far, these issues have been neglected by the literature.

Empirical results

The interviewed fund investors (N=22) are represented in advisory boards of an average of 35% of their funds. About a third is already represented in more than 50% of the advisory boards of their funds. Compared to other findings, this rather high number is probably attributable to the fact that the sample represents the top European investors.[443] They are often naturally choices for fund managers due to the typical size of their investments. The importance of the advisory board is demonstrated by the fact that 57% of the interviewed investors (N=21) would like to see their institutions represented in even more fund advisory boards in the future.

Three reasons are equally often stated by the interviewed partners when asked why they participate in advisory boards. Primarily, it is used as a source of information. Fund investors who attend board meetings feel that they are better informed about the

---

[439] See Thomson (2005), p. 16.

[440] This is especially true for larger buyout funds that may have more than 100 different investors.

[441] See Schell (2006), chap. 9, p. 36.

[442] See Thomson (2005), p. 19.

[443] HAGENMÜLLER for example finds that, on average, limited partners in his sample are represented in boards of around 20% of their funds. He also finds that about a third of them does not have any seat in these boards. See Hagenmüller (2004), p. 50.

development of the fund. Through the contact to other fund investors during these meetings, they can share their views. Secondly, it offers networking opportunities. The interviewed fund investors use the advisory board meetings to strengthen the relationship with the general partners. Furthermore, they believe the advisory board has a governance function. However, a couple of fund investors point out that some advisory boards have little governance content. Often, it is simply used as an efficient voting and investor relations instrument at best.

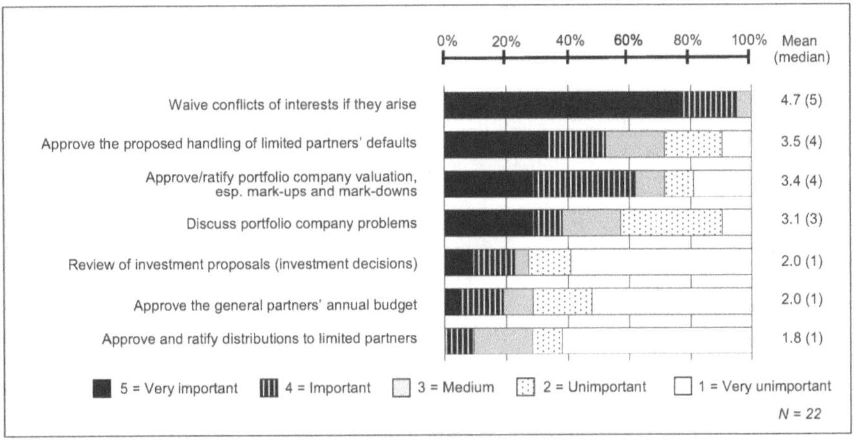

Figure 30: Purposes of funds' advisory boards

The most important purpose of an advisory board is dealing with conflicts of interests if any arise during the partnership's life-time. As can be seen in Figure 30, more than 90% of the interviewed investors rank this as important task. The approval of the proposed handling of potential limited partners' defaults and the approval and ratification of portfolio company valuations are ranked as nearly equally important purposes. Limited partners' default may affect the whole partnership structure and fund investors want to have influence on the decision about who will follow as investor.[444] Due to the uncertainty concerning the valuation of private companies, many fund investors believe an approval of the valuation by the advisory board may be of value.[445] The fund

[444] In case the defaulting investor needs to sell the partnership, the co-investors in the fund often have a right of first refusal. See Grabenwarter/Weidig (2005a), p. 153.

[445] Whether it should be the advisory board or a special valuation committee that would review the valuations, is a different topic.

managers have to disclose the underlying methodologies and assumptions. The board members then testify their appropriateness. Still 40% of the interviewed fund investors find it important to discuss portfolio company problems. However, the investment decisions should not be reviewed by the advisory board. More than 70% believe this is unimportant. The distribution of proceeds to fund investors is ruled out in the partnership agreement. Very few believe it is an issue that needs the board's approval.

3.5.2 Value Adding

It is industry standard that the management of portfolio companies is clearly within the responsibility of the fund managers. The limited partners should not be involved in the day-to-day operations of the fund.[446] However, the role of fund investors with respect to involvement and engagement on fund level must not be entirely passive. The competition for getting access to high quality funds has been increasing over the last years. Fund investors, therefore, may progressively think of what they can offer to their fund investments in addition to simple cash resources. They may also articulate and actively market their value proposition.[447]

The fund investor's value add may relate to the fund level or the individual portfolio companies of the fund. Active monitoring of the fund investments is the prerequisite to get involved in discussions and to be able to provide value add. Fund investors may have regular and intensive contact with the fund's management team. If they are aware of the current developments on fund and portfolio level, they can better understand the partnership's needs and provide better answers to these.

The interviewed limited partners have been asked about their engagement on partnership level. The research focuses on two questions: the issues on which limited partners are asked for advice from their fund managers, and the issues which the limited partners push themselves.

---

[446] See Meyer/Mathonet (2005), p. 273. In some jurisdictions, limited partners may even loose their status as limited partners or have to fear tax consequences when getting an influence on the day-to-day activity of the fund. See Grabenwarter/Weidig (2005a), p. 83.

[447] See McKinsey (2003), p. 21.

Empirical results

The first outcome is that in certain areas the general partners ask their fund investors pro-actively for advice. This concerns especially questions referring to the fund level. The value add which fund investors may offer substantially derives from their in-depth market knowledge, their experience, their reputation and their networks. Through intensive contacts to many fund managers, they have a broad understanding of the market developments. Fund managers know about that quality of their investors and take advantage of it.

A question is how often fund investors are asked for advice in specific actions by their fund managers. Partnership terms are an issue where fund investors are very often asked for advice. Many fund managers also seem to seek support in terms of fund raising by asking their fund investors to establish contacts to other potential limited partners. 40% of the interviewed investors are often approached on behalf of this issue. This can be explained due to the fact that fund investors with a market reputation offer some sort of endorsement to their funds.[448] Limited partners with experience might add value by helping the general partners to position themselves in the market, give guidance on investment strategy, and help develop and shape certain aspects of the team and the organization of the management company.[449] Furthermore, in the interviews, the fund investors added that they may be able to provide advice on best practice investor communication.[450]

Before the fund managers make portfolio company investments, some limited partners might be used as an information source, especially for investments in sectors where the limited partner has expertise. For example, pension funds as fund investors could establish contacts to experts within their organizations.[451] Overall, however, fund investors obviously are not of value in providing advice concerning potential new investments, and exits of existing investments. More than half of them claim that they are

---

[448] See Meek (2005a), p. 51.

[449] See Meek (2005a), p. 51.

[450] See Meek (2005a), p. 51. One interviewed investor mentioned the relevance of advice in terms of "best practice reporting, or pursuing annual meetings".

[451] See Fried/Hisrich (1989), p. 269.

hardly ever asked for this. These results are in line with the general view that the general partners should control the investment process (Figure 31).

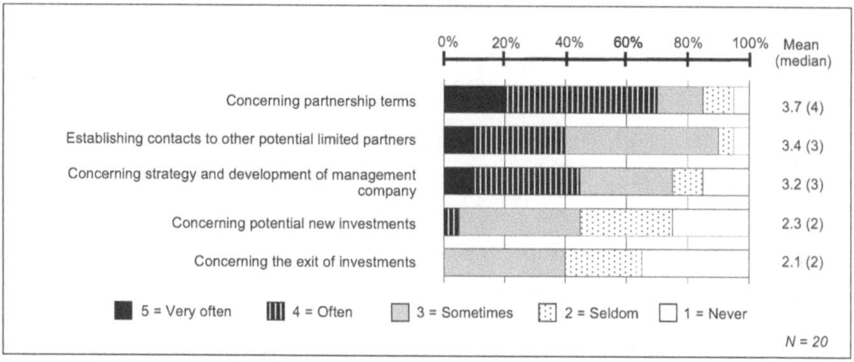

Figure 31: Issues on which limited partners are asked for advice from their fund managers

The second outcome of the interviews is that limited partners rarely get pro-actively involved. If any, the pro-active involvement of fund investors may be pushing their general partners in terms of strategy and development of the management company. 30% of the interviewed investors say this happens often. There have been also situations where fund investors were able to introduce fund portfolio companies to their network. After all, 20% of the interview partners state that they often try to establish contacts between portfolio companies, even of different general partners. It seldomly happens, that fund investors push or encourage their general partner to act on portfolio companies when they believe this is necessary. Less than 20% claim that this happens often. This is shown in Figure 32.

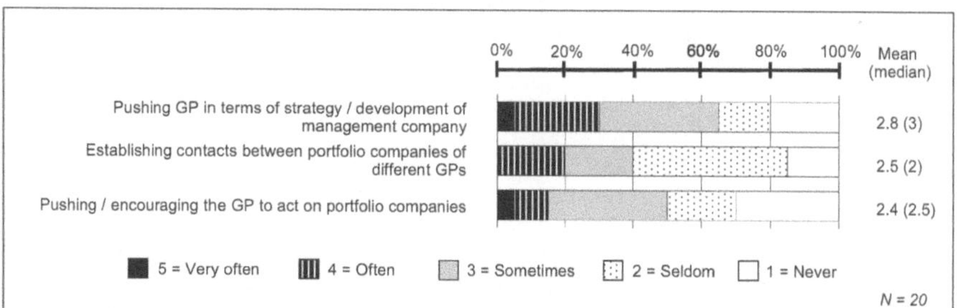

Figure 32: Pro-active involvement of limited partners

Being asked about their desired level of involvement in the future, only 23% of the interviewed investors (N=22) like to get more involved on the individual fund level. An overwhelming majority (77%) would like to see no change in the level of involvement in the future.

3.5.3 Crisis Management

The potential for fund investors to enhance the upside of their investments is limited. However, they may be able to prevent losses if investments get off track.[452] Monitoring the fund investments is therefore critical in order to early detect when things go wrong. Fund investors need to be clear about the following: First of all, they have to understand the early warnings signs, i.e. how they detect a fund crisis, and, secondly, how they can react to a fund crisis.

Detecting a crisis

There is no standard checklist that helps investors to become aware of any problems related to the individual fund investments.[453] However, there are some issues that fund investors should carefully monitor and analyze. The *stability of the team* and the *motivation of the individual professionals* are fundamental for the success of a fund. In case there are leavers, the fund investors should understand and evaluate the reasons why that is the case.[454] The development and implementation of succession plans for senior team members would corroborate the stability of the team.

Furthermore, fund investors should analyze the *new investments made by the fund.* The investment pace may be unusually slow or fast, the type of investment may not fit to the fund's declared strategy, or the investments may cause conflicts of interest with other funds managed by the fund managers. Reviewing the investment cases for these investments therefore allows the fund investors to get valuable insight in whether the fund is on track or not.

---

452 See Grabenwarter/Weidig (2005a), p. 84; Meyer/Mathonet (2005), p. 274.

453 See Grabenwarter/Weidig (2005a), p. 84. The following arguments are mainly based on Meyer/Mathonet (2005), pp. 282 et seq. and Grabenwarter/Weidig (2005a), pp. 84. et seq. For a catalogue of possible items that fund investors should assess in order to evaluate the operational status of a fund see Meyer/Mathonet (2005), p. 284.

454 The fund investors even need to check whether key-men-clauses are triggered.

Fund investors should also carefully follow the *development of the individual existing investments* within the portfolio of the fund. The reasons for unsuccessful investments, respectively write-offs, shed light on the capabilities and skill-set of the team. It may not be possible for the fund investors to track each individual portfolio company investment due to lack of resources. Fund investors should then identify and focus on those investments that will be key contributor - negatively as well as positively - to the performance of the fund.

Following the status of the portfolio company investments, the fund investors are enabled to *assess the potential performance of the entire fund.* This should be compared to their projections and benchmarked to the performance of their peers.

Finally, the *fund managers' quality of reporting and their transparency on issues relating to the investments and to the fund* are other valuable sources of information regarding the status of the fund investment. Changing valuation methods without reasonable explanation, limited disclosure of the progress of the portfolio, or portfolio companies going into bankruptcy without any warnings are signals for fund investors to be deeply concerned about.

Reacting to a crisis

Having identified a fund investment that is in trouble, there are several ways of how fund investors may react. The reaction of course depends on each specific situation. However, some general remarks should be provided here. Due to the lack of a liquid secondary market, the fund managers cannot easily and quickly sell the partnership. Especially, if the fund does not perform according to expectations, potential investors may not be willing to buy the stake or may require a substantial discount.

Therefore, the first thing a fund investor should do is to approach the existing general partner and to try to sort out the respective issue. This is often the quickest, most efficient and cheapest solution.[455] However, the interests of both parties may be contrary. The fund investors, for example, may want the fund manager to reduce the management fee or to release the limited partners from portions of their commitments. This is of course not the immediate interest of the fund managers. However, they still may

455 See Grabenwarter/Weidig (2005a), p. 87.

give in to the requirements of the fund investors, in order to make fundraising for future funds easier.[456]

If the fund managers do not agree to voluntary actions, limited partners could exercise their partnership rights including the right to remove the general partner. Depending on the partnership agreement, these removal clauses can be either exercised for cause or without cause.[457] The challenge is to act quickly and to find other limited partners to team up. If the general partner is confronted with more than one fund investor, his readiness to cooperate may improve.[458] The threat of action and the potential publicity may be very damaging for the fund managers. Their reputation and the chance to ever raise a fund again would be at risk.[459]

Very little is known about the possibilities for fund investors to secure their fund investments in case things go wrong. Therefore, this study addresses the questions whether the interviewed investors have faced such a situation and what their reaction was.

Empirical results

All of the interviewed fund investors have already faced a situation where a fund investment went off track. The reasons for the crisis were manifold including break-up of teams, death of key-men, or style drift with respect to new investments. Most of the fund investors stress the importance that limited partners act in concert in these situations. The larger investors in a fund need to take a leading role, as they very often have the resources to do so. Managing a crisis seems to be very time-consuming. One fund investor points to the difficulty of finding interim management teams. If the fund managers have been replaced, it is important to set the right incentives so that the new team is motivated enough. To sum up, the partnership agreements leave more room to act for limited partners than commonly known. In case of a crisis, the limited partners need to have processes in place that allow a timely and effective communication and coordination.

---

456 See Meyer/Mathonet (2005), p. 286.

457 Removal for cause requires approval from the majority of limited partners. Removal without cause is possible by a 75% qualified vote.

458 See Grabenwarter/Weidig (2005a), p. 87.

459 See Meyer/Mathonet (2005), p. 286.

This chapter has explained the relevance of monitoring in order to effectively govern private equity fund investments. But the role of monitoring is not only limited to the current fund, but is also an important basis for the re-investment decision. Many industry practitioners claim that a very powerful instrument is the threat not to commit to a follow-on fund of a fund manager. How monitoring and understanding the developments of the partnership support the decision about whether to re-invest or not, is subject of the next chapter.

3.6 Monitoring and Fund Re-Investing

3.6.1 Evaluating a Fund Investment Opportunity

Effective fund monitoring may support and enable a more successful decision about whether to re-invest in a new fund of an already existing fund manager relationship or not. In order to answer this question, it is first of all necessary to discuss and to understand the criteria on which fund investors evaluate an investment opportunity.[460] Fund investors focus on four key evaluation criteria: the investment strategy and market opportunity, the team, the team's track record, and the terms and conditions of the partnership.[461]

The analysis of the *investment strategy* enables the fund investors to project the nature and characteristics of companies that will be targeted by the fund managers. The investors need to judge on whether they believe there is a current *market opportunity* for the proposed strategy or not.[462] This is challenging and should be based on an assessment of the current economic environment in all respective geographic regions. The fund managers, on the other hand, must demonstrate their ability to execute the followed strategy by investing in respective and attractive portfolio companies. The fund managers must furthermore be able to generate a promising and sufficient deal flow.[463]

---

460 The fund selection process has been described in detail in chapter 2.5.3.

461 See Barnes/Menzies (2005), p. 219 et seq.; Bance (2004), pp. 13 et seq; Atkins/Giannini (2003), p. 222. Other authors suggest a slightly different classification of the due diligence criteria. See Tausend (2006), pp. 76 et seq; Hagenmüller (2004), p. 38; Schmidt (2003), pp. 257 et seq.

462 This may be indicated by the potential size of the market for this strategy, its specialization, or the historical risk-return generated through these strategies. See Grabenwarter/Weidig (2005a), pp. 44 et seq.

463 See Barnes/Menzies (2005), p. 221.

The experience of the individual team members and the mix and balance of the appropriate skill-set within the team to exploit the strategy is crucial for success. Therefore, the most important element of the due diligence for a fund investment may be the evaluation of the *fund manager's team* and its individual members.[464] However, it is not only a question of the capability of the team. Equally important is its consistency and continuity as most partnerships have a life-time of at least ten years. This includes an assessment of the future development of the team, taking into account any potential succession plans. The distribution of the carried interest among the team members should correspond to the work allocation in order to set the right incentives.[465]

The *track record analysis* is an assessment of the team's previous investment performance.[466] The main part is quantitative. Fund investors investigate in detail the generated internal rate of return, the investment multiples, the percentages of investments that are total losses, profitable exits, or still unrealized investments.[467] The volatility of portfolio company returns sheds light on the consistency of the overall performance of fund managers. Additional insight is gained by analyzing whether the returns can be attributed to individual team members, to specific industries, to regions where the investment has been made, or to the channels by which the investments were exited (so-called slice and dice analysis). The portfolio of former funds is seldom fully realized, so that the fund investors need to deal with the difficulties of valuing these unrealized investments. Finally, the achieved performance is regularly benchmarked in order to assess the success in comparison to peers.

An analysis of how the fund managers have actually generated the return is very important in order to determine whether this performance is sustainable. A crucial element is therefore the *value creation analysis*. From the perspective of the investor, the change in equity value (value creation) can be broken down into the determinants

---

464 See Atkins/Giannini (2003), p. 223. As fund investments are blind-pool investments and the fund investors normally have no influence on the portfolio company transaction, the selection of the fund management team is the most important element that a fund investor actively can control. See Grabenwarter/Weidig (2005a), p. 47.

465 Carried interest allocation mechanisms that are in favour of senior people who are actually no longer involved in the activities of the fund may lead to tensions in the team and, in extreme cases, to departures of team members. See Grabenwarter/Weidig (2005a), p. 54.

466 See Hagenmüller (2004), p. 38.

467 See Barnes/Menzies (2005), p. 220.

revenues growth and margin improvement (e.g. EBITDA growth), change of the valuation multiple (multiple expansion), and change in net debt.[468]

Revenues growth and margin improvements arise through operational and strategic improvements, or through changes in corporate governance including better incentivized and higher motivated management and employees. These changes directly lead to higher cash flows and thereby to higher company value. A change in the valuation of the company (multiple expansion) means that third parties are willing to pay a higher price for the asset. This may be caused by internal factors, such as changing expectations regarding the future financial performance of the company, or by external factors, such as changing expectations regarding the future success of the industry, or a general change in the valuation of public companies. In some cases, a multiple expansion can be realized by changing the new investors' perceptions to which industry the company belongs to. Furthermore, pricing differentials between public and private or national and international markets may be exploited by the investors.[469] Finally, cash flow generation at the target may lead to leverage/debt reduction.[470]

Buyout fund managers have achieved superior performance through financial engineering or multiple expansions.[471] However, HEEL/KEHOE stress the importance of operating performance as a main source of value.[472] Especially, in times, when external factors are not favourable, it is important that the operational performance offsets these negative influences. During their due diligence, fund investors should identify and evaluate if the fund mangers have the required operating skills to drive real operating improvements at portfolio companies.[473]

These capabilities are even more necessary for venture capital fund managers. Several researchers find that providing financial support, acting as sounding board to the management team, and supporting in developing the corporate strategy are ranked as very

---

468 See Berg/Gottschalg (2004), p. 22; Bance (2004), p. 13.

469 This is called *multiple arbitrage*. See Fingerle (2005), p. 40.

470 LOOS provides a detailed example how to deduct the relevance of each value driver in a specific investment case. See Loos (2005), pp. 57 et seq.

471 See Dresdale (2005), p. 2.

472 See Heel/Kehoe (2005), p. 24. The authors analyze 60 buyout deals from eleven leading private equity fund managers.

473 See Dresdale (2005), p. 2.

important activities.[474] Financial engineering does not play a role in value creation for early stage companies.[475]

Finally, the fund investors need to evaluate the *terms and conditions of the partnership*. Among others, this comprises the legal structure, the fund managers' compensation, profit distribution agreements, the governance mechanisms, or the reporting and transparency agreements.[476]

3.6.2 Differences to the First-time Decision

New and already existing fund investors have usually access to the same quantitative amount of information concerning a new fund. A private placement memorandum (PPM) is regularly provided which contains data on the strategy, the team, its track record and all necessary terms and conditions of the partnership.[477] Furthermore, the potential new fund investors themselves collect all required information by sending structured questionnaires to the teams.[478]

Former research, however, shows that existing fund investors are capable of using the information they have gained through monitoring existing investments to decide on whether to invest in the next fund of the managers or not.[479] Moreover, some of them are even better in forecasting the performance of follow-on funds than their peers.[480]

Very little is known why this is the case. Therefore, the interviewed fund investors were asked whether they feel that the re-investment decision is easier and, if yes, why.

---

474 See for example Deloitte & Touche (2002); Dotzler (2001); Feinendegen/Hommel/Wright (2001). FINGERLE provides an overview. See Fingerle (2005), p. 143.

475 See Fingerle (2005), p. 40.

476 See Atkins/Giannini (2003), p. 224.

477 See Hagenmüller (2004), p. 74.

478 For an illustrative questionnaire see Meyer/Mathonet (2005), pp. 203 et seq.

479 See Lerner/Schoar (2004), p. 37. For details of these studies see chapter 2.6.

480 LERNER/SCHOAR/WONG find out this is true for endowments and, to a lesser degree, corporate pension funds. See Lerner/Schoar/Wong (2005), p. 39.

Empirical results

Over 80% of the interviewed investors (N=23) say that the decision to re-invest in a subsequent fund of an existing fund manager relationship is easier than investing the first time in a fund manager's fund. They state basically two reasons for this.

The first reason that most fund investors mention is their *enhanced ability to assess the quality of the fund manager's team*. They have seen the team actually doing the transactions. They know whether they follow their declared strategy and whether that strategy delivers sustainable returns. They have also learnt about the processes that the fund managers employ. There may have been critical situations with respect to the portfolio companies that the fund managers needed to handle. There could have emerged conflicts of interests between the general and the limited partners. In all situations, the fund investors could see how the fund managers reacted. One investor points out that he usually gets a much better feeling about the team's soft skills. All in all, the fund investors have far more trust in the capabilities of the managers. This confidence leads to a lower risk factor when compared to the first-time decision.

The second reason that is brought up by the interviewed fund investors relates to the assessment of the track record. It is not that they have a better understanding of the actual performance figures. It is rather their gained knowledge about *how the portfolio companies' value has been created*. The special value drivers in certain transactions may have become visible to the fund investors. If a deal went wrong, there may be a reasonable explanation. Prerequisite for this is, however, that fund investors follow the development of portfolio companies during the fund's lifetime. Although they do not have an influence on the management of the portfolio companies, many of the fund investors therefore claim they closely monitor the developments. Another investor says that he learns about the fund managers' actual quality of client serving and reporting. The transparency and regularity of reporting and the willingness to provide the fund investors with required and necessary information may vary. However, it is the prerequisite for an effective monitoring.

One fund investor, however, mentions that the historical performance is no guarantee for the future. The due diligence may be easier. However, the final decision about whether to invest is not easier. He also points out that it is important not to get to familiar with the fund managers since this could influence the decision making in favor of the managers. In order to overcome this problem, some of the interviewed fund investors form a different team for the re-investment decision.

To summarize, dedicated monitoring of existing funds clearly provides a head start on the due diligence of follow-on funds. The whole due diligence process may be improved. Fewer questions regarding the quantitative analysis are probably necessary. This enables more relevant and intensive discussions about the strategy, organization, previous value creation, and expected performance of the next fund. All in all, the partners should be able to make better decisions and to finalize the contracts more quickly.

3.7 Monitoring and Fund Portfolio Management

3.7.1 Monitoring Portfolio Diversification

Limited partners construct their portfolio of private equity funds based on their optimal risk and return profiles.[481] Modern portfolio theory suggests that investors can diversify away specific risks, by combining investments with different risk and return characteristics.[482] This is also true for private equity. Diversification across the various different funds is a tool which limited partners use to manage the risk-return relationship and eliminate diversifiable risks.[483] The objective of monitoring with respect to the portfolio diversification is to identify any imbalances of the portfolio. The fund investors therefore constantly need to measure the diversification and compare the results with the intended strategy.

Figure 33 displays various ways of how to strategically diversify a portfolio of private equity funds. The fund investors typically balance their entire portfolio across different managers, stages or strategies, vintage years, sectors, geographies and targeted portfolio company sizes.[484]

---

481 See McKinsey (2003), p. 24.

482 See Atkins/Giannini (2003), p. 218. For the foundation of modern portfolio theory see Markowitz (1952).

483 See Meyer/Mathonet (2005), p. 90.

484 See Grabenwarter/Weidig (2005a), p. 126.

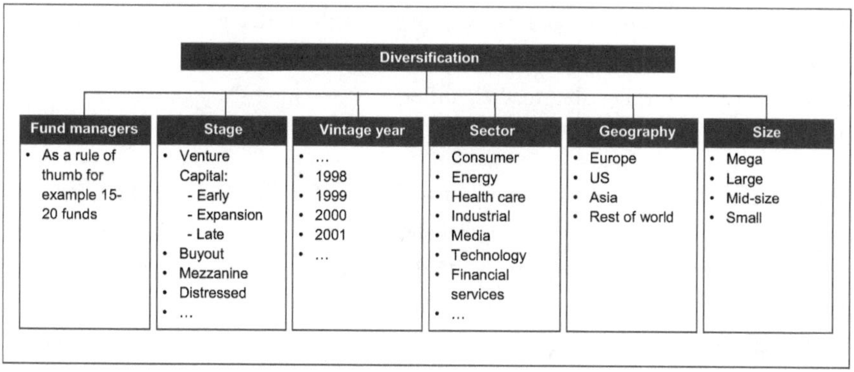

Figure 33: Diversification of a private equity portfolio[485]

An increasing number of *fund mangers* in a portfolio reduces the amount of overall volatility, i.e. risk, and increases the chance to get exposure to those managers that generate above-market returns.[486] Fund investors may select proven teams which already managed funds and new teams which raise their first fund. The diversification over different *stages* in the business life cycle offers different risk/return characteristics. Venture-stage companies are for example mainly subject to financing and market risks, whereas buyout strategies are mainly exposed to default and credit risk.[487] *Vintage year* diversification is important, as the performance of private equity fund investments depends on external economic conditions. These conditions, such as transaction valuations, the availability of investment opportunities and the ability to exit investments, e.g. via IPO, vary over time. By committing consistently through vintage years, the investor limits over-exposure to a down cycle.[488] Through the diversification over different industry *sectors*, the investor takes into account that these tend to perform differently in different market conditions. Achieving a diversified industry sector portfolio is challenging in private equity, as general partners often have a broad investment mandate which allows them to invest in a number of sectors.[489] Diversifica-

[485] The examples are non-exclusive.

[486] See Atkins/Giannini (2003), p. 218; Weidig/Kemmerer/Born (2003), p. 39.

[487] See Atkins/Giannini (2003), pp. 219. et seq.

[488] See Atkins/Giannini (2003), p. 221.

[489] See Bader (1996), p. 263. Many general partners explicitly require the freedom to choose their investment according to opportunities.

tion over different *geographical regions* cherishes the different cycles of economic markets and currencies.[490] Finally, as the targeted portfolio companies may have different risk return profiles due to their different *sizes*, fund managers diversify over funds that specify with respect to these characteristics.

The portfolio constantly changes due to two factors: The first factor is that funds and respective portfolio companies are added and liquidated. The cash flow and liquidity planning is therefore connected with the diversification planning. The next chapter provides more details. The second factor is the fact that the economic value of the fund investments fluctuates over time due to changes in the valuation of underlying portfolio company investments.[491] Investors therefore need to monitor the composition of their overall portfolio on an ongoing basis in order to identify unintended concentration across all funds.[492]

It is only possible to monitor the diversification when one has decided on an appropriate measure for the degree of diversification. This could be done on the fund level. First of all, it could be the simple number of funds per strategy. However, this would neglect the true economic exposure, i.e. the weighting of each fund in the portfolio. Secondly, the fund investor could therefore base the measurement on the total commitments to each fund per strategy. This would, however, ignore the actual development of the invested portfolio. Therefore, a sum of the undrawn commitment plus the net asset value seems to be the best estimate for each fund. To measure the diversification on sectors and geography, it is also suitable to base the measurement on the value of the single portfolio companies. Anyhow, it is obvious that the correct valuation of the current assets under management play an important role.

Two additional phenomena concern investors with respect to their diversification: the style drift risk of fund managers and potential club deals. The fund investors invest in a blind pool. Although their managers declare to follow a specific strategy, they do not necessarily adhere to it. *Style drift* can be defined as deviation from stated objectives of fund managers in terms of the focus for investments at particular stages of entrepreneurial development, their industry or geographical location. Style drift by a general

---

490 See Atkins/Giannini (2003), p. 220.

491 See Bader (1996), p. 302.

492 See Meyer/Mathonet (2005), p. 64.

partner can have serious consequences for the risk/return profile of the fund investors' portfolios.

So-called *club deals* could affect the fund investors' risk diversification. These are transactions where two or more private equity firms team up in a consortium or syndicate to make an acquisition.[493] Over the last couple of years, club deals have become increasingly common within the buyout industry.[494] From the general partners' perspective, several beneficial factors drive this trend: the opportunity - or need - to acquire ever larger companies[495], the recognition that different investors bring in specific knowledge or expertise, and the increasing competition for deals which offers an incentive to team up to reduce bidding wars.[496] Limited partners invest across several buyout funds in order to spread their risk. Clubs deals may therefore be counterproductive. Having assumed that they had diversified their exposure to the buyout asset class, the limited partners increasingly find themselves more concentrated in specific deals than they might like.[497] They have to be aware of these consequences and need to closely monitor the exposure to each deal relative to the overall exposure to private equity. In order to mitigate the risks, the number of invested funds with the same strategy, e.g. large buyouts, may be limited.

---

493 See Dresdale (2004), p. 1.

494 See McCurry (2006), 3. In venture capital, the syndication of deals has been already become the norm, however for slightly different reasons. For a discussion of the reasons see Nathusius (2005), pp. 75 et seq.

495 Most funds are restricted to invest a certain percentage in a single deal, often 15%. Even for bigger funds, it is therefore often not possible to acquire a large target alone. Club deals enable general partners to run the bigger deals without putting to much capital in one transaction. See McCurry (2006), p. 4.

496 If syndicates are formed early on in auction processes, they may prevent the price from spiraling upwards. See Dresdale (2004), p. 3. However, if regulators find that bidding teams were put together to reduce price competition and eliminate rivals, it will be a huge problem for the participating private equity firms. In October 2006, the U.S. Justice Department has started to investigate whether some of the recent very large private equity club deals were anticompetitive. Specifically, the government has been looking for evidence of collusion, bid rigging, or other antitrust violations. See Shearer (2006), p. 37.

497 See Dresdale (2004), p. 4. For large and well diversified fund investors, these concerns may be misplaced as the amount of money going into one deal relative to the total commitments of these fund investors to private equity is unlikely to have an impact on the portfolio outcome. See Schwartzman (2006), p. 101.

There are limits to the degree of diversification. Over-diversification may dilute the contribution of higher-performing investments to the portfolio's return. If an investor owns every fund in the market, he has effectively bought the market and his performance will inevitably regress to the mean.[498] This is contrary to why most investors decide to invest in private equity. In addition, a very large number of funds becomes an administrative burden.[499]

The monitoring and analysis of diversification is only the first step. Subsequently, fund investors who observe severe imbalances within their portfolios, need to re-act.[500] They could use the secondary market as a tool for active portfolio management. This will be discussed in chapter 3.7.3.

3.7.2 Monitoring Portfolio Liquidity

In public equity, investors can instantaneously and easily gain exposure to the asset class for the amount they desire to invest. This is very different to the private equity asset class.[501] Private equity fund investors also target the overall exposure as part of their long-term strategic asset allocation. An important issue that concerns them is, however, how to achieve and maintain this desired exposure to the asset class over time.[502]

The cash flow characteristics of the private equity investment process complicate the implementation of the targets. First of all, the commitments to funds are not instantaneously, but only gradually invested. It takes a couple of years before the general partners have called all capital and put the money to work.[503] Limited partners do not know in advance when and how much capital will be drawn down. Secondly, not all of the entire committed capital must be necessarily called by the general partners.[504] Last, it is uncertain when capital will be returned via distributions. Some distributions occur

---

498 See Dresdale (2004), p. 5.

499 See Atkins/Giannini (2003), p. 219.

500 See Bader (1996), p. 305.

501 Grabenwarter/Weidig (2005a), p. 125.

502 See de Zwart/Frieser/van Dijk (2006), p. 1.

503 See Nevins/Conner/McIntire (2004), p. 32. The investment period of a fund usually extends from one to five years. See chapter 2.2.2.

504 See de Zwart/Frieser/van Dijk (2006), p. 1.

already before the last drawdowns for a fund are made.[505] In sum, private equity fund investors need to recognize that commitments are not equivalent to investments. FREI/STUDER estimate that the maximum investment level (cumulative drawdowns minus cumulative distributions as a percentage of the fund size) is about two thirds.[506]

If the targeted investment level is not achieved and portions of the investors' capital remain in lower-yielding assets, there exists a risk that the portfolio's return will be diluted.[507] On the other hand, adequate liquidity is critical as the consequence of failing to meet a capital call from general partners may be severe.[508] Therefore, many fund investors implement sophisticated systems to manage the liquidity of their portfolio. The objective of such a system is to minimize the liquidity reserves and to achieve a desired allocation while - at the same time - avoiding liquidity shortfall which would be an inability to follow a capital call.[509]

	Cash flow planning	
	Short-term estimates	Long-term forecasts
Time horizon	• Typically up to one year	• More than one year
Primary objective	• To get an accurate picture of the liquidity needs over that period of time	• To determine an optimal commitment strategy to achieve a targeted portfolio allocation
Most important inputs	• Liquidity events from existing portfolio and potential new commitments including their possible first draw downs	• Historical cash flow data and assumptions about the parameters of future cash flow including scenarios of future environment
Predominant tasks	• Data gathering and analysis	• Quantitative modelling

Figure 34: Approaches to projecting cash flows[510]

---

[505] See Grabenwarter/Weidig (2005a), p. 125.

[506] See Frei/Studer (2003), p. 203.

[507] See Frei/Studer (2003), p. 204.

[508] See Kogelman (1999), p. 2. A liquidity shortage may have a severe impact on the reputation of the fund investor as a trustful partner.

[509] See Grabenwarter/Weidig (2005a), p. 124.

[510] Based on Meyer/Mathonet (2005), p. 135.

Depending on the timeframe of the cash flow planning, short-term and long-term approaches can be distinguished (Figure 34).[511] *Short-term cash flow estimates* are pursued for a period up to one year. The primary objective is to get an accurate picture of the liquidity needs over that period of time. Inputs to consider are on the one hand the expected liquidity events of the already existing portfolio of funds. This includes cash outflow, respectively drawdowns, e.g. due to new potential portfolio company investments. It also comprises cash inflow, respectively distributions, e.g. due to potential exits of existing portfolio company investments.[512] The needed information has to be gathered from the general partners. Any commitments into new private equity funds and their first anticipated drawdowns have to be taken into account. Therefore, fund investors need a good understanding of the current fund-raising environment, i.e. which general partners are coming to the market in the near-term and to which they intend to commit.

Long-term forecasts aim at predicting the portfolio cash flow over a period of time far beyond one year. Determining the right commitment strategy and maintaining it over the long term is critical to achieve the desired optimal allocation to private equity. General rules of thumb or "gut feeling" are not sufficient for that purpose.[513] Consequently, there has been growing effort from industry practitioners and academic researchers over the last years aiming at the development of quantitative models with the intention to reduce the uncertainty associated with private equity cash flows.[514] Inputs to these models are provided by studies on historical cash flow patterns.[515] Specific adjustments by the fund investors are necessary to incorporate the actual market development and the condition of the specific individual fund investments.[516]

---

[511] Most partnership agreements state that the general partner has to announce capital drawdowns two weeks in advance.

[512] See Meyer/Mathonet (2005), p. 135.

[513] See Frei/Studer (2003), p. 204. For example Takahashi/Alexander (2002); Weidig (2002).

[514] GRABENWARTER/WEIDIG provide a comprehensive overview of different cash flow models. See Grabenwarter/Weidig (2005a), pp. 131 et seq. Many practitioners' models are not publicly available. See Grabenwarter/Weidig (2005a), p. 127.

[515] Several studies examine the historical private equity cash flow patterns. See for example Kaserer/Diller (2004c); Ljungqvist/Richardson (2003); Cheung/Kapoor/Howley (2003); Cheung et al. (2003). Fund investors may derive the necessary input data from their own former fund investments or use the data services such as Venture Economics.

[516] See Grabenwarter/Weidig (2005a), p. 207.

One can distinguish between different types of models: (1) Models that are based on inputs and assumptions from the underlying portfolio companies, and (2) models that are based on inputs and assumptions on the fund level. The former models require direct access to detailed portfolio company information which the fund investors may not have. Furthermore, gathering and administrating all the portfolio company information may be burdensome for large investors.[517] Therefore, most cash flow modeling is done on the fund level. The fund and its content are thereby regarded as a black box. Typical parameters that are used are, for example, historical cash flow patterns of similar funds, the net asset values, the expected internal rates of return, or adjustments for the economic environment.[518]

The cash flow planning is even more complicated through the *impact of foreign exchange rates*. The entire fund investment or single portfolio company investments could not be done in the home currency. For contributions, a higher amount of cash in terms of home currency than expected may be necessary, if the respective currency of the fund has appreciated. Distributions from portfolio companies denominated in foreign currency could be reduced due to a depreciation of the foreign currency.[519]

Since liquidity planning of private equity fund investors has been so far rather neglected by the academic literature, this study addresses this issue in more detail. The interviewed investors were asked about the importance of cash flow planning, the models they use, and the satisfaction with the fund managers' information on potential company transactions.

Empirical results

Cash flow planning is of high relevance for fund investors, irrespective of their type. One could assume that cash flow planning for fund-of-funds is not very important as most of them simply manage the cash flow for their clients. However, their clients require this service from them. Most of them thus have very sophisticated models. As laid out in Figure 35, more than 70% of the interviewed fund investors think a long-term liquidity management is important.

---

517 See Grabenwarter/Weidig (2005a), p. 131. If a fund investor's portfolio consists of 100 funds, this may count up to 2,000 or more underlying portfolio companies.

518 See Grabenwarter/Weidig (2005b), p. 131.

519 See Meyer/Mathonet (2005), p. 124.

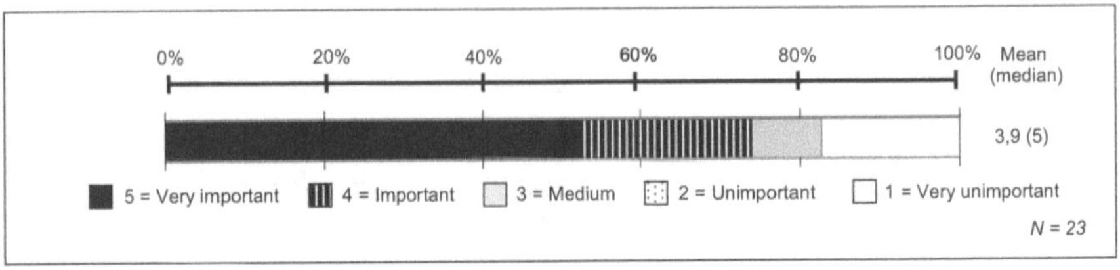

Figure 35: Importance of long-term cash flow planning

82% of the interviewed fund investors (N=22) apply a formal model for their long-term liquidity planning. However, there seems to be no standard model within the industry, since the mentioned approaches vary. The details of the different models are typically not disclosed by the fund investors.[520] With respect to the inputs, nearly all investors who use formal models base their forecast for the undrawn commitments on historical cash flows. The already invested part of the portfolio, however, is often forecasted based on assumptions of the expected internal rate of return. Some investors build different scenarios concerning the long-term performance of the individual portfolio companies. Half of the interviewed investors mention that they evaluate and discuss each portfolio company with their fund managers in order to get an estimate of the expected amount and time of the exits.

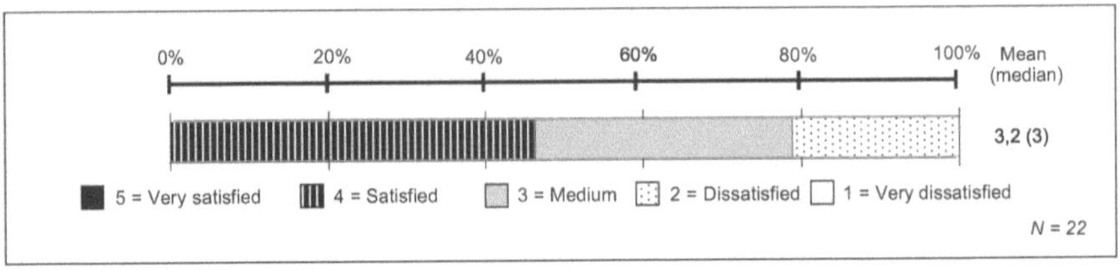

Figure 36: Fund investors' satisfaction with information on potential portfolio company transactions

Concerning short-term estimates, the fund investors depend on the disclosure of potential transactions that their fund managers plan. Many fund investors, however, acknowledge that it is difficult for fund managers to provide these details due to confi-

520 There are two explanations for this. Some fund investors say their models are proprietary knowledge which they do not want to share in detail. Some others acknowledge that they do not know the details of their models as the modeling is pursued by a separate quantitative team.

dentiality and competitive reasons. Only few more than 20% of the interviewed fund investors are dissatisfied with the availability of this data (Figure 36).

To sum up, estimating and forecasting the cash flow of the portfolio is very important for private equity fund managers. It enables to plan the liquidity of the portfolio and to determine the commitment strategy and lays the ground for portfolio projection. If the fund investors see the necessity to steer and manage the liquidity of the fund portfolio, they may use the market for secondary transactions which will be discussed next as a tool.

3.7.3 Portfolio Management with Secondary Transactions

Private equity fund portfolio management is about implementing a long-term investment that keeps the return and risk profile of the portfolio within the desired and defined boundaries.[521] The toolset for that fund portfolio management is comparatively restricted due to the illiquidity of the funds. It is therefore not possible that fund investors continuously rebalance their portfolio via active trading of the positions.[522] However, the secondary market for transactions may still offer interesting opportunities for them.

Over the last years, the secondary market for private equity partnerships has received increased attention by industry participants.[523] The market offers a way for active management at the portfolio of fund level.[524] Through buy-and-sell-transactions portfolio managers can change the structure and characteristics of their portfolios.

From a portfolio management perspective, there are different motivations why investors buy and sell on the secondary market.[525] Sellers may have overcommitted to pri-

---

521 See Grabenwarter/Weidig (2005a), p. 91.

522 See Meyer/Mathonet (2005), p. 286.

523 See Hansing (2005), p. 39; Kojima (2005), p. 39; Clark/Kojima (2003), p. 74; Wihite (2001), p. 1. The secondary market for limited partnership stakes should not be confused with the secondary market in private equity financed companies, e.g. so-called secondary buyouts.

524 See Meyer/Mathonet (2005), p. 64. An alternative to the direct sale of partnerships is the securitization of private equity assets. The typical structure of such a securitization is that owners of limited partnership stakes transfer their interests in these funds to a special purpose vehicle (SPV). The SPV then issues securities. For more information see, for example, Romer/Moise/Hrvatin (2003); Cheung et al. (2003); Cheung/Kapoor/Howley (2003); Erturk/Cheung/Fong (2001).

525 For the different motivations see among others Meyer/Mathonet (2005), pp. 297 et seq; Grabenwarter/Weidig (2005a), pp. 152 et seq; Hagenmüller (2004), p. 148.

vate equity in general and/or have sudden liquidity needs. Their desired overall asset allocation may change. Regulatory changes sometimes require fund investors to adjust their portfolios. There could also be the fund investors desire to re-balance their portfolio for diversification aspects. Fund investments typically perform differently leading to sub-optimal or unexpected cash flows. Some fund investors may also want to restructure their program by focusing on fewer fund manager relationships with increased investment sizes. The aim could be a decrease of the administrative burden. The secondary market then offers the opportunity to sell parts of the portfolio.

Buyers search investment opportunities with a discount to the fair value when buying private equity funds on the secondary market. However, there are also portfolio management reasons. If investors want to build up a private equity fund portfolio more quickly, they often use the secondary market. The secondary market offers the opportunity to immediately increase portfolio weightings to private equity funds. New entrants in that asset class could also wish to flatten the J-curve effect by adding funds that are already entering their cash distribution phases. Furthermore, fund investors may wish to rebalance underweight positions and optimize their diversification. Another reason for buying fund assets on the secondary market is the ability to invest in funds otherwise difficult to access.

Buyers and sellers that the secondary market attracts are typically faced by significant transactional issues leading to high costs of these transactions.[526] MEYER/MATHONET refer to the challenges of the due diligence, the confidentiality, and the structuring.[527] KOJIMA adds the challenges of the transfer process after closing the transaction.[528]

The *due diligence* requires similar assessments as a primary investment plus the analysis of the underlying, already existing portfolio companies.[529] Sellers of the fund investments as well as respective fund managers very often require absolute *confidentiality*. Fund investors who sell do not want to create the impression that they need to sell. This image could impede getting access to new funds. Fund managers on the

---

[526] See Kojima (2005), p. 45.

[527] See Meyer/Mathonet (2005), pp. 307 et seq.

[528] See Kojima (2005), p. 44.

[529] It still takes a considerable period of time until a transaction is really settled. The due diligence which the potential investors need to conduct in order to assess the value of the underlying investments may take up to six months. See Financial Service Authority (2006a), p. 25.

other side tend to view a sale as a negative judgment on their performance which it does not have to be. Sellers could simply have portfolio management motivations. Furthermore, the *structuring* of secondary transactions can be actually very complex in the effort to bridge the sellers' and buyers' expectations. This includes payment structures, sellers' participation in the upside of the portfolio, new structures to hold the fund assets, or the insertion of a new team to manage the assets.[530]

Having signed the purchase-and-sale agreement, the *transfer process* can still become complex and can require additional negotiations. The transfer must be approved on a fund-by-fund basis by each underlying general partner. In some cases, the existing other limited partners in the respective funds have a right of first refusal, i.e. an opportunity to first acquire the position being transferred.[531]

Concerning the valuation of the funds in secondary transactions, it can be referred to the challenges of valuing the interim status of the fund when analyzing the performance. In the past, many secondary buyers have simply applied broad discounts to the underlying net asset values. However, as discussed, the net asset values are not appropriate proxies for the true economic values. An appropriate assessment involves the valuing of each of the underlying portfolio companies and the evaluation of the potential of the undrawn part of the commitment. An evaluation of the general partners is therefore necessary. However, the information needed can be difficult to assess. If relevant and timely information about the portfolio companies' operations is not subject to the fund's quarterly reporting, it is rarely made available by the general partners without interacting with them.[532]

In order to understand the actual potential of the secondary markets as an instrument to actively manage the portfolio, this study addresses the two questions: First, it investigates whether the fund investors have been active on the secondary market in the past and, secondly, for what reason they would use it in the future.

---

530 See Meyer/Mathonet (2005), p. 308.

531 See Kojima (2005), p. 44.

532 See Kojima (2005), p. 44. The potential buyers very much depend on the willingness of the general partners to share the information.

Empirical results

Being asked whether the interviewed fund investors have been already active on the secondary market for limited partnership stakes *in the past*, 83% of them stated they had been active (N=24). Most of them were buyers and not sellers of fund assets. According to the fund investors, three rationales were behind these secondary transactions. First of all, they simply saw an attractive investment opportunity that was offered. Secondly, they pro-actively sought to influence their liquidity position, i.e. flatten the J-curve. Thirdly, the investors mention their desire to get a better diversification over vintage years.

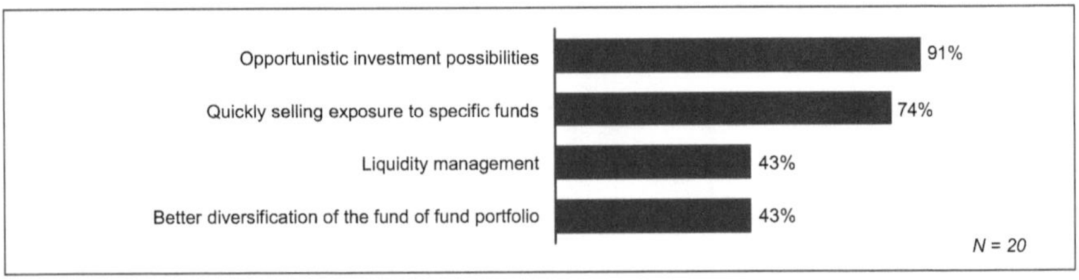

Figure 37: Reasons for using the secondary market for limited partnerships stakes in the future

Based on these experiences in the past, it is no surprise that the secondary market will be also of importance *in the future*. Figure 37 demonstrates that the interviewed fund investors will use arising opportunities to buy fund assets (91%) and also will sell assets when necessary (74%). However, there is more skepticism about the use of the secondary market for portfolio management, i.e. managing the liquidity and steering the diversification of the portfolio (43% each).

Those fund investors who are not planning to use the secondary market for portfolio management purposes in the future raise the issue of the high transaction costs and the limited number of available transactions as reasons. The transactions are still very expensive. Furthermore, they are limited by the rare number of opportunities to buy fund stakes.[533] However, the market has evolved significantly over the last years and is expected to do so in the future.[534] For an increasing number of sophisticated fund inves-

[533] See Meyer/Mathonet (2005), p. 64.

[534] See Kojima (2005), p. 45.

tors with the respective resources, there may arise opportunities to further optimize their fund portfolios.

3.8 Resulting Information Requirements

3.8.1 Information Sources

As has been demonstrated, private equity investors require a wide-ranging and high amount of information that allows them to monitor the developments of the individual funds and their portfolio of funds. They use different sources to gather this information. These sources are, on the one hand, their own fund manager relationships from which they pull specific *fund data* that is needed. On the other hand, they use additional market sources for relevant *market data*. Market data is publicly available.

From a monitoring perspective, gathering market data is necessary for two purposes. First, market data, such as performance figures, enables the fund investors to compare and benchmark their own fund investments with respect to the performance. Also the costs of the fund investment or the appropriateness of legal terms have to be assessed with respect to the current market trends. The second reason for gathering market data, i.e. especially historic cash flow market data and performance figures, is that it enables the fund investors to forecast and steer their portfolio of funds. It has been discussed in length how fund investors, for example, plan the liquidity and diversification of their portfolio. This may be based on a pool of historic cash flow data from similar funds. However, it is also important to have a clear understanding of the current market development. Who are the fund mangers that are currently raising new funds? What are the most attractive markets to invest in?

Both fund and market data can be gathered through *impersonal sources* or through *personal sources* (Figure 38). The main impersonal market data sources are databases provided by external data providers, private equity related publications, research reports, the financial press, or information provided by private equity industry associations. Through their own networks and the participation at conferences, the fund investors may get valuable informal information about the market in general or about specific fund managers. Reference calls about the quality of fund managers are standard tools to support the due diligence process. However, they are less common to gather information during the fund investment period.[535]

	Impersonal sources	Personal sources
Fund data	• Fund reports • Transaction summaries • Press releases	• Annual general meetings • Advisory board meetings • One-on-ones with fund managers • Monitoring calls • On-site visits
Market data	• Private equity databases • Private equity publications • Research reports • Financial press • Industry associations	• Own network • Conferences participations • Reference calls

Figure 38: Fund investors' information sources

In order to monitor the individual fund, the fund investors need to gather data from their fund managers, i.e. fund data. Fund investors are formally informed about the development of the partnership by fund reports. These reports are usually released on a quarterly basis.[536] In addition, some fund managers may send formal transaction summaries about new investments and exits to their investors or make press releases. In addition, the fund investors use the annual general meetings, the advisory board meetings, the direct one-on-ones, or on-site visits in the fund managers' offices to gather information about the fund investment. These personal sources may be important to enable the fund investors to interpret and assess the given "pure data" which is provided by the fund reports.[537] The different information sources are summarized in Figure 38.

In order to better understand how fund investors gather information, the study addresses the relevance of different information sources and the frequency and occasions of contacts with fund managers. In addition, it sheds light on the change of information requirements over the last years and the expectations concerning the future.

---

535 Reference calls are typically proceeded with other fund investors, investment bankers, management of portfolio companies, or former members of the staff of the fund manager. See Lauer (2006), p. 2.

536 See Kemmerer/Weidig (2005), p. 88.

537 See Grabenwarter/Weidig (2005a), p. 105; Private Equity Intelligence (2005), p. 4.

Empirical results

The interviewed fund investors were asked in an open question about the three most important sources of information on their fund investments during the investment period. According to their answers, the most important sources are fund reports, one-on-ones with the fund managers, and the attendance of both the annual general meetings and the advisory board meetings.

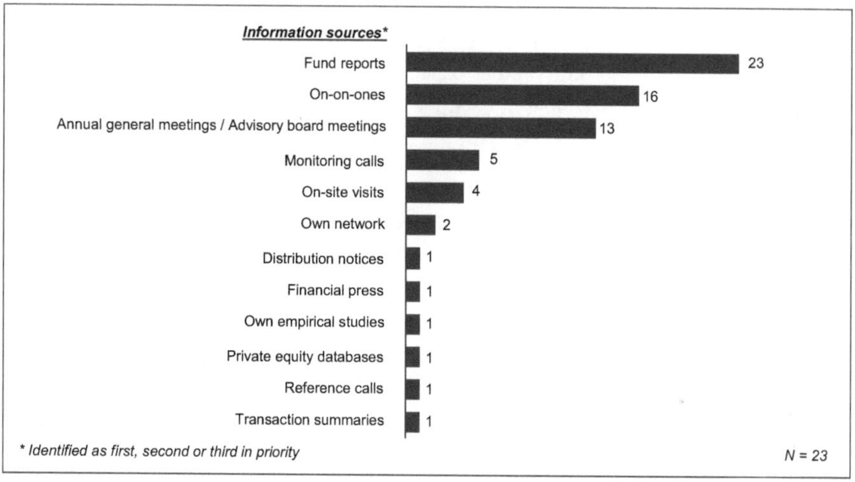

Figure 39: Importance of information sources

As Figure 39 shows, all interviewed fund investors regard the fund reports as one of the three most important sources of information. 78% of them actually rank fund reports as the most important source. These results clearly underline the importance of the reporting to investors. Personal contact through one-on-ones and/or attendance of governance bodies is also seen to be a key source in gathering information during the life of a fund. A handful of fund investors mention that monitoring calls and the on-site visits generate valuable insights.

The interviewed fund investors also indicate in % how much information to monitor the fund investment they typically obtain from impersonal sources in comparison to personal sources. They say that on average 62% (min. 10%, max. 70%) of the information is provided by impersonal sources and 38% (min. 30%, max. 90%) by personal sources. Some fund investors state that the quality of data gathered through personal contacts is usually higher. This high relevance of informal sources is not comparable with traditional asset classes. Private equity fund investors allocate significant time and financial resources to gather the relevant information, e.g. for advisory board meetings or on-site visits. However, one fund investor mentions that for the monitoring purposes, the formal sources are more important as they simply provide the quantity of data needed.

One third of the interviewed fund investors (N= 21) are in contact with their fund managers on a monthly basis, including meetings and calls. The rest usually gets in touch with them every quarter. The interviewed fund investors themselves approach the fund managers basically for three different reasons. First of all, they make standard monitoring calls (or meetings) on a regular basis. These calls are intended to get an update on the fund's portfolio, e.g. new investments, the companies' developments and exit projections. Typically, they also ask for the fund managers' perception of current market developments. Secondly, they contact fund mangers if any irregularities occur which cause their concern. The third reason for getting in touch with investors is when they need to clarify on administrative issues such as cash flow data or reporting content.

62% of the interviewed investors (N=21) claim that they have at least once faced a situation where they asked for specific information from their fund managers that they did not get. This has been especially the case with information that relate to detailed portfolio company data. U.S. venture capital fund managers seem to be most reluctant in providing information.

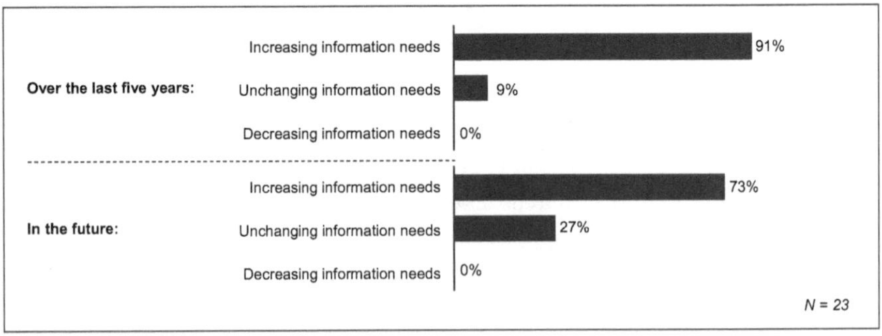

Figure 40: Fund investors' changing information needs

Overall, the information needs of the interviewed fund investors have been increasing over the last five years and will increase in the future. The evidence is provided in

Figure 40. 91% of the interviewed fund investors have required more details about their investments and still 73% believe that they will require even more in the future. The drivers are both increasing monitoring activities and increasing reporting requirements by the fund investors themselves.

3.8.2 Satisfaction with the Fund Managers' Reporting

Fund managers provide disclosure of the fund investment through fund reports and through informal communication. As has been stated by the fund investors, the fund's reports are perceived to be very important in fulfilling the information needs of investors. This is the case for basically three reasons.

First of all, the fund's reports are a mechanism to standardize the delivery of information to fund investors. Instead of directly talking to each investor individually, the fund mangers should use the reports to provide most of the required information in that rather low-cost manner.[538] With increasing fund sizes and a respective increasing number of fund investors, fund managers do not have the time to deliver all information in an individual way. Smaller fund investors may lack the time and financial resources to gather all the information in an informal way. Secondly, the data provided by a written report may be more reliable than orally exchanged information. Auditors may have to testify the prepared annual statutory accounts, thereby providing confidence that the disclosure is correct.[539] Thirdly, most fund investors themselves have to fulfill reporting requirements which need to be based on a reliable and verifiable basis. Fund reports offer this data input.[540]

Due to the importance of the fund managers' reporting, the satisfaction and potential areas of improvement have been addressed in the interviews with the fund investors.

Empirical results

According to the interviewed fund investors, the main role of the reporting is the creation of transparency about the performance, the current status and the assessment of

---

538 See Meyer/Mathonet (2005), p. 279.

539 See Böhler (2004b), p. 292. The auditing of the annual statutory accounts may be legally required or regulated by the partnership agreement.

540 See Böhler (2004b), p. 172.

the future development of the fund. Some interviewees also point out its relevance for their own reporting requirements.

The interviewed fund investors have been further asked that - presumed they are satisfied with 100% - how much of their information requirements in % are currently fulfilled by the funds' reporting. It fulfills an average of only 72% of the interviewed fund investors' information requirements (N=21). Many interviewed fund investors, however, stress that the variation is significant. Some funds only report 35% of what the fund investors require and some funds report up to 100%.

Furthermore, the relevance of the fund reporting for specific purposes has been addressed in the interviews with the fund investors. By asking whether more information in the reports would actually enhance their monitoring and what sort of additional reporting is needed, information gaps have been identified (Figure 41).

The first part of the results concern risk reporting and performance measurement. According to the interviewed fund investors, 63% of them would like to receive more data on the risks inherent in the fund investments. They complain that fund managers do not report about risks in a systematic way. However, a few fund investors express their skepticism about whether it is really possible to quantify and report the risks. Many of the interviewees therefore mention the importance of detailed information on the fund's portfolio companies. Based on this information, fund investors then can themselves identify the risks.

48% of the fund investors would like to receive more information on the fund investment's performance. This may enhance their ability to measure the performance more accurately. Especially, data on cash flows is missing. Instead of aggregated figures, one fund investor stresses the importance of getting "raw data" in order to be able to reconstruct the internal rate of return figures of the fund managers. Fund investors furthermore require detailed data on the fund investments' costs, the portfolio companies' developments, and the valuations of the investments.

The next outcomes relate to questions whether a more comprehensive reporting would enable better decisions of the fund investors. Clearly, the re-investment decision seems to be easier if more information is available. According to 74% of the interviewed fund investors, this is the case. Most of them point to the importance of disclosing underlying portfolio company data, as they need to understand how the value is created.

One fund investor emphasizes the relationship-building role of reporting. The better informed he is, the higher is his trust in the fund managers.

Still 55% of the fund investors believe that a more comprehensive reporting improves their ability to forecast the liquidity of the portfolio. More information of planned portfolio company transactions such as planned exits, more details on the valuations, and more qualitative information on the portfolio companies' business developments seem to support this task.

Only 43% of the interviewed fund investors believe a more comprehensive reporting would enhance the liquidity in the secondary market. Although this could make the market more transparent as prospective buyers of these assets could gather more information on their targets by analyzing the reports, the majority of fund investors claim that they still require the direct contact to the fund managers to gather relevant information.[541] Figure 41 summarizes the details.

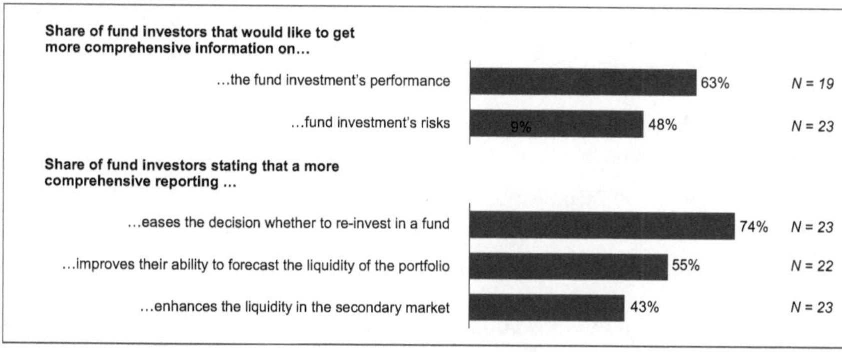

Figure 41: Relevance of reporting for monitoring purposes

These outcomes demonstrate that according to the interviewed fund investors, there is room for improvement in the fund managers' reporting.

541 Some fund investors even express their concern that, with more transparency, the prices on the secondary market for limited partnerships could increase. However, if that is the case this would mean that the market is becoming more efficient because the participants are better informed.

3.8.3 Implications for the Content of the Fund Managers' Reporting

Based on the analysis of the monitoring and the interviews with the fund managers, several implications for the content of the fund managers' reports can be drawn. Again, the objective of the analysis here is not to pinpoint average information requirements, but to identify the information that sophisticated and best-practice applying fund investors require.

In general, all information provided by fund managers should be of use for fund investors. Some general qualitative characteristics make reporting information useful to its users. Reported information must be relevant, reliable and comparable.[542] Information is *relevant* when it is capable of affecting decisions. Fund managers should report information that may influence the fund investors' decisions. The information is *reliable* if information is verifiable and neutral, and if an independent measurer of the information would agree.[543] Information is *comparable* if similar transactions and events are accounted for in the same way. This includes not only comparability over time of data from one fund, but also comparability between different funds. All information that is included into the fund managers' reporting should be relevant, reliable and comparable.

The reported information can be distinguished in information on fund level and information on portfolio company level. It can be qualitative or quantitative information. Qualitative information is difficult to be standardized as it is descriptive. However, it may be as important for fund investors as quantitative figures.

Based on the elaborated activities of monitoring and the interviews with fund investors the following five implications have been identified:

Fund investors require…

1. comprehensive information on the operating and financial situation of the fund, and on the performance of the fund investment,

2. detailed information on the fund investment's costs,

---

542 These characteristics are directly taken from the IASB Framework. See Ernst & Young (2004), pp. 91 et seq.

543 See Tuck (2003c), p. 30.

3. detailed information on the valuation of the unrealized underlying portfolio company investments,

4. information on the type of business, and the operating and financial situation of the underlying portfolio companies,

5. an assessment of the risks and the future development of both the fund and the underlying portfolio company investments.

Implication 1: Fund investors require comprehensive information on the operating and financial situation of the fund, and on the performance of the fund investment.

The fund investor needs comprehensive information on the fund level. The information on the operations of a fund comprises, for example, details of the fund manager's team, its strategy and the implemented investment processes. This information is of qualitative nature. It allows the fund investors to identify and assess any changes and the respective implications. Also, information on transactions with related parties, such as other funds of the fund managers, need to be known by the fund investors in order to judge whether any conflicts of interest can arise.

The information on the financial situation of the fund includes quantitative figures on total capital drawn down, total invested capital, total distributions and total value of remaining assets. In addition, all current, new and realized investments should be listed. A capital account statement informs the fund investors of their individual share of the total value of the partnership.[544]

Performance figures such as the internal rate of return demonstrate the success or failure of the fund investment. Therefore, internal rates of return and investment multiples are often provided. Due to differences in the method applied, the information should be complemented by notes indicating the methodologies used and, if adequate, the cash flows employed to calculate the figures.

This information should be included in the reporting as it forms the basis for all: the performance measurement, the governance of the funds, the re-investment decision and the portfolio management of the fund investors.

---

544 The balance of the capital accounts is increased by a partner's contributions and share of net income and decreased by a partner's distributions and net loss. See Schell (2006), chap. 9, p. 21.

Implication 2: Fund investors require detailed information on the fund investment's costs.

The fund investors need details on the management and performance fees that they have to pay to the fund managers. In addition, they require transparency about any additional income and expenses related to the fund's portfolio investments. The reporting, therefore, should include a comprehensive fee statement.

Fund investors have to carefully monitor these costs due to two reasons. First, they have a direct influence on the fund investors' net return of the investment. It is the return after all costs that the fund investors are interested in. The level of the management fee should be determined in relation to the team and the operations it is intended to support. Secondly, a conflict of interest between fund investors and managers may arise especially with respect to any additional income of the fund managers generated from the fund's investment. As discussed in chapter 3.4.5, fund managers may aim to maximize the fee income from portfolio companies which can result in a lower valuation of the companies. The partnership agreements usually comprise arrangements regarding the reimbursement of this fee income to fund investors. It is important to monitor the adherence to these agreements.

Implication 3: Fund investors require detailed information on the valuation of the unrealized underlying portfolio company investments.

The valuation of the unrealized underlying fund's portfolio company investments constitutes a central part of the reporting to fund investors. Getting an understanding of the current actual value of the portfolio companies is therefore a prerequisite not only for performance measurement. The valuations of the fund's portfolio investments are also necessary to monitor the true diversification of the total current portfolio of the fund investor. Furthermore, they may be input to liquidity planning models.

Key requirement is, however, that these valuations reflect the potential current market values as adequately as possible. As there are no market prices readily available for private equity investments, these valuations have to be derived by applying certain valuation methodologies.[545] However, due to the subjectivity in the valuation processes, different fund managers in the same portfolio company may report different

---

[545] The different models available are discussed in chapter 4.3.5.

valuations. It makes it therefore hard for limited partners to actually gauge how their investments are performing.

Fair values require that the reporting fund manager makes a choice about which valuation methodology to apply and which assumptions to make. Nearly 70% of the interviewed fund investors see the lack of consistency in using the fair value-based valuation methodologies as problematic. Industry associations have developed valuation guidelines to overcome this inconsistency and to support comparability. Nevertheless, a degree of subjectivity will remain even when using these guidelines. This subjectivity is problematic for also nearly 70% of the fund investors. However, the higher volatility in valuations caused by a fair value-based approach seems to be a minor issue. Only 38% of the interviewed fund investors find it disturbing that the valuation is time consuming for fund managers. Figure 42 shows the details.

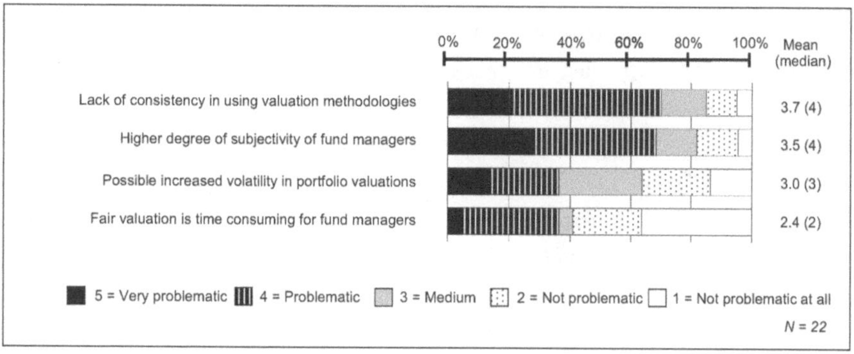

Figure 42: Problems with a fair value-based approach of portfolio company valuation

Given the problems with fair value measurement, it is important that fund managers act transparently with respect to the valuation methodologies and assumptions they use. As described earlier, certain fund investors adjust the reported valuations (*adjusted net asset value method)*. They analyze and challenge the partnerships' fair values of all significant underlying portfolio company positions. Thereby, they aim to obtain a consistent and reliable fair value at the level of the fund.[546] However, as Figure 43 demonstrates, only 24% of the interviewed fund investors are satisfied with the disclosure of the applied valuation methodologies and assumptions.

[546] See Kinsch/Petit-Jouvet (2006).

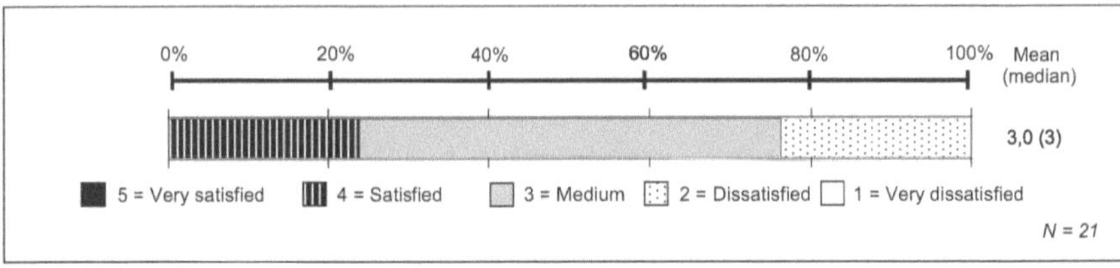

Figure 43: Satisfaction with disclosure of applied valuation methodologies and assumptions

Implication 4: Fund investors require information on the type of business, and the operating and financial situation of the underlying portfolio companies.

With respect to the portfolio company level, fund investors require more details than only the reported values. They need additional information on the operating and financial conditions of the companies. Given the difficulties to accurately value private equity companies and the conflicts of interest that arise between the fund investors and the fund managers regarding the valuation,[547] most fund investors try to assess the value and the respective performance of the portfolio companies based on these details by themselves. Even more important, they aim to understand how their fund managers have created value with the investments. For most fund investors, the quality of the fund managers and their performance depends on their ability to influence the operative development of the portfolio companies. Furthermore, the information on the operational and financial developments shed some light on the potential risks inherent in the fund investments. Typically, this sort of information forms the basis for fund investors to discuss the portfolio companies' issues at advisory board meetings or at one-on-ones meetings.

The description of the businesses and the industry of the portfolio company should be provided. Changes in the management team, or any other key events during the reporting period should be reported as well. Details are required on the financial structure such as the percentage of ownership and the used financial instruments are central to analyze the investment value.

---

547 See chapter 4.3.6.1 for the conflicts of interest with respect to valuations of portfolio companies between fund managers and investors.

These details are as important for buyout portfolio company investments as for venture capital portfolio company investments. However, there may be differences with respect to the information requirements. Buyout company investments are usually made in already established companies with positive cash flows and revenues. As discussed in chapter 3.6.1, the value creation for investors results from earnings increase, multiple expansion, or net debt repayments. In order to be able to analyze and assess the value created, fund investors therefore need to know at least the earnings development,

the entry, current or exit valuation multiples, and information on net debt. Historic information on revenues or earnings allows the fund investors to assess the development of the companies. By comparing earnings against their budget and against the original business plan, fund investors are able to evaluate whether the companies are performing as planned or whether they may face any not anticipated difficulties.

For venture capital portfolio companies, the quantitative financial figures are less relevant as most of these investments have no revenues, make losses and seldom have any additional debt when the investment is made. Therefore, qualitative information on the development of the companies such as the achievement of milestones, e.g. market readiness of products, is more important. Another key factor is to know whether the companies have enough liquidity to survive the next phase of their development. The cash burn rate and the liquidity reserves including information on any additional committed capital to these investments give implications on the status of the companies.

Implication 5: Fund investors require an assessment of the risks and the future development of both the fund and the underlying portfolio company investments.

The different types of risks that private equity fund investors face have been discussed in length in chapter 3.4.4. There is no systematic way to communicate these risks as their quantitative measurement is either very difficult or even impossible.[548] However, even if the risks are not measurable, the fund managers could report some qualitative remarks and their personal assessments. The communication of the risks increases the transparency, reduces asymmetric information and, hence, promotes the private equity firm's reputation.[549] It enables the fund investors to implement better diversification

[548] For example, the style drift risks or the manager risks on fund level are impossible to quantify.

[549] See Kemmerer (2005), p. 7.

strategies, makes fund investors' follow-on decisions less difficult and allows more reliable liquidity and investment planning.[550]

Referring to reporting, it is useful to distinguish between the risks on the fund level and on the underlying portfolio company level. On the fund level, the fund investors may be interested in aggregated information, for example, on the currency exposure. Also important are information on the fund managers' processes that are implemented to manage the risks.

Concerning the portfolio company level, fund investors should be informed about what are the specific risks of the individual investments, e.g. the achievement of a next product development stage, or the loss of an important customer. A qualitative assessment of the portfolio companies' status compared to the expectations at the time of the investments (i.e. "on track, not on track") shows the fund managers' evaluation of the developments.

Concerning an assessment of the future development of the fund investment, fund investors may want to get management projections such as worst or best case scenarios of portfolio companies' outcomes. This would support and assist the forecasting of the future performance. Discussions on near term investment liquidation events or write-offs with fund managers are important.[551] Many fund investors ask for these assessments in specific monitoring calls. Exit plans, exit horizons, or an estimated exit valuation could be provided.

Figure 44 summarizes the elaborated fund investors' information requirements implicated by their monitoring needs. It distinguishes between information on the fund level and the portfolio company level.

---

550 See Kemmerer (2005), p. 7.

551 See Atkins/Giannini (2003), p. 225.

Fund level	General operational information on fund level
	Financial information on aggregated investments
	Capital account information
	Performance measurement on fund level
	Risk reporting on fund level
	Information on fund investment's fees
Portfolio company level	General information on portfolio companies and role of fund
	Financial information on portfolio company
	Information on valuation and performance of portfolio investments
	Assessment of current situation, risks, and future development of investments

Figure 44: Summary of fund investors' required information

3.8.4 Limitations of Fund Managers' Reporting

In the two previous chapters, it has been demonstrated that providing information to fund investors is beneficial for them. The fund investors, however, seem to be dissatisfied - at least in some cases - with the level of disclosure they get.[552] Some market participants even claim there is an information deficiency in the private equity industry.[553] In the following, it will be therefore analyzed why fund managers may be reluctant to provide all the information that their investors may need.

Providing information to fund investors is costly from the perspective of the information provider. Typically, three types of costs are distinguished: the cost of competitive disadvantage attributable to disclosure, the cost of litigation attributable to information disclosure, and the cost of preparing and disseminating information.[554]

The *cost of competitive disadvantage* relates to the underlying investments of the funds as well as to the bargaining position of the fund managers. The release of information on patents, products and profitability of venture capital investments to competitors, for example, may hurt the portfolio companies' competitive positions.[555] Furthermore, a

---

[552] See Private Equity Intelligence (2005), p. 3; Böhler (2004b), pp. 269 et seq.

[553] See Diem (2002), p. 10.

[554] See Labhart (1999), pp. 226 et seq.

[555] See Gove (2005), p. 47.

depreciation of the investment value by the fund managers may be seen as a sign of weakness and may deter suppliers and customers of that company from doing business with them. Information on expected exit prices of existing portfolio companies provided to fund investors may actually disturb the bargaining position of the fund managers in transactions.[556]

In addition, fund managers may fear *the cost of litigation attributable to informative disclosure.* Fund managers may fear that fund investors are more willing to bring a claim against them if fund investors feel that they have been mislead or that the fund has been mismanaged.[557] The more information is provided to fund investors, the more details can be subject to disputes.

Finally, there is *the cost of preparing and disseminating information.* Developing reports and distributing them to the fund investors is costly and time consuming.[558] Some fund managers may simply try to avoid spending financial and time resources on the reporting process.

Fund managers may also *fear misinterpretation of the information* that is disclosed to their fund investors. They may claim that short-term interim data is misleading in private equity due to the J-curve effect.[559] A low or negative return in the first years of a fund's life time may not indicate the actually expected performance. Some fund investors, however, may also believe that the fund managers use this argument and try to hide the true performance by not providing comprehensive information to the fund investors. Especially in times in which the fund managers need to raise new funds, they may try to present their performance as favorable as possible to them.

There are differences between public equity markets and private equity partnerships. As the latter act in a private environment, the information exchanged between both parties should not be released to outside parties. If that is true, the participants should not fear any competitive disadvantages. However, due to the *Freedom of Information*

---

556 See Gove (2005), p. 47. If, for example, a potential buyer finds out that a private equity fund manager has marked down its portfolio company investment, the acquirer may downgrade its bid accordingly.

557 See Marsh (2004), p. 4.

558 See Private Equity Intelligence (2005), p. 3.

559 See chapter 3.4.2.1 for more details.

Act (FOIA) in the U.S., this has changed. Several public institutions got under legal pressure to disclose the performance of their private equity fund investments.[560] The argument for that case was that the public had a right to know the public institutions' performance and to hold its officials accountable.[561] Following a court ruling, the California Public Employees' Retirement Systems (CalPERS), for example, decided to open this information to the public.[562] Because of the rarity of private equity disclosure so far, the decision received a great deal of interest in the industry.

Under the FOIA, any written communication by a fund manager to a public fund investor would legally have to be disclosed. As a consequence, the fund managers could limit the documentation provided to public fund investors. If the fund managers become more cautious about providing fund investors with detailed information, the FOIA could limit the scope of information conveyed to fund investors. Rather than creating the intended effect of increased disclosure, the effect could be just the opposite.[563]

In order to get a better understanding which of the discussed reasons to be reluctant in providing information are indeed relevant, this question has been addressed to the interviewed fund investors.

Empirical results

As demonstrated in Figure 45, over 50% of the fund investors state that a relevant reason why fund managers are reluctant to provide information on the fund investment is that they fear that this information will be disclosed to the public due to the FOIA. This has implications for regulators and legislators dealing with the private equity markets. They should assure that the information exchange between fund investors and managers is possible without forcing fund investors to make information publicly available.[564] The interviewed fund investors also claim that another relevant reason not

---

[560] Fund managers fear that also information on the underlying portfolio companies has to be released. See Reyes (2005), p. 69.

[561] See Chaplinsky/Perry (2004), p. 3.

[562] See EVCA (2003c), p. 2. For more information on the FOIA see, for example, Reyes (2005); Chaplinsky/Perry (2004); Aragon (2002).

[563] See Chaplinsky/Perry (2004), p. 4.

[564] This is discussed in more details in chapter 5.2.

to disclose information could be the general partners' fear of a competitive disadvantage with respect to the businesses and the potential exits of portfolio companies. All the other potential reasons are perceived to be relevant only for a minority of the interviewed fund investors.

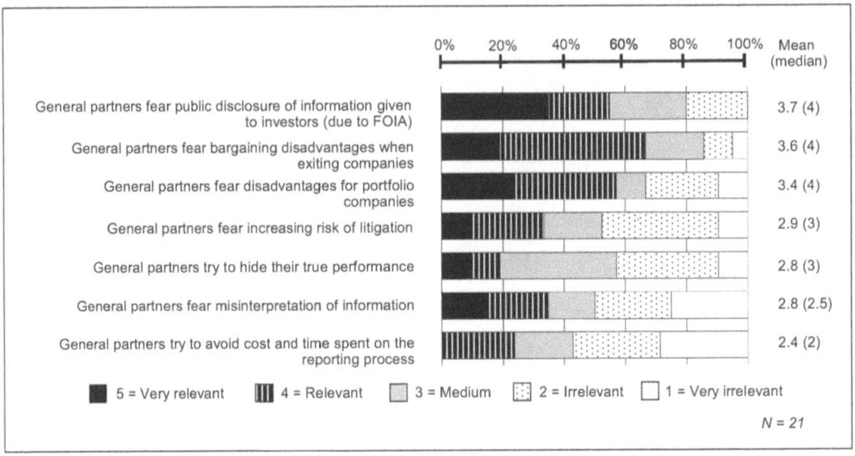

Figure 45: Potential reasons for the reluctance of fund managers to disclose information

To sum up, in chapter 3 the fund investors' monitoring activities have been addressed, and resulting information requirements have been elaborated. Especially, five implications regarding the specific content of the fund reports have been unfolded and discussed. The next chapter changes the perspective from the fund investors to the fund managers. The fund managers' reporting will be described in detail with specific consideration given to the fair value measurement of private equity fund portfolio companies. The actual reporting will be empirically tested and critically assessed. Based on these results, it can be discussed whether the fund investors' reporting requirements expressed in the five implications in this chapter are actually fulfilled or whether any information gaps still exist.

4 Fund Managers' Reporting

4.1 Introductory Remarks

Fund managers communicate in manifold ways with their fund investors in order to inform about the current status, the performance and the expected development of the funds. Regular reporting is an integral part of this communication and seen as one of the most important information sources for private equity investors.[565]

The fund reporting can be distinguished in statutory financial statements and additional investor reporting. Each partnership is required to prepare *statutory financial statements* according to either national or international 'General Accepted Accounting Principles (GAAP)'. These obligatory disclosure requirements arise from the national corporate and accounting legislation of the jurisdiction in which the private equity partnership is incorporated.[566] Constituent parts of statutory financial statements are a balance sheet, a profit and loss statement, a statement of changes in equity, a cash flow statement and additional notes.[567] Beyond this, no legal requirements for reporting to investors typically exist.[568]

Besides, fund managers provide *additional investor reporting* which aims at fulfilling fund investors' specific information needs. This additional disclosure is voluntary from a regulatory perspective. However, it is not only based on the discretion of the fund manager but might also arise from special agreements, e.g. the limited partnership agreement between fund managers and their investors.[569]

An essential input to both the statutory financial statements and the investors reporting are the *valuations of the portfolio company investments*. Fund managers are required to

---

565 See Hagenmüller (2004), p. 130.

566 See Thoen (2002), p. 23; Böhler (2004b), p. 169.

567 See Pellens/Fülbier/Gassen (2006), p. 151. These are, for example, the required components of financial statements according to IFRS which are prescribed in IAS 1.8.

568 See Brooks (1999), p. 114.

569 TUCK find through a survey among U.S. private equity market participants that about 50% of the U.S. private equity fund managers and about 75% of their U.S. fund investors wish the limited partnership agreement should govern the transparency and detail of fund and portfolio company valuation reporting. See Tuck (2004b), p. 16.

carry out periodic valuations of their investments.[570] They face the challenge to report a relevant and reliable value of the in most cases illiquid investments to its investors. It has been common practice among private equity fund managers to value private equity portfolio company investments at cost.[571] However, this approach is not any longer acceptable for statutory financial statements that are prepared according to international reporting standards.[572] Instead, a fair value measurement of the investments is required. In addition, fund investors also increasingly demand that the fund managers disclose fair values in the investor reports. Figure 46 provides an overview of the fund managers' reporting.

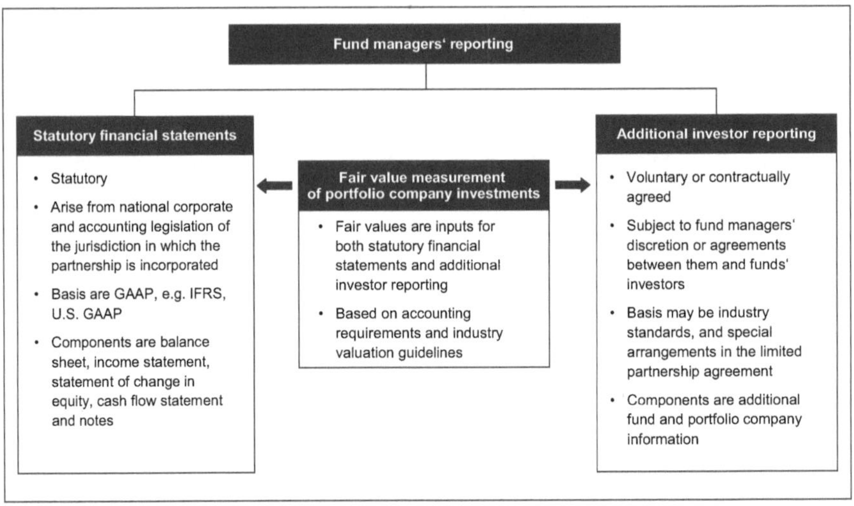

Figure 46: Overview of fund managers' reporting

This chapter proceeds as follows. At first, the requirements of the statutory financial statements are described with emphasis on the accounting for portfolio companies as important part (chapter 4.2). Since the fair value measurement of the portfolio company investments of the fund plays an increasingly more important and integral part of the reporting to fund investors, it will be subject to an in-depth analysis in chapter 4.3.

570 See AFIC/BVCA/EVCA (2004), p. 7; Böhler (2004b), p. 169.

571 See SECA (2006), p. 26.

572 This is true for both IFRS and U.S. GAAP. See AFIC/BVCA/EVCA (2004), p. 7; Snow (2006), p. 30.

Lastly, a detailed analysis of the actual content of the fund reports with respect to the additional voluntary disclosure will be provided (chapter 4.4).

4.2 Statutory Financial Statements

4.2.1 Relevance of International Financial Reporting Standards

The preparation of statutory financial statements is required and regulated by the corporate and accounting legislation of the jurisdiction in which a private equity fund is incorporated.[573] One set of internationally established accounting principles are the *International Financial Reporting Standards (IFRS)*.[574] The application of these standards varies globally but has grown over the last years.[575] Many countries adopt IFRS directly. Others allow the use of IFRS instead of existing national GAAP, or their standard setters are committed to let national GAAP converge with IFRS.[576] In the European Union, since January 1, 2005, IFRS is compulsory for consolidated accounts of companies which have listed securities.[577] Although few private equity funds exist that are listed, some private equity vehicles in the European Union are part of larger listed financial services organizations.[578] Furthermore, even if private equity funds are not legally required to prepare their financial statements in accordance with IFRS, fund investors increasingly ask for IFRS information because of their own reporting purposes.[579]

Given the growing importance of IFRS in private equity, these accounting standards are subject to the following analysis instead of any national GAAP. However, key conclusions that this analysis draws may be also relevant for U.S. GAAP. The latter standards are also commonly applied in the private equity industry, since many partner-

573 See Thoen (2002), p. 23.

574 See for more details on the development of international accounting standards Achleitner/Behr (2002), pp. 3 et seq.

575 See Bane (2005), p. 2.

576 See Thomson (2004), p. 25.

577 See European Commission (2002), article 4.

578 See McCurry (2005), p. 44. Examples are ABN AMRO Capital, Allianz Capital Partners, Barclays Capital.

579 See Bane (2005), p. 2. BÖHLER finds that around 70% of Swiss private equity fund investors favour IFRS as accounting standard for funds. 24% of the investors prefer U.S. GAAP. See Böhler (2004b), p. 186.

ships are structured according to U.S. law.[580] The standard setting boards, for IFRS the *International Accounting Standards Board (IASB)* and for U.S. GAAP the *Financial Accounting Standard Board (FASB)*, are committed to the convergence of U.S. GAAP with IFRS. A common set of high quality global standards is their long-term strategic priority.[581] It can be expected that for the most relevant topics concerning private equity funds, i.e. consolidation and fair value measurement, converged standards will be issued.[582]

The following analysis focuses specifically on the accounting for portfolio company investments in the statutory accounts according to IFRS.[583] This is relevant for private equity fund managers due to two reasons.[584] First, IFRS require funds to consolidate controlled investments. This procedure may not be appropriate for private equity vehicles as consolidated accounts do not inform the fund investors about the value that has been created through the fund's portfolio company investments.[585] Second, there has been a recent paradigm shift in investment valuation. Having valued most of their portfolio company investments at cost unless a new financing round or a realization provided evidence for an update of the old valuation, private equity fund managers today are required by IFRS to measure and present the fair value of their investment assets.[586] Both issues will be discussed in detail.

4.2.2 Elements of Statutory Financial Statements

Statutory financial statements are a structured presentation of the financial position and financial performance of an entity. Their objectives are to provide information that is useful for its users to make economic decisions. They show the results of the man-

---

580 See Böhler (2004b), p. 183.

581 See FASB/IASB (2006), p. 1. Both IASB and FASB agreed on a roadmap for convergence between IFRS and U.S. GAAP for the period from 2006 to 2008 and identified several issues where convergence should be achieved.

582 See FASB/IASB (2006), p. 3.

583 It is outside the scope of this analysis to elaborate and present detailed models of how to prepare statutory financial statements according to IFRS for private equity funds. The discussion should be rather focused on the major impacts of IFRS on private equity fund accounting.

584 See McCurry (2005), p. 43.

585 Consolidated accounts do not inform the investors of the financial position of their investment. Chapter 4.2.4.1 provides a detailed discussion.

586 U.S. GAAP also requires their fund managers to measure their investment at a fair value. See Snow (2006), p. 30.

agement's stewardship of the resources entrusted to it.[587] IFRS requires that the following elements of the statutory financial statements are presented (IAS 1.7): balance sheet, profit and loss statement, cash flow statement, statement of changes in equity and notes to the financial statements.[588]

The *balance sheet* presents the financial condition of a company at a specific point in time. It lists the company's assets, liabilities and the owners' equity (net worth). Naturally, due to the business of a private equity fund, its portfolio company investments are the most important items on the asset side of the balance sheet. Due to their importance, the question how to account for portfolio company investments is of special interest and is discussed in the next chapter. The amount of cash and cash equivalents is marginal in limited partnerships structures, since investors commit capital but usually do not contribute cash to the partnership unless the fund manager has identified an investment and has agreed to purchase it and therefore calls for the cash. As private equity funds are often restricted to take on debt,[589] the amount of liabilities is usually small.[590] The presented equity comprises the partners' capital accounts. It equals the net worth of the fund. Very often the term net asset value is used for the equity.[591] In limited partnerships, a capital account is established for each partner. The balance of the capital account is increased by the partner's contributions and share of net income and decreased by that partner's distributions and net loss.[592]

The *profit and loss statement* presents information on the financial performance within the reporting period. The main important source of income are capital gains or losses which should be differentiated in realized and unrealized positions. Unrealized gains and losses arise through revaluation of existing investments.[593] Whether these unrealized changes in value are recognized in the profit and loss statement or directly in the

587 See Ernst & Young (2004), p. 137.

588 For models of these elements for private equity funds see Böhler (2004b), pp. 187 et seq.

589 See Gompers/Lerner (1996), p. 485. The authors show that 95.6% of U.S. private equity funds are restricted to use debt.

590 To finance their investments, private equity investors use debt (financial leverage). However, the debt is taken on directly by the financed companies themselves. See Levin (2002) for detailed information on the structuring of portfolio company investments.

591 See Böhler (2004b), p. 192.

592 See Schell (2006), chap. 9, p. 21.

593 See Böhler (2004b), p. 194.

equity account as changes in the fair value reserve depends on the classification of the financial instruments in either 'fair value through profit and loss' or 'available for sale' assets (IAS 39.55).[594] Other sources of income are dividends or interests from investments. To a certain degree, additional fee income might be generated.[595] Expenses for private equity funds arise mainly through management and performance fees. The typical fund has no need for its own office space or personnel since its operations are all conducted by the general partner (or fund manager). However, the funds often incur material expenses relating to their portfolio company investments, especially so-called broken deal expenses that occur when an investment transaction is not consummated.[596]

The *cash flow statement* presents the amounts of cash and cash equivalents that enter and leave a company over the reporting period. All entities must prepare and present a cash flow statement which reports three types of cash flows during the reporting period, i.e. cash flows from operating, investing and financing activities (IAS 7.10). This break-down has been primarily developed for non-investment companies. For private equity funds compared to non-investment companies, a notable discussion relates to the question whether purchases and sales of investments should be rather operating cash flow than cash flow from investment activities.[597] However, according to IAS 7, these activities should be allocated to cash flow from investment activities.

The *statement of changes in equity* reflects and analyzes the increase or decrease in net assets between two balance sheet days (IAS 1.98).[598] This information is particularly interesting for private equity funds due to two reasons. First, the changes include total income and expense, i.e. both the part that is recognized in the profit and loss statement and the part that is recognized directly in equity. Fair value changes of 'available

594 Further details especially with respect to impairments and currency gains and losses are discussed in chapter 4.2.3.2.

595 The fee income, e.g. break-up, transaction or monitoring fees, could relate to the fund's investment transactions or it could relate to subsequent relationships with portfolio companies. See Schell (2006), chap. 2, p. 35.

596 See Schell (2006), chap. 2, p. 39.

597 See Böhler (2004b), p. 198.

598 Instead of preparing a statement of changes in equity, an entity might only show a statement that comprises the total of recognized income and expense (IAS 1.96). However, information of transactions with equity holders shall then be given in the notes (IAS 1.97).

for sale' assets are recognized directly in equity and could account for a significant part of total income. Second, it covers the amounts of transactions with equity holders. In private equity funds, there are usually frequent transactions with equity holders, especially contributions from and distributions to investors resulting from purchases and sales of investments.

Additional information about the basis of preparation and specific accounting policies, information that is not presented on the face of the statements but that is relevant to an understanding of any of them, and information that is required by other standards shall be presented in the *notes to the financial statements* (IAS 1.125).[599] IFRS 7 requires the provision of enough disclosures about the fund's financial instruments, especially its investments,[600] to enable users of the statements to evaluate their financial position and performance (IFRS 7.1).[601] Specifically, funds need to disclose details on the determination of the fair value of the financial instruments, e.g. methods and assumptions used (IFRS 7.25-30), and about the nature and extent of risks arising from the investments (IFRS 7.31-42). Furthermore, any transaction with related parties needs to be disclosed (IAS 24.5). Related parties to the fund may be for example the general partners or any additional advisors.[602]

The statutory financial statements are supposed to provide an overview of the private equity fund's business financial condition and profitability. As the business of private equity funds is the investment in companies for the purpose of achieving income and capital gains, the accounting for portfolio companies plays an important role in determining the structure and presentation of these financial statements. Therefore, it will be discussed in detail in the next chapter.

---

599 See Ernst & Young (2004), p. 168.

600 It does not deal with the investments that are accounted for in accordance with IAS 27 (subsidiaries), IAS 28 (associates) or IAS 31 (joint ventures). For more details on these types see chapter 4.2.3.

601 IFRS 7 is effective for annual periods beginning after January 1, 2007.

602 See Böhler (2004b), p. 200.

4.2.3 Accounting for Portfolio Company Investments

4.2.3.1 Financial Instruments and Level of Ownership

The way how a portfolio company investment is accounted for depends on two characteristics of the investment: the type of financial instrument that is used and - in case the financial instrument is an equity instrument - the level of ownership that is acquired. When providing financial resources to portfolio companies, private equity fund managers choose between various *financial instruments*[603] that can be broadly distinguished in equity[604], debt, or a combination thereof.[605] The choice of the financial instrument matters since this characteristic determines how a particular instrument is classified in the financial statements. The classification has important implications for the measurement of the assets, i.e. whether a fair value measurement is required or not and how the holder needs to account for changes in value. The latter may be recognized in the profit and loss statement or recognized directly in the equity position on the balance sheet.[606]

In private equity transaction structures different forms of financial instruments are used which represent equity, debt or a combination thereof. From an accounting perspective, it is necessary to identify whether the instruments have rather equity or debt characteristics.[607] Preferred stock has different investor rights than common stock.

---

603 A financial instrument is broadly defined as any contract that gives rise to a financial asset of one entity and a financial liability or equity instrument of another entity (IAS 32.11).

604 According to IAS 32.11 an equity instrument is any contract that specifies a residual interest in the assets of an entity after deducting all of its liabilities. Equity instruments are e.g. non-puttable ordinary shares or some types of preference shares (IAS 32.AG13).

605 Theoretical foundation of the use of different financial instruments in private equity transactions is based on the principal agent setting between the fund and the entrepreneurs. This is elaborated mainly in literature concerning venture capital contracting although some conclusion can be drawn also for buyout finance structures. See among others Bascha/Walz (2001); Bergemann/Hege (1998); Berglöf (1994); Hellmann (2006); Rudolph/Haagen (2004); Schmidt (2003). For a review see Jung-Senssfelder (2006), pp. 31 et seq. Empirical evidence about the financial instruments that are actually used is among others provided by Kaplan/Strömberg (2003) for the U.S., Bottazzi/Da Rin/Hellmann (2004) for Europe, and Bascha/Walz (2002), Hommel/Ritter/Wright (2003) for Germany. For a review see Jung-Senssfelder (2006), p. 42.

606 See Ernst & Young (2004), p. 938.

607 IAS 32, *Financial Instruments and Disclosure,* determines the differentiation of equity and liabilities from an issuer's perspective. The appliance of these rules for a holder of the instruments seems to be appropriate. See Löw/Lorenz (2005), p. 494. The differentiation between equity and debt according to IAS 32 is a complex issue. For a detailed discussion of the classification of fi-

These rights, e.g. special dividend, subscription, or voting rights as well as liquidation provisions, are directly linked to the ownership of the stock.[608] Typical for venture capital deals is the use of convertible preferred stock.[609] Preferred stocks take the legal form of equity but - depending on its rights - can be debt in substance. In determining whether the preferred share is a debt or equity instrument from the holder's perspective, IAS 32 requires to assess the particular rights attached to the preferred shares. Figure 47 provides an example relating to different types of preferred stock.[610]

Illustrative example – Classifying preferred stock as debt or equity according to IAS 32

The example: Type A is a *redeemable preferred stock* with a cumulative dividend of 6% p.a. that must be redeemed by the issuing company for face value plus dividend the sooner of an IPO or six years. This type is typically used by venture capitalists. Type B are *non-redeemable preferred shares* with no contractual right to receive a dividend.

Type A preferred stock has to be classified as debt instrument on the balance sheet by its holders. According to IAS 32.18(a), a preferred share that provides for mandatory redemption by the issuer for a determinable amount at a determinable future date is a liability. However, when there is no contractual obligation to deliver cash or another financial asset, the preferred shares are equity instruments. Distributions from the issuer of type B preferred stock are only at the discretion of the issuer. It is thus equivalent to an ordinary equity share and should be characterized as equity (IAS 32.AG26).

Figure 47: Illustrative example – Classifying preferred shares as debt or equity according to IAS 32

Shareholder loans are typically used by private equity funds to finance buyouts. They can be considered to be part of subordinated-debt. However, under certain conditions they might have to be classified as an equity position.[611] In the German venture capital

nancial instruments as equity or liability see among others Isert/Schaber (2005a) and Isert/Schaber (2005b).

608 See Fingerle (2005), p. 79; Jung-Senssfelder (2006), p. 22. Public and private preference shares should be distinguished. The former usually have special dividends and liquidation preferences but no voting rights whereas the latter carry additional investor rights, sometimes giving their holders a more powerful position in comparison to common stock holders. Traditional public preference shares show rather debt characteristics. Private preference shares are classified as mezzanine or equity. See Bagley/Dauchy (1999), p. 272; Wahl (2004), p. 162.

609 See Kaplan/Strömberg (2003), p. 286. Convertible preferred equity consists of preferred equity combined with an option to convert into straight equity. See Jung-Senssfelder (2006), p. 24. Typically, it automatically converts to common stock if the company makes an initial public offering. See Tuck (2003b), p. 4.

610 For the use of redeemable preferred stock in venture capital structures see Lerner/Hardymon (2005), pp. 289 et seq.

611 See Kühn (2006), p. 95.

market the use of so-called silent partnerships is often observable.[612] Depending on its characteristics a silent partnership is classified as equity or liability position.[613] As a rule, mezzanine instruments[614] can be separated either in debt-like or equity-like mezzanine. For the former, interest payments are the key feature. For the latter, participation in the value increase are more important.[615]

According to IFRS, the substance rather than the legal form of the financial instrument governs its classification on the entity's balance sheet (IAS 32.18). It is beyond the scope of this analysis to discuss the accounting of all various financial instruments that a private equity fund may use to finance the portfolio company transactions.[616] It will be focused rather on the most important ones, the use of equity investments, especially due to its inherent valuation difficulties.[617]

The accounting of equity investments depends, however, on another criterion, i.e. the investor's *level of ownership*. Private equity funds pursue different strategies with respect to the level of ownership they acquire in their portfolio companies. Buyout funds usually acquire a significant portion or controlling majority of a business. Venture capitalists typically hold minority interests. Often, private equity fund manager team up in a consortium or syndicate to make an acquisition.[618]

The level of ownership that a fund holds affects the *method* that the fund manager is required to use in order to account for the investment. Regarding that level and, ac-

---

612 Silent partnerships account for 19.6% of the investments by German private equity funds in 2005. See BVK (2006), p. 16.

613 A *typical* silent partner participates in company profits, has limited control rights, can be granted limited liability protection, and has a subordinated claim to debtholders. According to German commercial and tax law the silent partnership represents a liability position. An *atypical* silent partner participates in addition in company growth and in liquidation results. Therefore, German law assign the position to equity in the balance sheet. See Kühn (2006), pp. 24 et seq; Rudolph/Haagen (2004), p. 19.

614 Mezzanine instruments could be for example convertible debt, warrant-linked debt, or debt with equity kickers. For details of selected mezzanine instruments see Achleitner/Wahl (2004), pp. 65 et seq; Wahl (2004), pp. 140 et seq; Kühn (2006), pp. 99 et seq; Tuck (2003b), pp. 3 et seq.

615 See Kühn (2006), p. 99.

616 For a detailed discussion see for example Poole/Spooner (2006); Kuhn/Scharpf (2005).

617 See chapter 4.3 for the discussion of the fair value measurement of portfolio company investments.

618 See Nathusius (2005) for syndication in venture capital and Dresdale (2004) for so-called 'club deals' of buyout funds.

cordingly, the influence that investors have over their portfolio companies, three different types of equity investments have to be distinguished for accounting purposes: financial instruments, associates, and subsidiaries.[619] Financial instruments are accounted for by applying a fair value to the participation. Associates are partially consolidated, or the equity method is applied. Subsidiaries are fully consolidated. The next chapters discuss these different accounting methods for equity investments in portfolio companies in detail.

4.2.3.2 Accounting for Financial Instruments

Unless private equity investments are interests in subsidiaries, associates or joint ventures, they are financial instruments and have to be accounted for according to IAS 32 and IAS 39.[620] These standards regulate their classification, the initial and the subsequent measurement, the income recognition and the potential impairment.

Classification and initial measurement

IAS 39 states that at initial recognition financial instruments have to be classified into one of four different categories.[621] The initial classification is important as it determines the accounting treatment for the particular financial instrument. It sorts out the amount at which the investments are initially recognized, whether they are carried at historical cost or fair value in subsequent measurements and how any re-measurement gains or losses are accounted for.[622]

The four categories as defined in IAS 39.9 are (a) financial assets at fair value through profit or loss, including held-for-trading assets, (b) held-to-maturity investments, (c) loans and receivables, and (d) available for sale financial assets. Held-to-maturity investments and loans and receivables classifications are for debt instruments and, there-

---

619 See Böhler (2004b), p. 205.

620 See IAS 32, *Financial Instruments: Disclosure and Presentation,* and IAS 39, *Financial Instruments: Recognition and Measurement*. Additionally, IFRS 7, *Financial Instruments: Disclosures,* prescribes the disclosures about financial instruments in the financial statements. The additional disclosure allows users of financial statements to evaluate the relevance of financial instruments for the reporting entity's financial position and performance. It clarifies the nature and extent of risks arising from financial instruments to which the reporting entity is exposed and how the entity manages those risks. It was issued in August 2005 and replaced IAS 30 and some parts of IAS 32. See IASB (2005); Pellens/Fülbier/Gassen (2006), pp. 545 et seq.

621 See Kuhn/Scharpf (2005), p. 74.

622 See Ernst & Young (2004), p. 828; Bane (2005), p. 3.

fore, will not be discussed any further. Investments in equity instruments of portfolio companies by private equity funds can be classified either as financial assets at fair value through profit or loss, or as available for sale.[623] This is shown in Figure 48.

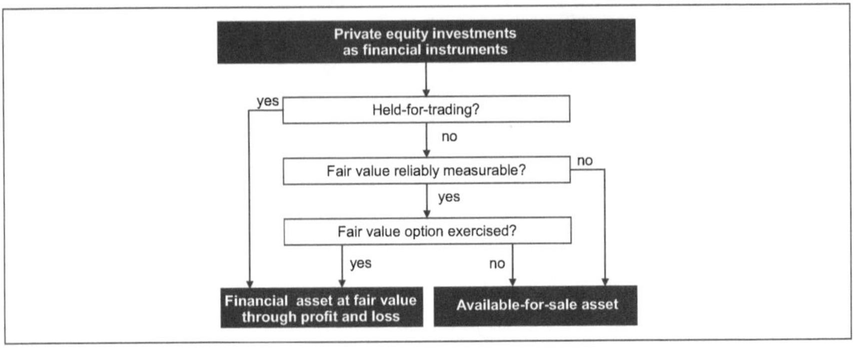

Figure 48: Classification of private equity investments according to IAS 39

A private equity fund must classify all its investments that are held-for-trading as financial assets at fair value through profit and loss (IAS 39.9a). Trading means active buying and selling, and financial instruments held-for-trading are used with the objective to profit from short-term changes in price (IAS 39.AG14).[624] Private equity investments are usually held for a period of three to five years and are therefore unlikely to fall in that category.

If a fair value of the portfolio company investment is reliably measurable, a fund may choose to designate all its private equity portfolio company investments as financial assets at fair value through profit or loss (IAS 39.9). This is the so-called 'fair value option'.[625] If the fair value option is not exercised or cannot be exercised as the fair

---

623 For a detailed discussion see Bane (2005), p. 4.

624 See Ernst & Young (2004), p. 830. For a detailed description about what constitutes an asset as held-for-trading see Löw/Lorenz (2005), p. 484; Ernst & Young (2004), p. 830

625 With its *Amendments to IAS 39 Financial Instruments: Recognition and Measurement – The Fair Value Option* (issued June 2005) the IASB limited the ability for an entity to designate any financial asset or financial liability as at fair value through profit or loss (FVTPL). It responded to a number of commentators, including the European Central Bank, the Basel Committee and the EU Commission that expressed concerns that the fair value option in the revisions to IAS 39 in December 2003, which permitted any financial instrument to be designated as at FVTPL on initial recognition, may be used inappropriately. See Deloitte (2005), p. 1. However, IAS 39.AG4I specifically states that venture capital organizations whose business is investing in financial assets

value is not reliably measurable, private equity funds have to classify these equity instruments as available for sale assets (IAS 39.9 and IAS 39.46c).[626]

The fair value option is not available for investments in equity instruments that do not have a quoted market price in an active market, and whose fair value cannot be measured reliably (IAS 39.9). According to IAS 39.AG80, the fair value of investments in equity instruments is *reliably measurable*, if (a) the variability in the range of reasonable fair value estimates is not significant for that instrument, or (b) the probabilities of the various estimates within the range can be reasonably assessed and used in estimating fair value.[627] The standard states that in many situations the variability in the range of reasonable fair value estimates is likely not to be significant and that it is usually possible to estimate the fair value of a financial asset that has been acquired from a third party (IAS 39.AG81).[628]

For private equity funds it is therefore difficult to argue why an investment should not be valued at fair value. For portfolio companies that have positive cash flows or earnings, e.g. later stage portfolio investments, valuation techniques may be applied. Only for those companies that have no revenues or where the future revenues are highly uncertain, e.g. early stage investments, the determination of a fair value may be more problematic. In practice, the application of the 'reliably-measured-test' will be subject to a degree of interpretation by management and auditors.[629] To conclude, when an investment is initially recognized, it shall be measured at its fair value. Only in few cases where the investment is not reliably measurable, it will be accounted for at cost.

For those investments that are classified as fair value through profit or loss, *transaction costs* have to be recorded immediately as expenses in the profit or loss statement.[630] For available for sale investments, these costs shall be capitalized as part of the cost of an investment (IAS 39.43). Transaction costs are incremental costs that are

---

with a view to profiting from their total return in form of interest or dividends and changes in fair value may chose to designate its investment as at fair value through profit and loss.

626 Theoretically, they might be classified as held-for-trading. See Ernst & Young (2004), p. 831.

627 IFRS give no further definition of the term 'significant'. See Böhler (2004b), p. 209.

628 See Ernst & Young (2004), p. 1024.

629 See Bane (2005), p. 5.

630 See Poole/Spooner (2006), p. 152.

directly attributable to the acquisition, issue or disposal of financial instruments. Incremental costs are those that would not have been incurred if the entity had not been acquired, issued or disposed of the financial instrument (IAS 39.9). They include fees and commissions paid to agents, advisors, brokers and dealers (IAS 39.AG13). In private equity transactions costs are usually high. However, whether a private equity firm that classifies its investments as available for sale can capitalize the actual costs of an acquisition of a portfolio company or not might be a matter of judgement. Many advisory, due diligence and legal costs could have been incurred even if the investment had not been acquired. Separating the costs that are direct attributable might be difficult.[631]

Subsequent measurement, income recognition and impairment

The subsequent accounting treatment of an equity instrument depends on its initial classification. All equity instruments are measured at fair value, except those that do no have a quoted market price in an active market and whose fair value cannot be reliably measured (IAS 39.46). The latter can only be classified as available for sale and measured at cost, less impairment. Figure 49 summarizes the requirements.

Classification	Initial recognition	Subsequent measurement	FV gains and losses	Dividends	Impairment	Foreign exchange
Fair value through profit and loss	Fair value (excl. transaction costs)	Fair value (excl. transaction costs)	Profit or loss	Profit or loss	---	Profit or loss
Available-for-sale	Fair value (incl. transaction costs)	Fair value (excl. transaction costs)	Equity	Profit or loss	Profit or loss	Equity
	At cost (incl. transaction costs)	At cost (incl. transaction costs)	---	Profit or loss	Profit or loss	---

Figure 49: Subsequent accounting treatment of equity instruments[632]

All gains and losses that result from any changes in the fair value of equity instruments classified as financial asset at fair value through profit and loss are recognised in the profit or loss statement (IAS 39.55a). Any change in fair value of an available for sale

631 See Bane (2005), p. 4.

632 Based on Ernst & Young (2004), p. 1021.

financial asset is recognized directly in equity.[633] Only when derecognized, which happens usually through as a sale of the asset, its cumulative change in value is recycled in profit or loss (IAS 39.55b). Dividends on an available for sale equity instrument are recognized in the profit and loss statement when the entity's right to receive payment is established (IAS 39.55).

Foreign exchange gains and losses for assets in fair value through profit and loss are accounted for in profit and loss. The recognition of those gains and losses for available for sale assets depends on whether the asset is a monetary item or not.[634] Equity instruments are not monetary items, the gain or loss that is recognised in equity includes any related foreign currency component (IAS 39.AG83).

For all assets that are not measured and classified at fair value through profit or loss an *impairment review* is required (IAS 39.46).[635] At each balance sheet date the private equity fund has therefore to assess whether there is any objective evidence that an equity instrument is impaired (IAS 39.58). Objective evidence of impairment of an equity instrument is given if (a) adverse effects have taken place in the technological, market, economic or legal environment in which the equity issuer operates, or (b) a significant or prolonged decline in the fair value of an investment in an equity instrument below its cost (IAS 39.61) has occurred.[636] If a decline in fair value of an available for sale asset has been recognized in equity and there is objective evidence that it is impaired, the cumulative loss is removed from equity and recognised in profit or loss (IAS 39.67). Reversals of past impairment are not permitted to be recognized in profit or loss (IAS 39.69). Overall it has been demonstrated that the classification can

---

633 The changes are then reported in a statement of changes in equity (IAS 1.99).

634 IAS 21: *The Effects of Changes in Foreign Exchange Rates* defines monetary items as units of currency held and assets and liabilities to be received or paid in a fixed or determinable number of units of currency (IAS 28.8). For monetary items the difference in value resulting from changes in exchange rates is recognized in profit or loss (IAS 39.55b and IAS 39.AG83). For a detailed description see Poole/Spooner (2006), pp. 157 et seq.

635 Assets that are classified as fair value through profit or loss but not measured at fair value, i.e. held-for-trading assets whose fair values cannot be reliably determined, are also subject to an impairment review. See Ernst & Young (2004), p. 1013.

636 See Poole/Spooner (2006), p. 184. Neither 'significant' nor "prolonged" is defined or further explained. A significant decline in value might be defined as a decrease of the present value by a certain percentage, e.g. 20% below the book value. A prolonged decline might be given if over a certain period of time, e.g. 9-12 month, the present value was below the book value.

have significant effects on the income in one specific period. This is illustrated in the example in Figure 50.

Illustrative example – Effect of classification of investments on income

In 2004, a private equity fund invests in three companies A, B and C €1m each. At the end of the year the fair values turn out to be as follows: Company A €3m, B €1.1m, C €0.5m. The decline in value of company C is assumed to be only temporarily, the asset is not impaired. In the next year 2005, company A is sold for €5m and C for €0.25m. Company B is still valued at €1.1m but paid a dividend of €0.5m during the year. Each year, the fund pays €1m of management fees to the fund manager.

In the following, it is presented how a fund account for the investments if it classifies a) all as *assets at fair value through profit and loss (FVTPL)* or b) all investments as *assets available for sale (AFS)*. Also, the income statements for 2004 and 2005 are compared.

	Classification at FVTPL			***Classification at AFS***		
2004:	Dr Investments at FVTPL	€1.6m		Dr Investments at AFS	€1.6m	
	Cr Gain or losses on financial assets		€1.6m	Cr Equity: Fair value reserve (A, B, C)		€1.6m
2005:	Dr Cash (sale A, C; div. B)	€5.75m		Dr Cash	€5.75m	
	Cr Investments at FVTPL		€3.5m	Dr Equity: Fair value reserve (A, B)	€1.5m	
	Cr Gains or losses on financial assets		€1.75m	Cr Investments at AFS		€3.5m
	Cr Dividend income		€0.5m	Cr Gains and losses on financial assets		€3.25m
				Cr Dividend income		€0.5m

Income statements

	2004	2005	2004	2005
Gains and losses on disposal of investments	-	€1.75	-	€3.25m
Unrealized gains and losses	€1.6m	€0	n.a.	n.a.
Dividend income	-	€0.5m	-	€0.5m
Management fee expense	-€1.0m	-€1.0m	-€1.0m	-€1.0m
Income*	€0.6m	€1.25m	-€1.0m	€2.75m

*The difference in total income over 2004 and 2005 is €0.1m and relates to the fair value change of company B which is not realized yet.

Figure 50: Effect of classification of investments on income[637]

The *use of the fair value option* eases the accounting for funds. If they designate private equity investments as assets at fair value through profit or loss rather than available for sale assets, no regular impairment tests are necessary.[638] Furthermore, foreign exchange effects on monetary instruments must not be separated. Probably more important in private equity investments, embedded derivatives do not need to be identified and separately treated. Normally, derivatives are recorded as assets held for trading on the balance sheet with any changes in value in profit or loss (IAS 39.9). Embedded derivatives are parts of hybrid or combined instruments that also include non-derivative host contracts. They have the effect that part of the cash flows of the hybrid instruments vary similar to stand-alone derivatives. In order to prevent that reporting

637 Based on an example on fund-of-funds level in Baker/Luff (2005), p. 6.

638 See Löw/Lorenz (2005), p. 493.

entities circumvent the accounting requirements for derivatives by embedding them in a non-derivative financial instrument, the IFRS require that embedded derivatives of financial instruments have to be accounted for separately as derivatives (IAS 39.BC37).[639] In practice, this concept proofed to be one of the most difficult for preparers as well as users of financial statements.[640] Private equity and venture capital entities regularly structure transactions that include derivative features, e.g. subordinated loans with equity kickers.[641] If these financial instruments are designated at fair value through profit or loss, a separation of the embedded derivative will not be necessary.[642]

In addition to these accounting simplifications when applying the fair value option, it might be argued that this concept best reflects the business and performance of private equity funds as changes in fair value of the investments are recorded in profit or loss.[643] All gains and losses are in one place. On the contrary, as long as those changes have not been realized, this procedure might artificially increase the volatility of earnings.[644] Some argue that it is more appropriate to defer unrealized gains in equity.[645] It will be interesting to follow up, how many private equity companies will actually choose to use the fair value option to account for their equity instruments.

4.2.3.3 Accounting for Associates and Joint Ventures

Accounting for associates and joint ventures under IFRS is dealt with in IAS 28 and IAS 31, respectively. According to IAS 28.2, an associate is an entity over which the investor has significant influence and that is neither a subsidiary nor an interest in a joint venture. *Significant influence* is defined as the power to participate in the financial and operating policy decisions of the investee but that is not control.[646] A stake of more than 20% or more in the voting power of a company is presumed to give rise to

[639] Not all embedded derivatives have to be separated, IAS 39.11 states when this rule has to be applied.

[640] See Ernst & Young (2004), p. 812; Poole/Spooner (2006), p. 105.

[641] See Ernst & Young (2004), p. 818 for an example.

[642] For more details on the accounting for embedded derivatives see Poole/Spooner (2006), pp. 105 et seq; Ernst & Young (2004), pp. 812 et seq.

[643] Bane (2005), p. 4.

[644] See Löw/Lorenz (2005), p. 493.

[645] In some jurisdictions, there might be potential tax consequences. This has to be separately evaluated.

[646] See chapter 4.2.3.4 for a definition of control.

significant influence (IAS 28.6).[647] In practice, it is very often the case that private equity companies have significant influence over their investments, even though the funds might hold less then 20% of voting rights. They normally have board representation rights and participate in policy-making processes.[648] If an investment is classified as an associate the reporting entity has to account for that investment by applying the equity method.[649]

Joint ventures are entities that are *jointly controlled* by the reporting entity and one or more third parties (IAS 31.3).[650] IAS 31 allows for two different accounting treatments, proportionate consolidation and equity method, for accounting for jointly controlled entities.[651]

Venture capital organisations[652], however, are explicitly excluded from applying IAS 28 and IAS 31 if their investments, upon initial recognition, are designated as at fair value through profit and loss or are classified as held for trading and accounted for in accordance with IAS 39. These investments shall be measured at fair value with changes in fair value recognised in profit or loss (IAS 28.1, IAS 31.1). The IASB justifies this exemption and notes that the use of the equity method or proportionate consolidation for venture capital investments often produces information that is not relevant to their investors and that fair value measurement produces more relevant infor-

---

647 See Ernst & Young (2004), p. 465. The standard further differentiates circumstances that will be usually evidence of significant influence, e.g. representation on the board of directors, participating in policy-making processes, material transactions between investor and investee (IAS 28.7).

648 See Bane (2005), p. 9.

649 IFRS describes the equity method in IAS 28.11. Essentially, it means that the investment is initially recorded at cost and adjusted thereafter for the post-acquisition change in the investor's share of net assets of the investee. The investor's share of profit and loss of the investee is recognized in the investor's profit or loss. For details see Ernst & Young (2004), pp. 469 et seq.; Baetge/Kirsch/Thiele (2004), pp. 397 et seq.; Pellens/Fülbier/Gassen (2006), pp. 742 et seq.

650 See Ernst & Young (2004), p. 487. It is somewhat more complex since three different types of joint ventures, i.e. jointly controlled operations, jointly controlled assets, and jointly controlled entities have to be distinguished.

651 See Ernst & Young (2004), p. 488. IFRS defines proportionate consolidation in IAS 31.3. Its application means that the balance sheet of the joint venturer includes its share of the assets that it controls jointly and its share of the liabilities for which it is jointly responsible. The profit and loss statement of the joint venturer includes its share of the income and expenses of the jointly controlled entity (IAS 31.33). See also Ernst & Young (2004), pp. 499 et seq.; Baetge/Kirsch/Thiele (2004), pp. 376 et seq.; Pellens/Fülbier/Gassen (2006), pp. 736 et seq. for details.

652 The IASB does not further define the term venture capital organizations (IAS 28.BC12, IAS 31.BC12.

mation (IAS 28.BC5, IAS 31.BC5). In addition, the IASB argues that possible frequent changes in the level of ownership in venture capital investments causes financial statements to be less useful (IAS 28.BC6, IAS 31.BC6).

These arguments would be also valid for interests in subsidiaries. However, the IASB does not exclude private equity entities from consolidating controlled investments as is discussed in the following.

4.2.3.4 Accounting for Subsidiaries

According to IAS 27.4, if an investment is "controlled" by another entity, the former is known as subsidiary and the latter as parent. Control is the power to govern the financial and operating policies of an entity so as to obtain benefits from its activities (IAS 27.4). A parent and its subsidiaries are collectively referred to as a group, and are accounted for according to IAS 27 using consolidated statements. Consolidated statements involve treating the net assets and activities of subsidiaries held by the parent as if they were part of the parent's own net assets and activities. The objective of consolidated statements is to present the results and state of affairs of the parent and its subsidiaries as if they were a single entity.[653]

IAS 27.13 states that *control* is presumed to exist when the parent owns, directly or indirectly through subsidiaries, more than half of the voting power of an entity unless it can be clearly demonstrated that such ownership does not constitute control. Control is also considered to exist when there is either:[654]

- power over more than half of the voting rights by virtue of an agreement,
- power to govern the financial and operating policies of the entity under a statute or an agreement,
- power to appoint or remove the majority of the members of the board of directors or equivalent governing body, and control of the entity is by that board or body, or

[653] See Ernst & Young (2004), p. 300.

[654] Currently, the IASB work on a new IFRS on consolidation to replace IAS 27 and SIC-12, *Consolidation – Special Purpose Entities*. The control criteria within a single IFRS should be developed for all entities, including special purpose entities. See IASB (2006a).

- power to cast the majority of votes at meetings of the board of directors or an equivalent governing body, and control of the entity is by that board or body.

As a result, in almost all situations where a private equity funds holds more than half the voting power of a portfolio company or controls its board, the fund is required to consolidate the individual company.[655] This might be often the case, especially for buyout funds. Their strategy is regularly to acquire control positions to influence management decisions within the companies. However, also venture capitalists might control a number of their investments without owning a majority stake. They usually require control rights that allow for influencing the operational and financial strategy of its investments.[656]

A previous version of IAS 27 included an explicit exemption from consolidating those subsidiaries which are held for sale.[657] This is not anymore the case.[658] However, substantially the exemption is still valid. If on acquisition a subsidiary meets the criteria to be classified as held for sale in accordance with IFRS 5, *Non-current Assets Held for Sale and Discontinued Operations*, it is accounted for in accordance with that standard (IAS 27.12 together with IFRS 5.11). The difference to the previous practice is, however, that the requirements under which an exemption was allowed have been now clearly specified. To be classified as held for sale, a subsidiary must be available for immediate sale and its sale must be highly probable (IFRS 5.7).[659] The management must be committed to a plan to sell the asset, usually within a one-year period after acquisition, and an active programme should have been initiated to locate a buyer. Furthermore, the asset must be actively marketed for sale at a price that is reasonable in relation to its fair value (IFRS 5.8 and IFRS 5.11).[660] If an investment qualifies as held for sale, it is measured at fair value less costs to sell (IFRS 5.16). An example is provided in Figure 51.

---

[655] See Bane (2005), p. 7.

[656] See Fingerle (2005), pp. 113 et seq.

[657] See Baetge/Kirsch/Thiele (2004), p. 142.

[658] Paragraph 13 of a previous version of IAS 27 required a subsidiary to be excluded from consolidation when control is intended to be temporary. The board considered this issue rather as part of a standard dealing with asset disposal which is IFRS 5. See IAS 27.BC13-14.

[659] See Baetge/Kirsch/Thiele (2004), p. 142.

[660] IFRS 5.9 states that some events and circumstances beyond the parent entity's control may extend the period to complete the deal beyond one year.

Illustrative example – Accounting for a private equity investment acquired exclusively with a view to resale
ValueAdd Investor, a limited partnership, is an investment entity that provides private equity. It holds 70% of the voting share capital of InvesteeComp and has board representation. ValueAdd, before investing in InvesteeComp, formulated an exit strategy to sell its holding in InvesteeComp in four years time, assuming that a number of key operating objectives are achieved.
ValueAdd's management considers not to consolidate InvesteeComp, since their intention is to sell it in the near future. However, ValueAdd needs to consolidate it. According to IFRS 5.8, an investment qualifies as a disposal asset held for sale at acquisition only if the one-year requirement is met. It must be highly probable that all other requirements for held for sale classification (plan to sell, active programme to locate a a buyer, asset actively market for sale) are met.

Figure 51: Illustrative example – Accounting for a private equity investment acquired exclusively with a view to resale[661]

Acquisitions through private equity funds are not intended to be permanent investments. A private equity fund invests only temporarily in a portfolio company.[662] Accordingly, before the changes to IAS 27 and IFRS 5 had been made, many funds did not consolidate their investments. They rather accounted for them according to IAS 39, arguing that the acquired control position would be only temporarily.[663] The IASB does not accept that position and explicitly notes that a subsidiary is not excluded from consolidation simply because the investor is a venture capital organisation (IAS 27.19).

EVCA shows the impact of the consolidation on private equity entities.[664] It concludes that between the date of the initial investment and the date of the exit an investor who relies on consolidated accounts gets a misleading picture of the performance of the investments. If the portfolio company needs to be consolidated and realizes losses - a situation typical for venture capital-backed companies - the value of the equity decreases. However, due to for example technical success in product development, the fair value of the investments may have actually increased.[665]

The previous chapters describe the accounting for private equity portfolio companies according to IFRS. Unless a portfolio company is a subsidiary, the private equity fund

661 Based on PWC (2006).

662 See Achleitner/Müller (2004), p. 15.

663 BÖHLER showed that eight out of eleven Swiss private equity companies that published annual reports in 2002 according to IFRS did not consolidate their investments. The remaining three funds did not invest in more than 20% of the equity stake. See Böhler (2004b), p. 211.

664 See EVCA (2003a).

665 See EVCA (2003a), p. 5.

manager may measure the investment at fair value. The accounting treatment is summarized by Figure 52. It is in line with the business model and the investors' information needs if the fund managers exercise the fair value option and classify all investments as fair value through profit and loss with changes in the fair value recognised directly in the profit and loss statements.

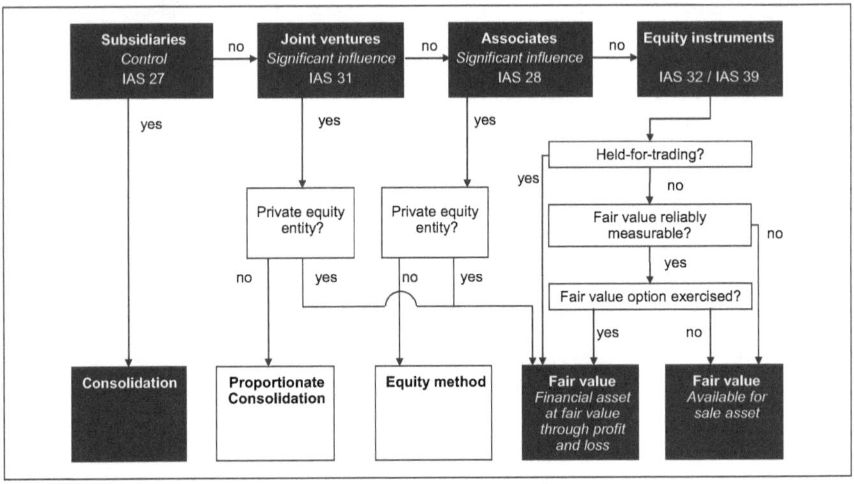

Figure 52: Accounting for portfolio companies according to IFRS[666]

The next chapters provide a critical assessment of the accounting according to IFRS with a special focus on the consolidation requirements.

4.2.4 Discussion of Financial Reporting Requirements

4.2.4.1 Consolidation of Portfolio Company Investments

Whether private equity portfolio company investments that are subsidiaries of private equity entities according to the control model in IAS 27 should be consolidated or instead be measured at fair value according to IAS 39 had been controversially discussed during the exposure period of the *IASB's improvements project*.[667] Although industry associations, especially the European Venture Capital & Private Equity Association

---

666 See Achleitner/Müller (2003), p. 5.

667 The improvements project included the revision of IAS 27 and IAS 28. See Ernst & Young (2004), p. 464.

heavily intervened and brought forward their arguments against this regulation, the IASB has not yet changed its position.[668] Basically, two different lines of argumentation can be identified. The IASB focuses on the ability to control whereas the private equity industry points out the needs of its specific business model.[669]

Against the background of recent accounting scandals for example at Enron[670], the IASB has been reluctant to make an exception for private equity probably because of the general need for strict rules to prevent off balance sheet items.[671] This is expressed in a statement by the IASB chairman, Sir David Tweedie, who said: "The worry is that a company won't have to set up a special purpose vehicle to hide stuff off the balance sheet. It can just become a venture capitalist and lump all the debt and losses in there instead".[672] *The IASB's position is that the requirement to consolidate is triggered by the parent's ability to control the investee* and should not depend on the basis of the nature of the controlling entity. The IASB draws a clear distinction between investments in controlled entities, i.e. subsidiaries, and those in uncontrolled entities. The fact that an entity is controlled is regarded as more important than that it is held as a as part of a portfolio of investments. Irrespective of the investor's industry, or its strategy for holding the investment, a consistent accounting approach, i.e. consolidation, should be applied to all controlled entities.[673]

In contrast, *the private equity industry refers to its specific business model* which is the management of a portfolio of investments. It argues that consolidation is not an appropriate basis for the type of investments private equity entities make and the accounting regulation should distinguish between traditional operating trade groups and private equity entities. Whereas trade groups usually invest for strategic reasons and initially

---

668 See EVCA (2002b), pp. 1 et seq; EVCA (2003b); Anonymous author (2003), p. 410; Becker (2004), p. 46. For the position of the IASB see IASB (2002), pp. 8 et seq.

669 Most of the following argumentation is relevant for all *investment companies* in general, not only private equity entities alone.

670 At the end of 2001, it was revealed that Enron, an American energy company, sustained its reported financial condition mostly by systematic and creatively planned accounting fraud. It finally filed for bankruptcy. For details on the case of Enron see Healy/Palepu (2003).

671 See European Commission (2006), pp. 23 et seq.

672 Quoted in Thomson (2004), p. 25.

673 See Ernst & Young (2004), p. 371. The IASB presents its view at some length in IAS 27, Basis for Conclusions (IAS 27.BC16-23).

plan to hold the new company for an unlimited period of time, private equity entities in comparison invest for a limited period of time with solely financial interests. They manage each of their investments separately from the rest of the portfolio on a *stand-alone-basis*.[674] Trade groups focus on current income from their subsidiaries, whereas private equity entities mainly focus on capital gains when they exit the investments.[675] The argumentation of the private equity industry is justifiable from two perspectives: the ultimate purpose of consolidated statements and the investors information requirements.

The *purpose of consolidated statements* is to show the accounts of a group, its results and state of affair, as if that group was 'one enterprise'.[676] Inter-company balances and unrealized profits on inter-company sales resulting from inter-company transactions need to be eliminated. Inter-company transactions are transactions between legal entities within a consolidated group of companies, not only between the parent and its subsidiaries but also, if more than one subsidiary exists, directly among subsidiaries.[677] These transactions would not become transparent by analyzing the separate financial accounts of the individual entities only. The more intense the linkages between the parent company and its subsidiaries are, the higher is the risk that the information provided through separate financial statements is misleading.[678] Through the preparation of consolidated accounts and the elimination of the mentioned inter-company transactions these imperfections should be overcome.[679]

---

674 See European Commission (2006), p. 12.

675 For a detailed differentiation of trade groups and private equity entities see Achleitner/Müller (2004), pp. 14 et seq.

676 See Elliott/Elliott (2005), p. 513.

677 Examples for inter-company transactions are interest- or non-interest-bearing loans, inventory or fix assets transfers, patent technology transfers, bond purchases, dividend payments, expense allocations, or inter-company sales.

678 See Achleitner/Müller (2004), p. 30.

679 For more details on the purpose of consolidated financial statements see among others Busse von Colbe et al. (2003), pp. 26 et seq.

In private equity entities these inter-company transactions usually do not occur.[680] Except from the financial resources that the private equity fund provides to its portfolio companies, no further inter-company transactions take place between the fund and portfolio companies and among portfolio companies. Each portfolio company is individually managed and financed.[681] There are no cross-holdings. Cash flow from one company cannot be used in another company. Neither is debt managed, negotiated or secured on a group basis, nor is there usually any other sharing of assets or other resources among the group. Purchasing activities are not co-ordinated or negotiated centrally. Taxes are not planned on a group basis.

If transactions happen between portfolio companies, the transaction prices will correspond to the market prices for at least two reasons. The management of each portfolio company is independent from other companies or the fund as a group and is incentivized with equity or quasi equity stakes which bring them, as well as the fund managers and their investors, a share of the profits directly related to the value created in the exit of the company.[682] Furthermore, the fund manager would not force their portfolio company to act against its interests as this would severely damage its reputation and would make finding new investment opportunities more difficult.[683] To conclude, given that private equity entities manage their investment portfolio on a stand-alone-approach, inter-company transactions and balances as in trade groups do not occur. If they occur, they are typically priced similar to market transactions. Consolidated accounts are therefore not relevant.

In addition, there is the private equity fund *investors' perspective* and the question whether consolidated statements do fulfil their information needs. The IASB states that consolidated accounts reveal the extent of the operations, the assets and liabilities of the entities the fund controls and concludes that users' information needs would not be

---

680 These conclusions might be different in the special cases of corporate venture capital funds. *Corporate venture capital funds* are a specific type of private equity entities. They are often established by corporates in order to invest under a strategic perspective ("windows on technology"). They can have both a strategic and financial focus and inter-company transactions might occur more frequently due to the strategic proximity of the portfolio companies and their corporate investors.

681 See Achleitner/Müller (2004), pp. 20 et seq.

682 See European Commission (2006), p. 12.

683 See Achleitner/Müller (2004), p. 23.

well served if those controlling investments were measured only at fair value. To be able to assess the financial position, results and cash flows of the group, the investors need consolidated statements (IAS 27.BC22). This may be true for traditional corporate investors. However, it is questionable how a line-by-line incorporation of the results and net assets of all companies in a private equity portfolio on an aggregated basis should be more useful for the predictability of the fund's cash flow than the fair value accounting of those investments. Private equity investments are managed on a stand-alone-basis and investors are interested in the individual fair value of the investments and how that has changed since the previous reporting date.[684] Sales, costs and profits are useful information on an individual company basis to support the valuation of the single investment but not on an aggregate basis on fund level.

Furthermore, fund investors as the users of financial statements wish to be able to compare the performance and financial position of their investments overtime and with other private equity funds. Consolidation on the fund level could distort that comparability.[685] The portfolio of a fund frequently changes since investments are added and disposed to the portfolio. Typically, the fund buys investments over the first half of its lifetime, and disinvests the holdings over the second half. Furthermore, the level of ownership in one company could also change during the life of the fund, especially in venture capital,[686] which potentially alters the accounting method that the fund might use. A line-by-line consolidation causes difficulties for a user of consolidated statements to understand the ongoing profitability of the group over time. The comparability between different private equity funds at the same point of time is also affected since they may pursue different strategies. The strategy of one entity might include investing in controlling stakes and therefore has to consolidate the investments whereas another only invests in minority stakes. Only fair value accounting ensures that the funds will be comparable on a consistent basis.[687]

---

684 See McCurry (2005), p. 44.

685 McCurry (2005), p. 45.

686 In venture capital, multiple financing rounds depending on the achievement of milestones (so-called staging) are commonly agreed on. The valuation of the company and the resulting ownership share of the entrepreneurs regularly depend on the achievement of milestones. See Engel (2003), p. 285. In buyout companies, multiple financing rounds are less common.

687 See Böhler (2004b), p. 219.

The Belgian listed private equity company GIMV N.V. is an illustrative example how private equity entities deal with the consolidation requirement today. It acknowledges that the consolidated accounts required by IFRS is not relevant and presents two sets of accounts. Their explanation is illustrated in Figure 53.

Illustrative example – Explanation why two sets of consolidated accounts are presented in annual reporting

Basis of preparation: "(...) GIMV is required to draw up its consolidated financial statements in accordance with the International Financial Reporting Standards (...). The Group has opted (...) to continue presenting two sets of consolidated accounts, that is the 'statutory' consolidation and a 'limited' consolidation. A significant impact of the transition to IFRS is that a number of companies in the investment portfolio which the Group is deemed to control in accordance with IAS 27 have to be fully consolidated. Given that these investments have been expressly made with a view to creating capital gains and generating income, we believe that the consolidation of enterprises included in the investment portfolio is not a relevant yardstick for measuring the Group's performance and can even be potentially misleading (...).

The limited consolidation is prepared using the same valuation rules as those used for the statutory consolidated financial statements of the group produced in accordance with the 'International Financial Reporting Standards', but not consolidating a certain number of companies (...) from the Group's investment portfolio, over which GIMV exercises control as defined by IAS 27 and which are therefore fully consolidated in the statutory consolidation. In the limited consolidation, these shareholdings are valued at fair value in accordance with the international valuation guidelines for private equity companies. The limited consolidation gives a more realistic view of the results and the value of the Group, and will enable investors and other stakeholders to understand and monitor the Group's financial performance."

Figure 53: Illustrative example – Explanation why two sets of consolidated annual accounts are presented in the annual reporting of GIMV group[688]

The IASB states that a parent could present information about the fair value of consolidated investments in the notes or in separate financial statements that might be prepared in addition to the required consolidated accounts (IAS 27.BC22). According to the IFRS framework, however, benefits derived from information should exceed the cost of providing it (IFRS Framework, paragraph 4). The costs that arise by preparing consolidated accounts can be substantial.[689] Knowing that the information provided by consolidated accounts is of limited use,[690] it might not be justified that private equity funds are required to prepare those.

---

688 GIMV (2006), p. 76.

689 See Bane (2005), p. 7. Obtaining the relevant financial information from subsidiaries can be difficult. Financial statements of parent and subsidiaries shall be prepared at the same reporting date (IAS 27.26). Furthermore, the accounting policies of parent and subsidiary must be consistent (IAS 27.29). Funds might need to invest in new accounting and reporting systems. See McCurry (2005), p. 44.

690 See Thomson (2004), p. 24.

In the United States, investment companies in general, and therefore also private equity funds, are currently granted an exemption from consolidation by the FASB.[691] It accepts the industry accounting practice which is formulated in *AICPA Audit and Accounting Guide: Audits of Investment Companies (the guide)* of the American Institute of Certified Public Accountants (AICPA). According to the guide, consolidation by an investment company of a non-investment company investment is not appropriate.[692] Investment companies shall report investments at fair value.[693] Currently, AICPA together with FASB work on a precise definition of 'investment companies' to clarify the scope of the guide.[694]

To sum up, there are valid arguments why private equity funds should be excluded from the requirement to present consolidated statements. It is therefore necessary to clearly identify private equity funds, or investment companies in more general, in order to be able to exclude these entities from parts of the regulation. The IASB notes that even if it had accepted the argumentation and had wished to make differentiations, it did not see how it could meaningful distinguish private equity entities from other entities (IAS 27.BC20). Clearly, this is a challenge but a solution to this will be discussed, as an excursus, in the following chapter.

4.2.4.2 Distinguishing Private Equity Funds from Non-Investment Companies

The IFRS do not define private equity funds.[695] If the standard setters, however, wish to make differentiations, it needs to be able to distinguish between private equity funds, or investment companies in more general, and non-investment companies.[696]

---

691 *FAS No. 94, Consolidation of all majority-owned subsidiaries,* does not specifically exclude investment companies from its scope. However, it acknowledges in paragraph 53 the existence of specialized industry practices for investment companies.

692 See AICPA (2000), paragraph 7.04.

693 See AICPA (2000), paragraph 1.32.

694 In December 2002, the Accounting Standard Executive Committee (AcSEC) of the AICPA issued an exposure draft of a statement of opinion (SOP) concerning the clarification of the scope of the as well as the accounting by parent companies and equity method investors, for investments in investment companies. An updated version of the exposure draft was issued in December 2005. See AICPA (2006).

695 This is somewhat odd since these entities are refrained from using the equity method or proportional consolidation when accounting for associate investments or joint ventures (IAS 28.1 and IAS 31.1). Explicitly named by the standards are 'venture capital organizations and similar enti-

In the absence of clear guidance, judgement shall be used to interpret the terms in the IFRS (IAS 8.10). In making this judgement, according to IAS 8.11-12 the requirements and guidance in similar standards, the definitions and concepts in the IFRS Framework, the most recent pronouncements of other standard setters that use similar conceptual frameworks, accounting literature and accepted industry practice shall be considered.[697] To elaborate a definition of private equity entities, it is therefore referred to two sources: AICPA's exposure draft to clarify the term investment companies[698] and a study of the CENTER FOR ENTREPRENEURIAL AND FINANCIAL STUDIES (CEFS) which elaborates differences between trade groups and private equity entities.[699] Aim of this chapter is to compile a checklist that can be used not only by accountants and auditors but also legislators and regulators to identify a private equity fund.

The question is whether the entity under consideration is rather a private equity fund, i.e. investment company, or a non-investment company. The underlying assumption is that non-investment companies have strategic interests in its investments. With respect to the consolidation issue the following is assumed: If entities have strategic interests in their investments, it is very likely that the related entities trade among each other and a consolidation of controlled investments by the investor would be appropriate. Therefore, in order to identify private equity funds, it needs to be proofed that they solely have financial interests.

To do this, two sets of factors should be checked. The first set contains requirements for a qualification as a private equity entity. If these requirements are fulfilled, a second set of factors needs to be considered. However, not all of these factors are individually required to be fulfilled but the overall assessment of all factors together may proof that the entity pursues financial interests only.[700]

---

ties', but private equity entities are subsumed. U.S. GAAP uses the term investment companies. See AICPA (2005).

696 Non-investment companies are any operating entities, or trade groups that do not solely invest for financial reasons.

697 See Ruhnke/Nerlich (2004), pp. 389 et seq.

698 See AICPA (2005).

699 See Achleitner/Müller (2004).

700 A similar approach is suggested by AICPA. See AICPA (2005).

Necessary for an entity to be identified as private equity fund is that its expressed business purpose is to invest in companies and thereby pursuing only financial interests, i.e. exclusively in order to realize capital gains or current income. Other than purely financial benefits could be for example the acquisition of intangible assets, the use of processes or technology that belong to the investee, or agreements to cooperate in developing, producing or distributing of products and services.[701]

Furthermore, private equity entities limit their risks through a diversification strategy. Most investment guidelines agreed upon between investors and private equity entities limit the investment of the fund's resources in a single portfolio company.[702] Holding multiple investments is therefore a second required factor.

Private equity funds usually pursue their financial interest by realizing a capital gain when exiting their investments and not by continuously obtaining current income. This entails that the investments will be sold again in the short- to medium-term (usually 3 to 8 years). An exit strategy for their investments is therefore an integral part of the initial investment decision and is another obligatory factor to consider.[703]

A last requirement is that the entity has no substantial activities, assets or liabilities unrelated to its investment activities. If an entity is part of a larger corporation, e.g. corporate venture capitalists, its investment activities have to be legally and organizationally separated from the unrelated business. A separate management responsibility for the investment activities and separate controlling and reporting systems are required.[704]

Other factors considered individually are not inevitable necessary to define a private equity entity but could give indications as to whether an entity is rather an entity with a strategic orientation or a solely financially oriented private equity entity. These factors relate to both the investors, i.e. limited partner in a partnership, and the investees. Private equity funds usually act as intermediaries, i.e. they collect capital from a number of investors. The more significant the influence of an individual investor in a fund, the

701 See Achleitner/Müller (2004), p. 31.

702 See Feinendegen/Schmidt/Wahrenburg (2003), p. 1180; Gompers/Lerner (1996), p. 485.

703 An agreement to exit the investment is usually documented in the financing contracts between the private equity entities and their investees. See Achleitner/Müller (2004), p. 31.

704 See Löw/Lorenz (2005), p. 498.

more likely is the possibility that this influence is used strategically. If an investor is also actively involved in the day-to-day management of the entity or decides about the investment strategy of the entity, it is likely that this engagement could be out of strategic motives. In these cases, it could be that the entity is not a private equity entity.[705]

With respect to the portfolio company investment, the level of ownership interest in the investees should be considered. If the entity has high level of ownership in its investments it is able to exercise control and could effectively follow strategic interests. The less majority holdings an entity has, the more likely is the existence of a private equity entity. Buyouts funds usually have only controlling interests in its investment companies and still classify as private equity entities. However, it is more likely that an entity with minority investments follows only financial interests. If a centralized management for investees exists on fund level that carries out service functions for portfolio companies, such as administration services, legal advice, procurement or similar, it is an indication that the entity is less likely a private equity entity. Correspondingly, the more often the entity is involved in the day-to-day management of the portfolio companies, the higher is the probability of a strategic interest. Another factor to be considered is that in private equity entities an internal capital market including financing guarantees or borrowing arrangements or a cash management within the group usually does not exist. Lastly, the compensation of the portfolio company's management should not depend on the investing entity's results. If it does, it is a signal that strategic goals of the entire group are more important and, respectively, strategic interests are pursued with the investment. Figure 54 presents this procedure in form of a checklist.

To sum up, a single factor of the second part of the present list gives only an indication but is not a proof whether an entity pursues only financial interests. All these factors have to be considered together and weighted to conclude whether an entity is a private equity fund or not. Based on the presented checklist and prudent judgement, it should be able to distinguish private equity entities from non-investment groups. Therefore, regulators, e.g. standard setters like the IASB, could grant exemptions from regulations. The checklist presented provides a feasible solution.

---

[705] Corporate venture capital investors could be involved in investment decisions but act only out of financial reasons. Typically, however, they have strategic goals.

Required factors to identify a private equity fund with solely financial interests		
1.	Business purpose is investing mainly for capital appreciation and not for strategic reasons	☑
2.	Entity makes multiple investments	☑
3.	Exit plans for each portfolio company investment exist	☑
4.	Entity has no other main activities than its investment activities and has no significant assets or liabilities other than those related to its investment activities	☑

Considered and overall weighted factors to identify a private equity fund with solely financial interests				
5.	Number of investors (limited partners) in the entity	High	☑ ☐ ☐ ☐ ☐	Low
6.	Type of investors (limited partners)	Passive	☑ ☐ ☐ ☐ ☐	Active
7.	Level of ownership interest in investees	Low	☑ ☐ ☐ ☐ ☐	High
8.	Centralized management for investees	No	☑ ☐ ☐ ☐ ☐	Yes
9.	Involvement in day-to-day management	No	☑ ☐ ☐ ☐ ☐	Yes
10.	Existence of internal capital markets	No	☑ ☐ ☐ ☐ ☐	Yes
11.	Cash management within the group	No	☑ ☐ ☐ ☐ ☐	Yes
12.	Investee's management compensation depends only on investee's results	Yes	☑ ☐ ☐ ☐ ☐	No
	Probability of being a private equity entity with solely financial interests	**High** ☑		**Low** ☐

Figure 54: Checklist to identify a private equity fund[706]

4.2.4.3 Information Gap of Statutory Financial Statements for Fund Investors

The relevance and appropriateness of information provided to fund investors through statutory financial statements prepared under general accepting accounting principles is minor. General accepted accounting principles, i.e. IFRS, have been developed for traditional companies. Statutory accounts alone are therefore insufficient to provide a full picture of the performance of private equity funds. They do not mirror special characteristics of the business model, i.e. its two-tier business model, the significant importance of the fund's management team, the value creation at individual investment level, and the challenging valuation of the underlying portfolio company investments.[707]

The private equity fund is characterized through a *two-tier business model.* It is an intermediary through which the investors' investments into the portfolio companies are channelled. The fund manager invests in a series of underlying companies to produce a

706 Based on Achleitner/Müller (2004), p. 33; AICPA (2005), pp. 14 et seq.

707 See for this and the following argumentation Böhler (2004b), pp. 263 et seq.

diversified portfolio based on a pre-agreed strategy with its investors. Therefore, as derived in the analysis in chapter 3.8.3, information separately on aggregated fund and individual investment level is essential for fund investors in order to follow the current status of their overall fund investment and to asses the historical and expected performance, including any costs related to it. Statutory financial statements do not explicitly distinguish between fund and portfolio information level.[708] Furthermore, according to IFRS, it is not required that each fund investor gets an individual capital account statement which displays his share of the partnership's net asset value.[709]

Financial statements also neglect that the *fund's management team is of significant importance.* The team members' quality and ability to source, exercise, manage and exit investments determine the success of the fund investments.[710] Non-financial information on the team and the processes they have implemented are necessary.

The *value creation occurs on individual portfolio company level.* In addition to providing financial funds, the private equity managers usually provide technical and management assistance to its investees as needed and requested. Investors want to understand the development of each portfolio company as this is important to be able to evaluate the fund manager's performance and his overall effort and appropriateness of the measures taken to create value. IFRS does not require that individual company figures and comments on single investments are disclosed. According to the standards, the reporting entity is the fund. The provision of detailed information on individual portfolio companies is not required.

Finally, the *valuation of private equity investments is challenging* but essential for fund investors to know. It has been elaborated in chapter 3.8.3, that the fund investors need to understand how the fund managers derive the valuations for each single investment. Therefore, the methodologies and assumptions that are used to calculate single investments value should be disclosed. IFRS 7 requires that a description is given how the fair values have been determined.[711] However, these are general measurement

---

708 See Böhler (2004b), p. 263.

709 See Böhler (2004b), p. 274.

710 KASERER/DILLER for example conclude that GP's skills have a significant influence on the fund's return. See Kaserer/Diller (2004d), p. 18.

711 See Kuhn/Scharpf (2005), p. 238.

guidelines and are not specific with respect to each single portfolio company investment.

Furthermore, IFRS do not require the disclosure of an internal rate of return. As statutory financial statements have a calendar year (or quarter of a year) perspective, no data since inception of the fund vehicle is required to be disclosed. However, data such as the cash flows both between the fund and the portfolio companies and the fund and the fund investors since inception would be helpful to understand and calculate performance figures.

It can be summarized that statutory financial statements do not meet private equity fund investors' information needs. Consequently, additional information has to be presented in the so-called "investor reporting" which will be subject to chapter 4.4. A significant part not only of the financial statutory statements but also the investor reporting concerns however the fair value measurement of private equity portfolio companies. Therefore, it is important to get a deeper understanding of the valuation of portfolio companies. The next chapter will specifically deal with the definition of 'fair value'. It will answer the question, *how* to determine a fair value of a private equity portfolio investment.

4.3 Fair Value Measurement of Private Equity Portfolio Company Investments

4.3.1 Definition and Concept of Fair Value

Over the last years, the valuation of unrealized private equity portfolio company investments has been subject of great discussion among the private equity industry participants, especially between fund managers, their investors and auditors.[712] The valuation of unrealized portfolio company investments is an integral part of the reporting process and the disclosure of the values is an important element of the information

---

712 It is necessary to distinguish the valuation for reporting purpose (post-investment stage) from the valuation that is carried out at a pre-investment stage. The latter is pursued in order to support the investment decision. It is different with respect to the level of information that is available, to the valuation techniques that can be used, and to the financial and time resources that the fund manager is able to spend. See Böhler (2004b), p. 220. Much more time and money can be spent when valuing the investment for investment decisions. For a general summary of the different valuation purposes and functions see for example Ballwieser (2004), p. 2; Achleitner/Nathusius (2004), pp. 14 et seq.

provided to fund investors. Performance reporting is of little value unless the underlying valuations are based on sound valuation principles.

The reason why the topic has been heavily discussed is that there has been a fundamental paradigm shift in the approach to valuation from a cost-based approach towards a fair value measurement approach. This shift has been triggered by two developments: The relevance of international general accepted accounting standards, which require fair value accounting, has been increasing over time.[713] Furthermore, the rising pressure from fund investors in private equity funds who themselves need to report the fair value of their private equity portfolio.

Until recently, the common private equity valuation practice for reporting purposes was based on a historical cost-based approach. Investments were carried at costs unless a material impairment indicated a write-down in value or a financing round with new investors supported a write-up.[714] This approach was regarded as appropriately conservative. By contrast, the fair value model requires regular revaluation of the investments.

According to IFRS, fair value is defined as 'the amount for which an asset could be exchanged, or a liability settled, between knowledgeable, willing parties in an arm's length transaction' (IAS 39.9).[715] Four elements constitute the term: the hypothetical transaction, the willing parties, the knowledgeable parties, and the arm's length transaction. [716] Fair value is established under the assumption of a *hypothetical transaction*. The result of that hypothetical transaction is an exchange price that reflects the price

---

713 See chapter 4.2.1. Funds that need to comply with accounting standards are required to disclose fair values of their investments.

714 See Blaydon/Wainwright (2004a), p. 45. This approach was based on a set of guidelines that had been proposed to the U.S. National Venture Capital Association (NVCA) in 1989. Chapter 4.3.4 provides details on industry valuation guidelines.

715 There are also definitions with the same meaning but with a slightly different wording in IAS 16.6, IAS 18.7, IAS 19.7, IAS 20.3 and IAS 40.5. U.S. GAAP defines fair value in the SFAS 157, Fair Value Measurement as follows: 'Fair value is the price that would be received for an asset or paid for a liability in a transaction between market participants at the measurement date.' See Lüdenbach/Freiberg (2006), p. 437. However, BIEKER demonstrates that despite the different wording the actual requirements are the same. See Bieker (2006), pp. 7 et seq.

716 See Dohrn (2004), p. 3. This is true for the definition of fair value according to IFRS as well as the definition according to U.S. GAAP. See Bieker (2006), p. 8; Feldman (2005), p. 2.

that would come out in an exchange between willing and knowledgeable parties.[717] Buyers and sellers are *willing parties* of a transaction if they are not forced to transact. Fair value measurement furthermore assumes that they have the *reasonable knowledge* of relevant facts.[718] With respect to company valuation that means that buyers and sellers are aware of the true financial condition of the firm and also have expectations of future performance consistent with those held by knowledgeable market participants.[719] The parties are furthermore assumed to be or to act as independent market participants, i.e. as if they were not related to each other. If that is the case, they pursue an *at arm's length transaction.*[720]

In perfect and complete markets, there would be only one price for an asset or a liability.[721] In reality, however, fair value is not well defined and alternative fair value constructs are likely to differ, e.g. entry value, exit value and value in use. The entry value of an asset is the cost to purchase the asset, the exit value is the price at which it could be sold for, and the value in use is the incremental entity-specific firm value attributable to an asset.[722] It has not been clearly communicated which value construct the IASB follows. However, it had expressed a preference for the exit price notion of fair value.[723]

4.3.2 Valuation Process

The valuation activity can be modelled as a sequential process with four general stages as described in Figure 55. These stages are information gathering, fair value measurement, approval and disclosure of values. In each stage different parties are involved.

---

717 See Dohrn (2004), p. 3; Feldman (2005), p. 2.

718 See Mercer (1999), p. 20.

719 See Feldman (2005), p. 3; Bieker (2006), p. 8.

720 See Bieker (2006), p. 8; Dohrn (2004), p. 126. U.S. GAAP refer to market participants whereas IFRS use the term at arm's length but the economic meaning is the same.

721 See Barth/Landsman (1995), p. 99.

722 See Beaver (1987), p. 67; Bieker (2006), p. 9.

723 See IASB (2006b), p. 2; Dohrn (2004), p. 121. This is equivalent to U.S. GAAP.

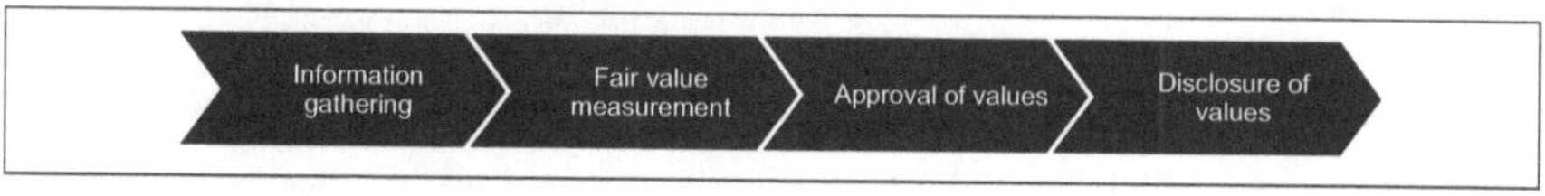

Figure 55: Valuation process

In order to determine the fair value of a portfolio company investment, the fund managers need to *gather information* from three different sources (Figure 56). The first data source is the company itself. Quantitative information such as sales, EBITDA, cash flow, net debt, actual and planned data and qualitative information on team, products and development is in general available through the constant monitoring of the investment by the fund managers. A second data source is the financial contract which includes information on the special type of financial instruments, total ownership, or additional contractual rights. Thirdly, capital market data are required such as market multiples or beta-factors, based on similar company transactions and similar market valuations. Whereas the data on the company and the contracts is usually gathered, stored and managed internally, information on capital market is supplied by external data providers.[724]

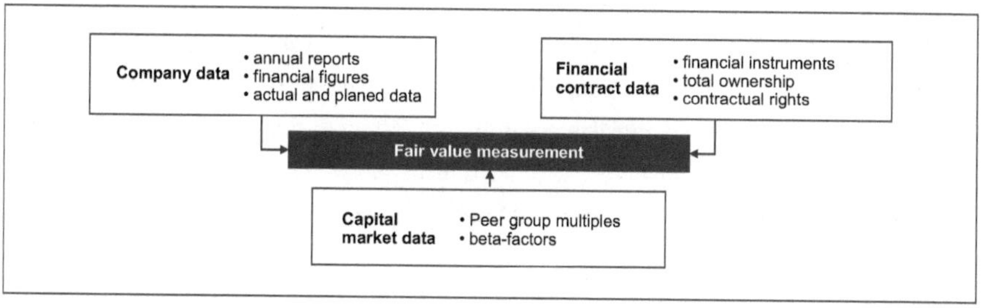

Figure 56: Data sources for fair value measurement

The second stage of the valuation process is the actual *fair value measurement* which means determining the fair value by applying one or more valuation techniques and making reasonable discounts and adjustments. Responsible for the valuation of the single investments is usually the investment manager who is in charge of monitoring the portfolio company. He is supported by the fund's chief financial officer and his

[724] External data providers are for example Bloomberg, Reuters, Thomson Financial, VentureXperts, or VentureOne.

team.[725] The finance team usually initiates the process because of its responsibility to prepare the quarterly and annual reports. Ideally, the valuation is documented on a valuation worksheet that comprises details on input data, assumptions, techniques, and additional comments on the company's financial and managerial aspects and the business development.[726]

An appropriate documentation is a prerequisite for the third stage of the entire valuation process, the *approval of values* by internal and external parties. Internally, the fund's managing partners typically approve the valuation in a so-called valuation meeting. Larger funds may have an additional internal valuation committee that finally decides about each valuation in the portfolio.[727] Externally, there may be an approval by the auditors on the one hand and the fund investors on the other hand. The valuation will be included in the balance sheet, so it is subject to an audit whenever the fund's annual statements are audited.[728] The respective auditors are looking for a well designed and documented process in order to be able to understand and concur with the rationale for each assumption and choice made by the fund managers.[729] In addition, the advisory board which represents the fund investors might review and ratify the valuations of the portfolio company investments as part of their governance role.[730]

The last stage of the valuation process comprises the *disclosure of values* and any relevant data on assumptions and inputs. The fair values have to be used in the fund's accounts, if these are prepared consistent with IFRS. Whether they are furthermore an integral part of the additional investors reporting depends on the decision of the fund managers as this part is not regulated. As long as the accounting values were prepared

---

725 See Achleitner et al. (2004b), p. 707. The authors find in a study among funds in German speaking countries that in 83% of the cases the investment managers, and in around 30% a special finance team, are involved in the valuation process. Percentages will not add up to 100% because respondents could check more than one answer.

726 See Böhler (2004b), pp. 245 et seq.

727 Good practice could be that the fund managers consult with co-investors on valuation issues. See Lerner/Hardymon/Leamon (2005), p. 418.

728 Investors usually ask for audited reports once a year. See PwC (2003), p. 23. Sometimes auditors specifically sign off on the valuations.

729 See Böhler (2004b), p. 251. In practice, the auditors will not test each valuation. They concentrate on the process and the internal controls. See PwC (2003), p. 23.

730 See Lerner/Hardymon/Leamon (2005), p. 418; Böhler (2004b), p. 251. As has been shown in chapter 3.5.1, this is a valuable task of advisory boards according to fund investors.

under the cost-based approach rather than the fair value approach, there were often different values in the accounts and in investors reporting.[731] However, to be consistent and more credible about the actual valuations, funds that measure their investments at fair value should present identical values in both parts of the reporting.

The valuation exercise plays also an important role in the fund manager's internal management of a private equity portfolio.[732] For internal purposes the fund managers have no external restrictions on the method and assumptions used for the valuation exercise. Valuation for reporting purposes, however, is regulated by accounting standards and international valuation guidelines. These requirements will be therefore discussed next.

4.3.3 Accounting Standards Requirements

The requirements to value private equity fund investments, i.e. equity instruments, according to IFRS are prescribed by IAS 39. Equity instruments have to be recognised and measured at fair value, no matter whether they are designated as financial assets at fair value through profit or loss or as available for sale assets (IAS 39.43).[733]

It is presumed when determining fair value that the business entity is valued within a going concern context, without any intention or need to liquidate, to materially curtail the scale of its operations or to undertake a transaction on adverse terms (IAS 39.AG69).[734] The fair value has to be determined at each respective reporting date.

---

731 See Snow (2004), p. 43. There could be even three kinds of reported valuations: valuations in financial statements, valuation projections in investors reporting, and valuation estimates in private placement memoranda of new raised funds. The latter are intended to get the attraction of potential new investors.

732 See Michas (1997), p. 1. Valuations may be important in internal evaluations of investment managers. See Thoen (2002), p. 6. They indicate the progress on a regular basis which may lead to strategic decisions about an investment's future. Having analyzed how comparable companies are valued in the public or private markets, fund managers may conclude to make adjustments to a planned exit strategy to take advantage of certain trends or market conditions. Valuation analysis reveals how the markets evaluate and reward particular attributes of companies in a given industry. Fund managers can then influence the corporate strategy to position the company to achieve the highest possible equity valuation upon an exit or public offering.

733 Exempted are equity investments that do not have a quoted market price in an active market and whose fair value cannot be reliably measured (IAS 39.46c).

734 See Bellavite-Hövermann/Barckow (2003), p. 78; Poole/Spooner (2006), pp. 169 et seq. Amounts that would be received or paid in a forced transaction, involuntary liquidation, or distress sale are therefore not a fair value (IAS 39.69).

However, the amount should reflect *adjusting events* after that date until the day when the financial statements are issued (IAS 10.8). Adjusting events provide more evidence of conditions that already existed at the balance sheet date and which have an influence on the value of the assets (IAS 10.3).[735]

For the purpose of measuring a financial instrument's fair value, IAS 39 distinguishes basically two types of instruments. On the one hand those instruments for which quoted prices in an active market exist, and on the other hand those instruments for which no such market is available (IAS 39.AG71-79).[736] Figure 57 provides an overview how to establish the fair value of an equity instrument. In general, the standard implies a valuation hierarchy that requires a market-based approach in setting the fair value and only allows the use of more entity-specific data and models if the former is not possible. Three levels are identifiable.

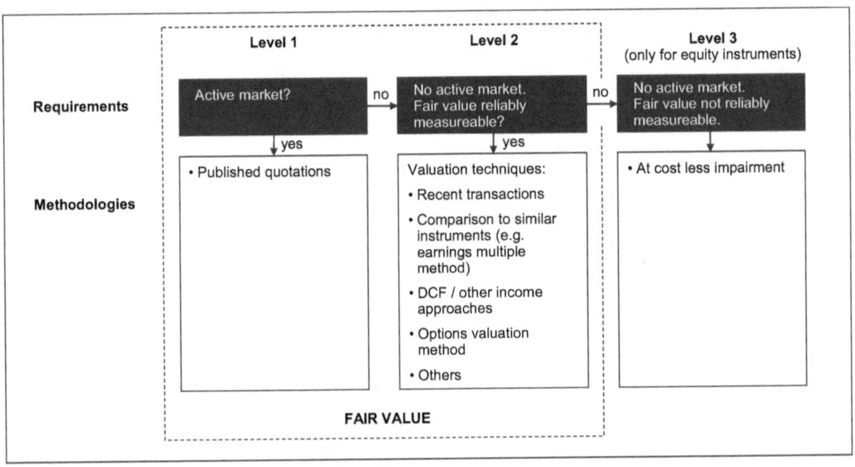

Figure 57: Valuation hierarchy for equity instruments according to IAS 39

If available, a *quoted market price in an active market* will give the best evidence of fair value (IAS 39.48a).[737] This constitutes the first level of the valuation hierarchy.

---

735 See Dohrn (2004), p. 147. Non-adjusting events are indicative of conditions that impact the value of the assets but that arose after the balance sheet date (IAS 10.3).

736 See Ernst & Young (2004), p. 1017.

737 The IASB concludes that quoted prices in active markets are superior to valuation techniques as evidence for fair value, given that fair value is defined as price agreed by a knowledgeable, willing buyer and a knowledgeable seller. Furthermore, it does not depend on entity-specific factors and therefore results in more consistent measurement across entities (IAS 39.BC96-97).

The term 'quoted prices in an active market' means that quoted prices should be readily and regularly available from an exchange, dealer, broker, industry group, or pricing service, and that those prices should reflect actual and regularly occurring market transactions on an arm's length basis (IAS 39.AG71).[738] Usually, it is straightforward to value listed private equity portfolio company investments. The value is the product of the number of shares in the companies and the price of the individual share in the market (IAS 39.AG72). If there are bid-ask spreads, the valuer should use the bid price for the shares held (IAS 39.AG72). According to IFRS, no adjustments should be made for the fair value of large holdings in an entity. Also no other premium or discount may be applied. As the fair value definition is drawn in a going concern context, the IFRS do not assume that the valuing entity needs to liquidate the whole position and accepts a discount to the market price by entering into a transaction on adverse terms.[739] However, private equity investments are usually not traded on an active market. This first level of the valuation hierarchy therefore rarely applies.[740]

For instruments without an *active market*, valuation techniques shall be used to establish fair values (IAS 39.AG74). According to IAS 39, there are various valuation techniques available, including using recent transaction prices, comparisons to similar instruments, discounted cash flow or option valuation methods. To choose an appropriate valuation technique requires a deep understanding of the market and involves subjective judgement.[741] The aim of applying one of them is to establish what the transaction price would have been on the measurement date in an arm's length exchange by normal business considerations (IAS 39.AG75). If market participants commonly use a

---

738 See Ernst & Young (2004), p. 1018.

739 See Poole/Spooner (2006), p. 6.

740 Exemptions are two different cases, so-called private investments in public equity (PIPE) and already public shares of private equity portfolio company investments that are under a legal or contractual restriction to sell (so-called lock-up period). PIPE transactions are usually structured as a minority investment in a publicly listed company. The investor does not receive the full array of control rights and protections that a private equity sponsor is used to receive in a common leveraged buy-out transaction. See Kuzneski/Landen (2006). The other case is where after filing for an IPO the private equity fund managers are restricted to sell their share for some period of time.

741 See Poole/Spooner (2006), p. 174. The valuer should consider the risk that a valuation techniques is incorrectly specified, that improbable assumptions are used, or that it does not mirror the true behaviour of the market.

particular technique to price an instrument and that technique has been proofed to provide reliable estimates of prices obtained in actual market transactions, that technique should be used (IAS 39.AG74). To ensure that the valuation techniques used have historically provided reliable estimates of prices obtained in actual transactions, the reporting entity shall regularly calibrate and test them for validity by comparing their results to prices from current market transactions or based on available observed market data (IAS 39.AG76).[742]

If for equity instruments quoted prices in an active market are not available and a *fair value cannot be reliably measured*, the instruments shall be measured at cost (IAS 39.46c). This third level of the valuation hierarchy is explicitly only acceptable for equity instruments.[743] A regular impairment test is still required. The fair value is reliably measurable if the variability in the range of reasonable estimated values is not significant or the probabilities of the various estimates within the range can be reasonably assessed (IAS 39.AG80-81). IAS 39.AG81 states that it is usually possible to assess fair value especially if the reporting entity has acquired that asset from an outside party. This is regularly the case for investments by private equity funds and, therefore, this third level should be used only in very few cases.[744]

Conceptually, the valuation techniques can be broadly classified in mark-to-market or mark-to-model valuation approaches. In a *mark-to-market valuation,* current market values of identical financial instruments (published quotations) or, if not available, similar ones are applied to assign a fair value for an asset (recent transactions and comparison to similar instruments). In a *mark-to-model approach,* one relies on models to estimate the market values. For companies, these are income approaches that convert future amounts, e.g. cash flows or earnings, to a single discounted present value.

IAS 39 does not explicitly constitute a ranking of the appropriateness of these techniques. However, the standard states that those techniques shall be used that use a

---

742 See Poole/Spooner (2006), p. 174.

743 It is also available for derivatives that are linked to unquoted equity instruments and that must be settled by delivery of unquoted equity instruments (IAS 39.46c).

744 See SECA (2006), p. 28.

maximum of observable market data and a minimum of entity-specific data.[745] The discounted cash flow or income approaches might need more entity-specific data on future income, growth rates and risk assumptions and could be therefore seen as less reliable to measure fair value for equity instruments. Valuation techniques that make maximum use of observable data and rely as little as possible on entity-specific data, such as the earnings multiple method are considered to be more objective. IFRS assume that the use of market inputs, as opposed to entity specific data, will contribute to consistent measurement across entities.[746]

An ongoing project at the IASB aims at developing a general standard on fair value measurement. The FASB has already released such a fair value measurement standard in December 2006.[747] These standards intend to provide a general framework. In the case of IFRS, fair value measurements are required by several individual standards, e.g. by IAS 39, and guidance on measuring is currently located in multiple standards.[748] The IASB notes the confusion that exists as a result of the lack of consistent, integrated guidance on measurement fair value when required. The objective of its project is to define fair value more clearly, and to provide guidance on measuring fair value in general.[749] When adding the project to its agenda, the IASB considered that the FASB was nearing completion of its fair value measurements project, and decided that it would issue the FASB's final statement on fair value measurement as soon as it is released as an IASB's paper for discussion.[750] Due to this effort, there may be changes to the fair value measurement requirements of IAS 39 in the future.[751] In gen-

---

745 See Poole/Spooner (2006), p. 169. The underlying assumption of the predominant request to use market data is that markets are efficient.

746 See Lüdenbach/Freiberg (2006), p. 440; Poole/Spooner (2006), p. 169.

747 In June 2003, the FASB added the fair value measurement project to its agenda to address concerns that guidance is dispersed among the many pronouncements that require fair value measurements in U.S. GAAP. The final publication of the *FASB Statement No. 157: Fair value measurements*, occurred in December 2006. The IASB set a fair value measurement project on its agenda in September 2005.

748 For an overview of the use of fair value accounting in IFRS see Dohrn (2004), p. 116.

749 See IASB (2006c), p. 4. The project is explicitly not intended to require additional fair value measurement or to increase the use of fair value in IFRS.

750 See IASB (2006b), p. 2.

751 There is, for example, divergent guidance in FAS 157 and IAS 39 with respect to the fair value at initial recognition. FAS 157 clearly postulates that the fair value is conceptually an *exit value*. It defines fair value of an asset as the price that would be received in a transaction between knowledgeable market participants. See Hitz (2006), p. 361. IAS 39 accepts the transaction price of an

eral, the FASB standard clearly postulates a hierarchy based on the input data to valuation exercise. Those methods and techniques shall be used that primarily rely on market inputs. FAS 157 is slightly more explicit in postulating market approaches than IAS 39 and therefore may increase the relevance of market-based approaches such as the earnings multiple technique over model-based techniques, e.g. the discounted cash flow methods.[752]

Besides these accounting standard requirements, the private equity industry has a tradition of developing self-imposed guidance on how to value investments for reporting purposes. These industry valuation guidelines provide a more detailed prescription of appropriate valuation techniques in different circumstances. If consistent with the general requirements of IFRS, which is, for example, the case for the so-called *International Private Equity & Venture Capital Valuation Guidelines*, these guidelines adequately supplement the more generic accounting standards.

4.3.4 Private Equity Industry Valuation Guidelines

4.3.4.1 Objectives of Industry Valuation Guidelines

Private equity industry valuation guidelines set out recommendations for general partners on the bases, methodologies and procedures in valuing private equity investments.[753] They provide fund managers with a framework which can be applied when assessing the value of investments for reporting purposes.[754] However, industry valuation guidelines cannot impose a legal obligation on fund managers to adhere to the requirements.[755] Industry valuation guidelines generally have various objectives. They

- standardize valuation bases, methodologies and procedures,

asset as fair value at initial recognition (IAS 39.AG64) which is conceptually different. See IASB (2006b), p. 3. As a result of an approval of the exit price definition of fair value, in circumstances where an asset is required to be measured at fair value on initial recognition a day-one gain or loss may be identified.

752 See Lüdenbach/Freiberg (2006), p. 440.

753 See Böhler (2004b), p. 224.

754 All relevant industry guidelines are intended to guide valuation for reporting purposes and not to influence the valuation when entering the investment or negotiating with potential sellers or entrepreneurs. See Achleitner/Nathusius (2004), p. 23.

755 See Thoen (2002), p. 20. So far, no industry association require its member to apply guidelines. Fund investors sometimes insist on having their general partners follow those guidelines.

- increase transparency and promote confidence between fund managers and their investors,
- represent best practice,
- decrease transaction costs, and
- pre-empt regulatory interference.

First of all, valuation guidelines limit the fund manager's scope for action by defining a framework within which he should value the unrealized portfolio company investments. The interim performance, e.g. the reported IRR, heavily depends on unrealized values.[756] Determining valuation in a consistent way across industry participants thus facilitates the comparability between funds for investors.

Secondly, the common and consistent application of a set of guidelines leads to more transparency of valuation results and thereby increases confidence among fund investors that fund managers' reported values are reliable. This will strengthen the asset class in the long term.

Furthermore, guidelines intend to represent industry's best practice on the valuation of private equity investments. They set a benchmark by which general partners can relate their own valuation methodologies and procedures to.[757] However, to be accepted as standard by the market participants, issuers of the guidelines need to permanently adjust them to new changes driven by amendments in accounting standards and new demands of the fund investors.

Fourthly, industry valuation guidelines lower transaction costs. Investors and fund managers can refer to the industry guidance when designing the contract regarding their relationship, i.e. limited partnership agreement, without having to negotiate bilateral valuation guidelines each time.

Lastly, valuation guidelines may pre-empt potential demands for greater transparency and uniformity from regulators. Against the background of recent corporate scandals

---

[756] See Schefczyck/Pankotsch (2005), p. 312.

[757] See Thoen (2002), p. 20.

some industry participants are concerned that regulators may extend their focus to issues like private equity fund valuations.[758]

Some market participants have expressed their scepticism concerning the development of uniform valuation standards. They don't believe in artificially valuing private equity investments. They argue that it is an illiquid asset class in which always subjective judgements of the fund managers are required.[759] Fund investors might be misled into believing that consistency and comparability has been achieved by implementing a standard. Too much emphasis on standardization of valuations and a potential existence of a single correct value could lead to lawsuits against those firms that do not report this correct value.[760]

Notwithstanding all the difficulties, valuation guidelines fulfil an important role within the private equity industry. Therefore, industry associations in Europe and the U.S. have developed and proposed those guidelines as discussed in the next chapter.

4.3.4.2 Development of Industry Valuation Guidelines

The first set of valuation guidelines for venture capital and private equity investments was introduced in the United States. Initiated by some of its members who recognized the need for a more consistent valuation policy, the *U.S. National Venture Capital Association (NVCA)* proposed valuation guidelines in 1989.[761] Although never officially adopted, they became a de facto standard.[762] The NVCA guidelines are considered to be a conservative framework as they basically only specify that a portfolio company investment of a fund should be carried at cost unless a material impairment indicated a write-down in value or a follow-on financing round including a new outside investor supported a write-up in value.[763]

---

758 See Harrell/Spiegel (2004), p. 16. Guidelines foster that the industry provides a solution itself rather then having regulators step in imposing them. See Boersma/Brown/Franklin (2005), p. 33.

759 See Meyer/Mathonet (2005), p. 160. Some discussants maintain that "valuation is an art, not a science." See Harrell/Spiegel (2004), p. 17.

760 See Harrell/Spiegel (2004), p. 17. For example, a general partnership might be sued by investors for presenting fraudulent information on valuation during its fundraising.

761 See Lerner/Hardymon/Leamon (2005), p. 410, for a reprint of the propositions of the NVCA.

762 See Lerner/Hardymon/Leamon (2005), p. 413; Blaydon/Wainwright (2004a), p. 45.

763 See Blaydon/Wainwright (2004a), p. 45; Blaydon/Horvath/Wainwright (2002), p. 97.

This historical cost based approach for valuing private equity portfolio company investments does not comply with U.S. GAAP which prescribe the use of fair values when valuing assets.[764] Therefore, the *Private Equity Industry Guidelines Group (PEIGG)* issued U.S. Private Equity Valuation Guidelines in December 2003 and supported and urged general partners to apply the fair value concept.[765] In March 2007, it made modifications to these guidelines and issued an updated version to ensure compliance with the newly issued FASB Statement No. 157 "Fair value measurement".[766] PEIGG is an informal institution which was founded in February 2002 in the United States. It is a volunteer group of industry wide representatives, including general partners, limited partners and service providers participating in both the venture and buyout segments of the private equity industry in the U.S. and overseas.[767] The NVCA has encouraged its members to review the PEIGG guidelines. However, it has not yet officially endorsed them.[768]

In Europe, the first set of valuation guidelines dated back to 1991 when the British Venture Capital Association (BVCA) published their standards shortly followed by the EVCA in 1993. Due to changes in the private equity market and, in particular a higher demand for standardization from limited partners, EVCA substantially revised its standards in 2001 and BVCA in 2003, respectively.[769] Both associations acknowledged that the distinctions and categories of investments in the old original guidelines had become out-dated.[770] The enormous growth in the asset class during the 90s, the internationalization of the industry, and the shortening of the business and investment cycle lead to a substantial increase in the demand for the quality and availability of information.

---

764 See Lerner/Hardymon/Leamon (2005), p. 419.

765 See Blaydon/Wainwright (2004a), p. 46.

766 See PEIGG (2007).

767 See PEIGG (2006); Borell (2003b), p. 33.

768 See NVCA (2006); Braunschweig (2004), p. 25. Another important industry group in the U.S. is the Institutional Limited Partners Association (ILPA) which organizes the interests of limited partner investors in the global private equity industry. It endorsed the PEIGG guidelines. See ILPA (2004).

769 See Harrell/Spiegel (2004), pp. 20 et seq.

770 See Crawford-Ingle/Kempen/Vickery (2003).

A joint revision of the up to then individually published valuation guidelines in Europe has been triggered in 2005. First of all, the revision was driven by the developments and requirements of international accounting rules, in particular IFRS but also U.S. GAAP. The old guidelines did not comply.[771] In this respect, new valuation guidelines should also serve to protect against government interference and support an argument for self-regulation of the industry.[772] In addition, the participating associations acknowledged the need to create truly uniform conditions for international investors by harmonizing different guidelines worldwide.[773] Therefore, EVCA and BVCA together with Association Française des Investisseurs en Capital (AFIC), the French private equity association, set up a joint working group and released common *International Private Equity & Venture Capital Valuation Guidelines* in March 2005.[774] All industry associations worldwide have been asked to join the initiative and to support the valuation guidelines. Since their launch, these guidelines have been endorsed by 35 regional and national private equity associations including the associations that developed them.[775] Only in the U.S., the NVCA is still hesitant and reluctant to finally endorse any guidelines.

Another set of guidelines was developed by the Chartered Financial Analyst (CFA) Institute.[776] Its *Global Investment Performance Standards (GIPS)* were initially developed with a focus on traditional asset classes, meaning public equity and fixed-income

---

771 EVCA suggested either a conservative value or fair value approach for valuing portfolio company investments, depending on the development stage of the company. Furthermore, the guidelines proposed discounts for illiquidity that were not in line with IFRS. For a detailed discussion why the former EVCA guidelines were not compatible with IFRS see Böhler (2004b), pp. 225 et seq.

772 In an industry panel conducted by EVCA, half of the participants expected future regulation on European or national level to be targeted towards more transparency, reporting and governance. See EVCA (2006a), p. 3.

773 See Achleitner/Müller (2005), pp. 69 et seq.

774 See Private Equity Valuation (2006). There has been a new release of the AFIC/BVCA/EVCA guidelines in 2006. However, the changes were mainly driven by wording issues. Therefore, in this analysis it is only referred to the issue released in 2005.

775 Endorsements as of June, 2006. See Kuan (2006), p. 8; Private Equity Valuation (2006); Guennoc (2006), p. 126.

776 The CFA Institute is a professional association that, among other tasks, developed and proposed policies, practices, and standards that improve the integrity of the global capital markets. It comments on important issues impacting investor protection, corporate disclosures, market regulations, ethics, and professionalism in the investment community worldwide. See Borell (2003a), p. 34; Kennedy (2005), p. 24.

portfolios. They have been expanded and today include also provisions dealing with private equity.[777] They are intended to be global standards and are primarily designed to provide prospective clients during fundraising with critical pieces of information about the firm's performance rather than reporting performance to existing clients.[778] GIPS valuation guidelines for private equity recognize the fair value as a basis of valuation which is conforming to U.S. GAAP and IFRS. As full convergence of existing valuation guidelines has yet to be achieved across the world, GIPS outline rather high-level valuation principles which shall supplemented by the more detailed regional guidelines developed by AFIC/BVCA/EVCA or PEIGG.[779] The development of the major industry valuation guidelines is summarized in Figure 58.

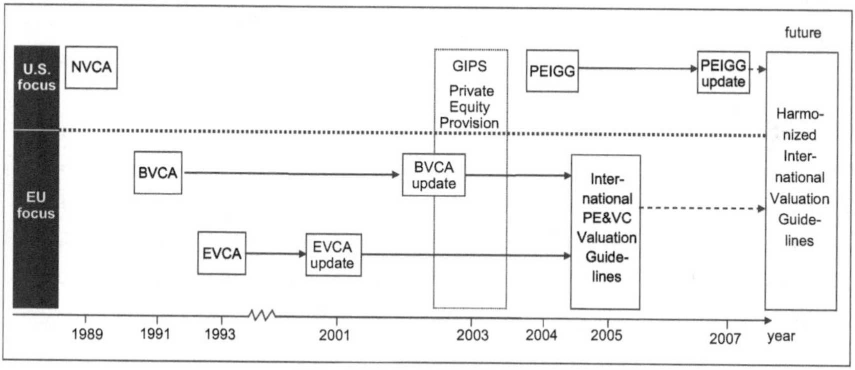

Figure 58: Development and harmonization of major industry valuation guidelines[780]

The fair value measurement project at the IASB is currently still ongoing but is expected to be finished soon. It is very likely that the IASB issue nearly converged guidance with the FASB aimed at providing consistency in the application of existing fair

---

777 See Boersma/Brown/Franklin (2005), p. 33; CFA Institute (2005). The CFA Institute recognized that performance standards have little value if the underlying valuation of portfolio company investments is unclear. Consequently, it developed also valuation guidelines as part of its standards. Additionally, it issued Interpretive Guidance for Private Equity to facilitate the application of its rules. See CFA Institute (2006).

778 See CFA Institute (2004), p. 6; Boersma/Brown/Franklin (2005), p. 34.

779 See CFA Institute (2006); Kennedy (2005), p. 24; Boersma/Brown/Franklin (2005), p. 34.

780 There are no valuation guidelines with an Asian focus due to the short history of private equity investments in Asia. Many Asian private equity industry associations endorsed, however, the International Private Equity & Venture Capital Valuation Guidelines.

value requirements.[781] This development, coupled with an increasing demand from globally active private equity investors that desire harmonized information, might further reinforce the consistent use of fair value standards worldwide. As discussed in the following chapter, the differences between the PEIGG and International Private Equity & Venture Capital Valuation Guidelines are not significant. Therefore, the development of a joint, truly international version might be achievable.[782]

4.3.4.3 Comparison of Industry Valuation Guidelines

To be accepted as relevant valuation standard for the industry, any guidelines should be in line with international accounting standards requirements. As the conservative approach of the rather old NVCA guidelines in the U.S. does not comply with the fair value accounting of the standard setters, only the guidelines developed by AFIC/BVCA/EVCA and PEIGG are seen to be relevant and are compared here.[783]

In general, both valuation guidelines are fairly similar. With respect to the fair value requirement and suggested valuation methodologies there are only minor differences. This is proofed in detail in a synopsis in Figure 59.[784] PEIGG guidelines state that they are compliant with U.S. GAAP. The International Private Equity & Venture Capital Valuation Guidelines explicitly state that they are compliant with both IFRS and U.S. GAAP.

Nevertheless, two dissimilarities shall be highlighted. First, the International Private Equity & Venture Capital Valuation Guidelines' provisions are more detailed. Application guidance is given in addition to suggested methodologies. Not only are they intended to demonstrate how to select an appropriate methodology but also to deal with specific issues, e.g. how to value mezzanine loans. They also provide more examples where appropriate.

---

781 See chapter 4.3.3 for more details on the fair value measurement projects at IASB and FASB.

782 However, in a survey among U.S. fund managers, 46% of venture capitalists and 29% of buyout fund managers believe that convergence will not happen. Overall, many GPs think it will take at least 5-10 years until convergence might be achieved. See Tuck (2005), p. 18.

783 The GIPS Private Equity Provisions shall not be discussed here as their focus is fundraising. See the previous chapter.

784 Similar attempts to compare valuation guidelines have been made by several researchers. These studies however cover outdated guidelines rather than the new developed ones as shown here. See for example Harrell/Spiegel (2004), pp. 18 et seq; zu Knyphausen/Kittlaus/Seeliger (2003), p. 555; Hagenmüller (2004), p. 172.

	International Private Equity & Venture Capital Valuation Guidelines	U.S. Private Equity Valuation Guidelines
General aspects		
Developed by	AFIC/BVCA/EVCA	PEIGG
Status	Finalized March 2005; effective January 2005	Updated March 2007
Principles	Degree of caution, judgement, substance over form, consistency	Consistency, transparency, prudent basis, judgement, substance over form
Level of details	Very detailed provisions	Detailed provisions
Measurement basis	Fair value	Fair value
Stated compatibility with	IFRS, U.S. GAAP	U.S. GAAP
Definition of fair value	Fair value is the amount for which an asset could be exchanged between knowledgeable, willing parties in an arm's length transaction	Fair value is the price that would be received to sell an asset or paid to transfer a liability in an orderly transaction between market participants at the measurement date.
Valuation process		
Frequency of valuation	Not specified	Generally on a quarterly basis
Review of valuation	Not specified	Valuation policy committee is recommended
Valuation of private companies		
Suggested methodologies	Flexibility in selecting the method, no hierarchy but preference for market-based methods: price of recent investment, earnings multiple, net assets, DCF (from underlying business or investment), industry benchmarks	Market approach including comparable company transactions and performance multiples is preferred. Cost / last round of financing may indicate fair value. In addition DCF, net assets, industry benchmarks may be used
Change in valuation methodologies	Only if a change results in a better estimate of fair value. Changes have to be made transparent to investors	Only if a change results in a better estimate of fair value. No frequent changes are expected
Marketability discount if compared to public equity	Marketability discount is a question of judgement; discount rate between 10% and 30% is generally used in practice; factors to be considered given and examples provided	Marketability discount might be appropriate; could be between 0% to 30% or even higher. No further guidance
Treatment of carrying at cost	Cost less impairment is only allowed if fair value is not reliably measurable. Costs (or price of recent investment) remains appropriate as fair value typically for a period of one year, unless an material event implies a change in value	Costs (or latest round of financing) may approximate fair value for some period of time. Managers need to assess whether circumstances indicate a change in fair value
Events to consider for impact on value	Non-exlusive list that may lead to a positive and negative adjustment provided; extent of adjustment can be based on intuitive and analytical process. If insufficient information, then a decrease in tranches of 25% may be applied.	Non-exclusive list that may lead to a positive and negative adjustment is provided; extent of adjustment can be estimated using intuituve and analytical process
Valuation of publicly listed securities		
Valuation reference	Bid price, if given. Otherwise at closing price	Closing price or bid price
Marketability discount	IFRS allows marketability discounts only for securities that have restriction that limits a sale (typical discount 20% for a six-month lock-up period). Recommendation to use a discount if possible, and details provided how to estimate it	Marketability discounts only for securities that have a formal/legal restriction that limits sale (typical discount 0%-30%). If marketability discounts are allowed by accounting standards, they should be applied

Figure 59: Comparison of major industry valuation guidelines[785]

785 The synopsis is based on the text of the guidelines. See AFIC/BVCA/EVCA (2004); PEIGG (2007).

Second, for the care and further development of the International Private Equity & Venture Capital Valuation Guidelines, a Valuation Guidelines Board was appointed. It shall observe market trends as well as the evolution of international accounting standards. Furthermore, it is responsible for answering concrete questions of practitioners, investors or regulators on how to use the Valuation Guidelines. In addition to smaller current adjustments, every three years a formal procedure for the revision of the Valuation Guidelines is planned. The composition of the nine-member board is decided by the founding associations and those associations that joined the initiative later on.[786] The PEIGG lacks such an institutionalized board although this is important to promote and further develop the guidelines.

The level of acceptance and application of valuation guidelines is investigated by only a few studies. MATHONET/MONJANEL find that 80% of European funds apply the International Private Equity & Venture Capital Valuation Guidelines in 2005.[787] For the U.S., a study by TUCK SCHOOL OF BUSINESS shows that 19% of funds have formally adopted the PEIGG guidelines. Over 50% of respondents have adopted some form of valuation guidelines, either PEIGG Valuation Guidelines, the International Private Equity & Venture Capital Valuation Guidelines, or a modified version of these guidelines.[788] Nearly 50% of the respondents that explicitly have not adopted PEIGG Valuation Guidelines state as reason that they prefer write ups only after a new round of financing. It demonstrates clearly the hesitant attitude of U.S. fund managers concerning the fair value approach.[789]

---

786 See Achleitner/Müller (2005), p. 71.

787 They base their study on the portfolio of the European Investment Fund (EIF) which comprises more than 200 European mainly venture capital and mid-market funds. The authors state that 91% of all funds value their investments in compliance with IAS 39. See Mathonet/Monjanel (2006), pp. 4 et seq. Previous studies found similar results with respect to the old EVCA guidelines. HIELSCHER/ZELGER/BEYER show that 75% of European funds applied the guidelines in 2002. See Hielscher/Zelger/Beyer (2003), p. 504. HAGENMÜLLER finds that 80% of European general partners apply EVCA valuation guidelines. See Hagenmüller (2004), p. 174.

788 See Tuck (2005), p. 8.

789 See Tuck (2005), p. 9. Increased volatility in valuations and little interest from LPs are important factors to at least a quarter of respondents that do not adopt PEIGG (23% and 28%, respectively).

4.3.5 Valuation Techniques for Private Equity Investments

4.3.5.1 General Considerations

Conceptually, two different approaches can be distinguished, when determining a value for an investment in a company: the direct valuation of the investment or the indirect valuation by valuing the entire company as an initial step.

The former procedure ascribes a value *directly* to the investment itself. The question that the valuation exercise answers is which price someone would hypothetically pay for that particular stake in the company.[790] The distribution of ownership might affect the value of an investment. The valuing entity needs to consider whether the particular business interest is a minority or majority position in the company. Depending on this, a minority discount or control premium adjustment in addition to a marketability discount might be appropriate.[791]

Under the second approach the value of the investment is determined rather *indirectly* by valuing the entire company first and by then ascribing to each share the pro rata portion of the overall enterprise value.[792] Differently to the direct approach, an adjustment factor considering the different ownership distribution would be inappropriate and is not applied. The second procedure is considered more suitable for private equity investments. The value of an investment for a private equity fund and its investors is regularly created by a sale or flotation of the entire company. If all parties that have an interest into the portfolio company agree that the company will be sold, this approach is considered to be appropriate. Of course, conflicts may arise between management, other shareholders and private equity investors about the terms and timing of an exit.[793] The interests of all participants in a private equity financing relationship, how-

---

[790] See Moll (2004), p. 16.

[791] See Kustner (2002), p. 193. A controlling investment is considered to be of greater value than a minority investment as the controlling shareholder has the ability to effect changes in the overall business structure and to influence the company's business policies. See Feldman (2005), p. 105.

[792] See Moll (2004), p. 18.

[793] FINGERLE provides a comprehensive overview of the *risks of exit obstruction* that venture capitalists face. Management and other shareholders could oppose an exit for any reason. They might refuse an exit via certain exit channel, e.g. if the entrepreneur does not want to sell to a specific competitor out of personal reasons. Also, the timing of the exit or its valuation might be issues of argumentation. See Fingerle (2005), pp. 109 et seq.

ever, are usually aligned through the contractual design of the transaction.[794] For private equity funds, it is therefore in most of the cases more appropriate to value the entire business first.[795] The indirect approach is presented in the following and is mapped in Figure 60.

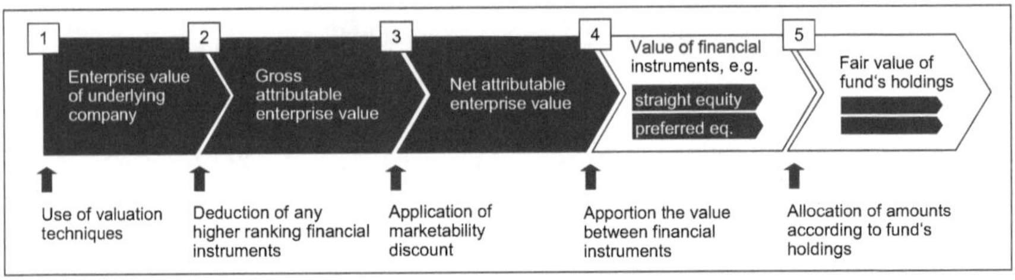

Figure 60: Derivation of fair value of private equity portfolio company investments[796]

The initial step in order to derive the fair value of a fund's holding in the portfolio company is the determination of the enterprise value of the underlying business. Different valuation techniques, either market-based or model-based, can be used and are described below. The enterprise value is the market value of the equity plus the market value of its net debt.[797]

Second, any financial instruments ahead of the highest ranking instrument of the fund are deducted. Any instruments that may dilute the fund's investments shall be taken

[794] See Greenberger (2001), p. 47. Alignment of interests means that the economic value of all investors is tied together so that the value derived from the investment is shared strictly pro rata by all investors. Various disinvestment rights protect the private equity fund: Tag-along rights assure that the private equity manager can participate in any sale of the management, usually on a pro rata basis. See Greenberger (2001), p. 49. Drag-along rights require the management and/or other shareholders to sell their shares to a third party if the private equity manager sells its interests. See Greenberger (2001), p. 51. For other disinvestment rights see Fingerle (2005), pp. 132 et seq.

[795] Only in rare situations where the fund has little ability to influence the timing of the realization and the likelihood of a realization is low, fair value will be directly derived mainly from the expected cash flows and risks of the relevant financial instruments. See AFIC/BVCA/EVCA (2004), p. 12.

[796] Based on the process described in AFIC/BVCA/EVCA (2004), p. 9.

[797] The value derived by the valuation techniques needs to be adjusted for surplus assets or unrecorded liabilities and other factors that are not covered by a valuation technique. See AFIC/BVCA/EVCA (2004), p. 9. In effect, the enterprise value is a theoretical takeover price, i.e., in the event of a buyout an acquirer would have to take on the company's debt but would pocket its cash.

into account.[798] The resulting gross attributable enterprise value is the value that can be attributed to the financial instruments that are part of the fund's investment.

Third, an appropriate marketability discount should be applied in order to derive the net attributable enterprise value.[799] The level of adjustment is a matter of judgement and may vary from case to case. Not only the specific situation of the investments, such as the remaining time to a planned realization, the level of influence of the reporting but also the circumstances and the condition of the capital market are relevant. The influence of the fund on the realization depends on the interests of other shareholders, the existence of any exit strategies, the distribution of any contractual rights that are potentially relevant to the exit decision and the intention of the management to support or hinder any exit plans. In practice, a discount between 10% and 30% is considered to be appropriate.[800]

Fourth, the resulting net attributable enterprise value needs to be finally apportioned between the portfolio company's different financial instruments. This happens according to their ranking where the most senior ones are considered first. Any options and contractual rights that are attached to the financial instruments should be considered. Their importance is discussed in more detail in chapter 4.3.5.6. Fifth, to derive at the fair value of the instruments that the fund owns, the amounts are allocated according to the fund's holdings.

In order to determine the enterprise value in the first step, numerous valuation methods have been developed, either from theoretical or practical origin.[801] The objective of the next chapters is to shortly present the valuation techniques that are available for managers according to the guidelines and accounting requirements. Figure 61 summarizes those suggested by the industry valuation guidelines or the accounting standards. The valuation techniques that are presented in the following are consistent with both the

---

798 Examples how contractual rights influence the portfolio company investment values are provided in chapter 4.3.5.6.

799 According to IFRS, a marketability discount for *listed* companies is not allowed.

800 See AFIC/BVCA/EVCA (2004), p. 19. PRATT/REILLY/SCHWEIHS estimate the marketability discount for privately held companies to be in a range of 25% to 30%. See Pratt/Reilly/Schweihs (2000), p. 402.

801 See Thoen (2002), p. 4.

industry valuation guidelines and the accounting standards requirements according to IAS 39.[802]

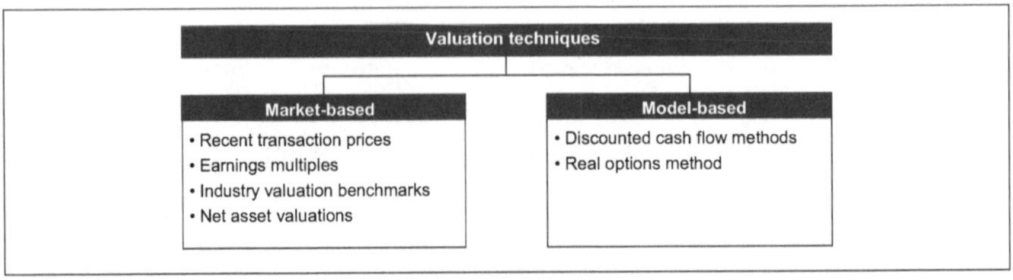

Figure 61: Valuation techniques for private equity portfolio company investments

4.3.5.2 Market-based Valuation Techniques

In *mark-to-market valuations,* current market values of identical financial instruments or, if not available, similar ones are applied to assign a fair value to an asset. Relevant valuation techniques are the recent transaction prices, the earnings multiple techniques, the industry valuation benchmarks, or the net asset valuation.

Recent transaction price

The price of recent transactions in identical instruments of the portfolio company may reasonably approximate the fair value in subsequent measurements. It is the most straightforward valuation technique.[803] Relevant transactions might be either the initial acquisition of the investment itself or any third-party transaction in the company afterwards.[804] As long as there has been no change in economic, market and company-specific conditions since the transaction occurred, a transaction price provides evidence of fair value. If conditions have changed, the value needs to be adjusted to re-

802 See Baker/Luff (2005), p. 4.

803 See Poole/Spooner (2006), p. 175. Sometimes the method is called 'price of recent investment', 'latest round of financing', or simply 'cost'.

804 Third party transactions in venture capital are usually additional financing rounds.

flect these changes by using a different valuation technique. As time passes following the transaction, the appropriateness of the method generally diminishes.[805]

It is necessary to analyze the background of the transaction as the price might not be representative of fair value in certain situations.[806] For example, if the transaction occurred between related parties, i.e. an investment of an existing investor, if the amount was insignificant, if new investors have strategic interests[807], if one or both parties experiences financial difficulties[808], or different rights are attached to the new and exiting investments, prices would not be considered to be reliable.[809]

This recent transaction method is considered to be appropriate for all private equity investments for a limited period of time after the transaction has taken place. However, for early-stage investments in venture capital financing relationships it is more relevant than for buyout investments because of the typically frequent financing rounds.

Earnings multiples

Another commonly used market-based valuation technique establishes fair value by applying an earnings multiple to the earnings of the business that shall be valued (target firm).[810] At first, this method identifies a set of firms that are comparable to the company being valued and then calculates their average earnings multiple. An earnings multiple is the result of dividing a numerator, which represents the prices of simi-

---

805 It depends on the specific circumstances for how long this methodology stays appropriate for a particular investment. In practice, a period of one year is often used. See AFIC/BVCA/EVCA (2004), p. 15. Chapter 4.3.5.5 provides more details.

806 See Poole/Spooner (2006), p. 176. IAS 39.AG74 requires a price in an arm's length market transaction between knowledgeable, willing parties to be representative of fair value.

807 ACHLEITNER shows in an example of a pharmaceutical company that the price an acquirer is willing to pay heavily depends on how the targeted company fits into its strategy. See Achleitner (2002b), p. 206.

808 IAS 39.AG69 states that fair value is not an amount paid or received in a forced transaction, involuntary liquidation or distress sale.

809 The list is not exclusive. See for more Tuck (2003c), p. 30; AFIC/BVCA/EVCA (2004), p. 14; Poole/Spooner (2006), p. 177; Ballwieser (2004), p. 191.

810 This method can be simply called 'method of multiples'. See Feldman (2005), p. 45. This includes also multiples of revenues or other performance indicators, e.g. customers. According to the International Private Equity & Venture Capital Guidelines, however, these methods are subsumed under the valuation technique 'industry valuation benchmarks'. More generally, IAS 39.AG74 refers to 'the current fair value of another instrument that is substantially the same'.

lar companies, by a denominator, which usually represents a financial earnings variable of a company. The multiplication of the derived multiple by the target firm's earnings equals the target firm's value.[811]

Two basic categories of multiples need to be distinguished depending on the earnings figures that are applied. Equity multiples, e.g. price/earnings (P/E), reflect the value of equity, whereas enterprise multiples, e.g. enterprise value/earnings before interests and taxes (EV/EBIT) or enterprise value/earnings before interests, taxes, depreciation and amortization (EV/EBITDA), reflect the total value of the entity.[812] The latter take into account that different financing structures and resulting costs affect after-tax profits. They are therefore usually more appropriate and common in private equity.[813] Multiples can further be derived by reference to comparable traded companies or comparable transactions.[814] The former involve gathering data from publicly listed companies. The latter involve the private transfer of whole companies and might therefore be seen as more relevant to value private equity investments than traded comparables. However, valuers using private transactions as comparables face especially data gathering problems.[815]

One of the key issues of earnings multiple techniques is the appropriate selection of similar companies with respect to risk profile and earnings growth. Criteria commonly applied to select are industry, geography, market position size, or development stage of the companies.[816] For venture capital investments this task is especially challenging. On the one hand they are typically riskier than other companies. They are smaller than

---

811 See Pratt (2001), p. 4.

812 See Achleitner/Nathusius (2004), p. 127. Enterprise multiples are sometimes also called invested capital multiples. It is critical that the calculation of the multiple for the market transaction is done on a basis that is consistent with the manner the multiple is applied to data for the target company. See Pratt (2001), p. 4.

813 See AFIC/BVCA/EVCA (2004), p. 16. EBITDA figures eliminate the impact of depreciation of fixed assets on valuation. However, different level of capital expenditures for fixed assets or the growth by acquisitions might affect the company's value. Valuers should carefully take that into account.

814 See Achleitner/Nathusius (2004), p. 123. The latter is also called recent acquisitions approach. See Böcking/Nowak (1999), p. 174.

815 See among others Pratt (2001), pp. 33 et seq. for a discussion of the different approaches.

816 See Böhler (2004b), p. 239. BALLWIESER criticizes that a detailed analysis of the comparability is necessary which requires as much entity-specific data assumptions as model-based valuation techniques such as discounted cash flow analysis. See Ballwieser (2004), p. 192.

comparable traded companies, they may rely on few key employees, or they are dependent on one customer or product.[817] On the other hand, their growth potential is typically higher. Another key issue is that the earnings which are used in the earnings valuation methodology are sustainable and reliable. It is a matter of judgement to select either historic but audited data or forecast figures, and to adjust the earnings for non-recurring and extraordinary items.[818]

Industry valuation benchmarks

Based on experience, various different industry-specific valuation benchmarks have been developed and are commonly applied by practitioners. In some situations they might be appropriate as a basis to estimate fair value of a business.[819] Their general approach is similar to earnings multiples. Instead of earnings, however, the denominator may be revenues or some physical variable of a company measured other than in dollar terms, e.g. subscribers for a cable operator.[820]

The basic assumptions when applying industry benchmarks for valuation are on the one hand that investors are willing to pay for revenue or market share and on the other hand that the profitability on average does not vary much across different companies.[821] For venture capital-backed companies that have no positive earnings or cash flow, the application of industry benchmarks could be justifiable.[822] Nevertheless, it is unlikely that this technique is very reliable. It might be rather used as a cross-check of values produced by other techniques.

---

817 AFIC/BVCA/EVCA (2004), p. 17. Multiples need to be adjusted to reflect this. See Achleitner/Nathusius (2004), p. 125.

818 See AFIC/BVCA/EVCA (2004), p. 18. Again, it is essential that the earnings used to calculate the multiple used must correlate to the earnings of the company that is to be valued.

819 According to IFRS, if a valuation technique commonly used by market participants to price a financial instrument has been proofed to provide reliable estimates prices obtained in actual market transactions, the entity may apply that technique (IAS 39.AG74).

820 See Pratt (2001), p. 4. AMIR/LEV for example find that in the wireless communication industry non-financial information is of more value than traditional, financial indicators. They expect this to be the case in other science-based, high-growth sectors, too. See Amir/Lev (1996), p. 5.

821 See AFIC/BVCA/EVCA (2004), p. 23.

822 See Achleitner/Nathusius (2004), p. 133 and therein cited literature for a profound discussion.

Net asset valuation

The net asset valuation technique identifies a firm's tangible and intangible assets and their market values. The sum of these values equals thc fair value of the entity.[823] This approach is considered to be appropriate for private equity investments whose underlying business value derives mainly from its assets rather than from its earnings, e.g. property holding companies or investment businesses. It is also applicable for businesses that do not make an adequate return and that would generate a greater value by liquidating the business and selling all its assets.[824]

4.3.5.3 Model-based Valuation Techniques

Among the model-based techniques two methods can be identified that could be applied to value private equity investments: the discounted cash flow methods and the real options approach.

Discounted cash flow methods

Discounted cash flow valuation methods belong to the income-based approaches to valuation and are very popular both in valuation theory and in practice.[825] According to these methods, the value of the company depends on the future cash flow that will accrue to it.[826] The future cash flows are discounted back at an appropriate discount

---

[823] See Pratt/Reilly/Schweihs (2000), p. 45. Any off-balance sheet or contingent assets and liabilities should be included. The technique is also generally called *asset-based approach*. For a detailed description of the valuation procedure see Pratt/Reilly/Schweihs (2000), pp. 311 et seq.

[824] See AFIC/BVCA/EVCA (2004), pp. 20 et seq.

[825] See Böhler (2004b), p. 236. For an overview of DCF techniques in general see Copeland/Koller/Murrin (2000) or Ballwieser (2004). For its application to closely-held companies see Pratt/Reilly/Schweihs (2000), and with respect to the valuation of high-growth companies see Achleitner/Nathusius (2004). Other income-based approaches can be distinguished based on the income stream that the valuer applies. Accounting earning figures that accrue to the equity holder could for example be used (discounted earnings approach). Other future income streams may be dividends, interests, security sale proceeds. See Pratt/Reilly/Schweihs (2000), p. 154.

[826] This described model is the *entity approach* to valuation which results into the value of both equity and debt. An appropriate discount factor is therefore a weighted average cost of capital. Alternatively, one could estimate the flow to equity (*equity approach*) but would then need to discount the cash flow with the equity costs only. See Copeland/Koller/Murrin (2000), pp. 131 et seq. for the details of these different frameworks.

rate and the sum of these discounted values equals the present value of the company.[827]

Using this approach requires an estimation of the expected stream of cash flows and an identification of a required rate of return. The methods are useful for any businesses that have a predictable stream of positive cash flows. Usually, this is true for rather mature businesses but not venture capital investments. The methods can be applied to any stream of cash flows. Due to this flexibility they might be applied where the companies go through a process of great change, e.g. turnaround situations, strategic repositioning, or loss-making phases.[828] However, there are risks in applying DCF methods. First, the forecasted cash flow streams needs to be estimated and therefore might be not reliable. Second, the terminal value which also has to be estimated contributes significantly to the entire value.[829] Third, an appropriate discount factor needs to be applied. All these entity-specific inputs require substantial subjective judgement.[830] Because of this high level of subjectivity, the discounted cash flow methods should be only used to estimate fair value if techniques with more market-based inputs cannot be applied.

It is normally appropriate to apply the discounted cash flow methods to the entire underlying company first and deriving the value of the investment according to the process described in chapter 4.3.5.1. However, where a realization of the underlying investment is foreseeable and the pricing has been agreed, the value of the investment can be calculated by discounting the cash flow to the investment directly.[831]

Real options method

Discounted cash flow methods can be deficient in situations where managers or investors of a company have flexibility, for example to increase or decrease the rate of production, defer development, or abandon a project.[832] A real options method to valua-

---

827 See Pratt/Reilly/Schweihs (2000), p. 153.

828 See AFIC/BVCA/EVCA (2004), p. 21.

829 This is especially true if constant growth of the cash flows is assumed.

830 See AFIC/BVCA/EVCA (2004), p. 21.

831 See AFIC/BVCA/EVCA (2004), pp. 22 et seq.

832 See Lerner/Willinge (2005), p. 214.

tion takes this flexibility explicitly into account.[833] According to this approach, a project or company value comprises of two parts. The first part is a passive and option-free company value which is usually valued using the standard cash flow method. The second part is an active company value which presents the value of options related to the project or company. The latter can be estimated by applying option pricing models.[834] Theoretically, the approach is very interesting in private equity financing situations. One example: Venture capitalists financing relationships are often characterized by a multistage investment approach to motivate the entrepreneurs to get to the next financing stage. The right but not the requirement to make a follow-on investment has similar characteristics as a financial call option.[835]

Although theoretically appropriate, the real option method proofs to be very complex and time consuming in practice. It requires that the valuing entity makes many assumptions with respect to the data input. Although IAS 39.AG74 explicitly mentions option pricing models, they cannot be regarded as an appropriate and reliable method for valuing private equity investments for reporting purposes.[836] Consequently, and as demonstrated by ACHLEITNER et al., it is virtually not applied in practice.[837]

4.3.5.4 Selecting a Valuation Technique

When selecting an appropriate valuation technique in order to estimate fair value of a private equity portfolio company investment, the specific situation that requires the valuation of a company needs to be considered. Each investment should be considered individually.[838] The valuation issue in this analysis is tied to the external reporting be-

---

833 For details on the real option approach see among others Brealey/Myers (2005), pp. 597 et seq; Copeland/Koller/Murrin (2000), pp. 399 et seq; Dixit/Pindyck (1995); Achleitner/Nathusius (2004), pp. 67 et seq.

834 Option pricing models have been developed to value financial options. Examples are the Black-Scholes formula or the binomial method. See for details among others Brealey/Myers (2005), pp. 565 et seq; Achleitner/Nathusius (2004), pp. 76 et seq. There are only few limited situations where option pricing can be applied to value entire companies. See Copeland/Koller/Murrin (2000), p. 399.

835 See Lerner/Willinge (2005), p. 214.

836 However, it might be very useful as additional approach to value an investment opportunity.

837 In their study investigating the valuation approaches of German private equity funds, the authors find that only 7-8% of the funds use the real options approach. See Achleitner et al. (2004b), p. 702.

838 See AFIC/BVCA/EVCA (2004), p. 27.

haviour of private equity fund managers. However, before elaborating on this situation in detail, some general remarks are necessary.

In general, the selection depends on various factors. The most important factors are the *quantity and quality of available data* for the valuation purpose. On the one hand, data from the entity itself is necessary. Due to their role as investors, the fund managers have usually access to the available financial and operational data.[839] However, some companies might lack input data for special valuation techniques because of the current stage of the business. For example, if they do not have revenues or profits yet, e.g. in early stage or turnaround situations, it is difficult to apply earnings multiple methods. On the other hand, the fund managers need data related to the market of the underlying company, i.e. industry private transactions and public company data. A large quantity of publicly available data regarding mergers and acquisitions transactions or publicly traded companies might be available for some industries.

The *industry of the company* is another factor that influences the selection of a valuation technique. Certain industries have specific rules of thumb that industry participants apply as quick estimates of the value.[840]

The *nature of the assets*, e.g. tangible versus intangible asset-intensive, is also a factor that should be considered when selecting a valuation technique. For companies with significant tangible assets such as real estate, the net asset valuation method may be appropriate.

Furthermore, the *nature of the interest in the company* is relevant. The valuation of a marketable, controlling ownership interest is a different task from the valuation of a non-marketable, non-controlling interest. Some valuation techniques are more relevant for overall enterprise valuation, while other may be more appropriate for the analysis of minority ownership interest positions.[841]

---

[839] Given the close relationship between investor and company in the investment holding period, it can be expected that the fund manager has usually close access to information. See Thoen (2002), p. 7.

[840] See Pratt/Reilly/Schweihs (2000), p. 440. An example for a rule of thumb is the number of subscribers of a cable operator.

[841] See Pratt/Reilly/Schweihs (2000), p. 440.

In the specific situation where a valuation is carried for the external reporting of private equity fund managers, managers cannot simply select a valuation technique by themselves. The subjective element in selecting a technique is reduced as fund managers have to comply with IFRS. The valuation methods chosen and the way that they are implemented is highly influenced by both the accounting requirements and the applied industry valuation guidelines compliant with the respective accounting standards. The International Private Equity & Venture Capital Guidelines echo the approach of IAS 39 methods to derive fair value. The valuation techniques set out in the guidelines are in general the same as those in IAS 39.[842] Market-based approaches and inputs are preferred. However, the valuation guidelines promote the use of discounted cash flow methods with lesser prominence than IAS 39 as they are less reliable.[843] There are circumstances where the discounted cash flow method can be considered appropriate according to IFRS. If, for example, infrastructure investments with rather steady cash flow streams are subject to the valuation, income approaches might result in more reliable results.

In order to facilitate consistency in the selection of valuation techniques used by private equity fund managers, the International Private Equity & Venture Capital Valuation Guidelines provide application guidance on the selection issue. The selection of a valuation technique shall be based on the *ability of the underlying business to generate sustainable revenues and profits*. The guidelines distinguish between three categories:[844] First of all, early stage companies or companies without or with insignificant revenues; secondly, companies with revenues but without either significant profits or significant positive cash flows; thirdly, companies with revenues, maintainable profits and/or maintainable positive cash flows. For all three categories, the recent transaction price method is regarded as the most appropriate method to indicate fair value for a particular period of time following the transaction, in practice usually one year. After

---

842 See Baker/Luff (2005), p. 4.

843 See Baker/Luff (2005), p. 4. According to the International Private Equity & Venture Capital Valuation Guidelines, discounted cash flows and industry benchmarks methods are rarely used in isolation and if, only with extreme caution. They are rather useful as a crosscheck of estimated values resulting from market-based techniques. See AFIC/BVCA/EVCA (2004), p. 14.

844 See AFIC/BVCA/EVCA (2004), pp. 27 et seq. Fund managers following these guidelines are expected to use the prescribed techniques unless it can be proven that another methodology provides more reliable results.

that limited period, the use of valuation techniques depends on the companies' ability to generate revenues and profits or positive cash flows.

For companies of the first category which are typically in a seed, start-up or an early stage situation the fund managers should evaluate whether there is material evidence of an increase or decrease in value.[845] If not, the fund manager usually should carry forward previous values.

For companies of the second category with revenues but no reliable earnings, e.g. in a turnaround situation, industry valuation benchmarks could provide additional support for fair value but should not be used alone. For these cases, a valuation according to the net assets method may be appropriate where a resulting liquidation value is greater than the going concern value. Discounted cash flow methods are highly subjective due to the high risks in forecasting the development of these companies and should rarely be used. Earnings multiple methods are inappropriate for both categories when there are no earnings.

For companies of the third category that show revenues, maintainable profits and positive cash flows, however, the earnings multiple and discounted cash flow methods usually provide the best estimate of fair value after a certain period of time.

The use of valuation techniques should be consistent over time.[846] Generally, a change is only appropriate if the result proofs to be a better estimate of fair value. If a transaction price can not any longer be accepted as recent, or the business development of the underlying company makes it possible to use earnings multiples, a change is acceptable but should be disclosed and substantially justified.

In some cases it might be obvious that the fund managers should rely on the indication of a single valuation technique. Often, however, it is appropriate to apply alternative valuation techniques that result in a range of acceptable solutions.[847] A study finds that in practice, fund managers use on average 1.4 techniques to value a portfolio company

---

845 An overview of potential value indicators is provided in chapter 4.3.5.5.

846 See AFIC/BVCA/EVCA (2004), p. 13.

847 This could be for example the use of market-based approaches and in addition a discounted cash flow model. See Baker/Luff (2005), p. 4.

investment.[848] The outcome of the different techniques could then be considered together to determine fair value.[849]

4.3.5.5 Considering other Indicators of Value

In some situations the described techniques are not applicable to value the equity investments. This could be, for example, the case for an underlying company that does not have any positive profits or cash flows, for which no true comparables can be identified and where the latest round of financing becomes less reliable as an approximation of fair value. Notwithstanding, there might be indications that a change in the carrying value of the investment is appropriate and that a fair valuation measurement would require to make a positive or negative adjustment to it. In a first step, a fund manager therefore needs to systematically review whether any indicator gives notice of a value change and, if this is the case, in a second step determine how to quantify the effect, respectively.[850]

Identifying value indicators

Numerous events and circumstances regularly indicate and justify a change in value. According to Figure 62, they can be categorized in company-related indicators and environment-related indicators.

Concerning these categories, the valuer may ask a list of questions to identify if any change in value has occurred.[851] With respect to the *liquidity and financing* of the company one should clarify whether the amount of the remaining cash - which depends on the cash burn rate - is adequate. Does the company have the ability to generate cash? What is the status and progress of the actual financing rounds? Are any new financing rounds planned? In case there are only a few remaining months left in which

---

848 See Achleitner et al. (2004b), p. 703. The study bases on a survey among private equity funds in German speaking countries.

849 See AFIC/BVCA/EVCA (2004), p. 13. Alternative results could be either used as a cross-check for the result of one technique or weighted to get one final result. See Pratt/Reilly/Schweihs (2000), p. 443.

850 See Böhler (2004b), p. 240.

851 The following questions are based on AFIC/BVCA/EVCA (2004), pp. 31 et seq; Böhler (2004b), pp. 240 et seq; PEIGG (2004c), p. 6 and are related to the list of loss events to test for impairment of a financial instrument in IAS 39.59 and IAS 39.61.

the company has sufficient available cash, e.g. less than six, the fund manager might feel impelled to write-down its investment.

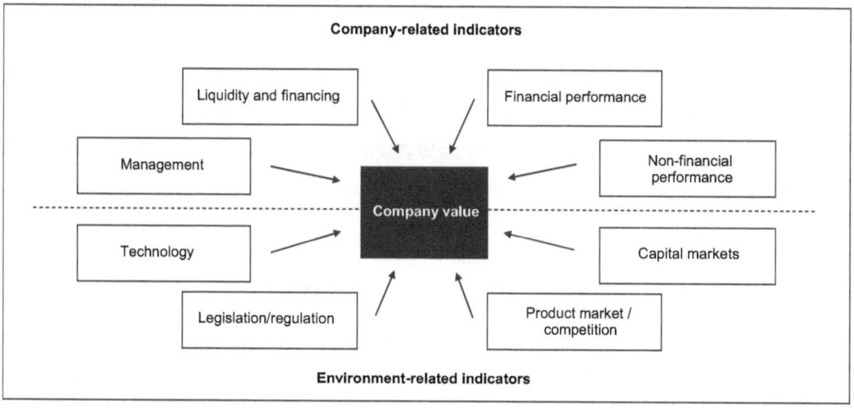

Figure 62: Categorization of value indicators[852]

With respect to the *financial performance* one could ask whether the portfolio company has achieved any important financial milestones, e.g. the first revenues, or not. Does it fail or exceed the budgets? Does any breaching of banking covenants, or default on obligations occur?

The *non-financial performance* may be tested by identifying whether any restructuring plans have been successfully completed or not. Has the company achieved non-financial milestones, e.g. with respect to product development? Has it achieved any technology breakthroughs or developed proprietary technology? Are any major lawsuits pending? Are there any disputes over commercial matters, e.g. concerning the intellectual property rights of the company? Do any material changes in the strategic direction occur?

As the *management* is very important, the valuer should elaborate whether any material changes in the management happened. Are there any issues that may influence the quality of the management? How high is the turnover of key employees? Does any fraud exist within the company?

852 Own exhibit based on AFIC/BVCA/EVCA (2004), pp. 31 et seq; Böhler (2004b), pp. 240 et seq; PEIGG (2004c), p. 6.

Concerning environmental-related indicators, the valuer should take into account whether any changes in the *legal and regulatory environment* happened or not. Are there any significant changes in the *product markets*, e.g. new *competitors* entering the market? Are substitutes for the company's products arising? Are there any changes in the *technological environment*, e.g. new competitors with new competing technology? And, finally, are there any changes in the *capital market* environment, e.g. the valuation of comparable companies that also indirectly influence the value of the company? A fund manager needs to take all these events and circumstances into account when valuing a company.

Determining the impact

Having identified the value indicators, the impacts of these events and circumstances on the carrying value have to be determined in a second step. However, it is a challenge to quantify the effects if a use of a valuation technique is impossible.[853] BÖHLER suggests that fund managers should apply a scoring model.[854] Following this approach would allow for a certain systematic approach. However, the construction of the model and the assignment of points to certain events remain highly subjective. The IASB acknowledges that in certain cases the data required to estimate the amounts on impairment losses may not be available and suggests that in these situations one uses experienced judgement (IAS 39.63). If there is insufficient information to accurately assess the adjusted fair value, it is common practice among private equity managers to decrease the value in steps of 25 percent.[855]

There has been a lot of discussion among private equity industry practitioners about potential write-ups without any new financing rounds. This has caused concerns especially among venture capitalists.[856] Following the fair value approach, if there is reli-

---

853 With respect to IFRS impairment requirements, there is a degree of circularity in the definition of impairment for those equity investments whose fair value cannot be reliably measured. They should be carried at cost unless the assets are impaired (IAS 39.46c). But no guidance is given how to estimate the impairment amount. See Bane (2005), p. 5.

854 See Böhler (2004b), p. 242. He applies his model to quantify the effect of any deterioration.

855 The International Private Equity & Valuation Capital Valuation Guidelines suggests tranches of 25 percent unless the valuer has information to more accurately assess fair value in tranches of 5 percent. See AFIC/BVCA/EVCA (2004), p. 32.

856 In a study by TUCK among U.S. private equity funds, 59% of the venture capital fund managers who have not adopted the PEIGG guidelines cites as their primary reason for not implementing them that they prefer write-ups only if a new round of financing has occurred. See Tuck (2005), p. 10.

able evidence of value creation this should be recognized in the reported valuation even though there has not been any new third party financing round that provided unambiguous evidence for the new valuation. This widens the discretionary scope of action for fund managers to influence reported values. In practice, therefore, write-ups without any financing rounds or profit generation, that would facilitate the use of market-based techniques such as the earnings multiples, should be made only in cases where there is clear support for such an increase.[857] It is assumed that this is rarely the case.

To sum up, indicators of value creation or diminution should be reviewed and, if clear evidence is provided, recognized in reported valuation. Decreases will be more likely than increases. The consideration of indicators will be more relevant for venture capital companies. Later stage companies usually show positive earnings or cash flows so that any change in valuation can be reliably justified by the results of the use of valuation techniques.

4.3.5.6 Considering the Impact of Options and Contractual Rights

In chapter 4.3.5.1, the general process how to derive the fair value of an investment has been described. In step four of this process, the net attributable enterprise value is allocated between the different financial instruments. The fund managers need to consider the various options and specific rights attached to the different types of securities. In private equity transactions the use of complex capital structures including options and specific rights is common.[858] Options and contractual rights that are attached to the securities may either enhance or diminish the value of the fund's portfolio company investments depending on the value of the underlying investments and depending on who owns these rights.[859] When assessing the fair value of the fund portfolio company

---

857 See AFIC/BVCA/EVCA (2004), p. 32. In a guidance letter on the criticized paragraph 30 which deals with non-financing valuation increases, PEIGG makes clear that for seed and early stage companies such a write-up would be unlikely within the first two years. Furthermore, in isolation examples like 'the build out of a management team' or 'the acquisition of a key customer' should not lead to a write-up. In addition, increases should be reviewed by the advisory board or a valuation policy committee. See PEIGG (2004d).

858 See for an overview of deal structuring among others Lerner/Hardymon (2005); Tuck (2003b).

859 Typically the rights are attached to preferred stock. See Pratt/Reilly/Schweihs (2000), p. 534.

investments, the value of the options and contractually rights needs to be considered. It is suggested by the valuation guidelines to assume that options and warrants are exercised, when the fair value is in excess of the exercise price.[860]

Especially in venture capital transactions, the fund managers ask for liquidation preferences.[861] A liquidation preference generally entitles its holder upon liquidation, which typically includes the sale of the company[862], to receive some specified value before other investors of more junior securities receive any payments. In its basic form, investors hold convertible preferred stock with a single liquidation preference, which is equal to the initial investment.[863] When allocating the net attributable value to the different securities, the preferred stock's conversion value should be compared to the estimated liquidation value. If the former is lower, it is assumed that the holder of the preferred stock does not convert. The value of the stocks would then equal the value of the liquidation preference.[864]

Figure 63 demonstrates the impact of different rights on the value of the investment. In this example, the private equity fund holds less than 50% of the company as the initial investment (I_0) is less than the post-money valuation including the initial investment (V_0). However, the fund has been granted preferred stock for its investment. The management team holds the other stake in the company but only common stock. In the first case (dashed line), the fund's investment is convertible preferred stock with a single liquidation preference. The dashed line represents the value of the investment of the private equity fund's preferred stock contingent on the net enterprise value attributable to both preferred and common equity. As long as the net attributable enterprise value

860 See AFIC/BVCA/EVCA (2004), p. 11. The valuer should consider any surplus cash arising in the underlying portfolio company through the exercise of options.

861 See Woronoff/Rosen (2005), p. 8. In the U.S. market liquidation preferences are used in 98% of venture capital financing rounds. See Kaplan/Strömberg (2003), p. 290. The use of these rights is also standard in German financing transactions. See Hoffmann/Hölzle (2003), p. 113.

862 See Woronoff/Rosen (2005), p. 7. The definition of 'liquidation' is negotiated between the parties involved.

863 See Fingerle (2005), p. 127. This can be linked with cumulative dividends. Furthermore, even multiple liquidation preferences have been negotiated where the investor asks for the repayment of double or triple of his investment.

864 This is suggested by both the International Private Equity & Venture Capital Valuation Guidelines and PEIGG Valuation Guidelines. See AFIC/BVCA/EVCA (2004), p. 33 and PEIGG (2004c), p. 11.

is higher than the post-money valuation, the preferred stock's value equals the value of the direct participation in the stock of the company. If the net attributable enterprise value is lower than V_0 but higher than I_0, the preferred stockholder would exercise the liquidation preference and would get its initial investment back. If the net attributable value is below I_0, the preferred stockholders receive the full net attributable enterprise value.

In the second case (solid line), the investor has been granted participating preferred stock which is demonstrated by the solid line. The contractual provision here is that after the liquidation preference is paid, the preferred shareholders share any remaining proceeds pro rata with the common shareholders. The fund does not only get its investment back but participates with common stockholders in the remaining payments as if they had converted.[865] The allocated value to participating preferred stock is consequently higher than for the convertible stock.

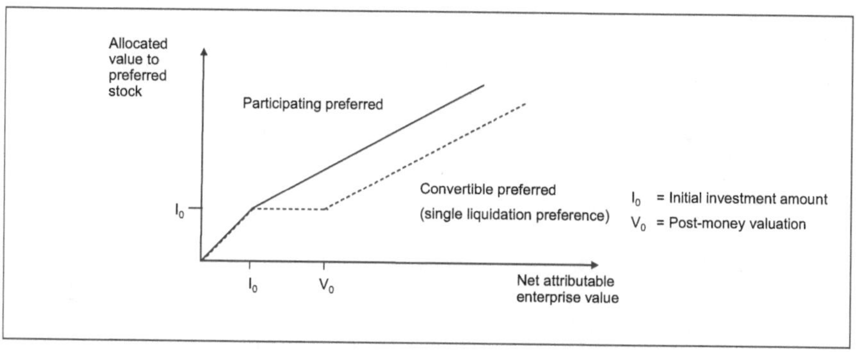

Figure 63: Impacts of different contractual rights on the value of the portfolio company investment[866]

Other typical contractual rights include but are not limited to anti-dilution clauses[867], or ratchet clauses.[868] All these rights should be reviewed on a regular basis to assess

865 See Fingerle (2005), p. 128. Participation features are very common for U.S. venture capital deals. See Blaydon/Wainwright (2006), p. 41.

866 Based on Blaydon/Wainwright (2006), p. 42.

867 Private equity investors typically protect their investments against share and price *dilution provisions*. Share dilution provisions protect the ownership of an investor against dilution in events

whether they are likely to be exercised and have any impact on the value of the fund's investment.[869] However, further research is still required to fully understand and demonstrate in detail how these contractual rights may impact the value of the investments. So far, it must be acknowledged that it has been neglected by academics.

4.3.6 Discussion of the Appropriateness of Fair Value Measurement for Private Equity Investments

4.3.6.1 Incentives to Manage Valuations

Even if the fund managers elaborate a well thought-out valuation process and apply valuation guidelines suggesting consistent and comparable methodologies, valuations always require an element of judgment that can not be avoided.[870] The fair value only estimates the potential values that may be realized by selling the portfolio company investments. It does not represent actual market transactions.[871] Therefore, it might be possible that fund managers, intentionally or unintentionally, exploit their discretion in determining fair values. An assessment and discussion of the appropriateness of the fair value measurement of private equity portfolio companies requires that the incentives for fund managers to manage valuations have been identified.

The risk that fund managers report overstated valuations of their unrealized investments is of special concern to fund investors. The performance of the funds would be overstated and may cause fund investors to make wrong decisions.[872] Overstated

---

where new shares are issued. Primarily, private equity investors are concerned with down-rounds which are financing rounds that value a company's stock at lower price per share than previous rounds. So called price dilution provisions protect the holders' shares from sales of shares at lower valuations in down-rounds. See Fingerle (2005), pp. 128 et seq; Tuck (2003b), p. 8; Harris (2002), p. 35.

868 *Ratchet clauses* are used in venture capital contracts to incentivize the management team. In case the management team does not meet a performance target, a ratchet-down agreement specifies that the management's equity share will be reduced by transferring shares from management to the private equity investors. A ratchet-up agreement conversely sorts out that if management meets its target on time, it will receive shares from the investor. See Fingerle (2005), p. 123.

869 See AFIC/BVCA/EVCA (2004), p. 33. For an overview of contractual rights that are typically used in venture capital financing relationships see Fingerle (2005), pp. 103 et seq.

870 See Michas (1997), p. 1.

871 See Kaserer/Wagner/Achleitner (2003), p. 262.

872 Based on a mislead performance, the fund investors may re-invest in subsequent funds of the fund managers although the true performance is actually not good enough.

valuation might be the result of several actions. Fund managers could choose inadequate valuation techniques, improper discounts, wrong estimates of future events and conditions which are used as input to valuation techniques, or inappropriate benchmarks for market comparables. They could also avoid or postpone write-downs or write-offs.[873]

Explanation why fund managers may overstate the valuation of unrealized investments can be distinguished in rational explanations, which assume that fund managers intentionally act,[874] and unintentional, rather behavioural-related explanations. The most prominent factor among the *rational explanations* relates to fund managers' future fundraising plans. In order to present a notable track record to potential fund investors, fund managers that are raising or planning to raise a new fund have an incentive to present higher portfolio company valuations on unrealized investment.[875] Higher unrealized valuations artificially increase the current fund's performance and thereby could enhance the probability of closing the next fund. This incentive is especially relevant for younger funds that lack a long track record.[876] Older funds normally have a higher reputation at stake which they could lose.

Fund investors themselves could also have an interest in high unrealized valuations. Therefore, even without any immediate fundraising plans, fund managers might try to keep investors happy by presenting positive performance generated by creative valuations during the lifetime of the fund.[877] Their fund investors may not like write-downs of portfolio company investments since these would immediately affect their own results. Public pension funds are under special scrutiny not to risk employee pensions.[878] Fund-of-funds as investors worry that through write-downs their own investors could

---

[873] See Kaneyuki (2003), p. 508. The author also points out that funds might use new investments rounds not conducted at arm's length by independent third party investors as indication for an increase in value. This is not allowed by the international valuation guidelines which are assumed to be applied in this analysis.

[874] Kaneyuki calls this creative valuation. See Kaneyuki (2003).

[875] See Kaneyuki (2003), p. 507; Gompers/Lerner (2000), p. 251.

[876] See Cumming/Walz (2004), p. 9. They provide evidence that younger funds overstate their valuations.

[877] See Kaneyuki (2003), p. 507.

[878] The public disclosure of fund performance data in the U.S. due to the Freedom of Information Act (FOIA) furthermore increased the pressure on the trustees. See chapter 3.8.4 for more details on the FOIA.

be deterred from re-investing.[879] On a personal level, the individual professionals on the fund investors' side could have their compensation and bonuses tied to the unrealized net asset values.[880] Therefore, they may prefer that their fund managers do not write-down portfolio company investments.

Furthermore, the valuation results may be biased by portfolio company-related factors which the general partner considers. The valuations are intended to inform fund investors and should be kept confidential between both parties. However, they may get known to other stakeholder of the portfolio companies and then may have severe consequences for the portfolio companies.[881] Write-downs send signals to suppliers or customers that the portfolio companies face difficulties. Any business with them consequently bears the risk of financial distress of the transaction partner.

With respect to potential exits of the portfolio companies, fund managers might want to gain a better bargaining position by presenting higher book values of their investment positions.[882] Potential buyers may take the book values as reference price, as the fund managers are insiders and owners of the respective companies and should know most about the businesses and their prospects. Contradicting this argument, fund managers might not want to raise their own fund investors' expectations by reporting high valuation but want to be sure to meet or, even better, to exceed them.

If the net asset values are the bases for calculating the management fee of the partnership, the general partners could intend to maximise their fee income by overstating valuation.[883] In addition, the individual fund managers responsible for the individual investments might have their own interests in higher valuation of their investments. New partners, or those that may get promoted, might be reluctant to take a loss as they fear to loose their standing within the partnership.[884]

---

879 See Lerner/Hardymon/Leamon (2005), p. 417.

880 See Tuck (2003c), p. 7; Lerner/Hardymon/Leamon (2005), p. 417.

881 See Michas (1997), p. 5. The larger the number of investors in a fund, the higher the likelihood that information could be passed to third parties.

882 See Michas (1997), p. 5.

883 See Böhler (2004b), p. 125. During the first years of a fund cycle, the so-called investment period, the management fee is usually a percentage of the committed capital. After that, however, it might be tied to the remaining net asset value.

884 See Lerner/Hardymon/Leamon (2005), p. 414.

Beside these rational factors there also exist *behaviour-related explanations* for overstated portfolio company valuations. Fund managers may have a tendency for searching information that rather supports their positive beliefs or preferences. That is called *confirmation bias*. If fund managers believe that the value of a specific portfolio company is high, they may actively seek out evidence in support for this proposition such as comparable companies that have high multiples.[885] Equally plausible evidence suggesting comparable companies with lower multiples is rather ignored.

The fund managers could also become emotionally tied to their companies. They could fear that a write-down would cause the partnership and his colleagues to lose their interest in the investment.[886] Some fund managers therefore automatically write down portfolio companies after a specific period of time, e.g. four years of investment.

Another factor that leads to overstated valuations is the *overconfidence bias* which can arise in two types.[887] Fund managers may overestimate the likelihood that their favoured outcome with the portfolio company will occur. They might also have overconfidence in the validity of their judgment abilities.[888] Both are explanations for overstating the investment values.

Little empirical evidence has been provided so far on the issue whether fund managers actually overstate valuations in practice.[889] Only CUMMING/WALZ consider the reporting of unrealized returns to fund investors and compare the reported internal rate of returns on unrealized investments to the returns the authors would predict for such investments based on an analysis of realized investments.[890] They provide evidence that inexperienced fund managers tend to report significantly higher valuations than their more experienced colleagues. Furthermore, they find that early stage investing fund managers are more eager to overvalue their investments than later stage fund manag-

---

885 See Martin/Rich/Wilks (2006), p. 295.

886 See Lerner/Hardymon/Leamon (2005), p. 414.

887 See Griffin/Varey (1996), p. 228.

888 See Zacharakis/Shepherd (2001), p. 313; Müller (2003), p. 129. MÜLLER provides an overview of behavioral finance aspects in the valuation process of young companies.

889 This is the case, because researchers rarely have access to the required data.

890 See Cumming/Walz (2004). They base their analysis on a dataset collected by the Center for Private Equity Research (CEPRES) consisting of 221 funds, 72 management companies and 5040 entrepreneurial firms.

ers. In early stage investments the informational asymmetries between fund managers and investors are more pronounced, and therefore greater scope for exaggerating returns exists.[891] Interestingly, the authors also found that the likelihood for overstating valuations is greater in environments where less legal and accounting requirements exist.[892] This has implications for the industry itself and the regulatory agenda. More stringent accounting rules reduce significantly the incentives and possibilities to manage the valuations. This is a strong case demonstrating how valuation guidelines provided by the private equity industry associations benefit the industry as a whole.

Knowing that fund managers may have incentives to intentionally manipulate and overstate valuation or that they may be unintentionally biased in setting these valuations is important for fund investors in order to assess the quality of the reported values. It also leads to the question whether the fair value is actually the appropriate measurement basis for private equity portfolio company investments. This will be discussed in the next chapter.

4.3.6.2 Fair Value as Measurement Basis

In the private equity industry, there has been a long-lasting and controversial debate about the right measurement bases. The measurement can be defined as the process of determining the values at which assets and liabilities are to be recognised and carried in the balance sheet and profit and loss statement.[893] The measurement basis of valuation is different to the valuation technique or methodology. The measurement basis defines what the carrying amount purports to represent, whereas the valuation technique describes in detail how to derive the valuation.

It has been elaborated how the fair value of private equity portfolio company investments can be generated by applying valuation techniques. The valuation of portfolio companies is challenging due the special characteristics of private equity. Both venture capital and buyout portfolio company investments are usually not listed. An efficient

[891] See Cumming/Walz (2004), p. 21.

[892] See Cumming/Walz (2004), p. 22.

[893] See for example the definition in the IFRS Framework, para. 99; Ernst & Young (2004), p. 121.

and liquid capital market that provides continuously reliable prices based on active trading is not available.[894]

Venture capital investments typically have a short operating history and lack data or track records that can be projected.[895] As their young businesses rarely produce positive cash flows or earnings, it is very difficult to apply traditional valuation methods.[896] In addition, the valuation of these companies heavily depends on the appraisal of their intangible assets, such as intellectual property rights or entrepreneurial skills, abilities and knowledge.[897] Significantly high risks inherent in venture capital investments are difficult to be quantified.[898] In comparison, buyout investments are usually easier to value.[899] These portfolio companies generally operate in mature industries, have a longer history and produce steady cash flow and income.[900] Hence, their future outlook is more predictable.[901] However, also for buyout investment valuations, fund managers need to make assumptions concerning the input data.

Due to these difficulties in determining fair values of private equity portfolio company investments, many industry participants prefer the cost-based approach as valuation basis instead. According to the cost-based approach, all investments are carried at costs unless a material impairment indicated a write-down in value or a financing round with new investors supported a write-up.[902] The key difference with the fair value approach is that it allows and requires write-ups of portfolio company investments even if no third party transaction has occurred.

---

894 See Ick (2005), p. 18; Böhler (2004b), p. 221; Tyebjee/Bruno (1984), p. 1052.

895 See Gompers (1995), p.1463; Tyebjee/Bruno (1984), p. 1051; Black (2003), p. 48.

896 See Meyer/Mathonet (2005), p. 43.

897 See Meyer/Mathonet (2005), p. 43; Achleitner/Nathusius (2004), p. 5; Michas (1997), p. 4. Intellectual property rights are patents, copyrights, trademarks, design rights or certain specialist rights. See Artley et al. (2003), p. 247. For the challenges of valuing intangible assets see Achleitner/Nathusius/Schraml (2007).

898 See Meyer/Mathonet (2005), p. 43. FINGERLE provides a valuable classification of risks in high growth companies. See Fingerle (2005), pp. 44 et. seq.

899 See Achleitner et al. (2004b), p. 702.

900 This may be, however, different for turnaround investments. See Kraft (2001).

901 See Black (2003), p. 48.

902 See Blaydon/Wainwright (2004a), p. 45.

Proponents of the cost-based approach cite a number of reasons why the approach may be more appropriate for valuing private equity portfolio companies. First, they claim that a regular revaluation of the company investments which is required by the fair value approach may lead to more volatility in carrying values.[903] However, fund investors may accept the volatility knowing that any changes in the valuations are only realized upon disposition of the company.

Secondly, fund manager state that it may be impractical especially for some venture investments to come up with an assessment of the value. However, when it comes to marketing their existing fund performance in order to raise a new fund, very often they actually do not hold their investment at cost and cite that cost would not reflect the 'true' value. Fund investors do not want to see inconsistencies between valuations in marketing documents and fund reports.[904] Fund managers therefore should rather use consistent values in all documents.

Third, applying the conservative cost-based approach prevents the fund managers using their discretion in valuing to overstate the valuations. However, valuation guidelines and accounting requirements provide a framework that set limit to the discretion of the fund managers. In addition, fund managers should provide details on the assumptions and models used to estimate the fair values. If this is the case, fund investors have the possibility to make their own judgments on the appropriateness of these assumptions.

Fourth, frequent determination of valuations can be costly and time-consuming for fund managers. Not every fund managers may be able to afford this exercise. Those, who can, may be diverting resources away from other more important investment activities.[905] However, fund managers themselves need the information for their own controlling and portfolio management.[906]

903 See Tuck (2003c), p. 7.

904 See Snow (2004), p. 44; Harrell/Spiegel (2004), p. 20.

905 See Harrell/Spiegel (2004), p. 20.

906 The maximization of the portfolio company value is the aim of the private equity investors and is therefore typically integrated in internal management systems. See for example Achleitner et al. (2004a), p. 37; Schenk (2004), p. 155.

Overall, there are important reasons why the fair value approach is much more appropriate. The most important one is probably that fund investors want to measure and compare the fund performance which is reflected in the valuations. Conservative valuations do not reflect current performance adequately and make it impossible for fund investors to benchmark their investments.[907]

Furthermore, it has been elaborated in the chapter on fund investors' monitoring that the fair values of the fund portfolio company investments may be input variables for fund investors in their portfolio management approaches.[908] In order to steer the liquidity and the diversity of the fund-of-fund portfolio, fund investors need to assess the actual values as accurate as possible. Therefore, they need the fair values provided by the fund managers. Also, the secondary market of private equity fund investments may benefit from more accurate and current valuations.[909]

Lastly, fund investors face own reporting requirements. If they have to comply with fair value requirements themselves, which is typically the case for many institutional private equity fund investors such as insurance companies or pension funds, they need information of the fair values from their fund managers.

While this debate may still go on, the accounting requirements are more or less clear. As has been shown, preparing accounts according to IFRS or U.S. GAAP requires presenting the fair value of the portfolio company investments. Educated guesses of the values of portfolio company investments take precedence over holding everything at cost.[910] Knowing all the difficulties that a fair value approach entails, it is very important that the fund managers are transparent with the information that relates to the valuation techniques to derive the fair values. If fund investors know the models and assumptions that the fund managers use, they can make their own assessment and judgment on whether the reported values are appropriate or not.

---

907 See Harrell/Spiegel (2004), p. 17.

908 See chapter 3.7 for more details.

909 See Harrell/Spiegel (2004), p. 17. For the secondary market see chapter 3.7.3.

910 See Snow (2006), p. 30.

4.4 Investor Reporting

4.4.1 Introductory Remarks

Statutory financial statements alone do not provide a comprehensive picture of the performance and current state of private equity fund investments.[911] Fund managers therefore need to disclose additional information, which can be called *investor reporting*. Reporting guidelines have been developed by private equity industry associations that include not only a framework for the specific content of the additional disclosure but also a template for its presentation and layout.[912]

This chapter presents an empirical analysis of the content of disclosure in the investor reporting. The objectives of this analysis are:

- to describe the actual disclosure of individual information items in private equity fund reports,
- to measure the average level of disclosure in private equity fund reports, and
- to identify relationships between the level of disclosure and selected fund characteristics.

Disclosure in reports per se is an abstract concept that cannot be measured directly.[913] A research instrument that aims to show the level of disclosure and that has been used in several studies dealing with the disclosure of publicly listed companies is the so-called *disclosure index* of information.[914] A disclosure index is constructed as a function of the number and, in some cases, the relevance of the items provided in the reports.[915] It is calculated by the number of information items contained in a given report divided on a pre-defined list of possible index items.[916] It only provides an indirect and to some extent subjective measure of the underlying concept. However, it has been

---

911 See chapter 4.2.4.3 for more details.

912 See EVCA (2006b); PEIGG (2005); CFA Institute (2005); BVCA (2003).

913 See Wallace/Naser (1995), p. 326; Marston/Shrives (1991), p. 197. According to COOKE/WALLACE, disclosure "does not possess inherent characteristics by which one can determine its intensity or quality like the capacity of a car." Cooke/Wallace (1989), p. 51.

914 See Marston/Shrives (1991), p. 195.

915 See Prencipe (2004), p. 328.

916 See Bukh et al. (2005), p. 719.

proven to be a valid research methodology.[917] The use of disclosure indices is still very common in empirical accounting research.[918] However, for the first time, it is employed to analyze the additional disclosure to investors in private equity fund reports.

The *selection of items* for investigating the extent of disclosure is the first step and a major task in the construction of a disclosure index.[919] A general theory on how to select the items does not exist. As a result, the usefulness of the disclosure index methodology depends on the critical and cautious selection. The user of the private equity fund reports are the fund investors. Therefore, items should be selected which are seen as important by them.[920] The implications of reporting requirements discussed in chapter 3.8.3 thus form the basis for the choice of information items in this study. In addition, a thorough inspection of the literature as to the reporting of private equity funds has been conducted. Finally, disclosures recommended by reporting guidelines developed by private equity industry associations have been considered.[921] Feedback from practitioners has been incorporated and assures the relevance and appropriateness of the selected information items.

The remainder of this chapter is organized as follows: Based on the review of the literature (chapter 4.4.2.1) and the recommendation in reporting guidelines (chapter 4.4.2.2), a comprehensive private equity investor reporting framework will be developed in chapters 4.4.2.3 until 4.4.2.5. This framework contains and groups the information items that are considered to be relevant for investors in private equity funds reports. Various fund characteristics may influence the extent of disclosure (chapter 4.4.3). In chapter 4.4.4 the actual extent of disclosure is measured based on a sample

---

917 The validity has been proved by consistent and corroborative results documented by previous studies on the determinants of disclosure. See Ahmed/Courtis (1999) for a summary.

918 For a review of accounting studies that employ disclosure indices see Ball/Foster (1982); Marston/Shrives (1991); Ahmed/Courtis (1999). The disclosure index has been first applied to quantify the extent of disclosure in annual reports in general. See for example Cerf (1961); Buzby (1975), Singhvi/Desai (1971). Recently, more specific types of information have been analyzed, e.g. segment information, information on intellectual capital, social and environmental disclosures. See for example Prencipe (2004); Bukh et al. (2005).

919 See Marston/Shrives (1991), p. 201.

920 See Marston/Shrives (1991), p. 201. It is, however, questionable whether consensus within the user group is established.

921 This corresponds with processes that researchers use who develop disclosure indices for public companies. See for example Cooke (1989a), pp. 181 et seq; Prencipe (2004), p. 329. The challenge here is, however, that nobody before has developed an index for private equity fund reports.

of funds and by using the developed framework. The results will finally be presented and discussed.

4.4.2 Framework for the Analysis of Investor Reporting

4.4.2.1 Overview on Existing Literature

In comparison to the vast research that exists on disclosure in public capital markets[922], the reporting and information disclosure of private equity funds towards their investors has been virtually neglected by academics to date. This can be explained mainly with the fact that academics lack an access to appropriate data. Very little is known about the content of these reports. Most of the existing surveys have been carried out and analyzed by practitioners.

BÖHLER and PRICEWATERHOUSECOOPERS provide a comprehensive study about the reporting of private equity funds.[923] Based on a questionnaire which was discussed with around 50 Swiss private equity investors, the authors analyze the relevance, satisfaction and the desired reporting interval of 24 different information elements within the formal reports sent to investors. By comparing the relevance and satisfaction of those information elements for investors, information gaps are identified. According to their findings, gaps exist especially with respect to non-financial and forward-looking information.[924]

A slightly different approach based on questionnaires was utilized in a study conducted by PEIGG.[925] In order to get feedback from the industry and to assist the group in developing and promoting its reporting guidelines, the group asked investors as well as fund managers about a variety of aspects concerning the content of and the process related to the reporting.[926] 35 U.S. investors give information on their requirements concerning specific pre-selected information elements. 55 U.S. fund managers offer

---

[922] HEALY/PALEPU provide a review of empirical disclosure literature. See Healy/Palepu (2001). Reviews of studies of the level and determinants of disclosure are provided for example by Ahmed/Courtis (1999); Marston/Shrives (1991).

[923] See Böhler (2004b); PwC (2003).

[924] See PwC (2003), p. 6.

[925] See PEIGG (2004a).

[926] It is explicitly stated that the results are not scientific but are intended to provide PEIGG with an understanding of the views of various industry participants. See PEIGG (2004a), p. 3.

information on their reporting behaviour in respect to these elements as well as about the difficulty to disclose those items within the reports. The combination of both surveys reveals disclosure deficiencies for individual information elements. The authors find that an information gap is most significant in the area of portfolio company financial performance information and fund level performance disclosure.[927]

However, there is criticism as to the usefulness of surveys. This criticism is derived from the human information processing literature. This literature suggests that revealed answers of respondents to surveys usually do not represent what the respondents actually do.[928] For example, weighting the relevance of specific information has no real economic consequences so that investors might tend to weight all information as equally important. Fund managers might misstate their actual disclosure level.

Thus, the application of a content analysis of reporting documents offers a promising approach of investigating the actual reporting behavior instead.[929] KEMMERER/ WEIDIG examine reports of nearly 200 European private equity funds.[930] The study focuses mainly on the reporting interval and the delivery time of reports and concludes that the European private equity industry improved their reporting qualitatively and quantitatively, especially in terms of shorter delivery times for reports. The authors, however, do not analyze details of the actual reporting content.

Other studies only partially address the question of the reported content to investors. HAGENMÜLLER uses a survey among fund managers and investors to investigate the investor relations of European private equity partnerships.[931] His results indicate the important role of reporting as an investor relationship instrument. Furthermore, he shows that industry guidelines are applied by the majority of funds.[932] HIELSCHER/ZELGER/BEYER explore the methods of performance measurement and its presentation in the reporting among German private equity companies.[933] They show het-

---

927 See PEIGG (2004a), p. 6.

928 See for example Libby (1981), pp. 40 et seq.

929 See Hagenmüller (2004), p. 196.

930 See Kemmerer/Weidig (2005), p. 87.

931 See Hagenmüller (2004), p. 130.

932 See Hagenmüller (2004), pp. 174 et seq.

933 See Hielscher/Zelger/Beyer (2003); Haarmann Hemmelrath/Universitaet Leipzig (2002).

erogeneous reporting behaviour concerning the information on portfolio companies and the transparency of fees charged to investors.[934] Based on 14 semi-structured interviews with fund-of-fund managers, DIEM enquires the technical aspects of investment monitoring, i.e. the possibility to standardize the information flows between investors and funds. He concludes that by means of improved automation and the establishment of common standards within the industry, the private equity asset class can be further promoted. ROBBIE/WRIGHT/CHIPLIN examine the fund investors' monitoring process. They look at investors' information requirements, but focus only on the means through which funds provide information to investors, e.g. reports, annual meetings, and on how often specific information is given to investors, e.g. quarterly or annually.[935] Overall, they observe that fund investors have increasing needs for more information. In a survey on limited partnership agreements conducted by the TUCK SCHOOL OF BUSINESS, limited and general partners were asked about the importance and satisfaction of the several reporting aspects concerning the governance of the partnerships.[936] A major finding of the study is that limited partners are more disposed to strengthening the limited partnership agreement as a governance document – especially regarding disclosure.

Overall, these studies only allow some insight into the actual reporting content of private equity partnerships. Further details for the matter at hand are provided by reporting guidelines that have been developed by private equity industry associations.

4.4.2.2 Industry Reporting Guidelines

Due to the specific characteristics of a private equity fund's business model, the financial accounting only offers an incomplete picture for investors.[937] Industry associations have thus developed reporting guidelines over the last years that set out detailed recommendations for funds outlining content and how it should be disclosed as additional information to investors.

The role of reporting guidelines is similar to the role of valuation guidelines. Overall, they serve to improve the information sharing process between funds and their inves-

934 See Haarmann Hemmelrath/Universitaet Leipzig (2002), pp. 13 et seq.

935 See Robbie/Wright/Chiplin (1997), pp. 19 et seq.

936 See Tuck (2004b), p. 15.

937 See Thoen (2002), p. 19.

tors by raising and standardizing the quality of reporting content. They facilitate confidence and trust between both parties. Guidelines shall present best practice, but also aim at pre-empting possible regulation and increase efficiency.[938] Complying with guidelines could reduce the number of special information requests fund managers have to respond to.

For Europe, EVCA was the first industry association issuing reporting guidelines in March 2000 which have been widely adopted across the private equity industry.[939] In June 2006 an update was released.[940] EVCA distinguishes between *requirements* that have to be applied if fund managers claim compliance with the guidelines and *recommendations* whose adoption is left to the discretion of the fund manager.[941] The guidelines cover general aspects, the timing of reports, the content with respect to the fund and portfolio level, the capital account, fees and carried interest. They require semi-annual reports but recommend to report quarterly. They also provide a template to exemplify the structure and layout of best practice reporting. Included is furthermore detailed guidance on how to measure performance. BVCA issued reporting guidelines in 2003 which were, with minor amendments, the so-called level one provision of the old EVCA reporting guidelines.[942]

In March 2005, PEIGG issued *Reporting and Performance Measurement Guidelines* for the U.S. private equity industry.[943] The guidelines were developed through a two-year joint effort among private equity industry participants and incorporate input from industry organizations including EVCA and BVCA. Similar to these guidelines, PEIGG reporting guidelines do not address the financial statements of private equity funds, but focus on additional reporting of fund level information, including capital

938 See PEIGG (2005), pp. 3 et seq.

939 For an overview of the old reporting guidelines see for example Hagenmüller (2004), pp. 167 et seq; Thoen (2002), pp. 22 et seq.

940 This was necessary in order to adopt the reporting guidelines to the new International Private Equity & Venture Capital Valuation Guidelines that have been endorsed in March 2005, and to reflect the evolution of reporting practices within the industry. See EVCA (2006b), p. 3. Most of the changes are due to the change to fair valuation practice. See Witney (2006).

941 See EVCA (2006b), p. 3.

942 See BVCA (2003), p. 3. EVCA's old level one provision specified a minimum reporting standard. See Hagenmüller (2004), p. 168.

943 See PEIGG (2005). The NVCA has not issued any reporting guidelines.

accounts. Details are provided to demonstrate how funds should calculate their performance, especially the IRR and various return multiples. They provide a framework for disclosing portfolio company information, but do not require it.[944] The appendix also illustrates how the guidelines might be incorporated into funds' reports by referring to examples. PEIGG guidelines require quarterly reporting.

With respect to report information requirements on fund level, EVCA and PEIGG reporting guidelines are relatively similar. To claim compliance with EVCA guidelines, however, funds *must* disclose far more information on portfolio company level. Only the disclosure of a few details, e.g. information on budget and forecast, exit plans, syndication partners or explanation of changes in valuation, is at fund managers' discretion. Whether or not to require portfolio-level disclosure was long-debated among PEIGG's members. On the one hand, limited partners wanted more granular information, on the other general partners were cautious about distributing this information, especially against the background of possible public disclosure due to the Freedom of Information Act.[945] A compromise was found: PEIGG reporting guidelines do not prescribe to disclose portfolio company data, but demonstrate a model how to provide it if the general partner voluntarily decides to do so. Interestingly, concerning portfolio companies' balance sheet information items, securities ownership, valuation, and other performance metrics, e.g. cash burn rate, PEIGG guidelines are more precise than EVCA.[946]

To conclude, both reporting guidelines are quite detailed when it comes to the level of information that should be provided to investors, but at the same time allow fund managers some flexibility. Investors therefore still need to agree on the degree of details in reports with their managers.

A third set of reporting guidelines are the *Private Equity Provisions* of the *Global Investment Performance Standards (GIPS)* issued by the CFA Institute in February 2005.[947] Unlike EVCA and PEIGG, these guidelines are primarily designed for fund-

944 See PEIGG (2004b).

945 See Snow (2005), p. 24. For more details about the FOIA see chapter 3.8.4.

946 See PEIGG (2005), p. 18; Snow (2005), p. 25.

947 See CFA Institute (2005), pp. 18 et seq. The revised GIPS standards that include the private equity provisions are effective from January 1, 2006. See Sormani (2005), p. 12. CFA Institute

raising purposes and should enable investors to compare investment performance using a consistent methodology.[948] They therefore address investment performance measurement and presentation issues and do not explicitly state which information items have to be disclosed in regular reports. If private equity funds claim compliance with GIPS, they must present their performance measured by gross and net IRR since inception of their activities, plus various multiples based on composites defined by strategy (e.g. early stage, buyouts, or turnaround) and by vintage year. Furthermore, they are required to disclose additional information on these composites, on valuation methodologies applied,[949] the valuation processes, benchmarks used and details of the IRR calculations.

Over the last years, the private equity industry has put a tremendous effort in standardizing the reporting and performance measurement which resulted in the release of the above reviewed guidelines. However, a logical next step would be the issuance of harmonized, truly global reporting guidelines. This requires an additional joint effort by the industry, especially from associations in Europe and the U.S., but would be in the interests of both fund managers and investors.[950]

4.4.2.3 Categories of Information in Fund Reports

The elaborated implications for fund managers' reporting in chapter 3.8, the review of the current literature and the discussion of the most important industry reporting guidelines indicate which information might be disclosed in private equity fund reports. A comprehensive and detailed framework is developed in the following that displays possible information items. The general categorization of the framework has been already presented in the discussion of the fund investors' information needs for monitoring purposes in chapter 3.8.3. In chapter 4.4.4 this framework will be tested against the actual reporting content found in a sample of reports.

---

also provides interpretive guidance on applying GIPS to private equity investments. See CFA Institute (2006).

948 See Sormani (2005), p. 12.

949 GIPS explicitly require a fair valuation of investments. See chapter 4.3.4.2 for details.

950 See Hagenmüller (2004), p. 173. International private equity fund investors do not prefer national standards. See Hielscher/Zelger/Beyer (2003), p. 505.

Based on the above described analysis, 114 potential information items have been identified in private equity fund reports.[951] In a first step, these information items can be broadly categorized into 62 information items on fund level and 52 information items on portfolio company level. In a second step, the information can be further categorized in six different information categories on fund level and in four information categories on portfolio company level. Figure 64 provides an overview.

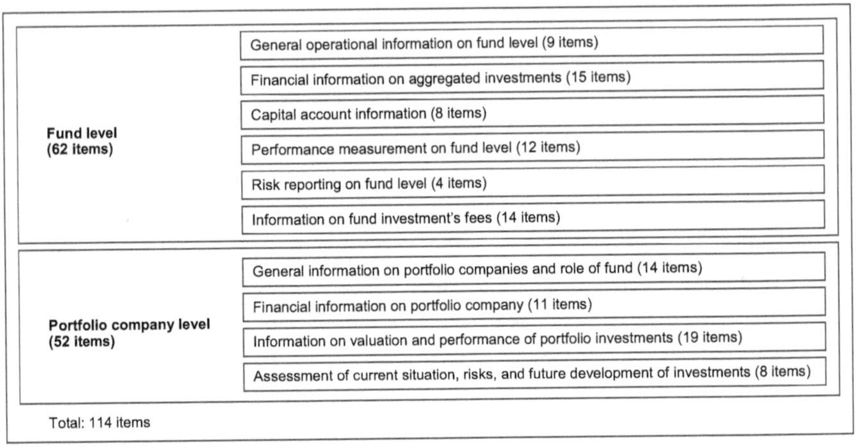

Figure 64: Reporting framework in private equity fund reports

4.4.2.4 Information on Fund Level

On the fund level, 62 information items have been identified which can be classified into six different information categories. The first category comprises the *general operational information on fund level*, e.g. domicile, legal form, strategy, or management. These information items provide a valuable overview of the fund investment.

---

951 The following summary and analysis of information items that could be included in funds' reporting does not mention anything about the actual presenting and the layout of reports. For an adequate template of how to present information in reports see the examples in EVCA or PEIGG reporting guidelines. See EVCA (2006b), pp. 13 et seq; PEIGG (2005), pp. 10 et seq.

General operational information on fund level (9 items)

- Fund's domicile
- Legal form
- Closing date
- Vintage year
- Portfolio or fund strategy (incl. any changes)
- Changes of GP's management
- Information about related party transactions
- Note on deal flow
- Note about the application of any reporting guidelines

Figure 65: General operational information on fund level

The second category contains the *financial information on aggregated investments*. The respective information items present a structured statement of the overall investment activity of the fund.[952]

Financial information on aggregated investments (15 items)

- Total commitments
- Total capital drawn down
- Total capital invested
- Total sum distributed
- Date of capital drawn down
- Total capital committed or reserved for follow-on-rounds
- Total value of remaining assets (NAV)
- List of all current investments
- List of all new investments
- List of all realizations
- Sum of net investment income or loss
- Sum of realized gains or losses
- Sum of unrealized gains or losses
- Note of any leverage to the fund (debt, guarantees, contingent liabilities)
- Average holding period of investments over the life of the fund

Figure 66: Financial information on aggregated investments

In addition to the aggregated information on the fund level, each individual investor should receive a statement of his own *capital account* that includes the changes in the fund investor's equity positions. It is adjusted for capital and operating activity during the current reporting period, such as capital contributions, distributions, income allocations, expense allocations, and realized and unrealized gain or loss allocations.[953] The capital account balance can be calculated with the remaining investment valued both at cost and at fair value,[954] and from inception to date or for the current reporting period only.[955] Some fund reports might provide the capital account of all individual investors and even include their names.

---

952 For an example see EVCA (2006b), p. 17.

953 See Böhler (2004b), p. 273.

954 See Hagenmüller (2004), p. 168.

955 See EVCA (2006b), p. 11; PEIGG (2005), p. 8.

Capital account information (8 items)

- Current capital account balance at cost
- Current capital account balance at fair value
- Capital account information since inception
- Capital account information for current period
- Detailed capital account statement (shows all investors)
- Investors' names
- Detailed information of investors' ownership
- Capital account information for General Partner

Figure 67: Capital account information

Evidently, fund investors are especially interested in the performance of the investment activity of the fund. The category *performance measurement on fund level* therefore comprises 12 information items that allow readers of the fund reports to assess the success of the fund managers. The internal rate of return (gross and net of fees) and various investment multiples are the most common measures. However, private equity funds may also provide information on the payback period on fund level and on how to benchmark their performance against other private equity funds or the public market.

Performance measurement on fund level (12 items)

- IRR of fund's realized investments (Gross IRR)
- IRR of fund's realized and unrealized investments (Gross IRR)
- IRR on fund investment net to investors (Net IRR)
- Detailed IRR (Gross IRR) by industry, geography, stage, lead partner responsible for investments
- Multiple on fund inv.: total value to paid-in capital (TVPI)
- Multiple on fund inv.: residual value to paid-in capital (RVPI)
- Multiple on fund inv.: distribution to paid-in capital (DPI)
- Detailed multiples by industry, geography, stage, lead partner responsible for the investments
- Payback period on fund level
- Comparison against an industry benchmark
- Information on calculation of benchmark
- Comparison with other asset classes

Figure 68: Performance measurement on fund level

Although risk reporting is an integral part of corporate annual reporting and of increasing importance for investors in public equity,[956] it seems to be rather neglected in private equity fund reports.[957] The EVCA reporting guidelines vaguely require that funds include information on material risks of the performance of the fund as a whole.[958] However, BÖHLER concludes that information on the risk management process is valuable for investors and should be disclosed.[959] Part of the *risk reporting on fund*

956 See for example Bungartz (2003) for a study among German public companies.

957 Only few general partners even measure the risks inherent in investments. Some do so by calculating loss ratios or applying scoring models. See Hielscher/Zelger/Beyer (2003), p. 503.

958 See EVCA (2006b), p. 6. PEIGG reporting guidelines do not address risk reporting at all.

959 See Böhler (2004b), p. 275.

level might be quantitative, e.g. loss ratios.[960] Currency risks are also quantitatively measurable. They are important to look at and should be easier to disclose than other potential risks. The other part may be qualitative information.

Risk reporting on fund level (4 items)

- Information on fund's currency exposure
- Quantitative risk measures on fund level
- Information on fund's risk management processes
- Qualitative information on fund's specific risks

Figure 69: Risk reporting on fund level

Additionally important content in reports on fund level are *information on fund investment's fees* that fund investors are charged by fund managers.[961] This comprises the actual sum of management fee plus its basis of calculation. EVCA guidelines require that the information is specified in a clear fee statement. Furthermore, fund managers charge consulting or monitoring fees on portfolio companies. This fee income is increasingly being split with limited partners to offset the management fees.[962] This means that fund managers reimburse the fund investors for part of this income. Reports should also include a statement of performance fee, i.e. information on the carried interest that has been paid to and the carried interest that has been earned by the fund managers during the reporting period.[963]

Information on fund investment's fees (14 items)

- Management fees
- Basis of calculation of management fees
- Detailed fee statement
- Deal fees
- Broken deal fees
- Consulting fees
- Monitoring / director fees
- Fund's compensation disclosed in total and by transaction
- Fund administration costs
- Detailed statement on expenses paid on individual transaction
- Total carried interest paid since inception
- Carried interest paid during reporting period
- Carried interest earned during reporting period
- Basis of calculation of carried interest

Figure 70: Information on fund investment's fees

960 The loss ratio could be the total amount of write-offs measured by the cost of the investments relative to the total invested capital.

961 See Böhler (2004b), p. 272.

962 See Mawson (2005), p. 18 for details. These fees can be significant. Blackstone, for example, is said to have charged more than $100m of transaction and monitoring fees in less than a year when it floated Celanese, a German chemicals company in 2005.

963 See EVCA (2006b), p. 12.

4.4.2.5 Information on Portfolio Company Level

The extent of private equity funds' reporting on underlying portfolio companies is subject to discussion between limited and general partners. With respect to the content, four different categories can be identified which comprise 52 single information items altogether.

The first category summarizes the *general information on portfolio companies and role of the fund* as investor. This information, e.g. legal name, location, brief description of business, should not frequently change. EVCA requires fewer details for already realized transaction.[964]

General information on portfolio companies and role of fund (14 items)

- Legal and trading name of portfolio company
- Location of head office or management
- Name of CEO and management
- Webpage
- Brief description of the business
- Summary investment thesis (investment rationale)
- Industry / sub-sector
- Current stage of investment
- Stage of investment at time of investment
- Company status (public, private)
- Statement of the fund's role in the investment (lead, co-lead etc.)
- Board representation (names and numbers of seats held compared to the total board seats, if any)
- Name of the responsible investment manager (partner, principal, personnel) of fund
- List of major co-investors in the deal

Figure 71: General information on portfolio companies and role of fund

Likely to be more subject to change is the potential *financial information on portfolio companies* that contains 11 possible items. This includes accounting figures, both income statement or balance sheet related, and other financial ratios. The information could be reported for the current period, could be compared to historic data or could be budgeted or forecast for the future.

Financial information on portfolio companies (11 items)

- Accounting standard (national GAAP, US GAAP, IFRS)
- Excerpt of income statement
- Excerpt of balance sheet
- Excerpt of cash flow statement
- Figures on sales
- Figures on earnings/income (EBIT, EBITDA, net earnings)
- Figures on capital structure and liquidity (cash, debt, etc.)
- Comparison against budget
- Budget or forecast for next year on income and balance sheet
- Historic data on income and balance sheet
- Non-financial figures (customers, suppliers, etc.)

Figure 72: Financial information on portfolio companies

With respect to the *information on valuation and performance of the portfolio company investments,* 19 different information items have been identified that could be

---

964 See EVCA (2006b), p. 8.

disclosed by the fund manager. First, these items include general descriptive information on the appliance of any valuation guidelines and on the valuation process. They comprise information about the questions whether different valuations are used in financial accounting and investors reporting and whether the fund manager notes the use of fair value. Secondly, the valuation methodology used to determine the investment value should be described: For each investment it should be stated whether the manager uses cost or a different value and which valuation methodology is used. What is the rationale for it? Does the manager provide the detailed calculation, e.g. the composition of applied multiples?[965] Are any changes in valuation explained? The third part then comprises rather hard figures on the valuation, e.g. percentage of ownership, date of initial investment, valuation of the investment at time of investment and at reporting date. Furthermore, any information on income, gains and losses and gross IRR or investment multiple could be given.

Information on valuation and performance of the portfolio investments (19 items)

- Note about the application of any valuation guidelines
- Description of the valuation process applied
- Note about whether different valuations are used in financial statements and investors' reporting
- Note about the use of fair value
- Note about the use of cost or a different value for each investment
- Valuation methodology used (e.g. earnings multiple, DCF)
- Rationale for used valuation methodology
- Detailed calculation of valuation provided (e.g. by disclosing peer group)
- Note on any changes in valuation methodologies
- Date of initial investment
- Percentage ownership of fund
- Valuation (cost) at time of investment
- Valuation at reporting date
- Net investment income or loss on investment
- Realized gains or losses on investment
- Unrealized gains or losses on investment
- Divestment or distribution amounts
- Gross IRR on portfolio company investment
- Multiple on investment: fair value divided by cost

Figure 73: Information on valuation and performance of the portfolio investments

The last group of information on portfolio company level *assesses the current situation, risks, and future development of the investments*. The fund manager could describe significant events during the reporting period, give a qualitative assessment of the current status (e.g. "on track"), and report the achievement of important milestones. Also specific risks to the investment could be revealed. Of importance for the investors are furthermore exit related information items.

965 For example, the companies included in the peer group could be disclosed.

Assessment of current situation, risks and future development of the investments (8 items)	
• Significant events during the reporting period • Assessment of the company's status compared to the expectation at the time of investment ("on track", etc.) • Milestones analysis (hard figures) • Quantitative risk measures on portfolio level	• Qualitative information on portfolio company specific risks • Exit plans (IPO, trade sale) • Exit horizon • Estimated exit valuation

Figure 74: Assessment of current situation, risks, and future development of the investments

4.4.3 Possible Influence of Fund Characteristics on the Disclosure

In the description of the reporting behaviour of private equity funds, it is interesting to analyze whether specific private equity fund characteristics have an influence on the extent of disclosure in private equity reports. As of today, no study exists that identifies this relationship. However, the relationship between the extent of disclosure and several firm characteristics has been examined for the reports of publicly listed companies.[966] When applicable, it will be referred to the results of these studies to develop hypotheses on the determinants of disclosure.

One aspect that could influence the extent of disclosure is the *strategy of the fund*, which shall be broadly classified into the two sub-segments of private equity, i.e. buyout and venture capital.[967] It is expected that buyout and venture capital funds provide the same extent of information on the fund level. However, concerning information on portfolio companies it is appropriate to assume that there are differences as venture capital investments are different to buyout investments. Investments in early stage companies are unlikely to show positive earnings. Financial information on those companies will potentially not be provided, although qualitative judgements on the current performance or the achievement of milestones should be alternatively disclosed. The non-financial information items should be far more important. Buyout fund managers may focus more intensively on key performance indicators which are based on financial accounting numbers, whereas venture capital fund managers may rely to a larger extent on the achievement of technical and contractual milestones.[968] Buyout fund managers typically control their portfolio company investment by setting-

966 For an overview see for example Ding et al. (2005) or Ahmed/Courtis (1999).

967 This relates to the question whether the type of industry has an influence on the level of disclosure. It has been confirmed for public reports by Adrem (1999), Cooke (1989b) or Cooke (1991) who find differences in the extent of disclosure for Swedish and Japanese companies depending on the industry type.

968 See Achleitner et al. (2004a), p. 34; Schenk (2004), p. 157.

up information systems, which should enable them to easily generate required information for their investors. Venture capital fund managers also base their controlling on information systems. However, the information systems and the reporting content are normally less comprehensive and less complex.[969] This may lead to a different level of disclosure in fund reports. To conclude, the first hypothesis is therefore:

H1: There are differences in the level of disclosure between reports of venture capital funds and reports of buyout funds.

The level of disclosure in private equity fund reports may also depend on the *geographic location of the fund manager.*[970] The major players are European and U.S. funds.[971] As the private equity industry has a longer history in the U.S.,[972] one could assume that market players are more sophisticated and information flow between fund investors and fund managers is more comprehensive. However, two factors may cause the opposite. There is a longer tradition of industry reporting guidelines that foster a more standardized and comprehensive reporting in Europe than in the U.S. It is assumed that the existing guidelines are much more prevalent among the fund managers in Europe.[973] Furthermore, due to the Freedom of Information Act, fund managers fear that their public investors, e.g. public pension funds, might be forced to publicly disclose information given to them. As a result, they might tend to report less. It is therefore concluded:

H2: There are differences in the level of disclosure between reports of European fund managers and U.S. fund managers.

The *size of funds* might be another important factor in explaining variability in the extent of disclosure in funds' reporting. The size can be measured in a number of ways. In this study, two variables are applied: total commitments of investors to the fund and

---

969 See Achleitner/Bassen (2004), p. 161.

970 Archambault/Archambault (2003) demonstrate that disclosure is influenced by social factors such as cultural, political, economic, and corporate ones. Jaggi/Low (2000) find that the legal system of a country plays an important role in financial disclosures.

971 The Asian private equity market is growing considerably. See Grabenwarter/Weidig (2005a), p. 15. However, the market is not yet as developed as in Europe or the U.S.

972 See Gompers (1994), pp. 5 et seq.

973 Unfortunately, there are no comparable studies about the actual application of reporting guidelines in the U.S. versus Europe.

number of investment professionals working for the fund manager. Buyout funds tend to be larger than venture capital funds, but might have the same number of professional investment managers. However, as the fund managers are responsible for producing the reports, the human resources that are available may be the same.

A positive relationship between size and extent of disclosure has been found for corporate reports in the public equity market,[974] and there are reasons to expect similar results for private equity funds. Fund managers that raise large funds might have an incentive to provide more information to satisfy their investors, especially if they plan to raise even larger sums in the future. Only those fund managers with an appropriate investor relations or reporting system in place may be able to raise large commitments. From an investor's monitoring perspective, larger funds are likely to be of more economic importance to them as the size of funds might correlate with the size of their individual commitments to the fund. Thus, they may demand from larger funds to deliver more information.[975] In addition, if one assumes that larger funds have more investors with diversified information needs, there is a greater incentive for their fund managers to increase the quality of the standardized information flow by disclosing more information through formal reports. For fund managers, the accumulation and dissemination of information is time consuming and costly. Smaller entities with fewer investment professionals may not possess the necessary resources for collecting and presenting an extensive array of information.[976] To summarize, the third and fourth hypotheses are the following:

H3: There is a positive relationship between the level of disclosure in the fund reports and the total commitments of the funds.

H4: There is a positive relationship between the level of disclosure in the fund reports and the number of investment professionals working for the management company of the fund.

Last but not least, the *age of the management company* may be a further factor that could influence the level of disclosure within the funds' reports. Younger funds proba-

---

974 See among others Cooke (1989a), p. 120 and Ahmed/Courtis (1999), p. 37 and therein cited studies.

975 See Cooke (1991), p. 176.

976 See Buzby (1975), p. 18.

bly lack resources that could be allocated to the reporting processes. High quality reporting might place a burden to the accounting and financial staff of younger fund managers.[977] Contrary, younger fund managers might realize that providing timely and comprehensive information to their investors could be an important differentiator in a competitive market and might compensate for their - up to then - lack of proven track record. [978] As both effects potentially offset each other, the fifth hypothesis is therefore:

H5: There is no relationship between the level of disclosure in the fund reports and the age of the management company.

4.4.4 Level of Disclosure

4.4.4.1 Research Methodology

To measure the disclosure of private equity fund reports in this study, a disclosure index consisting of the elaborated 114 quantitative and qualitative information items is applied. As shown above, the total disclosure index with 114 items is further subdivided into ten different categories.

The extent of disclosure in a single report is quantified as the percentage of recorded information items found in that report.[979] A dichotomous procedure is exploited, in which an item scores one if it is disclosed and zero if it is not disclosed.[980] This assumes that each item of disclosure is equally important. The question of weighting the items according to their varying degree of importance regularly arises in disclosure studies. The determination of weights could be based on the perceived relative importance by a user group.[981] These ratings are typically obtained through a survey without real economic consequences to the respondents and therefore might not fully reflect

---

977 Due to this argument, EVCA allows some discretion in their guidelines for fund managers to decide what information to report.

978 See Meek (2005b), p. 36.

979 Disclosure quality is difficult to assess. Therefore, researchers tend to assume quantity and quality are positively related. See Botosan (1997), p. 324.

980 See Cooke (1991), p. 179.

981 See Ahmed/Courtis (1999), p. 36.

the actual use and importance of the items.[982] COOKE argues furthermore that different classes of users attach different weights to different items and assumes that the subjective weights would offset each other.[983] The purpose of using an unweighted index is to reduce subjectivity. As it has become the norm in annual reports studies,[984] the unweighted method should also be applied here to analyze private equity fund reports.

The fact that certain items of disclosure may not be applicable to a particular company is another problem that usually arises in disclosure studies.[985] Disregarding whether an item is not disclosed because it is not relevant to the fund or whether the fund inappropriately excludes the item could distort the results of the analysis. Four of 114 information items have been identified for which it cannot be stated clearly whether they are relevant for a specific fund or not.[986] However, one should expect that the fund's report even makes a note on non-occurrence of the events, e.g. changes to the management or changes in valuation methodologies. With respect to all other items, it is either clear that they apply to all funds. Or by reading the whole fund report, one can judge that an item is not disclosed or even irrelevant at all.[987] Therefore, all 114 information items are included to show aggregated results of the disclosure level. But care must be exercised when interpreting results relating to each individual information item.

The disclosure of portfolio company level data depends on the availability of this data for the specific company. Different disclosure levels might be observable for different

---

982 See Chow/Wong-Boren (1987), p. 536; Wallace/Naser (1995), p. 331; Ball/Foster (1982), p. 201. Several studies use questionnaires to ask financial analysts about their perceived importance of selected items. See for example Buzby (1974); Prencipe (2004).

983 See Cooke (1989b), p. 182.

984 See Ahmed/Courtis (1999), p. 36. Empirical evidence has also demonstrated that using weighted or unweighted indexes produces equivalent results and therefore might be interchangeable. See Chow/Wong-Boren (1987), pp. 536 et seq; Prencipe (2004), p. 333.

985 See Marston/Shrives (1991), p. 204; Patton/Zelenka (1997), p. 609.

986 These are 'changes of GP's management', 'information about related party transactions', 'total capital committed or reserved for follow-on rounds', and 'note on any changes in valuation methodologies.'

987 This approach was suggested by COOKE. He acknowledges that this introduces an element of subjectivity into the dichotomous procedure, but is appropriate to overcome the mentioned problem. See Cooke (1989a), p. 115.

companies in one single report. This has been taken into account by crediting funds for the specific information item if it is displayed at least once in a report.

Formally, the actual total disclosure (TD) score for a private equity fund is calculated as follows:[988]

$$TD = \left(\sum_{i=1}^{M} d_i / M \right) \times 100\%$$

where $d_i = 1$ *if the item* d_i *is disclosed*

$d_i = 0$ *if the item* d_i *is not disclosed*

$M = 114$ *(maximum amount of information items)*

In order to control subjectivity, the private equity fund reports were read and carefully analyzed by two independent coders for evidence of various items. Any potential conflicts were resolved by joint investigation of the respective reports.

4.4.4.2 Sample Description

Private equity fund reports from limited partnerships are confidential data and are not publicly available. The sample of private equity reports that are analyzed comprises the portfolios of two established and leading European fund investors that invest in venture capital and buyout funds in Europe and U.S. It has been provided as data set for the purpose of this study.

The sample is taken from the original fund investments of the two fund investors. Fund-of-funds and mezzanine funds have been excluded. Also funds that have not yet invested in any portfolio company are excluded as these funds, of course, cannot yet report information on portfolio level. All funds in the sample have the legal structure of a limited partnership and are not publicly listed. The database includes 36 annual reports around the year 2004. It comprises financial statutory statements and additional investor reports.[989] The sample encompasses venture capital and buyout funds from Europe and U.S. as shown in Figure 75.[990]

---

988 See Bukh et al. (2005), p. 720 or for a slightly different notation Cooke (1989a), pp. 182 et seq.

989 Only those parts of the report have been considered that have been provided to all investors in the fund and which are not due to investors' possible role in advisory boards. Included in the sample are 27 funds' financial statutory statements and investor reports as of December 31, 2004. For one

		Total sample	Europe	U.S.
Total sample	*Number of funds*	36 100.0%	20 55.6%	16 44.4%
Buyout funds	*Number of funds*	20 55.6%	13 36.2%	7 19.4%
Venture capital funds	*Number of funds*	16 44.4%	7 19.4%	9 25.0%

Figure 75: Fund sample

In order to examine whether there are any relationships between certain characteristics of the funds and the actual level of disclosure, the following data has been collected for each fund: the committed capital, the age of the management company, and the number of investment professionals working for the management company. The smallest fund measured by its committed capital counts EUR 47 million and the largest one counts EUR 4,482 million.[991] The age of the management companies varies from four years to 33 years with an average age of 15.1 years. The number of investment professionals is on average 24.6 with a high range of three to 175. For a summary of the descriptive information of the sample see Figure 76.

Characteristics of the funds	Mean	Std. deviation	Min	Max
Committed capital [EUR million]	1,096	1,342	47	4,482
Age of management company [years]	15.1	8.4	4	33
Investment professionals [number]	24.6	30.3	3	175

Figure 76: Additional characteristics of the fund sample

fund, those documents are provided as of September 30, 2004, and for another fund as of December 31, 2003. For seven others funds, financial statutory statements as of December 31, 2004 in combination with investor reports for the first quarter 2005 are available. All other documents, e.g. quarterly reports that are provided by the fund managers, have been reviewed in order to assure that they do not contain different information content.

990 Funds that invest in both venture capital and buyout have been classified according to the prevalent focus.

991 Not EUR dominated fund commitments have been converted in EUR using the exchange rates as of December 31, 2004.

As mentioned before, annual reports of private equity funds are usually not publicly available.[992] Therefore, collecting data from all existing funds is almost impossible.[993] Completeness and representativeness of the data set cannot be doubtlessly assessed and, thus, should not be claimed.[994] The sample may contain a bias of atypical investment behavior of the fund investors' managers with respect to the average market. However, this effect should be mitigated since two independent fund investors have provided the data. Differences between venture capital and buyout funds on the one hand, and funds from Europe and the U.S. on the other, shall be especially examined. The data set is evenly distributed with respect to these attributes. Therefore, it can be concluded that, for the purpose of this analysis, the sample provides a valuable basis.

4.4.4.3 Results

The purpose of this analysis is to demonstrate the variability in the amount of reported information across different private equity funds and to understand, in which information categories the fund reports show a lack of information. This may indicate room for improvements. Relationships between the extent of disclosure and certain fund characteristics are explored. To test any significant relative disclosure score differences between buyout vs. venture capital funds and European vs. U.S. funds, the *Mann-Whitney U* test for two independent samples is applied.[995] This non-parametric test is rather used than the t-test due to concerns about the small sample sizes (36 fund

---

992 Exemptions are reports of private equity funds listed at stock exchanges, e.g. reports of Deutsche Beteiligung AG, 3i Ltd., or bmp AG. However, these publicly listed vehicles are not within the scope of this dissertation.

993 FEINENDEGEN/SCHMIDT/WAHRENBURG also note that problem in their paper on limited partnership agreements. See Feinendegen/Schmidt/Wahrenburg (2003), p. 1174.

994 Different approaches have been considered in former research on private equity in order to assess the completeness and representativeness of data sets. GOMPER/LERNER for example compare their sample of limited partnership agreements with a database compiled by Venture Economics. See Gompers/Lerner (1996), p. 477. FEINENDEGEN/SCHMIDT/WAHRENBURG match the fund volume of their sample with the total new funds raised within that period. See Feinendegen/Schmidt/Wahrenburg (2003), p. 1174. Due to the lack of data, the assessment cannot be done in this case.

995 For details on the Mann-Whitney U test see for example Bortz (1999), pp. 146 et seq. The tests in this analysis are performed with SPSS.

reports) and to avoid the assumption that the independent variables are normally distributed.[996]

The presentation of the study's results is structured as follows: First of all, the total disclosure indices for all fund reports and the distribution across the funds will be discussed. Then, a deeper look into the results of the ten different information categories, divided in fund and portfolio level, will be presented. Some interesting scores on the respective single information items shall be highlighted. Finally, the compliance of the funds reports with the EVCA reporting guidelines will be analyzed. Appendix C contains a comprehensive list of the scores of each individual information item. This list displays the respective differences for venture capital and buyout funds on the one hand, and European and U.S. funds on the other.

Total disclosure index

Figure 77 provides descriptive statistics for the distribution of the total aggregated disclosure index scores for the whole sample.

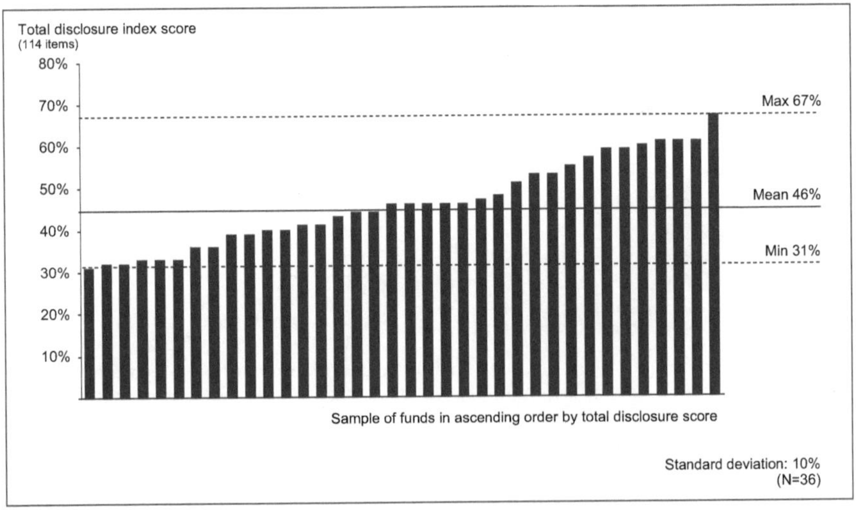

Figure 77: Total disclosure index scores

[996] The data in this study satisfies the three assumptions underlying the *Mann-Whitney U* test: (i) the two samples are random, (ii) the two samples are independent, and (iii) the scale of measurement is at least ordinal. See for example Eckstein (2000), p. 162; Janssen/Laatz (2003), p. 497.

The mean score across the 36 private equity funds for all 114 items is 46% with a standard deviation of 10%. The scores range from 31% (lowest score) to 67% (highest score), indicating a wide variation in the disclosure level of private equity funds. As can be seen in Figure 77, however, there are no extreme values but the scores are equally distributed over the whole range.

Buyout funds receive an average total disclosure score of 49% (*SD=9%*) and venture capital funds of 43% (*SD=10%*). The Mann-Whitney U test indicates that this difference is only slightly not statistically significant on a 5% level (*Mann-Whitney U=100.0, z=-1.915, p=0.056, two-tailed*). European private equity funds disclose on average 50% of the information items (*SD*=10%), whereas U.S. funds only disclose an average of 41% (*SD*=8%). This difference in disclosure between European and U.S. funds is statistically significant (*Mann-Whitney U=79.5, z=-2.569, p=0.010, two-tailed*).

As far as the relationship of the total disclosure score with the additional fund characteristics such as the committed capital, the number of investment professionals, and the age of the management company is concerned, no significant correlations can be detected. A relationship of these additional fund characteristics has also not been found with respect to any of the disclosure index scores of the individual information categories. Based on these results, there is no evidence for an influence of these fund characteristics and of the extent of disclosure in the private equity fund reports.

Disclosure on fund and portfolio company level

Next, the total disclosure index is divided in information on fund and on portfolio company level which can be seen in Figure 78.

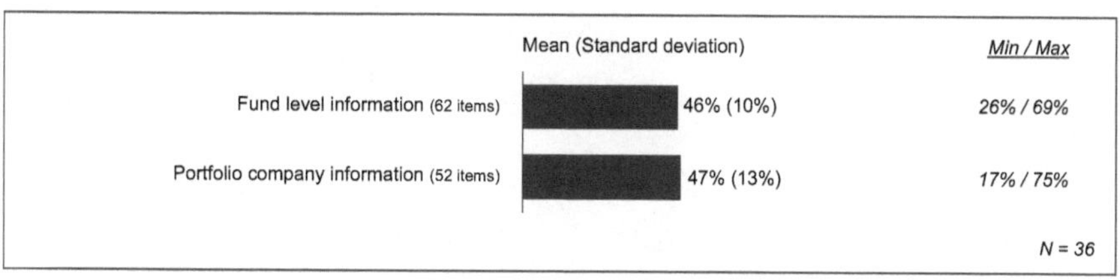

Figure 78: Disclosure scores on fund and portfolio company level

The average disclosure level of information items on fund level is 46% *(SD=10%)*, which is not different to the average disclosure level of information on portfolio companies (*M*=47%, *SD*=13%). However, one can see that the distribution is broader at portfolio company level. The minimum (maximum) level of disclosure is 17% (75%) in comparison to 26% (69%) on fund level. This indicates that the difference in total reporting behavior of all funds may be potentially explained by the difference in reporting on portfolio company level.

With respect to the overall disclosure on fund level, no significant differences between European and U.S. funds or between buyout and venture capital funds are found. There are also no differences between the disclosure indices of buyout and venture capital funds on portfolio company level. Prominent, however, is the significant difference between European and U.S. funds regarding the disclosure score on portfolio company information. European funds achieve a significant higher score (*M*=53%, *SD*=10%) than U.S. funds (*M*=40%, *SD*=13%, *Mann-Whitney U=55.5, z=-3.332, p=0.001, two-tailed*).

Disclosure in the information categories on fund level

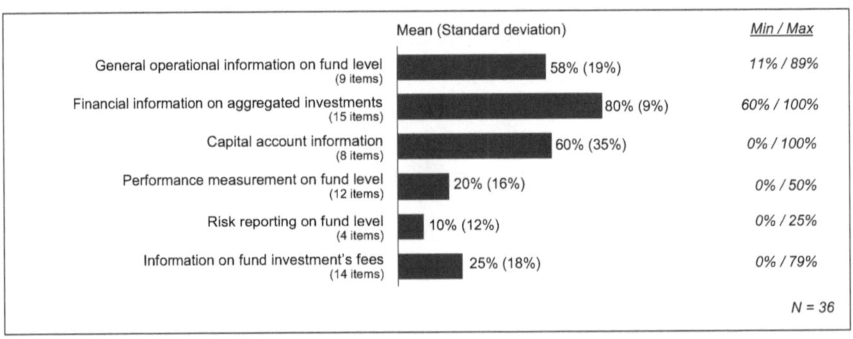

Figure 79: Disclosure category scores on fund level

As Figure 79 shows, the disclosure category score on *general operational information on fund level* is on average 58% (*SD*=19%) with a high range between the minimum score of 11% and the maximum score of 89%. Regarding the individual information item scores, only 14% of all funds and no U.S. fund at all state compliance with any industry reporting guidelines. Only 31% of the funds make a note on their actual deal flow, and only 39% report any changes of the general partner's management.[997]

On fund level, the category *financial information on aggregated investments* receives the highest average score with 80%. This category has also the lowest standard deviation with 9%. Looking at the individual information item scores within that category, one sees that only 14% of all funds report average holding periods, 17% report the information on total capital committed or reserved for follow-on funds. 47% of the funds display the date of capital draw downs, and 56% of all funds make a note on any leverage (debt, guarantees or contingent liabilities) to the fund. Buyout funds achieve a disclosure score of on average 83% (*SD*=9%), which is not significantly more than venture capital funds with an average of 77% (*SD*=8%). European funds report significantly more information (*M*=84%, *SD*=8%) than U.S. funds (*M*=75%, *SD*=7%, *Mann-Whitney U=68.5, z=-2.988, p=0.003, two-tailed*).

On average, 60 % of the possible *capital account information* is disclosed with no outliers regarding the individual information items. Interestingly, however, the range between the minimum (0%) and the maximum (100%) category disclosure score is the highest among all information categories. All of this, and the comparably high standard deviation of 35%, indicates that funds either disclose all of the information belonging to that category or nothing at all. The capital account information since inception is reported by only 42% of all funds whereas this information for the current period is reported by 72%.

The information category *performance measurement on fund level* receives a disclosure score of 20% (*SD*=16%). The maximum disclosure score achieved is only 50%. Whereas many funds still report a net IRR to investors (67%) and a TVPI multiple (53%), other information on performance is in general not provided. Almost no fund reports a detailed break-down of the IRR (3%) or multiple (3%) on meaningful subcategories such as industry, geography, stage, or lead partner responsible for the investment. Only 6% of the funds provide a comparison against an industry benchmark such as a potential peer group, and no fund at all discloses any information concerning a comparison against different asset classes.

---

[997] As has been noted earlier, information on changes on the general partner's management is an information item for which it cannot clearly be stated whether they are relevant for a specific fund or not.

The information category *risk reporting on fund level* comprises only four information items. The disclosure score for that category is 10% (*SD*=12%), which is the lowest score among all categories. No fund discloses any information on the risk management processes within the management company of the fund or any other quantitative risk information. The only risk that is actually mentioned in the reports is currency risk. 36% of the fund reports include information on the currency exposure. Nearly all of them are, however, European funds (57% versus 7% U.S. funds). This leads to significant overall differences in the disclosure of this category between European funds (*M*=15%, *SD*=13%) and U.S. funds (*M*=3%, *SD*=9%, *Mann-Whitney U=84.0, z=-2.864, p=0.004, two-tailed*).

The category *information on the fund investment's fees* receives a disclosure index score of 25% (*SD*=18%). Again there are large differences between the funds with a minimum score of 0% and a maximum score of 79%. Nearly all funds disclose the management fees that have to be paid. Approximately half of them report the basis of calculation on both the management fee and the carried interest. However, further details on the different types of expenses and income that the fund generates are only provided by between 10% and 20% of the fund sample. There are significant differences with respect to the category scores between buyout and venture capital funds. Buyout funds report a disclosure score of on average 31% (SD=21%), venture capital funds only of an average of 16% (*SD*=8%, *Mann-Whitney U=93.0, z=-2.163, p=0.031, two-tailed*).

Disclosure in the information categories on portfolio company level

The results of the four information categories on portfolio company level will be provided next and are summarized in Figure 80.

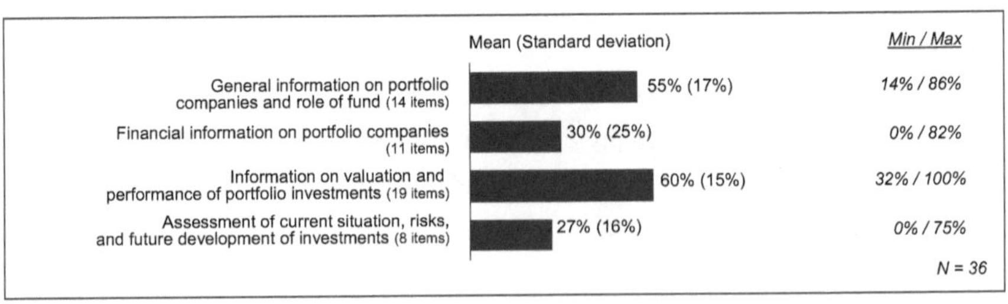

Figure 80: Disclosure category scores on portfolio company level

Regarding the category *general information on portfolio company and role of fund,* an average disclosure score of 55% (*SD*=17%) is achieved, again with a large range between the minimum score of 14% and the maximum score of 86%. Looking at the information item scores reveals a lack of information regarding the role of the fund in the portfolio company. Only 19% of the funds report the name of the responsible investment managers, and only 31% provide a statement of the fund management's role (lead, co-lead etc.) in the investment if it is a syndicate with other investors. This, however, may be important for fund investors when they assess how the fund managers actually contribute to the investments.

On average, the funds achieved a disclosure score of 30% (*SD*=25%) in the category *financial information on portfolio company*. The high standard deviation and the large range (minimum score 0%, maximum score 82%) indicate a high dispersion across the sample. Less than 20% of all funds present excerpts of the balance sheet, the profit and loss statement, or the cash flow statement of the portfolio companies. Only slightly more than 20% of all funds disclose budget or forecast figures on profit and loss statements or balance sheets or make a comparison of the budgeted figures with the actual outcomes. The large dispersion in the category can be explained by the significant difference between buyout and venture capital funds. Buyout funds, on average, have a disclosure score for that category of 43% (*SD*=21%). Venture capital funds only have a disclosure score of 14% (*SD*=20%, *Mann-Whitney* $U=49.5$, $z=-3.570$, $p<0.001$, *two-tailed*).

The category *information on valuation and performance of portfolio investments* receives an average disclosure score of 60% (*SD*=15%) with a minimum score of 32% and a maximum score of 100%. The maximum score is notably, since this category is the largest one comprising 19 information items, and since it includes detailed information items on the valuation of portfolio companies. Not much information is provided on the valuation of the portfolio companies. 92% of all funds state that they apply the fair value for their investments. However, only 58% indicate for each investment whether it is actually an 'at cost' valuation as proxy for fair value or a different valuation derived by applying a valuation methodology. Then, only 33% of the funds disclose which valuation methodology they have used to derive the fair value. Only 6% provide the rationale for using the valuation methodology, and only 8% give a detailed calculation of the valuation (e.g. by disclosing peer group data). 17% of the funds report changes in valuation methodologies. A description of the process of the valuation review is provided in only 14% of the fund reports. There are significant differences between the disclosure scores of European and U.S. funds in that category. European funds receive a significant higher disclosure index score (*M*=68%, *SD*=12%) than U.S. funds (*M*=50%, *SD*=12%, *Mann-Whitney U=43.5, z=-3.739, p<0.001, two-tailed*).

The fourth information category on portfolio company level, *assessment of current situation, risks and future development of investments*, achieves an average disclosure index score of 27% (*SD*=16%). Again, there is at least one fund which reports no information in that category at all (minimum score 0%), but also a fund with a maximum score of 75%. Almost all funds (97%) report on the significant events that occurred to their investments during the reporting period. 33% provide an assessment of the company's current status compared to the expectation at the time of the investment. However, all other information items such as further information on the risks that the portfolio companies may face or any exit plans and horizons are provided by less than 20% of the funds in the sample. Again, it is found that European funds (*M*=33%, *SD*=17%) achieve a significant higher disclosure score in this category than U.S. funds (*M*=19%, *SD*=12%, *Mann-Whitney U=83.5, z=-2.547, p=0.011, two-tailed*).

Compliance with EVCA Reporting Guidelines

An interesting question is whether the private equity funds' reporting is in compliance with respect to the existing reporting guidelines. This question is tested with a focus on the EVCA Reporting Guidelines due to the following reasons: As explained in chapter 4.4.2.2, there is a longer tradition of using private equity industry guidelines in Europe than in the U.S. For the first time, the U.S. PEIGG Private Equity Reporting and Performance Measurement Guidelines have been released in 2005 in comparison to year 2000 in Europe. PEIGG used the EVCA Reporting Guidelines as a foundation. The EVCA Reporting Guidelines can be regarded as best practice. The reporting content that is required by the EVCA Reporting Guidelines can therefore be considered as relevant to any fund investor around the world, and not only to European fund investors. It is consequently also tested, in what respect U.S. funds comply with the requirements of the EVCA guidelines.

For the EVCA Reporting Guidelines, the issue of compliance with these guidelines has been subject to various studies before.[998] In all of theses studies, either the fund managers have been asked whether they comply or not, or the fund investors needed to state how many of their funds comply with the guidelines. However, the results of these questionnaires may be biased. Through the analysis of actual reports, however, it is possible to get more objective results about the actual degree of the implementation of the guidelines.

In order to measure the disclosure that is relevant to comply with the EVCA reporting guidelines, those items out of the 114 information items of the total disclosure index have been selected that the EVCA guidelines require or recommend to be reported. As discussed in chapter 4.4.2.2, the EVCA Reporting Guidelines distinguish information items that are required to be reported and information items which the guidelines recommend to be reported.[999] In total, 84 information items have been identified (11 of them are only recommended) and their actual disclosure level has been analyzed.

As shown in Figure 81, the analyzed private equity reports provide on average 56% (*SD*=11%) of the required and recommended information according to the EVCA reporting guidelines.[1000] The maximum score is 77% (minimum 38%) which implies that actually no fund fully complies with the guidelines. Comparing buyout and venture capital funds reveals that buyout funds receive on average a higher score (*M=60%, SD=10%*) than venture capital funds (*M=53%, SD=12%*). This difference is sharply statistically significant (*Mann-Whitney U=98.5, z=-1.960, p=0.050), two-tailed*). European funds achieve a significant higher score (*M*=61%, *SD*=11%), with respect to the compliance with the EVCA guidelines, than U.S. funds (*M*=51%, *SD*=9%, *Mann-Whitney U=72.0, z=-2.805, p=0.005, two-tailed*).

998 See Hagenmüller (2004), p. 174; Haarmann Hemmelrath/Universitaet Leipzig (2002), p. 17.

999 See EVCA (2006b).

1000 The average disclosure scores on just the EVCA Reporting Guidelines' requirements have also been identified (74 information items): The average score was 60% (*SD=11%*) with a minimum score of 42% and a maximum score of 79%.

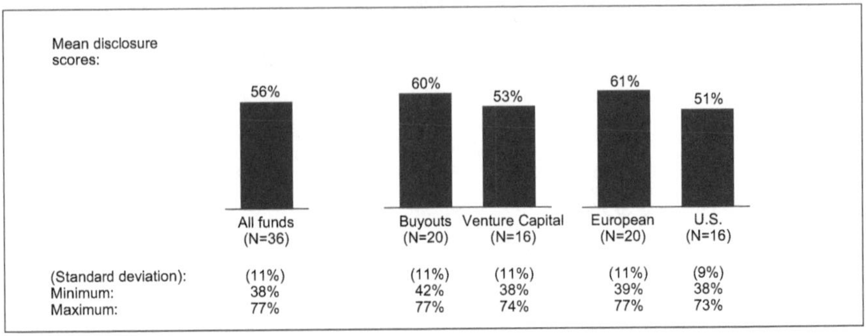

Figure 81: Disclosure index score for compliance with EVCA Reporting Guidelines

Conclusion on hypotheses

To summarize, weak support is found for *Hypothesis 1* that predicted differences in the level of disclosure between reports of venture capital funds and reports of buyout funds. On fund level, buyout funds disclose more information on the fund investment's fees. On portfolio level, buyout funds achieve a higher disclosure score with respect to financial information on the portfolio companies. However, with respect to the total disclosure score, no differences have been found. *Hypothesis 2* is supported more significantly. European funds disclose more information than U.S. funds. Their total disclosure index scores are significantly higher. In particular, they achieve higher scores referring to overall portfolio level information, and in the categories financial information on aggregated investments, risk reporting on fund level, valuation and performance measurement of portfolio company investments, and assessment of current situation, risks and future development of investments. In all categories, no relationship between the extent of disclosure and the total commitments to the funds (*Hypothesis 3*) or the number of professionals in the management companies (*Hypothesis 4*) has been found. Therefore, these hypotheses could not be verified. Furthermore, no relationship between the level of disclosure and the age of the management company has been identified. *Hypothesis 5* cannot be neglected.

4.4.5 Discussion of Results

The extent of disclosure provided in private equity reports shall be first assessed and discussed on the implications for the fund reporting requirements elaborated in chapter 3.8.3. Information gaps exist when fund investors regard certain information as important, but the information is not reported in enough detail.

The first implication was that fund investors require comprehensive information on the operating and financial situation of the fund, and on the performance of the fund investments. Concerning the operating and financial situation of the fund, it can be concluded that fund investors receive the information they require. Although the disclosure indices for the categories 'general operational information on fund level (58%)' and 'financial information on aggregated investments (80%)' do not achieve scores close to 100%, their scores are - in comparison to other categories - above average. This indicates that the fund reports provide a comprehensive summary of the current investment activities of the funds. However, with respect to some information items, e.g. information on any changes of the management team, information on deal flow or reserves for follow-on rounds, there is room for improvement. The fund investors that were interviewed for the study presented in chapter 3 mentioned that they especially require this rather qualitative type of information. These results support the findings of BÖHLER who identifies information gaps on fund level especially concerning information on non-financial issues, e.g. with respect to the corporate governance of the funds.[1001]

The results with respect to capital account information, i.e. a disclosure index score of 60%, with a high dispersion across the funds, suggest that some fund managers may report no details on the capital account, whereas other fund managers provide full disclosure. This result is also supported by BÖHLER.[1002] In contrast to these results, however, in a study by HAGENMÜLLER, fund investors state that 90% of all fund reports provide a true and fair view on the capital account information.[1003] The author's own interviews with fund investors revealed only in a few cases a lack of information concerning the capital account information.

Nevertheless, there is an information gap concerning information on the performance measurement of a fund. The information in this category is perceived as very important by fund managers. This is a clear result of the author's own discussion with the leading fund investors. It is also supported by findings of HAGENMÜLLER and BÖHLER.[1004] However, the disclosure index on that category is with 20% on average

[1001] See Böhler (2004b), p. 275.

[1002] See Böhler (2004b), p. 274.

[1003] See Hagenmüller (2004), p. 50.

[1004] See Hagenmüller (2004), p. 50; Böhler (2004b), p. 273.

very low. Very few additional information items other than the net internal rate of return and a total value to paid-in capital (TVPI) investment multiple are provided. It is actually questionable whether fund managers should provide information regarding the benchmarking of the performance of the funds at all. DIPIAZZA/ECCLES generally note that relevant information from external sources should be reported, if a company can draw a complete picture of how well it is performing only with this information.[1005] In interviews, some fund investors expressed the opinion that this is a standard task which they should pursue as they have the market overview and know better which funds are actually comparable. This argument is valid. Fund investors therefore have to rely on external sources, such as private equity data providers, to gather the information by themselves.

The second implication was that fund investors require detailed information on the fund investment's costs. Many of the interviewed fund investors for the study in chapter 3 note that there is very often an information gap concerning this issue. Based on the results of the disclosure study, this outcome can be confirmed. There is no transparency in most of the funds' reports surrounding the issue of fund investments fees. The needs of the investors concerning that issue are not satisfied. The quality of the reporting on the funds' costs very much varies across the funds. Almost all funds provide information on management fees. However, more detailed information on the carried interest is rarely released. A clear and detailed presentation of the fund's income and expenses separated by different fee types is lacking.

The results are supported by earlier findings. BÖHLER states that information on fees and profit participation paid to fund managers is regarded as the most important element to be disclosed in the fund reports, but that the satisfaction with the reporting is among the lowest.[1006] HAGENMÜLLER demonstrates that European fund investors believe that reporting on funds' costs is very important, but only 70% of the reports provide a true and fair view.[1007] HIELSCHER/ZELGER/BEYER survey German private equity fund managers and find that 30% do not report on fees at all.[1008] To conclude, there is

---

[1005] See DiPiazza/Eccles (2002), p. 113.

[1006] See Böhler (2004b), p. 273.

[1007] See Hagenmüller (2004), p. 50.

[1008] See Hielscher/Zelger/Beyer (2003), p. 504. According to their results, especially smaller funds forgo to report on fees.

room and a strong need for improvements concerning the issue in the private equity fund reporting.

The third implication was that fund investors require detailed information on the valuation of the unrealized underlying portfolio company investments. It has been demonstrated in chapter 3 that an assessment of these values is necessary, not only for their performance measurement, but also for portfolio management purposes such as liquidity management and diversification steering. Many of the interviewed fund investors say that information on the valuation of portfolio company investments is, however, limited. This conclusion can also be drawn based on the analysis of the fund reports. Only a fraction of the fund managers provide a deep insight into their specific approaches and explains how they come up with these values. The overall disclosure score on the category which comprises information on the valuation and performance of the portfolio companies is 60%. The information on the valuation aspect is, nevertheless, rarely provided. Especially, information on the valuation techniques and data inputs that are used are not reported. BÖHLER supports these findings. In his study, he reveals that the largest information gap relates to the issue of valuation principles and assumptions for each investment.[1009]

Fund investors recognize how difficult it is for private equity fund managers to value their illiquid investments. However, they like to see more frequent valuations both downward and upward.[1010] But as different funds typically have different approaches, the only way for fund investors to compare the reported valuations is to make their own judgment. Therefore, full transparency on the valuation is needed. The maximum disclosure score that was achieved in this category is 100%. This demonstrates that it is possible to provide comprehensive information on the valuation issue.

The fourth implication was that fund investors require information on the type of business, and the operating and financial situation of the underlying portfolio companies. The analysis of the private equity fund reports reveals that the reporting on portfolio company data is also very different across the reports and, overall, very limited. Standard information such as the description of the businesses and the industry is usually

---

[1009] See Böhler (2004b), p. 278.

[1010] See Gove (2005), p. 47.

given. Details on the role of the fund (e.g. lead or non-lead role, information on board presentation, name of responsible manager) are, however, less often provided.

Financial information forms the basis for the valuation of the portfolio company investments and is therefore of great importance. Fund investors ask for information on portfolio companies' earnings and debt levels in order to determine the fair values of the investments.[1011] This has been also discovered in own interviews with fund investors and already elaborated in chapter 3. Fund investors want to compare portfolio companies' earnings against their budgets and against the original business plan.[1012] This information is required to be able to make own judgments on the value creation of the private equity fund managers. Nonetheless, the disclosure score on the category financial information on portfolio companies is on average only 30% with a high standard deviation of 25%. The highest score of 82% demonstrates, however, that it is possible to provide this type of information. Some funds though do not report this data at all (minimum disclosure score of 0%).

These outcomes explain the relative dissatisfaction among fund investors concerning portfolio company information identified by BÖHLER.[1013] He shows significant gaps between the fund investors' perceived importance of that information and their satisfaction with the reporting content concerning portfolio company information. Also HAGENMÜLLER confirms that there is room for improvement with respect to information on portfolio company level. He finds that only 60% of all fund investors provide a true and fair view on that issue.[1014]

The fifth implication was that fund investors require an assessment of the risks and the future development of both the fund and the underlying portfolio company investments. Based on the analysis of the fund reports, however, it can be concluded that there is still a large gap with respect to this type of information. Risk reporting on the fund level is not provided. On the portfolio company level, less than 20% of the reports contain qualitative risk information. Concerning the information on risk management

---

1011 See Private Equity Intelligence (2005), p. 3.

1012 See Meek (2005b), p. 36.

1013 See Böhler (2004a), p. 276.

1014 See Hagenmüller (2004), p. 50.

of the fund, BÖHLER also identifies big information gaps.[1015] He states that private equity fund investors should know how the fund management handles and controls the risks inherent in their investment activities. This includes information on who is responsible for investment decisions, on what kind of internal controls exist within the fund, and on how the monitoring of portfolio company investments works. None of the analyzed fund reports in the sample of this study contains information on these issues. In addition to the risk information, fund investors require forward-looking information concerning the future development of the fund and the portfolio companies.[1016] However, also details on exit plans, expected exit valuations or any material risks to the performance outlook are rarely given. Some fund investors believe that this kind of information can only be acquired informally. They claim to have a good relationship with the fund managers and therefore are able to gather the information relevant to them.[1017] However, incomplete information increases the overall uncertainty. As a consequence, the risks for the fund investors rise. They, for example, may not be able to optimize their entire fund-of-funds portfolio, e.g. with respect to the desired diversification, if they lack information. It should be therefore in the interest of the fund managers that as much information as possible should be standardized and shared among all fund investors.

It has been found that U.S. funds lag behind European firms with respect to the extent of the disclosure. This is especially true with respect to the reporting on portfolio company level. There may be some U.S. private equity funds that hold back information because of concerns about the disclosure under the Freedom of Information Act.[1018] They could fear that information especially pertaining to portfolio companies could be released to the public. Fund managers therefore may have concluded that it is better to limit the flow of information instead.

The differences in the extent of disclosure between venture capital and buyout funds relates mainly to information on the fund investments' fees and the financial information on portfolio companies. Fund managers of buyout funds seem to be more aware of the fund investors' interest of getting information on fees. This might be explained

---

[1015] See Böhler (2004b), p. 275.

[1016] These findings have been also supported by BÖHLER. See Böhler (2004b), p. 177.

[1017] See Meyer/Mathonet (2005), p. 280.

[1018] See Meek (2005b), p. 37.

with the fact that the buyout funds typically charge higher fees and have more possibilities to generate additional income from portfolio companies as these are usually mature companies with positive cash flows. In general, buyout funds provide more financial information on their portfolio companies as these normally already have revenues and earnings.

No differences in the extent of information disclosed in fund reports have been found with respect to the size of the funds and the number of investment professionals working for the fund managers. This is astonishing, but demonstrates that also smaller funds with fewer time and management resources may be able to provide the necessary information to their fund investors. These findings indicate that it may be inappropriate to make distinctions between larger and smaller funds when it comes to reporting requirements by standard setters or regulators.

It can be summarized that the extent of disclosure provided in private equity fund reports very much varies across different funds and is on average not very comprehensive. The reporting guidelines such as the EVCA Reporting Guidelines[1019] provide a framework which entails most of the information that is required by fund investors. However, not all fund managers comply with the framework. As has been shown, on average only 56% of the information required by the guidelines is reported. HAGENMÜLLER finds that 80% of the European fund managers claim compliance with the EVCA reporting guidelines.[1020] Analyzing the reports reveals that the level of implementation may be actually lower.

Some private equity fund reports provide a comprehensive overview of both the state of the fund investment and the state of the portfolio companies. However, not all the fund investors' information requirements are fulfilled. This has been also demonstrated by the results of the interviews with fund investors. The fund investors mention that the variation of disclosure is significant. It can be therefore concluded, that there is still room for improvements in order to utilize the full potential of these reports as an effective communication tool between fund managers and fund investors.

1019 This should include any reporting provisions in the *International Private Equity & Venture Capital Valuation Guidelines*, which especially concern the valuation of the portfolio companies.

1020 See Hagenmüller (2004), p. 174.

4.4.6 Limitations of the Study

A few limitations should be taken into account when interpreting the disclosure study's results. First of all, the sample of analyzed reports is very small due to the fact that these reports are not publicly available. It might even be biased by the selection of the fund-of-funds managers that provided the reports. Representativeness can therefore not be claimed. However, the results give an indication of what private equity funds actually report and, in this respect, are very useful for further investigations of the issue.

Secondly, not only the content of private equity funds reports but also the way of how the information is presented is important. These issues are of course linked. However, the actual quality of the format and presentation of the reports have not been subject to the analysis at hand. The readability and clarity of the presented information is of significant importance.[1021] Many fund investors that were interviewed for the study about the monitoring of fund investments, have complained that a lot of the private equity fund reports they receive do not have a clear structure.[1022] The reading of unstructured and unorganized reports is very time-consuming.[1023] Reporting all the information that the fund manager has decided to disclose to fund investors in a logical and organized way is, however, a challenge. To support fund managers, industry associations offer blueprints and templates of the fund reports' layout.[1024] All these suggestions have in common that they recommend to clearly separate fund level and portfolio level reporting content.

Thirdly, it is very likely that in addition to the fund reports, additional information is provided to fund investors. Not all information must be included in the reports. It can be supplemented by extraordinary disclosures such as transaction summaries, extra fee statements, or extra information on the capital account. These documents, however, have not been subject to this research effort as they have not been provided.

1021 See Böhler (2004b), p. 296.

1022 See chapter 3.2 for more information on the interviews.

1023 See Böhler (2004b), p. 296.

1024 See EVCA (2006b), pp. 13 et seq. The EVCA Reporting Guidelines and the PEIGG Reporting and Performance Measurement Guidelines, for example, provide a template for the fund reporting. See PEIGG (2005), pp. 10 et seq. BÖHLER also offers a structure for the reporting content of private equity funds. See Böhler (2004b), p. 283.

Fourth, although fund reports are an important source of information for fund investors, as shown in chapter 3.8.1, there are also other sources. Both fund investors and fund managers equally stress the importance of the informal relationship. It can be assumed that a lot of the information that concerns the assessment of the current status of the portfolio companies, including valuation and risk analysis, may be provided in private conversations between fund managers and their investors rather than by written reports. This information flow based on the personal relationship was not within the scope of this analysis. The actual received information level including orally provided information may therefore be higher. Whether the information provided in this way is more reliable to fund investors is, however, questionable.

5 Conclusion

5.1 Summary

Over the last years, the private equity market has evolved extensively and has grown to a very significant size, compared to the small niche market it was 20 years ago. Today, it plays a crucial role in the economy by fostering the restructuring of companies, by boosting research and innovation, and by creating jobs.[1025] Prerequisites of this evolution are increasing investment inflows from institutional investors for whom private equity nowadays represents an important asset class.

The majority of these investments is pursued via independent private equity funds whose fund managers invest on behalf of their investors. The day-to-day business of the funds is solely managed by fund managers, whereas fund investors do not participate in the operational management at all. However, they are not simply passive investors: Once they have selected and invested in a fund, they carry out a number of important tasks. They measure the performance of the funds, they govern the fund managers, and they have to manage their entire portfolio of private equity funds. Therefore, they need information on the investments which has to be provided by the fund managers.

In the past, however, some fund managers seemed to be reluctant to create enough transparency towards their investors and to inform them about how they are investing the fund capital and managing the fund's portfolio company investments. This is astonishing as open communication and an appropriate level of information between fund managers and their fund investors is essential in order to further attract new fund investors, as well as to enhance or develop private equity as an asset class. An objective analysis of this information gap was therefore necessary, and consequently has been the subject of this dissertation. It elaborated in detail on the fund investors' monitoring of private equity partnership investments, the resulting information requirements and the fund managers' reporting intended to fulfill these information needs. In summary, a number of insights can be drawn from the preceding analysis.

[1025] See Achleitner/Kloeckner (2005), p. 5.

The first aim of the dissertation was to analyze the role of the information flow between private equity fund managers and their fund investors, after the fund investors have invested in the fund. The results of the analysis in chapter 2 clearly show that an information flow plays a crucial role in the relationship between fund managers and their investors. Three different roles of this information flow between fund managers and their investors have been expounded in detail: a decision-supporting role, a governance-enabling role, and a relationship-building role.

The first role, the decision-supporting role, arises from the fund investors' need to make decisions. These decisions include not only re-investment decisions in subsequent funds of existing fund manager relationships, but also decisions relating to steering the diversification and liquidity of the portfolio of funds. In order to be able to make these decisions, fund investors need information provided by their fund managers.

The second role, the governance-enabling role, results from the principal agent relationship between fund managers and their investors. As the management is delegated, fund managers may have incentives to exploit their positions. A continuous flow of information provided by fund managers towards investors allows the latter to monitor and control the appropriate use of the fund resources. Thus, the information directly lowers the information asymmetries and thereby the agency conflicts between the two partners. In addition, the information is used to fulfill the governance role in advisory boards and to control the adherence to the limited partnership agreements.

These two roles of information may be as important for investors in public equity markets as in private equity markets. However, in private equity, a third role, the relationship-building role, needs to be considered. Fund investors cannot easily sell their fund stakes, but are committed to the fund managers for a long time. A strong relationship with their partners is therefore essential. Communication and transparency between the partners in a private equity partnership may enhance trust and cooperation among them. Fund investors' willingness to cooperate is necessary for fund managers, as they need to raise subsequent funds and want that their existing investors also invest in the new fund investment. In some cases, fund investors may also provide advice to fund managers with respect to their strategy and the organization of the partnership. As fund access to very successful fund managers is typically limited, fund investors are furthermore interested in a good relationship with successful fund managers. They want to be 'investor of choice'. In the analysis, the prisoner's dilemma framework, procedural justice theory and trust-based theory approaches in addition to agency theory have been applied to explain how open communication and information can promote trust and strong relationships between the partners. It has been revealed that clear, direct and constructive communication is in the interest of both fund managers and fund investors.

Accepting the general role of information between fund managers and investors, there is still uncertainty in the private equity market about the specific information requirements of fund investors. These requirements clearly depend on the use of information by fund investors for their activities, and a deeper understanding of these activities was necessary. Therefore, *the second aim of this dissertation was to elaborate the current best practices of private equity fund investors with respect to monitoring their fund investments and to identify their specific information requirements.* An exploratory approach has been applied to achieve this aim. 28 leading European fund investors have been interviewed about their monitoring practices. The results reveal comprehensive and in-depth insights into current best practices. To point out some highlights one can state that fund investors spend around 42% of their entire time to monitoring the investments, however, disregarding any time spend to own fundraising purposes. They are represented in advisory boards by an average of 35% of their funds in order to closely monitor the fund's development. 80% of the interviewed fund investors say that the decision to re-invest in a subsequent fund is easier than the decision to invest the first time in a fund manager. They emphasize that they would have an enhanced ability to assess the quality of the fund manager, if they could monitor how the fund manager created the portfolio companies' value. 70% also think that a long-term monitoring and management of fund portfolio liquidity is important. As the basis of all decisions, the fund investors rely on an extensive performance measurement of the individual fund investment as well as of the entire portfolio of funds.

Based on these monitoring activities of fund investors, this dissertation identifies five implications for the reporting content: First of all, fund investors require comprehensive information on the operating as well as the financial situation, and on the performance of the fund. Secondly, they require detailed information on the costs associated with investing in the fund. Thirdly, fund investors need detailed information on the valuation of the underlying portfolio company investments. However, getting information on the valuation is not enough to understand how fund managers actually create value with the investment in the portfolio companies. Understanding the value creation is necessary to judge on the quality of fund managers. Fund investors thus need further information on the type of business and the operational and financial situation of the underlying portfolio companies. Last but not least, they require an assessment of the risks and the future development of both the fund and the underlying portfolio companies.

Fund managers should offer all these information. However, fund investors seem to be not always satisfied with their fund managers' delivery of the required information. A deeper understanding and evaluation of the actual reporting behavior of fund managers is essential. Therefore, chapter 4 of this dissertation turns to the perspective of the fund managers. *The third aim was to demonstrate whether or not fund managers actually fulfill the fund investors' informational needs with their fund reporting.* Fund reports are an integral part of the communication and seen as one of the most important information sources for fund investors. Due to the complexity of the issue, this aim was further subdivided into three subordinated aims. Fund reports can be distinguished in the statutory financial statements on the one hand, and the additional investor reporting on the other.

Statutory financial statements are based on national or international accounting standards. As the International Financial Reporting Standards (IFRS) are becoming more important for private equity funds, a *first subordinated aim was to describe and discuss the requirements of the IFRS especially with respect to the accounting for portfolio companies.* The results clearly show that statutory financial statements alone do not meet the private equity fund investors' informational needs.

With respect to the accounting for investments in private equity portfolio companies, IFRS states that all investments have to be reported at fair value except those investments that are interests in subsidiaries. Subsidiaries are investments where the investor has the ability to control the financial and operating policy of the companies. According to IFRS, subsidiaries have to be consolidated. However, the discussion in the dissertation presents several valid arguments why private equity funds should be excluded from the requirement to present consolidated statements. In a nutshell, the ultimate purpose of consolidated statements does not apply to private equity funds, and they do not fulfill the information requirements of investors. Even worse, they may provide a misleading picture of the performance of the funds. However, in order to grant an exemption to private equity, one has to be able to distinguish private equity funds from non-investment companies. This dissertation provides a practical solution to this task which takes twelve characteristics of the entities into account, such as the business purpose of the entity, the existence of exit plans for portfolio companies, or the number and influence of investors, upon which an evaluation and distinction can be pursued.

Apart from the consolidation requirement, statutory financial statements neglect the two-tier business model of private equity funds with the split into the fund and the portfolio company level. Therefore, they do not provide a comprehensive picture of the performance and current state of private equity investments. Furthermore, they disregard the relevance of providing information on the fund's management team and organization. In addition, the provision of detailed information on individual portfolio companies is not required, although for private equity fund investors it is important to understand the development of each portfolio company. Finally, information on valuation, e.g. the methodologies and assumptions that are used for individual valuations, is not required to be reported.

IFRS requires the measurement of portfolio companies at fair value. Given the importance and challenges to derive these fair values, *the second subordinated aim to achieve was therefore a detailed elaboration and discussion of the fair value measurement requirements of portfolio company investments.* Fair values may be generated by applying various valuation techniques. The accounting standards, but also various private equity industry valuation guidelines, provide guidance in order to promote the consistent application of these techniques within the industry. However, one has to admit that difficulties remain in deriving fair values. Portfolio companies are typically not listed. Especially in case of venture capital investments, a lack of reliable input data, such as earnings, affects the use of valuation techniques.

Therefore, the fair value requirements by IFRS are heavily discussed in the industry. Instead of the fair value approach, many industry participants prefer a cost-based approach which carries all investment at cost, unless a material impairment indicates a write-down in value or a financing round with new investors supports a write-up. They point out the difficulties in determining fair values, the artificial volatility in fund values to which the fair value approach may lead, the danger of overstating company valuations, and the significant resources necessary to carry out regular valuations of all portfolio companies. Notwithstanding these arguments, proponents of the fair value approach argue that it is appropriate. It delivers the information which fund investors need to measure the fund performance and which they also need as input for their portfolio management purposes and own reporting requirements. This dissertation reveals that fair values are clearly needed by fund investors as input for their monitoring activities and clearly argues that the presentation of fair values is reasonable. However, in order to deal with the difficulties that the approach entails, i.e. the subjectivity that the fund managers have in deriving fair values, it concludes that it is very important that fund managers maintain transparency regarding the techniques and assumptions they use to derive the fair values.

The analysis of the requirements of statutory financial statements revealed that these statements have to be supplemented by additional information provided to fund investors. Due to confidentiality issues and the lack of data, research on the extent of additional disclosure to private equity fund investors has been sparse or non-existing. *The third subordinated aim was therefore to develop a comprehensive framework for this additional investors reporting, to measure the level of disclosure in the fund reports based on this framework and to identify relationships between the level of disclosure and selected fund characteristics.* This study represents a very important addition to the existing knowledge in private equity. For the first time, a disclosure index has been developed and applied in order to measure the disclosure of private equity reports.

A comprehensive private equity fund reporting framework has been developed which comprises all information that fund investors may require. The choice of information items included in this framework is based on the elaborated implications regarding the reporting requirements presented in chapter 3, a thorough inspection of the existing literature on the reporting of private equity funds, and on the analysis of reporting guidelines developed by private equity industry associations. 114 information items were gathered and presented in ten information categories. These categories are broadly distinguished with respect to information on fund and portfolio company level in order to provide structure and clarity.

The selection of items was then used to construct the disclosure index. A thorough analysis of 36 private equity fund reports was pursued. These reports have been provided by two leading European fund investors. The extent of disclosure in a single report is quantified as the percentage of recorded information items found in that report.

The findings of the study indicate a wide variation in the overall disclosure level in private equity fund reports, measured through the number of reported items. Some fund managers provide a comprehensive picture of their fund investments. Others are very reluctant with the release of information. European funds on average disclose more information than U.S. funds, especially with respect to portfolio company data. This may indicate that the long-standing effort of the European private equity associations regarding industry wide reporting and valuation guidelines have been successful. Buyout funds report more information on the fund investment's costs and more financial information on portfolio companies than venture capital funds. Other characteristics, such as the size of the funds measured in commitments, the number of investment professionals, and the age of the management company, do not influence the disclosure level. Although having fewer resources available, smaller funds seem to be able to provide the same level of detail in reports as larger funds.

With respect to the fund investors' required content of the reports which has been elaborated in chapter 3, the disclosure study in chapter 4 has identified various information gaps. Generally, an information gap exists with respect to information on the performance measurement of the fund. Furthermore, there is a lack of transparency relating to fund investment's costs. Detailed information on the valuation of portfolio company investments is also very limited in fund reports. Financial information on the portfolio companies is rarely provided and, finally, information on the risks of the fund as a whole and the individual portfolio company investments is in general neither quantitatively nor qualitatively disclosed. These information gaps reveal room for improvement in order to utilize the full potential of these reports as an effective communication tool between fund managers and their investors.

5.2 Implications for Practitioners

Several implications for practitioners can be drawn out of the discussions in this dissertation. They provide solutions in order to overcome the perceived information gap between fund managers and their investors as well as to create enough transparency between the two parties. It is appropriate to distinguish implications for fund investors, for fund managers, for private equity industry associations, and, last but not least, for policy-makers.

By providing insights into the best practices of monitoring not only a single private equity fund investment, but also a portfolio of these funds, the findings of this study show how *fund investors may be able to add value to their portfolios after having committed to their funds.* This may guide less sophisticated new investors in the asset class. Through closely following the development of the individual fund investments, they are able to minimize the downside risk and are in a position where they can improve their decision making with respect to a re-investment in a follow-on fund of the fund managers. Monitoring the portfolio of funds enables an optimization of the diversification and the liquidity of their entire private equity investment program.

Fund investors monitoring is built on the provision of information from their fund managers. There is obviously a dilemma for fund investors when asking for more information. Since providing information is costly, fund managers may prefer those investors that are less demanding. If their fund is oversubscribed, they may exclude potential investors that ask too many questions. Therefore, *fund investors should clearly communicate and explain the relevance of receiving certain information from their fund managers*. The research findings of this study help in this respect as they give insight about how fund investors monitor and manage their portfolio of private equity fund investments and about the sort of information they desire. This is an important contribution, since only if the fund managers fully recognize the reasons for the increasing demand, they may be less reluctant or more open to provide the necessary information.[1026]

Fund managers need to recognize the growing demand from fund investors to get more rigorous and in-depth reporting. Their fund investors have evolved with the growth of the asset class and are thus more sophisticated than in the past. In addition, with increasing fund sizes, the number of investors in the funds has risen as well. Some of the largest buyout funds today may have 200 or more fund investors.[1027] Thus, the question the fund managers face today is not only how to cope with the more intensive information demands from their fund investors, but also how to manage all these relationships.

[1026] See Private Equity Intelligence (2005), p. 3.

[1027] See Thomson (2006), p. 46.

A solution to handle this increasing demand is the establishment and strengthening of an investor relations function within the fund managers' organizations.[1028] Key success factor for effective investor relations is, first of all, that *fund managers understand and respond to fund investors' information needs.* Knowing the information gaps is essential. The conclusions of this study foster the generation of knowledge in this respect. A promising way to know whether the fund managers adequately meet the information requirements of the fund investors is obviously to ask them.[1029] Furthermore, the developed private equity fund reporting framework in this dissertation presents a comprehensive set of key information items that could be potentially reported.

An important task of the investor relations function is the regular fund reporting. This instrument allows handling the many different investor relationships. *More formalization and standardization in providing information through fund reports may avoid that fund investors individually contact the fund managers in order to fill their information gaps.* This may free resources for more valuable activities at the fund managers' side. However, reporting itself is of course also very time-consuming. Thus, each fund manager needs to find the appropriate balance.

Fund managers should view their communication with fund investors as ongoing, not transactional.[1030] In good times, fund managers might be tempted to decrease the resources spent on back-office functions. Some fund managers might only increase their efforts shortly before they raise a new fund. However, only continuously providing transparency should support their ability to successfully raise funds. The market for private equity capital has become increasingly competitive. Fund managers may desire to stay ahead of the game or should at least follow best practices with respect to their fund reporting. However, top performing fund managers may resist increasing reporting demand, as they typically face enough interests from investors for their funds.

Transparency in a partnership supports building a good relationship. This has been elaborated in detail in this dissertation. *Fund managers should therefore pro-actively provide information to their fund investors*: To be as open as possible about the poten-

---

[1028] See Hagenmüller (2004), pp. 123 et seq. for different organizational structures of the investor relations departments in private equity firms.

[1029] See DiPiazza/Eccles (2002), p. 113.

[1030] For a similar argumentation see Gove (2005), p. 47.

tial risks inherent in portfolio company investments, including signalling when bad news are coming up, would certainly create trust in fund managers and their ability to control these risks.

Although formal reporting is of high importance, it needs to be acknowledged that the quality of the partnership between fund managers and investors very much depends on the ability of both parties to personally communicate. Private equity is unlike investing in mutual funds where fund investors typically have no contact with fund managers.[1031] Through direct interaction with the fund managers, fund investors may obtain information that may be otherwise not accessible.

The format and structure of the fund reports is very important as it eases the readability and comprehensiveness of the content. Fund managers and fund investors together may also think of solutions that supersede some of the paper-based communication formats which are currently standard within the industry. The use of new technology such, as the internet for submitting information, could be considered. Much of the private equity fund information can be standardized. As large fund investors invest in a large number of funds, getting the information via a digitalized interface may turn out to be an effective solution to the growing quantity and complexity of the information they have to deal with.

In recent years, the private equity industry associations, i.e. EVCA, AFIC and BVCA in Europe and PEIGG in the U.S., have made significant progress in improving the professionalism of the industry's reporting and valuation standards. The results of this dissertation indicate the success of these efforts in strengthening the relationship between fund managers and their investors and the self-regulation of the industry. However, these *industry associations should reinforce the further development and improvement of these guidelines.* For the International Private Equity & Venture Capital Valuation Guidelines for example, the involved industry associations appointed a dedicated Guidelines Board in order to take care of this issue.[1032] In addition, an important task of the industry associations is to further internationalize and to harmonize the guidelines. One set of truly global private equity guidelines would definitely benefit the asset class. In order to assure that the self-regulation of the industry works, the

---

[1031] See Peninion (2003).

[1032] See Achleitner/Müller (2005), p. 70.

industry associations may also think of developing certification processes that allow fund managers to clearly claim that they comply with the recommendations.[1033]

The results of this study could assist policy-makers in deciding whether the disclosure is adequate in meeting the needs of users. Policy-makers have a regulatory responsibility for transparency in the private equity investment industry, including valuation disclosure.[1034] They need to be concerned with ensuring that private equity fund investors receive appropriate disclosure to support informed and objective decision-making. However, based on the results on this study, policy-makers should *acknowledge that, on average, there is currently a relative high transparency between fund managers and their investors, and taking further action on this issue may not be necessary.*[1035] As has been discussed in detail, some fund managers may still improve the extent of their reporting.

When drafting new regulation and legislation, policy-makers should consider the special characteristics of the private equity industry. An example where this may be not the case and which has been discussed in detail in this study is the accounting regulation of IAS 27 that requires private equity funds to consolidate their portfolio company investments. The consolidation requirement produces a distorted view of the private equity fund's financial statements. It would be more appropriate to report all portfolio investments consistently at fair value.[1036]

Another example is the consequence of the Freedom of Information Act in the U.S. which also has been discussed in this dissertation. Regulators and legislators need to carefully evaluate the outcome. Much of the information in fund reports may be commercially sensitive which needs to be kept confidential between fund managers and

---

[1033] As a role model, the Global Investment Performance Standards (GIPS) issued by the CFA Institute may be taken. See chapter 4.4.2.2. To claim GIPS compliance, a firm must follow a series of requirements to achieve best practice in investment performance presentations. AGF Private Equity and AXA Private Equity were the first private equity firms in Europe to have their performance figures audited according to GIPS' private equity provisions. See Sormani (2005).

[1034] See Financial Service Authority (2007), p. 12.

[1035] This equals a conclusion that also the FINANCIAL SERVICE AUTHORITY (FSA) in the U.K. came up with in their feedback statement that responds to a discussion paper on more regulatory engagement in private equity. See Financial Service Authority (2007), p. 13; Financial Service Authority (2006b).

[1036] See Böhler (2004b), p. 316.

their investors. If there is a real danger that strategic and sensitive information about portfolio companies will be made public, it is highly reasonable that fund managers limit the information that is distributed in writing.

A promising way for policy-makers to incorporate the special characteristics of the private equity industry into the legislation and regulation is to involve the private equity industry in their efforts and to build on a mix of self-regulation and oversight. The private equity industry currently adheres to a set of self-imposed industry standards such as the Private Equity & Venture Capital Valuation Guidelines. These standards have been developed in conjunction with their investors and clients.[1037] An obligatory implementation of these self regulation mechanisms might be an appropriate answer to current calls for more regulation of the industry.[1038]

5.3 Implications for Further Research

This analysis allows also setting forth several important implications for further research. They relate to fund investors monitoring, fair value measurement of portfolio companies and additional investors reporting.

The analysis of the fund investors' best practices in monitoring private equity funds in this study reveals an explorative nature. While this was the aim of this dissertation, a more profound investigation concerning this issue using alternative empirical methods could evolve further valuable knowledge. A major limitation of the interview approach, for example, is that it fails to study the monitoring and management of the private equity funds in the organizational contexts of the fund investors. An approach that can deal with more complex social phenomena, e.g. case studies, could offer further insights into monitoring practices.[1039]

It would be, for example, highly interesting to compare the behavior of different types of private equity fund investors with respect to their monitoring. One could assume that there are clear differences between banks, insurance companies, pension funds,

---

1037 See European Commission (2006), p. 20.

1038 This equals what KASERER ET AL. propose in a report commissioned by the German Ministry of Finance in order to make suggestions how Germany should change the tax and legal environment for private equity. See Kaserer et al. (2007), p. 226.

1039 See Yin (1994), p. 3.

endowments or fund of funds as private equity fund investors with respect to the governance and incentive structure. LERNER/SCHOAR/WONG find that some institutional fund investors have superior reinvestment skills and may be better in using the information they obtain through their monitoring of the fund managers.[1040] A better understanding of this performance puzzle would be interesting. There is still a lack of knowledge concerning the specific agency problems within the organizations of the fund investors that may lead to superior or inferior results of the private equity investment programs.

A different interesting research direction relates to the fair value measurement of portfolio companies. Whereas this dissertation focuses on the analysis of the requirements of accounting standards and industry valuation guidelines, it would be interesting to investigate the actual implementation of these regulations. Auditors in different regulatory environments in Europe and the U.S. may interpret the rules differently.

The increasing application of the fair value measurement approach may furthermore have positive implications on the reliability and comparability of performance measurement methods in private equity. This in return may affect the allocation decisions of fund investors. It may also make intra-asset class and inter-asset class performance comparison of private equity more valid and reliable. Further research in this respect promises valuable insights.

A larger fund report sample may allow drawing additional conclusions with respect to the relevant factors influencing the extent of fund managers' reporting. Two directions of future research seem to be promising. On the one hand, it would be interesting to get a deeper insight in how fund investors actually value different information items in the fund reports relative to each other. The disclosure study equally weights the information content which may not be appropriate. On the other hand, the database for the empirical disclosure analysis comprises only fund reports from one year. A longitudinal approach may bring further insights of the increasing professionalization of the private equity industry and may allow identifying the driver of this development.

Finally, it may be interesting to analyze whether the results and conclusions of this study can be generalized. Subject of this dissertation has been the independent private

---

[1040] See Lerner/Schoar/Wong (2005), p. 39.

equity partnership. However, some private equity fund managers are publicly listed. It may be interesting to investigate the relationship with their investors and the respective reporting requirements.

Based on an improved understanding of the relationship between fund managers and fund investors in private equity partnerships, both parties can make an effort towards further professionalizing their activities. Enhanced communication between both parties can be expected to have a significant positive impact on the development of private equity partnership investments and on private equity as an asset class in general.

Appendix A: List of Interview Partners

Most of the interviews took place in 2006. Any subsequent changes of interview partners' titles or companies have not been considered.

FUND INVESTORS

Dr. Gerhard Bauer	Director Allianz Private Equity Partners, Germany
Sven Berthold	Investment Manager WEGAsupport GmbH, Germany
Tom H. Clausen	Co-Founder and Managing Partner Capvent, Switzerland
Mark Coppin	Vice President Capital Dynamics, Switzerland
Christophe de Dardel	Head of Private Equity Investments Unigestion, Switzerland
Layla Fear	Private Equity Analyst Standard Life Investments, UK
Stephan Grillmaier	Vice President Swiss Re Private Equity, Switzerland
Leon Hadass	Vice President Pantheon Ventures, UK
Adam Heaysman	Partner Altius Associates, UK
Bengt Hellström	Head of Alternative Investments AP-Fonden 3, Sweden
Dr. Stefan Hepp	Founding Partner and CEO SCM Strategic Capital Management, Switzerland
John A. Hess	CEO Altius Associates, UK
Tim Hoffert	Controller Private Equity Feri Institutional Advisors, Germany

Dr. Rüdiger Kollmann	Managing Director Solutio AG, Germany
Dr. Peter Laib	Managing Director adveq, Switzerland
Richard Lancaster	Director Golding Capital Partners, Germany
Monika Lauber	Stv. Leiterin Vermögensanlagen Pensionskasse Stadt Zürich, Switzerland
Dr. Katharina Lichtner	Managing Director Capital Dynamics, Switzerland
Detlef Mackewicz	Managing Partner AVIDA Advisors, Germany
Edwin Niers	CFO Bregal Investments, UK
Christina Schär	Controller Private Equity Winterthur Group, Switzerland
Robert Schlachter	Principal LGT Capital Partners, Liechtenstein
Jan-Philipp Schmitz	Investment Manager Axa Private Equity, Germany
Stephan Schnuerer	Investment Manager UBS Global Asset Management, Switzerland
Thomas Staubli	Partner Partners Group, Switzerland
Hans van Swaay	Head of Private Equity Pictet & Cie, Switzerland
Anna Vándor	Analyst Private Equity Funds F&C, UK
Maarten Vervoort	Partner AlpInvest Partners, Netherlands
Eberhard Witt	Executive Partner and CFO CAM Private Equity, Germany

FUND MANAGERS

Peter G. Nietzer	Partner GermanCapital, Germany
Bernd Seibel	General Partner, CFO European Operations TVM Capital, Germany

AUDITORS / ADVISORS

Sarah Baker	Director PricewaterhouseCoopers, UK
Anthony R. Cecil	Partner KMPG, UK
David L. Larsen	Partner, Transaction Services KPMG, U.S.
Dr. Theo Weber	Managing Director Deloitte & Touche, Germany

Appendix B: Interview Questionnaire

Center for Entrepreneurial and Financial Studies
TUM Businesss School

TECHNISCHE UNIVERSITÄT MÜNCHEN

Managing the Relationship with General Partners and Implications for Information Requirements

An Exploratory Study among European Private Equity Fund Investors (Limited Partners)

Prof. Dr. Dr. Ann-Kristin Achleitner Kay Müller

Objective

- We investigate limited partners' current practices of monitoring their portfolio of funds.
- We analyse limited partners' relationship towards the individual fund manager after the investment.
- We elaborate limited partners' information requirements from fund investments.

Methodology:

- Face-to-face or telephone interviews with limited partners.
- Structured questionnaire checklist, some open questions.
- All information provided will be treated fully confidential. No given information will be identified with your company.

Structure of the Interview:

Part A: Company profile

Part B: Monitoring a single fund investment

Part C: LP activism and re-investment decision

Part D: Limited partners' fund portfolio decisions

Part E: Reporting requirements

Part F: Team and remuneration

Contact Information:
Prof. Dr. Dr. Ann-Kristin Achleitner / Kay Müller
Center for Entrepreneurial and Financial Studies
Technische Universität München

Arcisstr. 21
80333 Munich
Germany

Email: Kay.Mueller@wi.tum.de
Phone +49 (0)89 289-25186
Fax: +49 (0)89 289-25188

Part A Company profile

A.1 Your **investments in private equity** are carried out through:

- ☐ Investments in private equity funds
- ☐ Co-investments directly in portfolio companies
- ☐ Secondary Investments
- ☐ Mandates given to fund-of-funds / use of managed accounts
- ☐ Others: ------------------------------------

Please provide some **general information on your institution** (all data as of end of 2005).

A.2 Year of first private equity fund investment ☐☐☐☐

A.3 Location of headquarter (country): --

A.4 Type:

- ☐ Pension Fund
- ☐ Bank (incl. Investment Bank)
- ☐ Family Office
- ☐ Endowment
- ☐ Fund-of-Fund
- ☐ Other ------------------------------
- ☐ Insurance Company

A.5 Total assets under management (only private equity commitments): ☐☐☐☐ million EUR

A.6 Please specify your allocation...

...in terms of stages:

Venture Capital	☐☐
Buyouts	☐☐
Others	☐☐
	=100%

...in terms of geographical regions:

EU	☐☐
USA	☐☐
Asia	☐☐
Rest of the World	☐☐
	=100%

A.7 Number of private equity funds in portfolio: ☐☐

Number of GP relationships ☐☐

Part B Monitoring a single fund investment

Information gathering

B.1 What are the **three most important sources of information** about your fund investment **during the investment period**?
(Open question)

B.2 Please indicate in % **how much information in order to monitor the fund investment** you obtain **from impersonal sources in comparison to personal sources** ?

Impersonal sources (e.g. fund reporting)	☐☐	%
Personal sources (e.g. GP calls)	☐☐	%
	= 100	

B.3 Some general partners are **reluctant to disclose information.**
In your opinion, what can be reasons? State whether the following reasons are relevant or not.

General partners...	very relevant 5	4	medium 3	2	very irrelevant 1
try to hide weak performance	☐	☐	☐	☐	☐
fear misinterpration of information	☐	☐	☐	☐	☐
fear competitive disadvantages for portfolio companies	☐	☐	☐	☐	☐
fear bargaining disadvantages when exiting companies	☐	☐	☐	☐	☐
fear increasing risk of litigation / legal action	☐	☐	☐	☐	☐
fear public disclosure of information given to investors (FOIA)	☐	☐	☐	☐	☐
avoid costs and time related to the reporting process	☐	☐	☐	☐	☐

Performance measurement

IRR and multiples are the most frequently used performance measures.

B.4 Do you use other measures to evaluate individual fund performance?
(Open question)

B.5 How do you benchmark your portfolio of funds?
(Open question)

B.6 Would you like to see funds to provide more information on performance measuring data?

☐ Yes ☐ No

If yes, what sort of information? (Open question)

B.7 The risk profiles of individual fund investments are different. Do you assess the risk of your fund investments?

☐ Yes ☐ No

B.8 If yes, how do you do that? (Open question)

B.9 How important are the following risks during the investment period?

	Very important 5	4	medium 3	2	Very unimportant 1
Currency risks	☐	☐	☐	☐	☐
Leverage / interest risks	☐	☐	☐	☐	☐
Liquidity / cash flow risks	☐	☐	☐	☐	☐
Valuation risks	☐	☐	☐	☐	☐
Style drift of fund management	☐	☐	☐	☐	☐
Operational risk within the fund managing company	☐	☐	☐	☐	☐

B.10 Would you like to see more information about the risks in fund's reporting?

☐ Yes ☐ No

B.11 If yes, please describe what sort of information? (Open question)

Resources for monitoring

B.12 On average, **how much of the time** of all investment professionals (in % of total time of investment professionals) does your institution spend on

Selecting *new* investments?	☐☐ %
Monitoring *existing* fund investments?	☐☐ %
Others	☐☐ %
	= 100 %

B.13 What do you think is an **optimal number of GP relationships per professional investment manager?**

☐☐ funds

Part C LP activism and re-investment decision

Advisory boards

C.1 In what percentage of your private equity funds does your institution take **a seat on the advisory board**? ☐☐ %

C.2 In your opinion and without regarding any legal/regulatory constraints, what **purposes / tasks** should an advisory board fulfill?

	Very important 5	4	medium 3	2	Very unimportant 1
Review of new investment proposals (investment decisions)	☐	☐	☐	☐	☐
Discuss portfolio company problems	☐	☐	☐	☐	☐
Approve / ratify portfolio valuation, esp. mark-ups and mark-downs	☐	☐	☐	☐	☐
Waive conflicts of interests if they arise	☐	☐	☐	☐	☐
Approve the general partner's annual budget	☐	☐	☐	☐	☐
Approve and ratify distributions to limited partners	☐	☐	☐	☐	☐
Approve the proposed handling of limited partner default	☐	☐	☐	☐	☐

C.3 What are **your** main reasons to **participate in advisory boards**?
(Open question)

C.4 In general, would you like to see your institution presented in more fund advisory boards in the future?

☐ Yes, more ☐ No, rather less ☐ No, rather the same as today

Enhancing value creation

C.5 On average, how often do you get in **contact with your fund managers**?

☐ Weekly ☐ Quarterly ☐ Others

☐ Monthly ☐ Yearly

C.6 On what occasion do you contact your fund managers?
(Open question)

C.7 From your experience, how often have you been **asked for advice** from your fund managers?

	Very often 5	often 4	sometimes 3	seldom 2	never 1
Concerning potential new investments?	☐	☐	☐	☐	☐
Concerning the exit of investments?	☐	☐	☐	☐	☐
Concerning partnership terms?	☐	☐	☐	☐	☐
Concerning strategy and development of management company?	☐	☐	☐	☐	☐
Establishing contacts to other potential LPs?	☐	☐	☐	☐	☐
Others ---	☐	☐	☐	☐	☐

C.8 How often have you **been involved** in the following actions?

	Very often 5	often 4	sometimes 3	seldom 2	never 1
Push/encourage the GP to act on portfolio companies (e.g. when portfolio companies face difficulties)	☐	☐	☐	☐	☐
Enabling contacts between portfolio companies of different GP	☐	☐	☐	☐	☐
Pushing GP in terms of strategy / development of management company	☐	☐	☐	☐	☐
Others ---	☐	☐	☐	☐	☐

C.9 In your opinion, how important are the following points in preventing **you** from being more engaged on fund level?

	Very important 5	4	medium 3	2	Very unimportant 1
Fear to loose your limited partner status	☐	☐	☐	☐	☐
Low level of influence due to little stake in fund (ownership structure)	☐	☐	☐	☐	☐
Few information / low transparency to judge about decisions	☐	☐	☐	☐	☐
No industry-know-how	☐	☐	☐	☐	☐
Costs and time restraints	☐	☐	☐	☐	☐
Not my job	☐	☐	☐	☐	☐

C.10 In the future, what **level of involvement** on individual fund level would you like to see?
(Only one answer)

We would like to be more involved ☐

We would like to be less involved ☐

No change in comparison to today ☐

Protecting value

C.11 Have you ever faced a situation where a fund investment went off track (crisis)?

☐ Yes ☐ No

C.12 If yes, please describe the situation briefly. What did you do to protect your investment? (open question)

Re-investment decision

C.13 From your experience, do you think the re-investment decision is easier than investing in a first time fund?

☐ Yes ☐ No

C.14 If yes, why? (open question)

C.15 Do you think better fund reporting would ease your decision to re-invest?

☐ Yes ☐ No

C.16 If yes, what information would you like to see? (Open question)

Part D Limited partners' fund portfolio decisions

Portfolio liquidity management / cash flow planning

Managing liquidity in private equity is difficult as drawdowns and distributions by funds are very difficult to predict.

D.1 For your institution, how important is the planning of cash flow in and out of private equity funds?

	5	4	3	2	1	
Very important	☐	☐	☐	☐	☐	Very unimportant

D.2 Do you **forecast the cash flow of your portfolio of funds** using a formal approach?

☐ Yes ☐ No

D.3 If yes, could you please **describe that model**, esp. with respect to model inputs? (Open question)

D.4 How **satisfied** are you with GP's **information on potential portfolio company transactions** (exits / new investments)?

	5	4	3	2	1	
Very satisfied	☐	☐	☐	☐	☐	Very dissatisfied

D.5 Would **better reporting enhance your ability to forecast** liquidity?

☐ Yes ☐ No

D.6 If yes, what information would you like to see? (Open question)

Secondary market transactions

D.7 **Active portfolio management**: Have you ever sold or bought fund stakes on the secondary market for limited partnerships? ☐ Yes ☐ No

If yes, why?

(Open question)

D.8 Would you **use the secondary market** in the future for…

	Yes	No
opportunistic investment possibilities (tactical asset allocation)?	☐	☐
quickly terminating exposure to specific assets?	☐	☐
better liquidity management?	☐	☐
better diversification of your assets under management?	☐	☐

For other purposes? --

D.9 Do you believe better reporting (more transparency) of funds would **enhance the liquidity on the secondary market?**

☐ Yes ☐ No

Part E Reporting requirements

Reporting content

E.1 What is for you the **main role of fund reporting**?
(Open question)

E.2 Given that you are fully satisfied with 100%: How much of your information requirements in % are currently fullfilled by funds' reporting?

_____ %

E.3 From your experience, **what sort of information do you expect to see more** in reports?
(e.g. information on valuation, risks, fees)
(Open question)

E.4 Do your **needs on portfolio company level information** depend on whether you are invested in a buyout or venture capital fund?
(Open question)

E.5 Have you ever been in the situation that you asked for but did not receive the information you needed?

☐ Yes ☐ No

E.6 If yes, what sort of information and what did you do? (open question)

E.7 On average, how have your **information needs changed over the last five years** and how will they change **in the future**?

Past five years:

☐ Increased ☐ Decreased ☐ Unchanged

Future:

☐ Will increase ☐ Will decrease ☐ Will not change

Valuation

E.8 Do you **check and adjust the reported portfolio company valuations** for your own reporting and information system?

(Open question)

E.9 Please indicate, whether you consider the **following effects** of using **a fair value-based approach** when valuing portfolio company investments as **problematic**?

	Very problematic 5	4	medium 3	2	Not problematic 1
Higher degree of subjectivity of fund managers	☐	☐	☐	☐	☐
Possible increased volatility in portfolio valuations	☐	☐	☐	☐	☐
Lack of consistency in using valuation methodologies	☐	☐	☐	☐	☐
Fair valuation is time consuming for fund managers	☐	☐	☐	☐	☐
Others --	☐	☐	☐	☐	☐

E.10 In general, how **satisfied are you with disclosure of applied valuation methodologies** and assumptions in funds' reporting?

	5	4	3	2	1	
Very satisfied	☐	☐	☐	☐	☐	Very dissatisfied

Part F Team and remuneration

F.1 Please provide some **information about the staff** of your institution:

Number of investment professionals ______

Number of administrative personnel ______

F.2 Is the responsibility for selecting and monitoring seperated between team members?

☐ Yes ☐ No

F.3 The **senior member of the team is compensated** on a ...

	Yes	No
performance based salary	☐	☐
If yes, what does the remuneration depend on?		
Cash-on-cash returns of fund investments	☐	☐
Net asset value (NAV)	☐	☐
Qualitative judgements of your board (investment committee) about your performance	☐	☐
On others --	☐	☐

Appendix C: Disclosure Index

Information item	All (N= 36)	Venture (N=16)	Buyout (N=20)	Europe (N=20)	U.S. (N=16)
	% of private equity funds making disclosure				
General operational information on fund level	**58%**	**58%**	**59%**	**62%**	**54%**
Fund's domicile	94%	94%	95%	100%	87%
Legal form	100%	100%	100%	100%	100%
Closing date	92%	81%	100%	90%	93%
Vintage year	50%	56%	45%	57%	40%
Portfolio or fund strategy (incl. any changes)	58%	69%	50%	67%	47%
Changes of GP's management	39%	31%	45%	52%	20%
Information about related party transactions	44%	31%	55%	33%	60%
Note on deal flow	31%	38%	25%	29%	33%
Note about the application of any reporting guidelines	14%	19%	10%	24%	0%
Financial information on aggregated investments	**80%**	**77%**	**83%**	**84%**	**75%**
Total commitments	97%	94%	100%	100%	93%
Total capital drawn down	100%	100%	100%	100%	100%
Total capital invested	100%	100%	100%	100%	100%
Total sum distributed	94%	88%	100%	100%	87%
Date of capital draw down	47%	38%	55%	62%	27%
Total capital committed or reserved for follow-on rounds	17%	19%	15%	29%	0%
Total value of remaining assets (NAV)	100%	100%	100%	100%	100%
List of all current investments	100%	100%	100%	100%	100%
List of all new investments	94%	94%	95%	95%	93%
List of all realizations	83%	81%	85%	86%	80%
Sum of net investment income or loss	100%	100%	100%	100%	100%
Sum of realized gains or losses	100%	100%	100%	100%	100%
Sum of unrealized gains or losses	97%	100%	95%	95%	100%
Note of any leverage to the fund (debt, guarantees, contingent liabilites)	56%	31%	75%	62%	47%
Average holding period of investments over the life of the fund	14%	6%	20%	24%	0%
Capital account information	**60%**	**59%**	**61%**	**61%**	**59%**
Current capital account balance at cost	69%	63%	75%	76%	60%
Current capital account balance at fair value	64%	69%	60%	57%	73%
Capital account information since inception	42%	50%	35%	38%	47%
Capital account information for current period	72%	63%	80%	71%	73%
Detailed capital account statement (shows all investors)	61%	63%	60%	67%	53%
Investors' names	53%	50%	55%	62%	40%
Detailed information of investors' ownership	61%	63%	60%	62%	60%
Capital account information for General Partner	58%	50%	65%	67%	47%
Performance measurement on fund level	**20%**	**18%**	**20%**	**24%**	**14%**
IRR of fund's realized investments (Gross IRR)	28%	19%	35%	38%	13%
IRR of fund's realized and unrealized investments (Gross IRR)	42%	31%	50%	57%	20%
IRR on fund investment net to investors (Net IRR)	67%	75%	60%	52%	87%
Detailed IRR (Gross IRR) by industry, geography, stage, lead partner responsible for investments	3%	6%	0%	5%	0%
Multiple on fund inv.: total value to paid-in capital (TVPI)	53%	56%	50%	62%	40%
Multiple on fund inv.: residual value to paid-in capital (RVPI)	22%	13%	30%	33%	7%

Information item	All (N= 36)	Venture (N=16)	Buyout (N=20)	Europe (N=20)	U.S. (N=16)
	% of private equity funds making disclosure				
Performance measurement on fund level	**20%**	**18%**	**20%**	**24%**	**14%**
Multiple on fund inv.: distribution to paid-in capital (DPI)	8%	0%	15%	14%	0%
Detailed multiples by industry, geography, stage, lead partner responsible for the investments	3%	6%	0%	5%	0%
Payback period on fund level	0%	0%	0%	0%	0%
Comparison against an industry benchmark	6%	6%	5%	10%	0%
Information on calculation of benchmark	3%	6%	0%	5%	0%
Comparison with other asset classes	0%	0%	0%	0%	0%
Risk reporting on fund level	**10%**	**9%**	**10%**	**15%**	**3%**
Information on fund's currency exposure	36%	31%	40%	57%	7%
Quantitative risk measures on fund level	0%	0%	0%	0%	0%
Information on fund's risk management processes	0%	0%	0%	0%	0%
Qualitative information on fund's specific risks	3%	6%	0%	5%	0%
Information on fund investment's fees	**25%**	**16%**	**31%**	**27%**	**23%**
Management fees	97%	100%	95%	95%	100%
Basis of calculation of management fees	50%	44%	55%	33%	73%
Detailed fee statement	14%	0%	25%	19%	7%
Deal fees	11%	0%	20%	10%	13%
Broken deal fees	14%	6%	20%	19%	7%
Consulting fees	31%	19%	40%	33%	27%
Monitoring / director fees	11%	0%	20%	10%	13%
Fund's compensation disclosed in total and by transaction	17%	0%	30%	14%	20%
Fund administration costs	19%	0%	35%	24%	13%
Detailed statement on expenses paid on individual transactions	8%	0%	15%	14%	0%
Total carried interest paid since inception	8%	13%	5%	10%	7%
Carried interest paid during reporting period	8%	6%	10%	5%	13%
Carried interest earned during reporting period	6%	6%	5%	10%	0%
Basis of calculation of carried interest	53%	38%	65%	38%	73%
General information on portfolio companies and role of fund	**55%**	**58%**	**52%**	**58%**	**51%**
Legal and trading names of portfolio company	100%	100%	100%	100%	100%
Location of head office or management	78%	81%	75%	81%	73%
Name of CEO and management	42%	50%	35%	43%	40%
Webpage	44%	63%	30%	48%	40%
Brief description of the business	92%	88%	95%	90%	93%
Summary investment thesis (investment rationale)	44%	25%	60%	48%	40%
Industry / sub-sector	72%	69%	75%	76%	67%
Current stage of investment	33%	38%	30%	29%	40%
Stage of investment at time of investment	17%	13%	20%	19%	13%
Company status (public, private)	97%	100%	95%	100%	93%
Statement of the fund's role in investment (lead, co-lead, etc.)	31%	31%	30%	33%	27%
Board representation (names and number of seats held compared to the total board seats, if any)	47%	63%	35%	48%	47%
Name of responsible investment manager (partner, prinicipal, personnel) of fund	19%	25%	15%	24%	13%
List of major co-investors in the deal	53%	75%	35%	52%	53%

Information item	% of private equity funds making disclosure				
	All (N= 36)	Venture (N=16)	Buyout (N=20)	Europe (N=20)	U.S. (N=16)
Financial information on portfolio companies	**30%**	**14%**	**43%**	**35%**	**23%**
Accounting standard (US GAAP, IFRS)	3%	0%	5%	0%	7%
Excerpt of income statement	17%	13%	20%	19%	13%
Excerpt of balance sheet	19%	13%	25%	19%	20%
Excerpt of cash flow statement	6%	0%	10%	5%	7%
Figures on sales	56%	25%	80%	67%	40%
Figures on earnings/income (gross profit, EBIT, EBITDA, net earnings)	67%	38%	90%	81%	47%
Figures on capital structure and liquidity (cash, debt, etc.)	50%	19%	75%	62%	33%
Comparison against budget	25%	6%	40%	33%	13%
Budget or forecast for next year on income and balance sheet	22%	6%	35%	24%	20%
Historic data on income and balance sheet	56%	19%	85%	67%	40%
Non-financial figures (customers, suppliers, etc.)	11%	13%	10%	10%	13%
Information on valuation and performance of portfolio inv.	**60%**	**57%**	**62%**	**68%**	**50%**
Note about the application of any valuation guidelines	47%	44%	50%	76%	7%
Description of the valuation process applied	14%	13%	15%	10%	20%
Note about whether different valuations are used in financial statements and investor reporting	19%	6%	30%	33%	0%
Note about the use of fair value	92%	100%	85%	95%	87%
Note about the use of cost or a different value for each investment	58%	56%	60%	76%	33%
Valuation methodology used (e.g. earnings multiple, DCF)	33%	13%	50%	48%	13%
Rationale for used valuation methodology	6%	0%	10%	10%	0%
Detailed caluculation of valuation provided (e.g. by disclosing peer group)	8%	0%	15%	14%	0%
Note on any changes in valuation methodologies	17%	19%	15%	24%	7%
Date of initial investment	94%	94%	95%	100%	87%
Percentage ownership of fund	97%	94%	100%	100%	93%
Valuation (costs) at time of investment	100%	100%	100%	100%	100%
Valuation at reporting date	97%	100%	95%	100%	93%
Net investment income or loss on investment	94%	94%	95%	100%	87%
Realized gains or losses on investment	92%	88%	95%	100%	80%
Unrealized gains or losses on investment	89%	94%	85%	95%	80%
Divestments or distribution amounts	89%	94%	85%	86%	93%
Gross IRR on portfolio company investments	44%	38%	50%	62%	20%
Multiple on investment: fair value divided by cost	47%	44%	50%	57%	33%
Assessment of current situation, risks and future develop. of inv.	**27%**	**25%**	**28%**	**33%**	**19%**
Significant events during the reporting period	97%	94%	100%	100%	93%
Assesment of the company's status compared to the expactation at the time of investment ("on track", etc.)	33%	25%	40%	57%	0%
Milestones analysis (hard figures)	19%	25%	15%	14%	27%
Quantitative risk measures on portfolio level	3%	0%	5%	5%	0%
Qualitative information on portfolio company specific risks	17%	13%	20%	19%	13%
Exit plans (IPO, trade sale)	19%	19%	20%	29%	7%
Exit horizon	17%	13%	20%	24%	7%
Estimated exit valuation	6%	13%	0%	5%	7%

References

Achleitner, A.-K. (2002a): Entrepreneurial Finance: Herausforderung auch in Deutschland, in: Betriebs-Berater, 57 (3), pp. 142-145.

Achleitner, A.-K. (2002b): Handbuch Investment Banking, 3rd edition, Wiesbaden.

Achleitner, A.-K. / Bassen, A. (2004): Venture-Capital-bezogenes Controlling: Wie unterscheiden sich die Aspekte der verschiedenen Ebenen, in: Jahrbuch zum Finanz- und Rechnungswesen 2004, ed. by C. Meyer / D. Pfaff, Zürich, pp. 149-168.

Achleitner, A.-K. / Bassen, A. / Jais, S. D. / Nietzer, P. (2004a): Controlling von Buyout-Transaktionen durch Private-Equity-Gesellschaften, in: ZFCM Controlling & Management, Sonderheft 1, pp. 32-45.

Achleitner, A.-K. / Behr, G. (2002): International Accounting Standards: Ein Lehrbuch zur Internationalen Rechnungslegung, 3rd edition, München.

Achleitner, A.-K. / Kloeckner, O. (2005): Employment contribution of private equity and venture capital in Europe, EVCA Research Paper, Zaventum.

Achleitner, A.-K. / Müller, K. (2003): Die bilanzielle Behandlung von Portfoliounternehmen nach IAS/IFRS: Sind Private-Equity-Gesellschaften Konzerne? Zur Notwendigkeit einer vergleichenden Studie, Konferenzbeitrag G-Forum 2003 - Doktorandenkolloquium.

Achleitner, A.-K. / Müller, K. (2004): Trade groups versus private equity entities: A comparative study, EVCA Research Paper, Zaventum.

Achleitner, A.-K. / Müller, K. (2005): International private equity and venture capital valuation guidelines: A milestone in strengthening the asset class, in: Financial yearbook Germany 2006, ed. by T. Anderer, Munich, pp. 66-71.

Achleitner, A.-K. / Nathusius, E. (2004): Venture Valuation: Bewertung von Wachstumsunternehmen, Stuttgart.

Achleitner, A.-K. / Nathusius, E. / Schraml, S. (2007): Valuation of platform technology based intangibles companies, CEFS Working Paper No. 2007-02, TU München.

Achleitner, A.-K. / Wahl, S. (2004): Private Debt als alternative Finanzierungsform für mittelständische Unternehmen, in: Private Debt: Alternative Finanzierung für den Mittelstand, ed. by A.-K. Achleitner / C. v. Einem / B. v. Schröder, Stuttgart, pp. 41-80.

Achleitner, A.-K. / Zelger, H. / Beyer, S. / Müller, K. (2004b): Venture Capital/Private Equity-Studie 2004: Company-(E)valuation und EVCA Valuation Guidelines, in: Finanz Betrieb, 6 (10), pp. 701-709.

Achleitner, P. / Fingerle, C. (2006): Investing in alternative assets, in: Management am Puls der Zeit: Festschrift für Prof. Wildemann zum 65. Geburtstag, Band 2, ed. by I. Hausladen, München, pp. 727-744.

Adrem, A. (1999): Essays on disclosure practices in Sweden: Causes and effects, Doctoral Dissertation, Lund Studies in Economics and Management, Vol. 51, Institute of Economic Research, University of Lund, Lund.

AFIC / BVCA / EVCA (2004): International private equity and venture capital valuation guidelines.

Ahmed, K. / Courtis, J. K. (1999): Associations between corporate characteristics and disclosure levels in annual reports: A meta-analysis, in: British Accounting Review, 31 (1), pp. 35-61.

AICPA (2000): AICPA audit and accounting guide: Audits of investment companies.

AICPA (2005): Statement of position: Clarification of the scope of the audit and accounting guide 'Audits of investment companies' and accounting by parent companies and equity method investors for investments in investment companies, Discussion Draft, December 27, 2005.

AICPA (2006): Project information: Scope clarification, investment companies guide - SOP, http://www.aicpa.org/members/div/acctstd/projects/scope_clarification.asp, 16.07.2006.

Akerlof, G. (1970): The market for 'lemons': Quality uncertainty and the market mechanism, in: Quarterly Journal of Economics, 84 (3), pp. 488-500.

Amir, E. / Lev, B. (1996): Value-relevance of nonfinancial information: The wireless communications industry, in: Journal of Accounting and Economics, 22 (1-3), pp. 3-30.

Amit, R. / Brander, J. / Zott, C. (1998): Why do venture capital firms exist? Theory and Canadian evidence, in: Journal of Business Venturing, 13 (6), pp. 441-466.

Anonymous author (2002): Beyond IRR, in: Private Equity International, Dec/Jan 2002/2003 (11), pp. 28-33.

Anonymous author (2003): EVCA warnt bei Einführung der IAS/IFRS vor Risiken für private Unternehmensfinanzierung in der EU, in: KoR, 3 (9), pp. 410-411.

Anonymous author (2004): Much needed clarity, in: Private Equity International (21), p. 42.

Aragon, L. (2002): Disclosure, in: Venture Capital Journal, 42 (11), pp. 20-25.

Archambault, J. J. / Archambault, M. E. (2003): A multinational test of determinants of corporate disclosure, in: International Journal of of Accounting, 38 (2), pp. 173-194.

Artley, R. / Dobrauz, G. / Plasonig, G. / Strasser, R. (2003): Making money out of technology, Zurich.

Artus, P. / Teiletche, J. (2004): Asset allocation and European private equity: A first approach using aggregated data, in: Performance Measurement and Asset Allocation for Private Equity Funds, ed. by EVCA, Zaventem, pp. 7-26.

Atkins, B. / Giannini, M. (2003): Risk management for private equity funds of funds, in: The new generation of risk management for hedge funds and private equity investments, ed. by L. Jaeger, London, pp. 215-227.

Avida Advisors (2005): Die alternative Anlageklasse Private Equity und ihr Einfluss auf die Portfolioallokation institutioneller Investoren in Europa, München.

Bader, H. (1996): Private Equity als Anlagekategorie, Bern, Stuttgart, Wien.

Baetge, J. / Kirsch, H.-J. / Thiele, S. (2004): Konzernbilanzen, 7th edition, Düsseldorf.

Bagley, C. / Dauchy, C. (1999): Venture capital, in: The entrepreneurial venture, ed. by W. A. Sahlman, Boston, pp. 262-303.

Baker, S. / Luff, J. (2005): IFRS and the private equity industry, EVCA and PwC Discussion Paper No. 2, Zaventem.

Balboa, M. / Marti, J. (2006): Factors that determine the reputation of private equity managers in developing markets, in: Journal of Business Venturing (forthcoming).

Ball, R. / Foster, G. (1982): Corporate financial reporting: A methodological review of empirical research, in: Journal of Accounting Research, 20 (Supplement), pp. 161-234.

Ballwieser, W. (2004): Unternehmensbewertung: Prozeß, Methoden und Probleme, Stuttgart.

Bance, A. (2004): Why and how to invest in private equity, EVCA Special Paper, Zaventem.

Bane, M. (2005): IFRS and the private equity industry, EVCA and PwC Discussion Paper No. 1, Zaventem.

Barnes, S. / Menzies, V. (2005): Investment into venture capital funds in Europe: An exploratory study, in: Venture Capital, 7 (3), pp. 209-226.

Barth, M. E. / Landsman, W. R. (1995): Fundamental issues related to using fair value accounting for financial reporting, in: Accounting Horizons, 9 (4), pp. 97-107.

Bascha, A. / Walz, U. (2001): Convertible securities and optimal exit decisions in venture capital finance, in: Journal of Corporate Finance, 7 (3), pp. 285-306.

Bascha, A. / Walz, U. (2002): Financing practices in the German venture capital industry: An empirical assessment, Center for Financial Studies, Universität Frankfurt, Working Paper, Frankfurt.

Beaver, W. H. (1987): Financial reporting: An accounting revolution, 3rd edition, New Jersey.

Becker, W. (2004): Konzernabschlüsse für Private-Equity-Fonds führen in die Irre, in: Börsen-Zeitung, 31.12.04, p. 46.

Bellavite-Hövermann, Y. / Barckow, A. (2003): IAS 39 Finanzinstrumente: Ansatz und Bewertung, in: Rechnungslegung nach International Accounting Standards (IAS): Kommentar auf der Grundlage des deutschen Bilanzrechts, 2. Auflage, ed. by J. Baetge / D. Dörner / H. Kleekämper / P. Wollmert / H.-J. Kirsch, Stuttgart, pp. 1-121.

Berg, A. (2005): What is strategy for buyout associations? Berlin.

Berg, A. / Gottschalg, O. (2004): Understanding value generation in buyouts, in: European Venture Capital Journal (114), pp. 22-24.

Bergemann, D. / Hege, U. (1998): Venture capital financing, moral hazard, and learning, in: Journal of Banking & Finance, 22 (6-8), pp. 703-735.

Berglöf, E. (1994): A control theory of venture capital finance, in: Journal of Law, Economics, and Organization, 10 (2), pp. 247-267.

Bieker, M. (2006): Ökononische Analyse des Fair Value Accounting, Frankfurt am Main.

Bishop, M. (2004): Kings of capitalism: A survey of private equity, in: The Economist, 373 (8403), pp. 1-16.

Black, E. L. (2003): Usefulness of financial statement components in valuation: An examination of start-up and growth firms, in: Venture Capital, 5 (1), pp. 47-69.

Black, F. / Scholes, M. (1973): The pricing of options and coporate liabilities, in: Journal of Political Economy, 81 (3), pp. 609-623.

Blake, J. (1999): Structuring venture capital funds for investment: The legal dimension, in: The venture capital handbook, ed. by W. D. Bygrave / M. Hay / J. B. Peeters, Harlow, pp. 79-93.

Blaydon, C. / Horvath, M. (2003): LPs need to trust general partners in setting valuations, in: Venture Capital Journal, 43 (3), pp. 48-49.

Blaydon, C. / Horvath, M. / Wainwright, F. (2002): The year of the valuation guidelines, in: Private Equity Annual Review 2002, Supplement of the Private Equity International, pp. 97-100.

Blaydon, C. / Wainwright, F. (2004a): The stage is set, in: Private Equity International (21), pp. 45-49.

Blaydon, C. / Wainwright, F. (2004b): Survey: GPs and LPs support idea for model LP agreement, in: Venture Capital Journal, 44 (7), pp. 19-21.

Blaydon, C. / Wainwright, F. (2006): It's time to do away with participating preferred, in: Venture Capital Journal, 46 (7), pp. 41-42.

Böcking, H.-J. / Nowak, K. (1999): Marktorientierte Unternehmensbewertung, in: Finanz Betrieb, 1 (8), pp. 169-176.

Boersma, J. A. / Brown, S. D. / Franklin, W. B. (2005): Appropriate pricing and valuation of portfolio companies, in: CFA Institute conference proceedings: Dimensions in private equity (2), pp. 33-38.

Böhler, C. (2004a): Bewertung von Private-Equity-Investitionen: Prozessorientierung zur Entschärfung der Objektivierungsproblematik, in: Der Schweizer Treuhänder (12), pp. 1113-1120.

Böhler, C. (2004b): Corporate Governance und externe Berichterstattung in Venture-Capital-Gesellschaften, Bern, Stuttgart, Wien.

Borel, P. (2004): Making private equity work, in: Private Equity International (30), pp. 44-48.

Borell, J. (2003a): Profile: AIMR, in: Venture Capital Journal, 43 (5), p. 34.

Borell, J. (2003b): Profile: PEIGG, in: Venture Capital Journal, 43 (5), p. 33.

Bortz, J. (1999): Statistik für Sozialwissenschaftler, Berlin.

Botosan, C. (1997): Disclosure level and the cost of equity level, in: The Accounting Review, 72 (3), pp. 323-349.

Bottazzi, L. / Da Rin, M. / Hellmann, T. (2004): The changing face of the European venture capital industry: Facts and analysis, in: Journal of Private Equity, 8 (1), pp. 26-53.

Braunschweig, C. (2004): NVCA balks at backing PEIGG standards, in: Venture Capital Journal, 44 (May), pp. 25.

Brealey, R. A. / Myers, S. C. (2005): Principles of corporate finance, 8th international edition, New York.

Brooks, J. (1999): Fund-raising and investor relations, in: The venture capital handbook, ed. by W. D. Bygrave / M. Hay / J. B. Peeters, Harlow, pp. 95-117.

Buchner, A. / Kaserer, C. / Wagner, N. (2006): Stochastic modeling of private equity - An equilibrium based approach to fund valuation, CEFS Working Paper No. 2006-02, TU München.

Bukh, P. N. / Nielson, C. / Gormsen, P. / Mouritsen, J. (2005): Disclosure of information on intellectual capital in Danish IPO prospectuses, in: Accounting, Auditing & Accountability Journal, 18 (6), pp. 713-732.

Bungartz, O. (2003): Risk Reporting, Sternenfels.

Burgel, O. (2000): UK venture capital and private equity as an asset class for institutional investors, Foundation for Entrepreneurial Management: London Business School, London.

Burton, J. / Schierschmidt, R. (2004): First-time venture fund raising: Challenges and best practices, in: Journal of Private Equity, 8 (1), pp. 9-21.

Bushman, R. M. / Smith, A. J. (2001): Financial accounting information and corporate governance, in: Journal of Accounting and Economics, 32 (1-3), pp. 237-333.

Bushman, R. M. / Smith, A. J. (2003): Transparency, financial accounting information, and corporate governance, in: Economic Policy Review, 9 (1), pp. 65-87.

Busse von Colbe, W. / Ordelheide, D. / Gebhardt, G. / Pellens, B. (2003): Konzernabschlüsse: Rechnungslegung nach betriebswirtschaftlichen Grundsätzen sowie nach Vorschriften des HGB und der IAS/IFRS, 7th edition, Wiesbaden.

Buzby, S. L. (1974): Selected items of information and their disclosure in annual reports, in: The Accouting Review, 49 (3), pp. 423-435.

Buzby, S. L. (1975): Company size, listed versus unlisted stocks, and the extent of financial disclosure, in: Journal of Accounting Research, 13 (1), pp. 16-37.

BVCA (2002): Limited partnership agreement, London.

BVCA (2003): Reporting guidelines (reprint 2005), London.

BVK (2006): BVK Statistik 2005: Das Jahr 2005 in Zahlen, Berlin.

Cable, D. / Shane, S. (1997): A prisoner's dilemma approach to entrepreneur-venture capitalist relationships, in: Academy of Management Review, 22 (1), pp. 142-176.

Cerf, A. R. (1961): Corporate reporting and investment decisions, University of California, Berkeley.

CFA Institute (2004): Private equity provisions for the global investment performance standards (GIPS).

CFA Institute (2005): Global investment performance standards (GIPS).

CFA Institute (2006): GIPS: Interpretive guidance for private equity.

Chaplinsky, S. / Perry, S. (2004): CalPERS vs. Mercury News: Disclosure comes to private equity, Case Study No. UVA-F-1438-SSRN, University of Virgina, Charlottesville.

Chen, P. / Baierl, G. T. / Kaplan, P. T. (2002): Venture capital and its role in strategic asset allocation, in: Journal of Portfolio Management, 28 (2), pp. 83-89.

Cheung, L. / Howley, C. / Kapoor, V. / Smith, A. (2003): Rating private equity CFOs: Cash flow benchmarks, CDO Research, Structured Finance Special Report, Standard & Poor's, New York.

Cheung, L. / Kapoor, V. / Howley, C. (2003): Rating private equity CFOs: Stochastic market cash flows, CDO Research, Structured Finance Special Report, Standard & Poor's, New York.

Chow, C. W. / Wong-Boren, A. (1987): Voluntary financial disclosure by Mexican corporations, in: The Accounting Review, 68 (3), pp. 533-541.

Clark, G. G. / Kojima, J. C. (2003): Opportunities and challenges in secondaries: Investing in the secondary market for private equity, in: The Journal of Alternative Investing, 6 (1), pp. 74-86.

CMBOR / Adveq (2005): Private Equity: A study of UK institutional investors.

Cochrane, J. H. (2005): The risk and return of venture capital, in: Journal of Financial Economics, 75 (1), pp. 3-52.

Cooke, T. E. (1989a): Disclosure in the corporate annual reports of Swedish companies, in: Accounting and Business Research, 19 (74), pp. 113-124.

Cooke, T. E. (1989b): Voluntary corporate disclosure by Swedish companies, in: Journal of International Financial Management and Accounting, 1 (2), pp. 171-195.

Cooke, T. E. (1991): An assessment of voluntary disclosure in the annual reports of Japanese corporations, in: The International Journal of of Accounting, 26 (2), pp. 174-189.

Cooke, T. E. / Wallace, O. R. S. (1989): Global surveys of corporate disclosure practices and audit firms: A review essay, in: Accounting and Business Research, 20 (77), pp. 47-57.

Copeland, T. / Koller, T. / Murrin, J. (2000): Valuation: Measuring and managing the value of companies, 3rd edition, New York.

Crawford-Ingle, A. / Kempen, S. / Vickery, C. (2003): Private equity and the valuation game, The European Union Banking and Finance Network Newsletter September 2003, http://www.eubfn.com/arts/pricewaterhouse.htm, 16.06.2006.

Cumming, D. / Fleming, G. / Schwienbacher, A. (2005): Style drift in private equity, Working Paper.

Cumming, D. / Walz, U. (2004): Private equity returns and disclosure around the world, Working Paper, University of Alberta, J.W. Goethe-Universität Frankfurt/Main.

de Zwart, G. / Frieser, B. / van Dijk, D. (2006): A recommitment strategy for long term private equity investors, Working Paper, January 2006.

Defusco, R. A. / McLeavey, D. W. / Pinto, J. E. / Runkle, D. E. (2001): Quantitative methods for investment analysis, Charlottesville.

Deloitte (2005): IAS Plus, Audit Newsletter, July 2005, Special Issue.

Deloitte & Touche (2002): 2. Deloitte & Touche Venture-Capital- und Private-Equity-Studie, Frankfurt am Main.

Diamond, D. (1984): Financial intermediation and delegated monitoring, in: Review of Economic Studies, 51 (3), pp. 393-414.

Diem, G. (2002): The information deficiency problem of private equity fund-of-funds: A risk and monitoring management perspective, University of Birmingham, MBA-Thesis.

Diller, C. (2007): Private Equity: Rendite, Risiko und Markteinflussfaktoren - Eine empirische Analyse, Bad Soden.

Ding, Y. / Fu, L. / Stolowy, H. / Wang, H. (2005): Disclosure and determinants studies: An extension using clustering methods (DIV), Working Paper.

DiPiazza, S. A. / Eccles, R. G. (2002): Building public trust: The future of corporate reporting, New York.

Dixit, A. K. / Pindyck, R. S. (1995): The option approach to capital investment, in: Harvard Business Review, 73 (3), pp. 105-115.

Dohrn, M. (2004): Entscheidungsrelevanz des Fair Value-Accounting am Beispiel von IAS 39 und IAS 40, Köln.

Dotzler, F. (2001): What do venture capitalists really do, and where do they learn to do it? in: Journal of Private Equity, 5 (1), pp. 6-12.

Dresdale, R. C. (2004): Private equity club deals: Risk and control, Institute for Fiduciary Education (IFE), Alternative Investment Seminar Paper.

Dresdale, R. C. (2005): Which private equity value creation strategies are best suited for the future? Institute for Fiduciary Education (IFE), Alternative Investment Seminar Paper.

Easterby-Smith, M. / Thorpe, R. / Lowe, A. (2002): Management research, London, Thousand Oaks, New Delhi.

Eckstein, P. (2000): Angewandte Statistik mit SPSS: Praktische Einführung für Wirtschaftswissenschaftler, Wiesbaden.

Eisenhardt, K. M. (1989): Agency theory: An assesment and review, in: Academy of Management Review, 14 (1), pp. 57-74.

Elliott, B. / Elliott, J. (2005): Financial accouting and reporting, 9th edition, Essex.

Engel, R. (2003): Seed-Finanzierung wachstumsorientierter Unternehmensgründungen, Sternenfels.

Ernst & Young (2004): International GAAP 2005: Generally accepted accounting practice under international financial reporting standards, London.

Erturk, E. / Cheung, L. / Fong, W. (2001): Private equity fund of funds: Overview and rating criteria, Standard & Poors Research, New York.

European Commission (2002): Regulation (EC) No 1606/2002 of the European Parliament and the Council of 19 July 2002 on the application of international accounting standards, in: Official Journal of the European Communities, L243.

European Commission (2006): Report of the alternative investment expert group - Developing European private equity, Internal Market and Services DG, Brussels.

EVCA (2002a): EVCA Yearbook 2002, Zaventem.

EVCA (2002b): Position statement: EVCA comments on exposure draft of proposed improvements to International Accounting Standards (IAS) and on exposure draft of proposed amendments to IAS 32 Financial Instruments: Disclosure and presentation and IAS 39 Financial instruments: Recognition and measurement, September 16, Brussels.

EVCA (2003a): Impact of consolidation on private equity and venture capital entities following the implementation of the improvements of IAS 27: A case study, Zaventem.

EVCA (2003b): Press relaease: EVCA welcomes the increased awareness on the impact of EU business on International Accounting Standards but warns oth the dangers of private financing of EU companies, July 18, Brussels.

EVCA (2003c): Press Release: Increased transparency professionalises the European asset class: But public disclosure pf portfolio company performance could endanger industry economics, June 4, Brussels.

EVCA (2004): Legal and regulatory aspects of marketing and promoting private equity funds across Europe: EVCA Tax & Legal Committee Paper, Zaventem.

EVCA (2006a): EVCA barometer March 2006, Zaventem.

EVCA (2006b): EVCA reporting guidelines, Zaventem.

EVCA (2006c): EVCA Yearbook 2006, Zaventem.

EVCA / Thomson Financial (2006): Pan-European survey of performance: From inception to 31 December 2005, Zaventem.

Fama, E. / Jensen, M. (1983): Separation of ownership and control, in: Journal of Law and Economics, 26 (2), pp. 301-325.

FASB / IASB (2006): A roadmap for convergence between IFRS and U.S. GAAP 2006-2008: Memorandum of understanding between the FASB and the IASB, February 27, London.

Feinendegen, S. / Hommel, U. / Wright, M. (2001): Stand der Beteiligungsfinanzierung in Deutschland, in: Finanz Betrieb, 3 (10), pp. 569-578.

Feinendegen, S. / Schmidt, D. / Wahrenburg, M. (2003): Die Vertragsbeziehungen zwischen Investoren und europäischen Venture Capital-Fonds: Eine empirische Untersuchung und Klassifizierung unterschiedlicher Vertragsmuster, in: ZfB, 73 (11), pp. 1167-1195.

Feldman, S. J. (2005): Principles of private firm valuation, New Jersey.

Fenn, G. W. / Liang, N. / Prowse, S. (1995): The economics of the private equity market, Federal Reserve Board Staff Study No.168, Washington.

Financial Service Authority (2006a): Financial risk outlook 2006, London.

Financial Service Authority (2006b): Private equity: A discussion of risk and regulatory engagement, Discussion Paper 06/6, London.

Financial Service Authority (2007): Private equity: A discussion of risk and regulatory engangement, Feedback on DP06/6, Statement 07/3, London.

Fingerle, C. (2005): Smart money: Influence of venture capitalists on high potential companies, Sternenfels.

Fort Washington (2006): A discussion of the J-curve in private equity, AltAssets Feature dated 05/04/2006.

Frei, A. / Studer, M. (2003): Quantitative private equity risk management, in: The new generation of risk management for hedge funds and private equity investments, ed. by L. Jaeger, London, pp. 201-214.

Frei, A. / Studer, M. (2004): Payback time, in: Private Equity International (30), pp. 30-33.

Frei, A. / Studer, M. (2006): Measuring private equity fund performance: The limited partner perspective, in: Structuring European private equity, ed. by I. Bassi / J. Grant, London, pp. 130-142.

Fried, V. / Hisrich, R. (1989): Venture capital from the investors' perspective, in: Frontiers of entrepreneurship research 1989: Proceedings of the ninth annual Babson College entrepreneurship research conference, ed. by R. H. Brockhaus / N. C. Churchill / J. A. Katz / B. A. Kirchhoff / K. H. Vesper / W. E. Wetzel, Wellesley, pp. 258-273.

Fried, V. / Hisrich, R. (1994): Toward a model of venture capital investment decision making, in: Financial Management, 23 (3), pp. 28-37.

GIMV (2006): Annual report 2005.

Gjesdal, F. (1981): Accounting for stewardship, in: Journal of Accounting Research, 19 (1), pp. 208-231.

Gompers, P. (1994): The rise and fall in venture capital, in: Business and Economic History, 23 (2), pp. 1-24.

Gompers, P. (1995): Optimal investment, monitoring, and the staging of venture capital, in: Journal of Finance, 50 (5), pp. 1461-1489.

Gompers, P. / Lerner, J. (1996): The use of covenants: An empirical analysis of venture partnership agreements, in: Journal of Law and Economics, 39 (2), pp. 463-498.

Gompers, P. / Lerner, J. (1997): Risk and reward in private equity investments: The challenge of performance assessment, in: The Journal of Private Equity, 1 (1), pp. 5-12.

Gompers, P. / Lerner, J. (1998): What drives venture capital fundraising? in: Brookings Papers on Economic Activity: Microeconomics, 1998 (July), pp. 149-192.

Gompers, P. / Lerner, J. (1999): An analysis of compensation in the U.S. venture capital partnership, in: Journal of Financial Economics, 51 (1), pp. 3-44.

Gompers, P. / Lerner, J. (2000): The challenge of performance assessment, in: Private equity and venture capital: A practical guide for investors and practitioners, ed. by R. Lake / R. A. Lake, London, pp. 249-259.

Gompers, P. / Lerner, J. (2001): Private equity and asset allocation: Clues to a puzzle, Salomon Smih Barney: Private Equity Research Initiative, Volume I Number III.

Gompers, P. / Lerner, J. (2004): The venture capital cycle, 2nd edition, Cambridge.

Gottschalg, O. (2006): Performance-Messung und Benchmarking von Private Equity-Investments, in: Handbuch Alternative Investments Band 2, ed. by M. Busack / D. G. Kaiser, Wiesbaden, pp. 189-212.

Gottschalg, O. / Phalippou, L. / Zollo, M. (2004): Performance of private equity funds: Another puzzle? Working Paper, INSEAD-Wharton Alliance Center for Global Research & Development.

Gottschalg, O. / Zollo, M. / Loos, N. (2004): Working out where the value lies, in: European Venture Capital Journal (113), pp. 36-39.

Gove, A. (2005): Toward transparency, in: Venture Capital Journal, 45 (10), pp. 47-48.

Grabenwarter, U. / Weidig, T. (2005a): Exposed to the J-curve: Understanding and managing private equity fund investments, London.

Grabenwarter, U. / Weidig, T. (2005b): Exposed to the J-Curve: Understanding and managing private equity fund investments: Summary and bibliography, Special Paper.

Greenberger, J. (2001): Minority investor rights in private equity transactions, in: Journal of Private Equity, 4 (2), pp. 47-53.

Griffin, D. W. / Varey, C. A. (1996): Towards a consensus on overconfidence, in: Organizational Behavior and Human Decision Processes, 65 (3), pp. 227–231.

Guennoc, D. (2006): Private equity performance and public equity returns, in: Structuring European private equity, ed. by I. Bassi / J. Grant, London, pp. 119-129.

Gull, J. (1999): Methodologies of marketing private equity returns, in: Venture Capital Journal, 39 (6), pp. 46-49.

Haarmann Hemmelrath / Universitaet Leipzig (2002): Performancemessung und Reporting bei Venture Capital-/Private Equity-Gesellschaften: Studie der RSM Haarmann Hemmelrath Wirtschaftsprüfung und des Instituts für Finanzen der Universitaet Leipzig, München.

Hagenmüller, M. (2004): Investor Relations von Private-Equity-Partnerships, Sternenfels.

Hansing, A. (2005): Sekundärmarkt für Private-Equity-Investments gewinnt an Bedeutung, in: Zeitschrift für das gesamte Kreditwesen, 58 (1), pp. 39-41.

Harrell, M. P. / Spiegel, J. A. (2004): To standardize or not to standardize: Recent developments, in: Debevoise & Plimpton Private Equity Report, 4 (3), pp. 16-22.

Harris, T. (2002): The antidilution death spiral, in: Journal of Private Equity, 5 (2), pp. 35-44.

Healy, P. M. / Palepu, K. G. (2001): Information asymmetry, corporate disclosure and the capital markets: A review of the empirical disclosure literature, in: Journal of Accounting and Economics, 31 (1-3), pp. 405-440.

Healy, P. M. / Palepu, K. G. (2003): The fall of Enron, in: Journal of Economic Perspectives, 17 (2), pp. 3-26.

Heel, J. / Kehoe, C. (2005): Why some private equity firms do better than others, in: The McKinsey Quarterly (1), pp. 24-26.

Hellman, R. / Katz, N. (2002): The evolution of partnership terms - aligning GP and LP interests, Institute for Fiduciary Education (IFE), Alternative Investment Seminar Paper.

Hellmann, T. (2006): IPOs, acquisitions, and the use of convertible securities in venture capital, in: Journal of Financial Economics, 81 (3), pp. 649-479.

Hellmann, T. / Lindsey, L. / Puri, M. (2004): Building relationships early: Banks in venture capital, NBER Working Paper, Stanford University, Arizona State University, Duke University and NBER.

Helwing, B. / Hummel, D. (2005): Risikobewertung von deutschen Kapitalbeteiligungsgesellschaften, in: Zeitschrift für das gesamte Kreditwesen, 58 (1), pp. 43-46.

Hielscher, U. / Zelger, H. / Beyer, S. (2003): Performancemessung und Reporting von Venture Capital-/Private Equity-Gesellschaften, in: Finanz Betrieb, 5 (7-8), pp. 498-505.

Hitz, J.-M. (2006): SFAS 15X, Fair Value Measurements: Zur Fortentwicklung der Fair-Value-Konzeption in der kapitalmarktorientierten Rechnungslegung, in: KoR, 3 (6), pp. 357-369.

Hoffmann, R. / Hölzle, A. (2003): Die "liquidation preference" in VC-Verträgen nach deutschem Recht, in: Finanz Betrieb, 5 (2), pp. 113-120.

Holmström, B. / Tirole, J. (1989): The theory of the firm, in: Handbook of Industrial Organization, ed. by R. Schmalensee / R. Willig, Amsterdam, pp. 61-133.

Hommel, U. / Ritter, M. / Wright, M. (2003): Verhalten der Beteiligungsfinanzierer nach dem "Downturn" - Ergebnisse einer empirischen Untersuchung, in: Finanz Betrieb, 5 (5), pp. 323-333.

IASB (2002): IASB Update December 2002, Board decisions on International Reporting Standards, London.

IASB (2005): Press release: IASB issues standards to improve disclosures about financial instruments and capital, August 18, 2005, London.

IASB (2006a): Active projects: Consolidations (inclusive special purpose entities), http://www.iasb.org/current/active_projects.asp?showPageContent=no&xml=16_205_116_08122005.htm, 15.07.2006.

IASB (2006b): IASB Update June 2006, Board decisions on International Reporting Standards, London.

IASB (2006c): IASB Update May 2006, Board Decisions on International Reporting Standards, London.

Ick, M. M. (2005): Private equity returns: Is there really a benefit of low co-movement with public equity markets? CEPRES Working Paper, University of Lugano.

ILPA (2004): Press release: ILPA endorses PEIGG U.S. Private Equity Valuation Guidelines, September 20, 2004.

Isert, D. / Schaber, M. (2005a): Zur Abgrenzung von Eigen- und Fremdkapital nach IAS 32 (rev. 2003), Teil I, in: KoR, 5 (7-8), pp. 299-310.

Isert, D. / Schaber, M. (2005b): Zur Abgrenzung von Eigen- und Fremdkapital nach IAS 32 (rev. 2003), Teil II, in: KoR, 5 (9), pp. 357-364.

Jaggi, B. / Low, P. Y. (2000): Impact of culture, market forces, and legal system on financial disclosures, in: International Journal of Accounting, 35 (4), pp. 495-519.

Janssen, J. / Laatz, W. (2003): Statistische Datenanalyse mit SPSS für Windows, Berlin.

Jensen, M. C. / Ruback, R. S. (1983): The market for corporate control, in: Journal of Financial Economics, 11 (1-4), pp. 5-50.

Jones, C. / Rhodes-Kropf, M. (2003): The price of diversifiable risk in venture capital and private equity, Working Paper, Columbia University.

Jugel, S. (2003): Benchmarking von Beteiligungsgesellschaften, in: Private-Equity-Investments: Die Praxis des Beteiligungsmanagements, ed. by S. Jugel, Wiesbaden, pp. 3-16.

Jung-Senssfelder, K. (2006): Equity financing and covenants in venture capital, Wiesbaden.

Kaneyuki, M. (2003): Creative valuation techniques for venture capital fund reporting, in: Finanz Betrieb, 5 (7-8), pp. 506-511.

Kaplan, S. / Schoar, A. (2005): Private equity performance: Returns, persistence, and capital capital flows, in: Journal of Finance, 60 (4), pp. 1791-1823.

Kaplan, S. / Strömberg, P. (2003): Financial contracting theory meets the real world: an empirical analysis of venture capital contracts, in: Review of Economic Studies, 70 (2), pp. 281-315.

Kaserer, C. / Achleitner, A.-K. / von Einem, C. / Schiereck, D. (2007): Private Equity in Deutschland - Rahmenbedingungen, ökonomische Bedeutung und Handlungsempfehlungen, Norderstedt.

Kaserer, C. / Diller, C. (2004a): Cash-flows und Performance von europäischen Private-Equity-Fonds, in: Finanz Betrieb, 6 (5), pp. 400-407.

Kaserer, C. / Diller, C. (2004b): European private equity funds: A cash flow based analysis, CEFS Working Paper No. 2004-01, TU München.

Kaserer, C. / Diller, C. (2004c): European private equity funds: A cash flow based performance analysis, in: Performance measurement and asset allocation for private equity funds, EVCA Research Paper, ed. by EVCA, Zaventum, pp. 27-71.

Kaserer, C. / Diller, C. (2004d): What drives cash flow based European private equity returns? Fund inflows, skilled GPs, and/or risk? CEFS Working Paper 2004-04, TU München.

Kaserer, C. / Wagner, N. / Achleitner, A.-K. (2003): Managing investment risk of institutional private equity investors: The challenge of illiquidity, in: Risk management: Challenge and opportunity, 2nd Edition, ed. by M. Frenkel / U. Hommel / M. Rudolf, Berlin, Heidelberg, pp. 259-277.

Kemmerer, A. (2005): A model to measure portfolio risks in venture capital, Working Paper, University of Frankfurt.

Kemmerer, A. / Weidig, T. (2005): Reporting value to the private equity fund investor, in: Journal of Financial Transformation, 15 (12), pp. 87-95.

Kennedy, C. (2005): Wake-up call on GIPS, in: Private Equity Manager, 2 (10), pp. 24-25.

Kinsch, A. / Petit-Jouvet, G. (2006): Funds of private equity funds valuation: A sum of equals? http://www.ey.com/global/content.nsf/Luxembourg_E/media_press_articles_Funds_of_Private_Equity_funds_valuation_a_sum_of_equals, 15.06.2007.

Kogelman, S. (1999): The importance of asset allocation in managing private equity, Goldman Sachs Investment Management Paper.

Kojima, J. C. (2005): Liquidity solutions and the secondary market in private equity, in: CFA Institute Conference Proceedings (2), pp. 39-45.

Kothari, S. P. (2001): Capital market research in accounting, in: Journal of Accounting and Economics, 31 (1-3), pp. 105-231.

Kraft, V. (2001): Private Equity für Turnaround-Investitionen: Erfolgsfaktoren in der Managementpraxis, Frankfurt am Main.

Kuan, J. (2006): Guidelines go global, in: Private Equity Manager, 3 (6), pp. 8-9.

Kühn, C. (2006): Capital structure decisions in institutional buyouts, Wiesbaden.

Kuhn, S. / Scharpf, P. (2005): Rechnungslegung von Financial Instruments nach IAS 39, 2nd edition, Stuttgart.

Kustner, C. (2002): Beteiligungsbewertung im Konzernabschluss, Bamberg.

Kuzneski, J. / Landen, R. (2006): Looking through the PIPE: Opportunities for private equity investors, Altassets Newsletter, June 28, 2006.

Labhart, P. A. (1999): Value reporting: Informationsbedürfnisse des Kapitalmarktes und Wertsteigerung durch Reporting, Zurich.

Lai, R. K. (2005): Why fund of funds? (Version March, 25, 2005), Working Paper.

Laib, P. (2003): Private Equity für institutionelle Investoren: Anforderungen, Potenziale, Erfolgsfaktoren, in: Private Equity Investments: Praxis des Beteiligungsmanagements, ed. by S. Jugel, Wiesbaden, pp. 17-29.

Lauer, J. (2006): Due diligence - Deal attribution & determinants of value creation, Institute for Fiduciary Education (IFE), Alternative Investment Seminar Paper.

Lerner, J. / Hardymon, F. (2005): A note on private equity securities, in: Venture capital and private equity: A casebook, ed. by J. Lerner / F. Hardymon / A. Leamon, Boston, pp. 288-295.

Lerner, J. / Hardymon, F. / Leamon, A. (2005): Between a rock and a hard place: Valuation and distribution in private equity, in: Venture capital and private equity: A casebook, ed. by J. Lerner / F. Hardymon / A. Leamon, Boston, pp. 404-431.

Lerner, J. / Schoar, A. (2004): The illiquidity puzzle: theory and evidence from private equity, in: Journal of Financial Economics, 72 (1), pp. 3-40.

Lerner, J. / Schoar, A. / Wong, W. (2005): Smart institutions, foolish choices? The limited partner performance puzzle, MIT Sloan Research Paper No. 4523-05, Januar 2005, Harvard University, Boston.

Lerner, J. / Willinge, J. (2005): A note on valuation in private equity settings, in: Venture capital and private equity: A casebook, 3rd edition, ed. by J. Lerner / F. Hardymon / A. Leamon, Boston, pp. 204-223.

Levin, J. S. (2002): Structuring venture capital, private equity and entrepreneurial transactions, New York.

Libby, R. (1981): Accounting and human information processing: Theory and application, Prentice Hall.

Lin, T. / Smith, R. (1998): Insider reputation and selling decisions: The unwinding of venture capital investments during equity IPOs, in: Journal of Corporate Finance, 4 (3), pp. 241-263.

Ljungqvist, A. / Richardson, M. (2003): The cash flow, return and risk characteristics of private equity, Working Paper, Stern School of Business, New York University.

Long, A. / Nickels, C. (1995): A method for comparing private market internal rates of return to public market index returns, Working Paper.

Loos, N. (2005): Value creation in leveraged buyouts, Dissertation of the University of St. Gallen, Liechtenstein.

Lossen, U. (2006): The performance of private equity funds: Does diversification matter? Munich Business Research Working Paper Series No. 2006-14, Munich.

Löw, E. / Lorenz, K. (2005): Ansatz und Bewertung von Finanzinstrumenten, in: Rechnungslegung für Banken nach IFRS, 2nd edition, ed. by E. Löw, Wiesbaden, pp. 415-604.

Lüdenbach, N. / Freiberg, J. (2006): Zweifelhafter Objektivierungsbeitrag des Fair Value Measurement-Projektes für die IFRS-Bilanz, in: KoR, 6 (7-8), pp. 437-445.

Markowitz, H. (1952): Portfolio selection, in: Journal of Finance, 7 (1), pp. 77-91.

Marsh (2004): Private equity management liability, Research Report 2004/2005, London.

Marston, C. L. / Shrives, P. J. (1991): The use of disclosure indices in accounting research: A review article, in: British Accounting Review, 23 (3), pp. 195-210.

Martin, R. D. / Rich, J. S. / Wilks, T. J. (2006): Auditing fair value measurements: A synthesis of relevant research, in: Accounting Horizons, 20 (3), pp. 287-303.

Mathonet, P.-Y. / Monjanel, G. (2006): New international valuation guidelines: a private equity homerun, Paper published by the European Investment Fund, May 2006, Luxembourg.

Mawson, J. (2005): Investors train their sights on better terms and conditions, in: Financial News: Private Equity News, 07.03.2005.

Mayer, C. / Schoors, K. / Yafeh, Y. (2003): Sources of funds and investment activities of venture capital funds: Evidence from Germany, Israel, Japan, and the U.K., Working Paper No.9645, National Bureau of Economic Research.

McCurry, P. (2005): Keeping up standards? in: European Venture Capital Journal, March (120), pp. 43-45.

McCurry, P. (2006): Club deals, in: European Venture Capital Journal (June Supplement), pp. 2-5.

McKinsey (2003): Private Equity Canada: Adapting to the new market reality, Volume 2, Toronto.

Meek, V. (2005a): Getting yourself a reputation, in: European Venture Capital Journal (122), pp. 50-51.

Meek, V. (2005b): GP reporting: are LPs getting what they want? in: European Venture Capital Journal (121), pp. 36-37.

Mercer, Z. C. (1999): Fair market value vs. the real world, in: Business Valuation Review, 18 (1), pp. 16-25.

Meyer, T. / Mathonet, P.-Y. (2005): Beyond the J curve: Managing a portfolio of venture capital and private equity funds, West Sussex.

Michas, A. P. (1997): LBO portfolio valuation practices, Institute for Fiduciary Education (IFE), Alternative Investment Seminar Paper.

Moll, D. K. (2004): Shareholder opression and fair value: Of discounts, dates, and dastardly deeds in the close corporation, in: Duke Law Journal, 54 (2), pp. 1-82.

Müller, S. (2003): Die Bewertung junger Unternehmen und Behavioral Finance, Köln.

Nathusius, E. (2005): Syndizierte Venture-Capital-Finanzierung, Sternenfels.

Nevins, D. / Conner, A. / McIntire, G. (2004): A portfolio management approach to determining private equity commitments, in: The Journal of Alternative Investments, 6 (4), pp. 32-46.

NVCA (2006): Valuation Guidelines, http://www.nvca.com/val_guidelines.html, 16.06.2006.

NVCA / Financial, T. (2006): Press release: Long term private equity performance consistent in Q4 2005, http://www.nvca.org/pdf/PeformanceQ405final.pdf, 16.09.2006.

Osnabrugge, M. v. / Robinson, R. J. (2001): The influence of a venture capitalist`s source of funds, in: Venture Capital, 3 (1), pp. 25-39.

Patton, J. / Zelenka, I. (1997): An empirical analysis of the determinants of the extent of disclosure in annual reports of joint stock companies in the Czech Republic, in: The European Accounting Review, 6 (4), pp. 605-626.

PEIGG (2004a): PEIGG reporting and performance measurement survey results.

PEIGG (2004b): Press release: Industry group releases exposure draft of private equity reporting and performance measurement guidelines, August 30.

PEIGG (2004c): U.S. private equity valuation guidelines.

PEIGG (2004d): Valuation guidelines: Guidance on paragraph 30: Non-financing valuation increases, released July 26, 2004.

PEIGG (2005): Reporting and performance measurement guidelines.

PEIGG (2006): Who are we, http://www.peigg.org/pages/1/index.htm, 08.06.2006.

PEIGG (2007): Updated U.S. private equity valuation guidelines.

Pellens, B. / Fülbier, R. U. / Gassen, J. (2006): Internationale Rechnungslegung, 6th edition, Stuttgart.

Peng, L. (2001): Building a venture capital index, Yale ICF Working Paper No. 00-51, Yale School of Economics.

Peninion, D. (2003): The GP-LP relationship: At the heart of private equity, Altassets, 02.08.2003.

Phalippou, L. (2007): Investing in private equity funds: A survey, Paper for the Research Foundation of CFA Institute.

Phalippou, L. / Zollo, M. (2005): The performance of private equity funds, Working Paper, University of Amsterdam.

Poole, V. / Spooner, A. (2006): iGAAP 2006: Financial instruments: IAS 32, IAS 39 and IFRS 7 explained, Kingston.

Povaly, S. (2006): Private equity exits: An analysis of divestment process management in relation to leveraged buyouts, Dissertation No. 3238, St. Gallen.

Pratt, S. (2001): The market approach to valuing businesses, New York.

Pratt, S. P. / Reilly, R. F. / Schweihs, R. P. (2000): Valuing a business: The analyses and appraisal of closely held companies, 4th edition, New York.

Prencipe, A. (2004): Proprietary costs and determinants of voluntary segment disclosure: Evidence from Italian listed companies, in: European Accounting Review, 13 (2), pp. 319-340.

Private Equity Intelligence (2005): Europe's limited partners report 2005: Report no. 18, London.

Private Equity Intelligence (2006): The 2006 limited partner universe, London.

Private Equity Intelligence (2007a): The 2007 global fundraising review, London.

Private Equity Intelligence (2007b): The 2007 private equity performance monitor, London.

Private Equity Valuation (2006): International private equity and venture capital valuation guidelines, http://www.privateequityvaluation.com/index.php, 16.06.2006.

Prowse, S. D. (1998): The economics of the private equity market, in: Federal Reserve Bank of Dallas Economic Review (Third Quarter), pp. 21-34.

PwC (2003): External reporting and corporate governance of private equity funds: A survey of Swiss private equity investors, Zurich.

PWC (2006): Applying IFRS - Solution No. 121.4, http://www.pwc.com/gx/eng/about/svcs/corporatereporting/05Solution121_4.pdf, 15.07.2006.

Quigley, J. M. / Woodward, S. E. (2003): An index for venture capital, University of California, Department of Economics, Working Paper No. E03-333, Berkely.

Reilly, F. K. / Brown, K. C. (2003): Investment analysis and portfolio management, 7th edition, Mason.

Reyes, J. (2005): FOIA cause and effect, in: Private Equity International, April (34), pp. 68-69.

Robbie, K. / Wright, M. / Chiplin, B. (1997): The monitoring of venture capital firms, in: Entrepreneurship Theory & Practice, 21 (4 Summer), pp. 9-17.

Robbie, K. / Wright, M. / Chiplin, B. (1999): Funds providers´ role in venture capital firm monitoring, in: Management buyout and venture capital - Into the next millenium, ed. by M. Wright / K. Robbie, Cheltenham, pp. 202-217.

Romer, M. / Moise, M. / Hrvatin, R. (2003): Hedge fund and private equity securization, in: The new generation of risk management for hedge funds and private equity investments, ed. by L. Jaeger, London, pp. 327-344.

Röper, B. (2003): Corporate Venture Capital: Eine emprirische Untersuchung des Beteiligungsmanagements deutscher und US-amerikanischer Corporate Venture Capital-Investoren, Bad Soden.

Rouvinez, C. (2003a): Beating the public market, in: Private Equity International (December), pp. 26-28.

Rouvinez, C. (2003b): Private equity benchmarking with PME+, in: Venture Capital Journal, 43 (8), pp. 34-38.

Rudolph, B. / Haagen, F. (2004): Die Auswirkungen institutioneller Rahmenbedingungen auf die Venture Capital-Finanzierung in Deutschland, Münchner Betriebswirtschaftliche Beiträge Nr. 2004-8, Working Paper, München.

Ruhnke, K. / Nerlich, C. (2004): Behandlung von Regelungslücken innerhalb der IFRS, in: Der Betrieb, 2004 (8), pp. 389-395.

Sahlman, W. (1990): The structure and governance of venture-capital organizations, in: Journal of Financial Economics, 27 (2), pp. 473-521.

Sanders, W. G. / Boivie, S. (2004): Sorting things out: Valuation of new firms in uncertain markets, in: Strategic Management Journal, 25 (2), pp. 167-186.

Sapienza, H. / Korsgaard, A. (1996): Procedural justice in entrepreneur-investor relations, in: Academy of Management Journal, 39 (3), pp. 544-574.

Schefczyck, M. (2000): Erfolgstrategien deutscher Venture Capital-Gesellschaften, 2nd edition, Stuttgart.

Schefczyck, M. / Pankotsch, F. (2005): Corporate Governance bei Venture-Capital-Beziehungen, in: Entrepreneurial Finance, ed. by C. J. Börner / D. Grichnik, Heidelberg, pp. 301-324.

Schell, J. M. (2006): Private equity funds: Business structure and operations, New York.

Schenk, G. (2004): Beobachtungen zum Controlling von VC-Beteiligungen, in: Finanz Betrieb, 6 (2), pp. 154-157.

Schmidt, D. / Wahrenburg, M. (2004): Contractual relations between European VC–funds and investors: The impact of reputation and bargaining power on contractual design, RICAFE Working Paper No. 008.

Schmidt, K. M. (2003): Convertible securities and venture capital financing, in: Journal of Finance, 58 (3), pp. 1139-1166.

Schmidt, W. (2003): Understanding and managing risk in leveraged buy-out fund investing, in: The new generation of risk management for hedge funds and private equity investments, ed. by L. Jaeger, London, pp. 246-262.

Schwartzman, E. (2006): What it takes to make a consortium work, in: International Financial Law Review, Special Issue Private Equity & Venture Capital, pp. 99-106.

SECA (2006): Swiss private equity & corporate finance association yearbook 2005/06, Zug.

Sharpe, W. (1992): Asset allocation: management style and performance measurement, in: Journal of Portfolio Management, 18 (2), pp. 7-19.

Shearer, B. (2006): Antitrust inquiry probes club deals, in: Mergers & Acquisitions: The Dealmakers Journal, 41 (12), pp. 37-37.

Shepherd, D. / Zacharakis, A. (2001): The venture capitalist-entrepreneur relationship: Control, trust and confidence in co-operative behaviour, in: Venture Capital: An International Journal of Entrepreneurial Finance, 3 (2), pp. 129-149.

Singhvi, S. S. / Desai, H. B. (1971): An empirical analysis of the quality of corporate financial disclosure, in: The Accounting Review, 46 (1), pp. 129-138.

Skypala, P. (2005): Private equity opaçity is a top risk, in: Financial Times, 29.09.2005.

Sloan, R. G. (2001): Financial accounting and corporate governance: A discussion, in: Journal of Accounting and Economics, 32 (1-3), pp. 335-347.

Smith, J. K. / Smith, R. L. (2004): Entrepreneurial finance, 2nd Edition, Hoboken.

Smith, P. (2007): Secretive sector steps into the glare of publicity, in: Financial Times, 24.04.2007.

Snow, D. (2004): That's not fair, in: Private Equity International (21), pp. 43-44.

Snow, D. (2005): End of the affair, in: Private Equity Manager, 2 (5), pp. 24-25.

Snow, D. (2006): Audit wars, in: Private Equity Manager, 3 (7), pp. 30-31.

Sormani, A. (2005): GIPS make French PE debut, in: European Venture Capital Journal, (128), pp. 12-13.

Sormani, A. (2006): Management fees: Alignment of interests, in: European Venture Capital Journal (133), pp. 45-47.

Steir, L. / Greenwood, R. (1995): Venture capitalist relationships in the deal structuring and post-investment stages of new firm creation, in: Journal of Management Studies, 32 (3), pp. 337-357.

Takahashi, D. / Alexander, S. (2002): Illiquid alternative asset fund modelling, in: Journal of Portfolio Management, 28 (2), pp. 90-100.

Tausend, C. (2006): Die Selektion von Venture-Capital-Gesellschaften durch institutionelle Investoren, München.

Thoen, V. (2002): Valuation and reporting requirements faced by venture capitalists, Department of Applied Economics, Katholieke Universiteit Leuven, Leuven.

Thomson, A. (2004): The IASB's road to hell, in: Private Equity Manager, 2 (7), pp. 24-25.

Thomson, A. (2005): Pulling punches, in: Private Equity Manager, 2 (10), pp. 16-19.

Thomson, A. (2006): Intimate relations, in: Private Equity International (47), pp. 46-49.

Timmons, J. / Bygrave, W. (1986): Venture capital's role in financing innovation for economic growth, in: Journal of Business Venturing, 1 (2), pp. 161-176.

Toll, D. M. (2003): Private equity partnership terms & conditions: For venture capital, LBO, mezzanine, and funds of funds, Research Report, London.

Troche, C. (2004): Development of a rating system for private equity funds, The European Investment Fund (EIF).

Tuck (2003a): A note on private equity asset allocation, Center for Private Equity and Entrepreneurship at Tuck School of Business, Dartmouth.

Tuck (2003b): A note on private equity deal structures, Center for Private Equity and Entrepreneurship at Tuck School of Business, Dartmouth.

Tuck (2003c): Private equity valuation and reporting conference: Proceedings, June 18-19, 2003, Center for Private Equity and Entrepreneurship at Tuck School of Business, Dartmouth.

Tuck (2004a): Limited partnership agreement conference: Proceedings, Center for Private Equity & Entrepreneurship at Tuck School of Business, Dartmouth.

Tuck (2004b): Limited partnership agreement project: Results of GP, LP surveys, Center for Private Equity and Entrepreneurship at Tuck School of Business, Dartmouth.

Tuck (2004c): Limited partnership agreement: Survey results GPs, Center for Private Equity and Entrepreneurship at Tuck School of Business, Dartmouth.

Tuck (2004d): Limited partnership agreement: Survey results LPs, Center for Private Equity and Entrepreneurship at Tuck School of Business, Dartmouth.

Tuck (2005): Results of Survey of Valuation Practices, Center for Private Equity & Entrepreneurship at Tuck School of Business, Dartmouth.

Tyebjee, T. / Bruno, A. (1984): A model of venture capitalist investment activity, in: Management Science, 30 (9), pp. 1051-1066.

Urwyler, A. / Wilde, C. (2001): Private Equity in der Asset Allocation - ein Portfolio-Ansatz, in: Private Equity und Hedge Funds: Alternative Anlagekategorien im Überblick, ed. by A. Grünbichler / S. Graf / A. Gruber, Frankfurt am Main, pp. 201-223.

von Daniels, H. (2004): Private Equity Secondary Transactions: Chancen und Grenzen des Aufbaus eines institutionalisierten Secondary Market, Wiesbaden.

Wahl, S. (2004): Private Debt: Private Fremdkapital- und Mezzanine-Kapital-Platzierungen bei institutionellen Investoren, Sternenfels.

Wallace, O. R. S. / Naser, K. (1995): Firm-specific determinants of the comprehensiveness of mandatory disclosure in the corporate annual reports of firms listed on the stock exchange of Hong Kong, in: Journal of Business Finance & Accounting, 14 (4), pp. 311-368.

Weidig, T. (2002): Towards a risk model for venture capital funds: Liquidity and performance forecasting, Working Paper.

Weidig, T. / Kemmerer, A. / Born, B. (2003): The risk profile of private equity funds-of-funds, in: Journal of Alternative Investments, 7 (4), pp. 33-42.

Weidig, T. / Mathonet, P.-Y. (2004): The risk profiles of private equity, Working Paper, Luxembourg.

Weitnauer, W. (2001): Rahmenbedingungen und Gestaltung von Private Equity Fonds, in: Finanz Betrieb, 3 (4), pp. 258-271.

Wihite, G. A. (2001): Private equity secondary investment, Institute for Fiduciary Education (IFE), Alternative Investment Seminar Paper.

William M. Mercer Inc. (1997): Investment officer in-box: A glossary of key terms and conditions for private equity investing, in: Investment Policy, 1 (2), pp. 102-121.

Witney, S. (2006): The importance of open relationships, Altassets, May 16, 2006.

Woodward, S. E. / Hall, R. E. (2003): Benchmarking the returns to venture, Working paper series, National Bureau of Economic Research, Stanford University.

Woronoff, M. / Rosen, J. (2005): Effective vs nominal valuations in venture capital investing, in: New York University Journal of Law and Business, 2 (1), pp. 1-22.

Wright, M. / Pruthi, S. / Lockert, A. (2005): International venture capital research: From cross-country comparisons to crossing borders, in: International Journal of Management Reviews, 7 (3), pp. 135-165.

Wright, M. / Robbie, K. (1998): Venture capital and private equity: A review and synthesis, in: Journal of Business Finance & Accounting, 25 (5-6), pp. 521-570.

Yin, R. (1994): Case study research, 2nd edition, Thousand Oaks, CA.

Zacharakis, A. / Shepherd, D. (2001): The nature of information and overconfidence on venture capitalists' decision making, in: Journal of Business Venturing, 16 (4), pp. 311-332.

Zehmke, I. (1995): Die Unternehmensverfassung von Beteiligungskapitalgesellschaften: Analyse des institutionellen Designs deutscher Venture Capital-Gesellschaften, Wiesbaden.

zu Knyphausen, D. / Kittlaus, D. / Seeliger, C. (2003): Internationale Standardisierungstendenzen bei der Renditeberechnung von Venture Capital-Fonds, in: Finanz Betrieb, 5 (9), pp. 548-555.

FSC
www.fsc.org
MIX
Papier | Fördert
gute Waldnutzung
FSC® C083411

Kolibri 360 GmbH
Ferdinand-Jühlke-Straße 7
99095 Erfurt, Deutschland
produktsicherheit@kolibri360.de